AWS Cloud Migration:
A Modern Approach

LICENSE, DISCLAIMER OF LIABILITY, AND LIMITED WARRANTY

By purchasing or using this book and companion files (the "Work"), you agree that this license grants permission to use the contents contained herein, including the disc, but does not give you the right of ownership to any of the textual content in the book / disc or ownership to any of the information or products contained in it. *This license does not permit uploading of the Work onto the Internet or on a network (of any kind) without the written consent of the Publisher.* Duplication or dissemination of any text, code, simulations, images, etc. contained herein is limited to and subject to licensing terms for the respective products, and permission must be obtained from the Publisher or the owner of the content, etc., in order to reproduce or network any portion of the textual material (in any media) that is contained in the Work.

MERCURY LEARNING AND INFORMATION ("MLI" or "the Publisher") and anyone involved in the creation, writing, or production of the companion disc, accompanying algorithms, code, or computer programs ("the software"), and any accompanying Web site or software of the Work, cannot and do not warrant the performance or results that might be obtained by using the contents of the Work. The author, developers, and the Publisher have used their best efforts to ensure the accuracy and functionality of the textual material and/or programs contained in this package; we, however, make no warranty of any kind, express or implied, regarding the performance of these contents or programs. The Work is sold "as is" without warranty (except for defective materials used in manufacturing the book or due to faulty workmanship).

The author, developers, and the publisher of any accompanying content, and anyone involved in the composition, production, and manufacturing of this work will not be liable for damages of any kind arising out of the use of (or the inability to use) the algorithms, source code, computer programs, or textual material contained in this publication. This includes, but is not limited to, loss of revenue or profit, or other incidental, physical, or consequential damages arising out of the use of this Work.

The sole remedy in the event of a claim of any kind is expressly limited to replacement of the book and/or disc, and only at the discretion of the Publisher. The use of "implied warranty" and certain "exclusions" varies from state to state and might not apply to the purchaser of this product.

AWS Cloud Migration:
A Modern Approach

Mukesh Kumar Das

MERCURY LEARNING AND INFORMATION
Boston, Massachusetts

Copyright ©2025 by MERCURY LEARNING AND INFORMATION.
An Imprint of DeGruyter Inc. All rights reserved.

This publication, portions of it, or any accompanying software may not be reproduced in any way, stored in a retrieval system of any type, or transmitted by any means, media, electronic display, or mechanical display, including, but not limited to, photocopy, recording, Internet postings, or scanning, without prior permission in writing from the publisher.

MERCURY LEARNING AND INFORMATION
121 High Street, 3rd Floor
Boston, MA 02110
info@merclearning.com

M. Kumar Das. *AWS Cloud Migration: A Modern Approach.*
ISBN: 978-1-5015-2378-6

The publisher recognizes and respects all marks used by companies, manufacturers, and developers as a means to distinguish their products. All brand names and product names mentioned in this book are trademarks or service marks of their respective companies. Any omission or misuse (of any kind) of service marks or trademarks, etc. is not an attempt to infringe on the property of others.

Library of Congress Control Number: 2025937798

242526321 This book is printed on acid-free paper in the United States of America.

Our titles are available for adoption, license, or bulk purchase by institutions, corporations, etc.

All of our titles are available in digital format at various digital vendors.

Contents

Preface		*xxxi*
Acknowledgments		*xxxiii*
Chapter 1:	**Introduction to Cloud Computing**	1
	What Is Cloud Computing?	1
	On-Premises/Traditional IT Infrastructure with Associated Problems	2
	Benefits of Cloud Computing	4
	3-4-5 Principles of Cloud Computing	5
	Cloud Computing Service Models	5
	Infrastructure as a Service (IaaS)	6
	Platform as a Service (PaaS)	7
	Software as a Service (SaaS)	8
	Deployment Models of the Cloud	9
	Public Cloud	9
	Here are some examples of a public cloud:	10
	Private Cloud	11
	Hybrid Cloud	12
	Community Cloud	13
	Pros and Cons of Community Cloud	14
	Different Cloud Deployment Model Characteristics	14
	The Five Characteristics of Cloud Computing	16

	On-Demand Self-Service	16
	Broad Network Access	17
	Multi-Tenancy and Resource Pooling	17
	Rapid Elasticity and Scalability	17
	Measured Service	17
	Summary	18
	References	18
	Knowledge Check: Multiple-Choice Q&A	20
Chapter 2:	**Introduction to Amazon Web Services (AWS)**	**23**
	Overview of Amazon Web Services (AWS)	23
	The Gartner Magic Quadrant for Strategic Cloud Platform Services	23
	AWS Cloud History	25
	Overview of AWS Services and Key Characteristics	26
	AWS Key Characteristics	29
	AWS Global Infrastructure: A Digital Ecosystem	29
	Regions	31
	Availability Zones	32
	Edge Locations	33
	Regional Edge Caches	33
	Method to Choose the Right AWS Region	34
	Different Methods to Access or Connect to AWS	35
	AWS Management Console	35
	AWS CLI	35
	AWS SDKs	35
	AWS Mobile App	36
	AWS SAML Provider	36
	AWS SSO	36
	Lab: Creating an AWS Account Using the AWS Management Console	36
	Summary	37
	References	38

	Knowledge Check: Multiple-Choice Q&A	39
Chapter 3:	**AWS IAM and Compute Services**	**41**
	Identity and Access Management	42
	IAM Benefits	43
	IAM: Users, Groups, and Roles	43
	What Is a User?	44
	Lab: AWS IAM User Creation	44
	What Is a Group?	45
	Lab: AWS IAM Group Creation	46
	Lab: Adding a User to an Available Group	47
	What Is a Role?	47
	AWS IAM Role Creation	48
	Lab: AWS IAM Role Creation	49
	What Is a Policy?	50
	MFA in IAM	51
	Lab: Enabling MFA in the IAM Console	52
	What Is an Access Key?	52
	AWS Compute Services	53
	Amazon EC2	55
	Different Types of Amazon EC2 Instances	56
	Different Pricing Models for Amazon EC2 Instances	58
	Amazon Machine Image	59
	Amazon Instance User Data and Instance Metadata	60
	Classic Port in Windows and Linux	62
	What Is SSH?	63
	Preparation for the Use of Amazon EC2	65
	Key Pairs	66
	Security Groups	66
	Root Volume	67
	Additional Volumes	67
	Volumes	68

	Lab: Creation of an EC2 Instance in AWS	68
	Step 1: Sign Up for an AWS Account	68
	Step 2: Create a Key Pair	68
	Step 3: Create a Security Group	69
	Step 4: Launch an Instance	69
	Step 5: Get Information About the Newly Created Instance	70
	Step 6: Connect to the Newly Created EC2 Instance	71
	Connecting to an EC2 Instance Using PuTTY	74
	Summary	78
	References	78
	Knowledge Check: Multiple-Choice Q&A	80
Chapter 4:	**Storage Services and Virtual Private Cloud (VPC)**	**83**
	AWS Storage Systems	83
	Object Storage	84
	Block Storage	85
	File Storage	85
	AWS Storage Gateway	85
	AWS Snow Family	86
	Amazon Glacier	86
	Amazon ECR	86
	Amazon S3	87
	What Is a Bucket in S3?	88
	S3 Features	88
	S3 Storage Classes	89
	Data Security Using Access Control Lists and Bucket Policies	91
	Access Control Lists (ACLs)	91
	S3 Bucket Policies	92
	Amazon S3 Versioning	94
	S3 Lifecycle Policies	95
	How to Create an S3 Lifecycle Policy	98

	Lab: Amazon S3 – Bucket Creation	101
	Bucket Creation Using the S3 Console	101
	Key Points for Bucket Naming	102
	Viewing the Properties of an S3 Bucket	103
	Uploading Folders and Files to an S3 Bucket	104
	Emptying a Bucket	105
	Deleting an S3 Bucket	105
	Amazon S3 Transfer Acceleration	105
	Lab: Enable S3 Transfer Acceleration for a Given Bucket	107
	Amazon Virtual Private Cloud (VPC)	107
	Overview of Amazon VPC	107
	Amazon VPC Components	108
	Subnets	109
	Route Tables	109
	Security Groups	110
	Network ACLs	110
	Internet Gateways	110
	Elastic IP (EIP) Addresses	111
	Endpoints	111
	Peering Connections	112
	NAT Instances and NAT Gateways	112
	Virtual Private Gateways (VPGs)	112
	VPC with All Components	113
	AWS Transit Gateway	114
	AWS Site-to-Site VPN	116
	Summary	117
	References	118
	Knowledge Check: Multiple-Choice Q&A	119
Chapter 5:	**AWS Database Services**	**123**
	Overview of AWS Databases	124
	Relational Databases	125

	Non-Relational Databases	126
	Key-Value Stores	127
	Document Stores	127
	Column-Family Stores	128
	Graph Databases	129
	Different AWS Databases	130
	Choosing the Right AWS Database	131
	EC2-Hosted Databases	131
	AWS-Managed Databases	132
	Deciding When to Use EC2-Hosted Databases or AWS-Managed Databases	133
	Amazon RDS	133
	Features of Amazon RDS	134
	Advantages of RDS over Deploying a Database on EC2	135
	Amazon Aurora	136
	RDS Solution Architecture	136
	Single-AZ RDS Deployment	136
	Multi-AZ RDS Deployment	137
	RDS Deployment with Read Replicas	138
	Lab: Creating an RDS Database Instance	138
	Lab: Deleting an RDS Database	140
	Lab: Modifying an RDS Database	141
	Summary	142
	References	143
	Knowledge Check: Multiple-Choice Q&A	144
Chapter 6:	**Miscellaneous AWS Services**	**147**
	Amazon CloudFront	147
	How Does CloudFront Work?	148
	Benefits of Using CloudFront	148
	Amazon CloudWatch	149
	Amazon CloudWatch Metrics	151

Amazon CloudWatch Alarms	152
Amazon CloudWatch Logs	153
CloudWatch Logs for EC2	154
AWS CloudTrail	155
CloudTrail Working Methodology	156
Auditing with AWS CloudTrail, AWS Audit Manager, and AWS Config	157
AWS Systems Manager	157
What Is AWS Systems Manager?	158
Capabilities of AWS Systems Manager	160
Key Benefits of AWS Systems Manager	160
Accelerated Problem Detection	161
Streamlined Automation	162
Enhanced Visibility and Control	162
Seamless Hybrid Environment Management	162
Robust Security and Compliance	163
Core Technical Concepts of AWS Systems Manager	163
Managed Nodes	163
Systems Manager Agent (SSM Agent)	163
Resource Groups	164
Systems Manager Documents	164
Parameters and Parameter Store	164
Patch Manager and Baselines	165
Compliance and Configuration Management	165
Key Use Cases of AWS Systems Manager	165
Patch Management	166
Session Management	166
Operations Management	167
Configuration Management	167
How AWS Systems Manager Facilitates AWS Cloud Migration	167
Pre-Migration Assessment	168

	Automation of Repetitive Tasks	168
	Resource Management	169
	Integration with other AWS Migration Tools	169
	Compliance Monitoring	169
Summary		169
References		170
Knowledge Check: Multiple-Choice Q&A		171

Chapter 7: Cloud Migration and Strategies — 173

Cloud Migration Workloads	173
Data Migration	174
Application Migration	174
Database Migration	175
Infrastructure Migration	175
Configuration Management	175
Testing	175
Change Management	175
Compliance	176
Cost Management	176
Traditional Approach to Cloud Migration	176
Data Collection and Analysis	176
Servers	177
Application	177
Software	178
Mappings and Dependencies	178
Network Dependencies	178
Application Mappings	179
Planning and Assessment	179
Application Sizing	179
Total Cost of Ownership (TCO) Reports	180
Wave Plans	180
Migration Project Plans	180

	Execution and Migration	181
	Migration Execution	181
	Common Cloud Migration Strategies	182
	What Is a Migration Strategy?	182
	Discovery	183
	Migration Path Decision	183
	Validation	183
	Cutover	183
	Operate	184
	Rehost (Lift and Shift)	185
	Relocate	186
	Replatform (Lift and Reshape)	187
	Refactor (Re-architect)	189
	Repurchase (Drop and Shop)	191
	Retire	192
	What Are the Risks of Retiring?	193
	When to Retire Applications	193
	Retain (Revisit)	193
	Identifying the Right Migration Strategy	196
	Summary	198
	References	199
	Knowledge Check: Multiple-Choice Q&A	200
Chapter 8:	**Cloud Migration Framework and Different Phases**	**203**
	What Is a Cloud Adoption Framework?	203
	Key Components of a Cloud Adoption Framework	204
	Strategy and Planning	204
	Governance	204
	Technology	205
	People and Processes	205
	Adoption and Migration	206
	Optimization and Innovation	207

Different Cloud Adoption Frameworks	207
AWS CAF	208
Business Perspective	209
Governance Perspective	209
Operations Perspective	210
Security Perspective	210
People Perspective	210
Platform Perspective	211
Well-Architected Frameworks	211
AWS Well-Architected Framework	212
AWS Well-Architected Framework for Migration	212
Different Phases of AWS Cloud Migration	215
AWS Well-Architected Framework with AWS Migration Phases	216
AWS Migration Key Activities by Phase	217
Assess Phase	218
Mobilize Phase	220
Migrate and Modernize Phase	222
Migration Phases and Associated Tools	225
Assess Phase	226
Mobilize Phase	226
Migrate Phase	226
Modernize Phase	227
Well-Architected Framework	227
Cloud Migration Success Mantra: People, Process, and Technology	228
People: Building Trust and Equipping Your Team	229
Understanding Change Management	229
Skills and Expertise	230
The Role of Leadership	230
Process: Charting a Clear Path with Flexibility	231

	Migration Strategy	231
	Phased Approach	231
	Technology: Choosing the Right Tools and Prioritizing Security	231
	Cloud Assessment Tools	231
	Migration Tools	232
	Security Measures	232
	Summary	232
	References	233
	Knowledge Check: Multiple-Choice Q&A	234
Chapter 9:	**Assess Phase of AWS Migration**	**237**
	Overview of the Assess Phase	237
	Why We Are Migrating to the Cloud	237
	Business Needs	238
	Current IT Snapshot	238
	Performance Information	238
	What We Want to Migrate	238
	How Ready We Are for Migration	239
	Where We Stand Currently	239
	Different Tools Used in the Assess Phase	240
	Cloud Adoption Readiness Tool	242
	Migration Readiness Assessment	245
	Comparison Between CART and MRA	246
	Migration Evaluator	247
	Obtaining Access	248
	Using Migration Evaluator	248
	Workflow of AWS Migration Evaluator	249
	AWS Migration Evaluator Reports	250
	AWS Migration Quick Insights Sample Report	250
	AWS Migration Details Sample Report	251
	Migration Portfolio Assessment	254

	Data Inventory	255
	Data Collection	255
	Portfolio Analysis	255
	Migration Planning	256
	Business Case Development	256
Comparison Between Migration Evaluator and MPA		257
Summary		257
References		258
Knowledge Check: Multiple-Choice Q&A		259
Chapter 10:	**AWS Migration Mobilize Phase**	**263**
	Overview of the Mobilize Phase	263
	Different AWS Cloud Migration Mobilize Tools	265
	Introduction to AWS Control Tower	265
	Understanding the Landing Zone	266
	Building a Landing Zone	266
	How to Build a Landing Zone	267
	Greenfield vs. Brownfield Deployments	267
	Setting Up a Landing Zone with AWS Control Tower	268
	Establishing the AWS Organization	268
	Creating AWS Accounts and Deploying Resources	269
	Consolidated Management and Governance	269
	Optional Components	269
	Benefits of Using AWS Control Tower	270
	AWS Application Discovery Service	270
	What Is Application Discovery Service?	270
	AWS ADS Process	271
	Agent-Based Application Discovery Process	272
	Agentless Application Discovery Process	272
	Manual Import	272
	Overall ADS Architecture	272

	Data Collection	273
	Data Storage and Processing	275
	Data Analysis and Visualization	276
	Key Features and Considerations	276
	Data Security	277
	Region Selection	277
	Integration with Migration Tools	277
	Agent-Based vs. Agentless Collection	277
	Benefits of ADS	278
	Lab: AWS Application Discovery Service Tutorial	279
	Lab: Agent-Based Application Discovery Tutorial	280
	Application Discovery Service Agentless Collector	284
	AWS Migration Hub	284
	Benefits of Cloud Migration with AWS Migration Hub	284
	Understanding the Migration Process with AWS Migration Hub	285
	Preparing for Cloud Migration with AWS Migration Hub	286
	Managing and Tracking Your Migration with AWS Migration Hub	286
	Best Practices for a Successful Cloud Migration with AWS Migration Hub	287
	AWS Migration Hub Tutorial	287
	Summary	289
	References	289
	Knowledge Check: Multiple-Choice Q&A	290
Chapter 11:	**AWS Migration Migrate Phase**	**293**
	Overview of the Migration Phase	293
	Understanding the Migrate Phase	293
	Workload Migration	293
	Data Migration	294
	Optimization and Modernization	294

AWS Prescriptive Guidance in the Migrate Phase	294
Utilizing Prescriptive Guidance	296
Different AWS Migration Phase Tools	297
AWS Application Migration Service (MGN)	298
AWS Database Migration Service (DMS)	298
AWS Services for Data Migration	298
Workload Migration vs. Data Migration	298
Workload Migration	298
VMware Cloud on AWS	299
AWS MGN	299
Data Migration	299
AWS Transfer Family	299
AWS Database Migration Service (DMS)	300
AWS DataSync	300
AWS Snow Family	300
VMware to AWS Cloud Migration	301
Relocate Strategy and Its Association with VMware Cloud Migration to AWS	301
Overview of the Relocate Strategy	301
VMware SDDC	302
VMware Cloud on AWS (VMC on AWS)	303
Different Migration Types	304
Cold Migration	304
Warm Migration	304
Live Migration	305
AWS Application Migration Service	305
Benefits of Application Migration Service	306
Application Migration Service Lifecycle	308
Keys to the Successful Implementation of AWS MGN	309
Server Migration Service (SMS) and Its Comparison with MGN	310
AWS MGN Architecture	311

Setting Up Network Connectivity to Run AWS MGN Properly	318
KPIs for Successful Implementation	319
Implementation	320
Initial Replication	320
Ready for Testing	320
Testing	320
Cutover	321
Lab: AWS Application Migration Service Tutorial	321
Case Study	321
Prerequisites	322
Step 1: Creating an IAM User	323
Step 2: Accessing the Application Migration Service Console	323
Step 3: First Time Setup (Replication Template/Tags)	323
Step 4: Configuring the Launch Template	324
Step 5: Creating the WordPress Content and Installing the AWS Replication Agent	326
Step 6: Configuring the Launch Settings	327
Step 7: Launching a Test Instance	329
Step 8: Launching a Cutover Instance	330
Step 9: Applications and Waves	331
Step 10: Post-Migration Modernization	332
Step 11: Cleaning Up After Final Cutover	334
Database Migration	335
Overview of Amazon Database Migration (DMS)	335
Determining the Right Tool or Approach for Database Migration	336
Three-Phase Approach to Database Migration	337
Assess Phase	337
Mobilize Phase	338
Migrate and Modernize Phase	338

Native Database Migration Tools	339
Different Types of Database Migration	339
Homogeneous Migration	340
Heterogeneous Migrations	341
Key Concepts in Database Migration	341
Transaction Logs	342
Change Data Capture (CDC)	342
Key Features of AWS DMS	342
Different Challenges During Database Migration	343
Database Migration Patterns	344
Lift and Shift	344
Replatforming	345
AWS DMS Architecture Types	345
AWS DMS Homogeneous Architecture	345
Lab: Getting Started with Homogeneous AWS Database Migration Service	347
Step 1: Create an AWS DMS Replication Instance	347
Step 2: Create AWS DMS Source and Target Endpoints	349
Step 3: Create and Run an AWS DMS Migration Task	350
Heterogeneous AWS Database Migration Service	351
Heterogeneous Database Migration	352
AWS Schema Conversion Tool	354
What Is a Database Schema?	354
Lab: Heterogeneous AWS Database Migration Service	355
Prerequisites	355
Step 1: Configure the Oracle Source Database	356
Step 2: Configure the Aurora Target Database	358
Step 3: Create an AWS DMS Replication Instance	358
Step 4: Create the Oracle Source Database Endpoint	359
Step 5: Create the Aurora MySQL Target Endpoint	360

Step 6: Create a Migration Task	361
Step 7: Monitor the Migration Task	362
AWS DMS Serverless	362
AWS DMS Fleet Advisor	364
AWS DMS Fleet Advisor Architecture	364
Data Migration to AWS	366
Data Migration Process Overview	367
Understanding Online and Offline Data Migration	367
Understanding Your Data Portfolio (Source Environment)	369
Targeting AWS Storage Services	369
Large vs. Medium vs. Small Data Based on Terabyte Size	370
Large-Scale and Small-Scale Data Migrations to AWS	371
Large-Scale Data Migration Challenges in AWS	372
Data Migration Framework and AWS Data Storage Mapping	375
File Systems (Source Storage Systems)	377
AWS Migration Services (Migration Tools)	377
AWS Storage Services (Target Storage Systems)	378
Key AWS Data Migration Services	378
AWS DataSync	379
When to Use AWS DataSync	382
AWS Storage Gateway	383
What Is Amazon S3 File Gateway?	383
Amazon S3 File Gateway Architecture	384
What Are the Benefits of Amazon S3 File Gateway?	385
When Should You Use Amazon S3 File Gateway?	385
AWS Snow Family	386
What Is AWS Snowball Edge?	387
AWS Snowball Edge Workflow	387

	What Are the Benefits of AWS Snowball Edge?	388
	When Should You Use AWS Snowball Edge?	389
	Summary	390
	References	390
	Knowledge Check: Multiple-Choice Q&A	392
Chapter 12:	**AWS Migration Modernization Phase**	**397**
	Overview of the Modernize Phase	397
	Key Objectives of Modernization	398
	Agility	399
	Scalability	399
	Cost Saving	399
	Innovation	399
	Collaboration	400
	Why Is AWS the Best Choice for Application Modernization?	400
	Modernization Stages	401
	IT Modernization	402
	Application Modernization	402
	Different Modernization Strategies	404
	Refactoring for Cloud-Native Design	405
	Replatforming on Managed Services	406
	AWS Managed Services in Cloud Modernization	408
	Scalability and Elasticity	408
	Cost Optimization	409
	AWS Cost Management Tools	410
	Monitoring and Logging	410
	Centralized Logging	411
	Security Best Practices	411
	AWS Security Services	411
	Rehosting	412
	Replacement of Legacy Applications	412

	Challenges and Solutions in Modernization	412
	Technical Debt	413
	Challenges	413
	Solution	413
	Data Migration	414
	Challenges	414
	Solution	414
	Security	414
	Challenges	414
	Solution	415
	Compliance	415
	Challenges	415
	Solution	415
	Summary	416
	References	417
	Knowledge Check: Multiple-Choice Q&A	418
Chapter 13:	**Generative AI in AWS Cloud Migration**	**421**
	What Is Artificial Intelligence?	421
	Common AI Workloads	422
	Machine Learning	423
	Deep Learning	424
	Computer Vision	425
	Natural Language Processing	426
	Robotic Process Automation	426
	Generative AI	427
	Different Applications of Generative AI	428
	Relationship Between AI, ML, DL, and Generative AI	429
	ML Model Creation Process	430
	Feature Selection	430
	Feature Engineering	432

Model Training	433
Model Evaluation	434
Putting It All Together	434
Types of ML	435
Supervised Learning	436
Unsupervised Learning	437
Reinforcement Learning	438
Comparative Characteristics and Applications	439
Machine Learning Building Blocks	440
Problem Definition	441
Data Gathering and Preparation	442
Data Collection	442
Data Preparation	442
Model Selection or Hypothesis Generation	443
Data Training and Evaluation	444
Hyperparameter Tuning	445
Epochs Parameter	446
Learning Rate	446
Accuracy and Loss	446
Batches	446
Batch Size	447
Iterations	447
Epochs	447
Predictive Modeling	448
Model Deployment/Implementation	448
Generative AI Definition and Components	449
How Does Generative AI Work?	450
Training	450
Sampling	450
Refinement	450
Different Applications of Generative AI	451
Art and Image Generation	451

Language Models	452
Audio and Video Synthesis	452
Medicine and Healthcare	453
Finance and Business	453
Manufacturing and Design	453
Defining Foundation Models, Prompts, and Prompt Engineering	454
Large Language Models	454
Multimodal Capabilities	454
Understanding Prompts	454
Building Generative AI Applications	454
Prompt Engineering	455
Defining Tokens, Embeddings, Vectors, and Transformers	455
Tokens	456
Embeddings	456
Vectors	456
Transformers	456
Different Types of Generative AI	456
GANs	457
VAEs	458
Recurrent Neural Networks	459
Popular Tools and Web Sites for Exploring Generative AI	459
ChatGPT by OpenAI	459
DALL·E by OpenAI	459
RunwayML	460
Midjourney	460
SOUNDRAW	461
GitHub Copilot	461
Key Generative AI AWS Services	461
Amazon SageMaker	462

Amazon Bedrock	462
Amazon Q	463
Unified Security and Access Control	463
Amazon SageMaker for Generative AI	463
Key Features for Generative AI	464
Flexible Pricing Model	464
Customization and Control	464
Amazon Bedrock for Generative AI	465
Key Features of Amazon Bedrock	465
Benefits of Using Amazon Bedrock	466
Amazon Q for Generative AI	466
Core Applications of Amazon Q	466
Benefits of Choosing Amazon Q	468
Generative AI in AWS Cloud Migration	468
How Generative AI Accelerates AWS Cloud Migration	468
Automated Analysis of Existing Infrastructure	468
Streamlined Re-Architecting and Replatforming	468
Simplified Redeployment and Validation	469
Evaluating Emerging AI-Assisted Migration Solutions	469
StackPulse	469
Transposit	469
Astro	469
PolyAI	470
Platform9	470
Generative AI in Different AWS Cloud Migration Phases	470
Generative AI in the Assess Phase of AWS Cloud Migration	470
Data Analysis	472
Cost Estimation	472
Risk Assessment	473

	Documenting Current Architectures	474
	Optimizing Target Architectures	475
	Generative AI in the Mobilize Phase of AWS Cloud Migration	476
	Automated Migration Tools	477
	Resource Allocation	478
	Monitoring and Optimization	479
	Generative AI in the Migrate and Modernize Phase of AWS Cloud Migration	480
	Architectural Enhancement	481
	Continuous Improvement	482
	Enhanced Decision-Making	483
	Predictive Maintenance	484
	Summary	485
	References	486
	Knowledge Check: Multiple-Choice Q&A	487
Chapter 14:	**Additional AWS Services for Migration**	**491**
	What Is AWS Organizations?	491
	What Problems Does AWS Organizations Solve?	492
	Centralized Management	492
	Governance	492
	Compliance	492
	Resource Sharing	493
	What Are the Benefits of AWS Organizations?	493
	Centralized Management Across Multiple Accounts	493
	Cost Optimization and Savings	493
	Customizable Environment Through Policies and Controls	493
	Enhanced Security with IAM Integration and Support	494
	Global Operations with Unified Access Across Regions	494

Secure and Comprehensive Auditing	494
Efficient Resource Sharing Across Teams	495
No Additional Cost for Using AWS Organizations	495
AWS Organizations: Centralized Governance and Management	495
Key Components of AWS Organizations	495
Organizational Units	496
Root	496
Policies	496
Management Account	497
Member Accounts	497
Hierarchical Structure and Policy Application	497
OUs: Grouping for Governance and Security	498
Foundational OUs	499
Specialized OUs	499
Basic Technical Concepts of AWS Organizations	500
Organization	500
Account	501
Invitation	501
Handshake	501
Features of AWS Organizations	502
Service Control Policies	502
Management Policies	502
AWS Organizations Use Cases	503
Organizing a Multi-Account Environment	503
Centralized Security and Monitoring	503
Resource Sharing Across a Multi-Account Environment	503
Cost Management and Centralized Billing	503
AWS Organizations Role in AWS Cloud Migration	504
Centralized Management: Streamlined Migration Across Multiple Accounts	504

Cost Reduction and Efficiency: Reducing Migration Costs	505
Enhanced Governance and Security: Policy Enforcement and Compliance	505
Simplified Resource Allocation: Efficient Resource Management	505
AWS Service Catalog	505
Overview of AWS Catalog	505
Why We Need AWS Service Catalog	506
Different AWS Service Catalog Features	507
Self-Service Provisioning	507
Workflow Automation	508
Version Control	508
Tagging and Reporting	508
Multi-Account Support	508
Benefits of AWS Service Catalog	508
Improved Governance	509
Increased Efficiency	509
Cost Savings	509
Enhanced Security	510
AWS Service Catalog in AWS Cloud Migration	510
Assess Phase: Understanding Your Current Environment	510
Mobilize Phase: Preparing for Migration	511
Migrate Phase: Executing the Transition	511
Optimize/Modernize Phase: Enhancing Your Cloud Environment	512
Summary	512
References	513
Knowledge Check: Multiple-Choice Q&A	514
Answer Sheet: Knowledge Check	517
Index	539

Preface

Cloud computing is making waves in the digital world, changing the way companies operate. It offers scalability, flexibility, and cost-effectiveness, addressing the challenges faced by traditional IT infrastructure. In the quest for business modernization and operational excellence, cloud migration has become a strategic necessity for many organizations. Among the leading cloud service providers, Amazon Web Services (AWS) stands out with its comprehensive suite of tools and services designed to facilitate a smooth transition to the cloud.

AWS Cloud Migration: A Modern Approach is a practical handbook tailored for IT professionals, cloud architects, and decision-makers looking to confidently navigate the complex journey of cloud migration.

This book offers an innovative approach to AWS cloud migration by the adoption of a structured method that includes fundamental concepts, strategic planning, and practical implementations.

The book is divided into three main sections:

1. *Introduction to Cloud Computing and Concepts*: This section lays the foundation by explaining cloud computing concepts, including the principles behind it, the implications of this system, and the key factors that organizations must consider when embarking on a cloud migration journey.

2. *Introduction to AWS and Its Processes/Tools*: This section explores AWS services and frameworks that work with cloud migration, including a brief description of the AWS Well-Architected Framework and the three main cloud migration phases: Assess, Mobilize, and Migrate and Modernize.

3. *AWS Migration Strategies and Tools*: This section explores various migration strategies, including rehosting, replatforming, and refactoring. It also provides practical guidance on using AWS migration tools at each stage of the process, ensuring an optimized and seamless transition to the cloud.

This book will offer the audience and readers a practical handbook that works. I hope that this will enable them to become well-informed to make the right decisions and successfully implement their cloud migration project. Whether you are a beginner looking to understand the fundamentals or an experienced professional seeking advanced strategies, this book serves as a comprehensive resource to enhance your cloud migration expertise.

Acknowledgments

I wish to thank Jennifer Blaney and Steven Elliot for their unconditional support, and also for giving me an opportunity to write this book under MERCURY LEARNING AND INFORMATION. They have been my main encouragement and have demystified the most abstract ideas and made them practical.

Thank you to my colleagues, Shrihari Prasad and Mohan Gowda, for their cooperation, and my family, whose support and motivation have been instrumental in completing this book.

Last but not least, readers who are searching for a path to a more focused cloud solution in AWS, and IT professionals who have embarked on their own journey to the cloud, will find this book to be instructive.

Happy reading!

Mukesh Kumar Das

June 2025

CHAPTER 1

Introduction to Cloud Computing

WHAT IS CLOUD COMPUTING?

Cloud computing refers to the delivery of IT resources and various services via the Internet. All these services are available on demand via self-service, with pay-as-you-go pricing.

In cloud computing, users and organizations can access servers, storage, databases, and applications without having to build and maintain their own infrastructure, as seen in Figure 1.1.

FIGURE 1.1 Cloud Computing Ecosystem (AI-generated image).

Here are some applications of cloud computing:

- *Web and application hosting*: Cloud computing can host a wide range of Web sites and applications, from basic personal Web pages to large business programs.
- *Data storage*: We can store many forms of data, including files, databases, and backups, in a cloud computing environment.
- *Software development and testing*: We can build and test software using cloud computing, eliminating the need for expensive on-premises hardware and software.
- *Execute High-Performance Computing (HPC) workloads*: We can use cloud computing to run HPC tasks such as scientific simulations and video rendering. Businesses can gain insights more quickly by using high-end computational resources that can execute numerous calculations quickly and in parallel.

ON-PREMISES/TRADITIONAL IT INFRASTRUCTURE WITH ASSOCIATED PROBLEMS

Traditional on-premises models consist of physical hardware and software components that businesses use to run their applications, handle computational aspects, and store their data. This underlying infrastructure can be expensive to purchase and maintain. It can also be difficult to scale up or down to meet the organization's changing needs.

The traditional on-premises model vs. the cloud model can be seen in Figure 1.2.

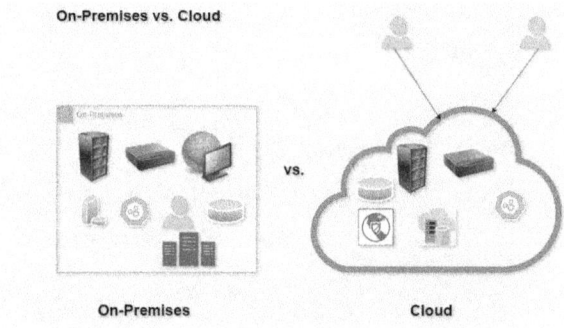

FIGURE 1.2 Cloud Computing vs. On-Premises Infrastructure.

The following are some issues related to dealing with conventional IT infrastructure:

- *High initial Capital Expenditure (CapEx)*: Traditional IT infrastructure can be expensive to buy and deploy. This can create a significant delay for small enterprises and startups trying to get into the market and do business.
- *Operational Expenditure (OpEx):* Traditional IT infrastructure requires constant maintenance and support to manage it effectively and efficiently, which can result in significant expenses over time.
- *Lack of scalability*: Conventional IT infrastructure creates challenges when it comes to changing existing capacity to accommodate fluctuating and changing demands. This can be a challenge for businesses that encounter periodic variations in demand.
- *Security risks*: Traditional IT infrastructure can be vulnerable to security attacks due to the absence of proper security preventive mechanisms in place. Businesses need to invest in security measures to safeguard their data and processes.
- *Complexity*: Traditional IT infrastructure can be complex and difficult to manage. This might need a team of expert IT professionals.

When working in an on-premises model, it's important to consider and resolve issues related to network speed, power supply, air conditioning, and physical security.

So, the bigger general questions are:

Do we have a solution for all these challenges?

Is there any other solution besides leveraging data centers for IT infrastructure?

The answer for both is: *cloud computing*.

Cloud computing can help different organizations overcome most of the issues associated with traditional on-premises data centers. Because cloud computing is a pay-as-you-go service, businesses do not need to make significant initial capital investments or reduce or manage operational expenses.

BENEFITS OF CLOUD COMPUTING

Cloud computing has several advantages as compared to traditional IT infrastructure, as shown in Figure 1.3.

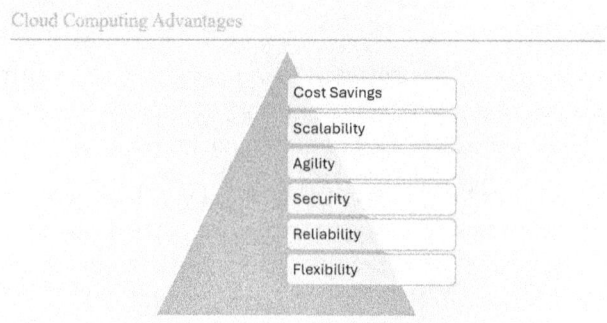

FIGURE 1.3 Advantages of Cloud over Traditional IT Infrastructure.

- *Cost savings*: Cost saving is one of the important benefits of cloud computing. It eliminates the CapEx as well as the necessity of businesses procuring and managing their own hardware and software. It also helps with the reduction of day-to-day operational costs.
- *Scalability*: Users can quickly and easily scale their computing resources up or down, based on their business requirements. It is a Just-in-Time (JIT) service and enables users to respond to changes in demand quickly, without incurring the costs and complexity of maintaining their own computing infrastructure. Hence, it removes the burden of the management of computing inventory and increases productivity.

   There are two types of scaling:
   1. Horizontal scaling
   2. Vertical scaling
- *Agility*: In this modern competitive world, businesses need to be more agile. Cloud computing helps businesses be more agile and responsive to change. In a cloud computing environment, users can quickly deploy new applications and services or scale their resources up or down as needed.

- *Security*: Cloud service providers provide a range of security solutions to safeguard the data and systems of their customers and respective organizations.
- *Reliability*: Cloud companies implement multiple systems and architecture to guarantee exceptional availability and dependability.
- *Flexibility*: Cloud computing provides users with the flexibility to choose the computing resources and services they need, without the need to invest in expensive hardware or software.

In essence, cloud computing is a rapidly growing industry, and it is changing the way that businesses of all sizes use computing resources and infrastructure. If you are looking for a way to improve your IT efficiency and agility, cloud computing is one of the best options to consider.

3-4-5 PRINCIPLES OF CLOUD COMPUTING

The 3-4-5 principles of cloud computing is a conceptual model that is used to explain the key aspects of cloud computing in a structured manner. It describes cloud computing as having three core characteristics, four deployment models, and five essential service models. The following are the main components of cloud computing as described by the 3-4-5 principles of cloud computing:

- Three (3) essential and fundamental services
- Four (4) deployment models used to describe the cloud computing architectural models
- Five (5) essential characteristics needed in a cloud computing environment

CLOUD COMPUTING SERVICE MODELS

Cloud computing offers different service models, each providing access to resources in distinct ways. Understanding these models empowers you to choose the best fit for your specific needs. The three main types of cloud computing are seen in Figure 1.4.

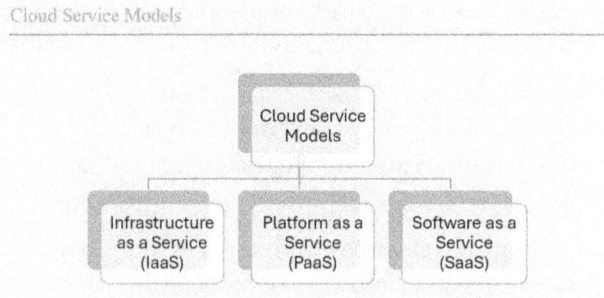

FIGURE 1.4 Cloud Computing Service Models.

1. Infrastructure as a Service (IaaS)
2. Platform as a Service (PaaS)
3. Software as a Service (SaaS)

Infrastructure as a Service (IaaS)

The abbreviation *IaaS* means *Infrastructure as a Service*. IaaS provides the basic building blocks in a cloud computing environment and includes computing, storage, networking, and other computing resources having access to facilities using the Internet.

IaaS customers or users can provision and maintain these resources on an on-demand basis, without having and managing their own inventories such as hardware and software. In a nutshell, IaaS is like renting a space in a data center and having access to all the necessary resources, such as servers, storage, and networking, without worrying about the management and maintenance of these underlying resources. This can be a very effective approach to saving money and performance improvement, especially for small businesses or enterprises.

One of the key benefits of IaaS is enhanced scalability, which allows users to easily add or remove resources according to varied business and demands. This is beneficial for businesses that face seasonal traffic fluctuations or are expanding and reducing rapidly.

In IaaS, consumers do not need to manage and control the underlying cloud infrastructure but they do have control over operating systems, storage, and deployment of applications, and potentially limited control over selected networking components (e.g., host firewalls).

It is also a very secure environment to store and process data. Cloud providers also provide multiple security features to protect their customers' data, including encryption, access control, and intrusion detection. The IaaS service can be represented as seen in Figure 1.5.

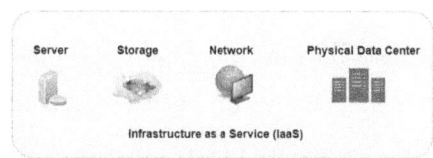

FIGURE 1.5 Overview of Infrastructure as a Service (IaaS).

Amazon Web Services (AWS), Microsoft Azure, and Google Cloud Platform (GCP) are examples of widely used IaaS providers.

Platform as a Service (PaaS)

The abbreviation *PaaS* stands for *Platform as a Service*. PaaS provides a platform for developers to build, deploy, and manage applications. PaaS customers can focus on developing their applications, without having to worry about the underlying infrastructure.

The PaaS service can be represented as seen in Figure 1.6.

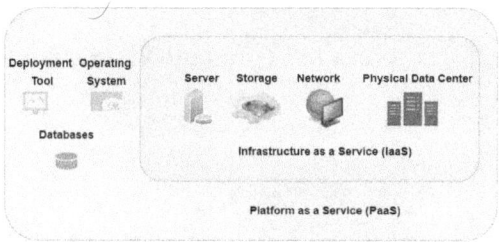

FIGURE 1.6 Overview of Platform as a Service (PaaS).

Users are responsible for application development and operational work, and they are not troubled by the technological aspects behind it. PaaS is a complete package that supports both deployment and application development. Its core services consist of application hosting, database administration, middleware, development tools, and other components. Developers can easily build, verify, and distribute applications by leveraging the preconfigured components and services provided by the platform.

In layperson's terms, PaaS enables developers to focus exclusively on application development while the provider of the cloud service handles all the necessary infrastructure such as storage, networking, and servers, which are essential to the operation of the platform. Thus, it is possible to achieve quick development cycles and scalability and ensure smooth teamwork.

Software as a Service (SaaS)

The abbreviation *SaaS* stands for *Software as a Service*.

SaaS distributes software applications over the Internet. SaaS customers can access and use these applications without having to install or manage any software on their own devices. The provision of software applications is managed by a cloud service provider, who has the responsibility of hosting and delivering this software to users through the Internet, instead of installing and executing software on personal computers or servers.

In the case of a SaaS application, the login process takes place in the cloud, whereas a non-SaaS application runs on the user's computer.

A browser or an app can access SaaS applications. SaaS applications are visible to the general public, and SaaS software such as Facebook, Netflix, Zoom, and Microsoft 365 are very popular and have a global reach of millions of users. Additionally, with cloud computing, building SaaS applications has become faster, which further helps increase its popularity in the developer community.

The SaaS service can be represented as seen in Figure 1.7.

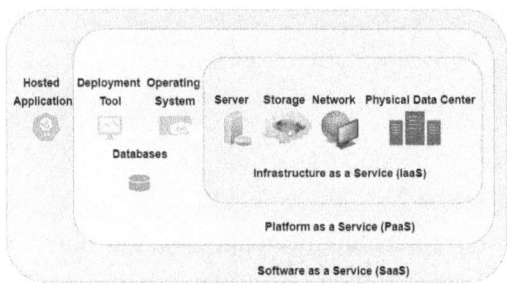

FIGURE 1.7 Overview of Software as a Service (SaaS).

SaaS users, instead of purchasing and installing needed software and applications, subscribe to them as per their needs. Users can log in to and use a SaaS application from any compatible device over the Internet. Cloud servers, typically located in the vendor's data centers, host the actual application and its data

Depending on organizations' and businesses' needs, they can choose to use one or more types of cloud computing in all three cloud services. For example, a small business might use SaaS for all its IT needs, while a large enterprise might use a combination of IaaS, PaaS, and SaaS.

DEPLOYMENT MODELS OF THE CLOUD

In cloud computing, a deployment model refers to the method of deploying and managing servers, storage, and other resources for their customers, depending on the organizational structure and the provisioning location. It explains the implementation and hosting of cloud computing platforms, as well as the users' access rights and accessibility.

There are four main deployment models for the cloud:

1. Public cloud
2. Private cloud
3. Hybrid cloud
4. Community cloud

Public Cloud

Public cloud refers to cloud computing resources and services that are available to the public over the Internet. Public cloud providers, such as AWS, Microsoft Azure, and GCP, offer a range of computing resources, including virtual machines, storage, databases, and applications, that users can access on a pay-as-you-go basis.

A public cloud deployment model (or public cloud) provides on-demand availability of all kinds (for example, IaaS, PaaS, and SaaS) of cloud services worldwide, as seen in Figure 1.8.

A public cloud generally has massive computing resources and storage, is easily available, and is easily scalable.

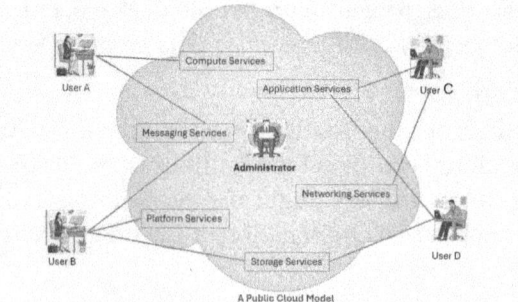

FIGURE 1.8 A Public Cloud.

The public cloud has the following key characteristics:

- Flexible
- Accessible
- Scalable

Getting accessibility from public cloud providers is much more straightforward than getting cloud services in any other type of cloud deployment model (private or hybrid). The reason is that accessibility limits or permission issues are much more moderate in the public cloud than in any other cloud deployment model.

A public cloud provides the advantages of cloud computing, such as a pay-as-you-go pricing model and on-demand availability of all cloud services worldwide, whereas the main drawback of a public cloud is that the cloud provider owns all the computing resources, which may create challenges when the provider goes out of business.

Here are some examples of a public cloud:

- *Netflix*: Netflix is an AWS public cloud platform developed for streaming movies and TV series to people all over the world. Netflix manages fluctuating demand due to the scalability and cost-effectiveness present in the public cloud environment.
- *Dropbox*: Dropbox uses GCP to store users' files and folders for over a million people worldwide. The public cloud model allows Dropbox to provide cost-effective storage solutions without having to manage its own infrastructure.

- *Airbnb*: Airbnb uses Microsoft Azure to connect guests with accommodation around the world. This cloud service offers the computing power and network resources necessary for managing bookings and listings around the globe.

Private Cloud

A single organization, consisting of various consumers such as different business units, can exclusively design a cloud infrastructure under the private cloud deployment model. The organization, a third-party service provider, or a collaborative effort can own, oversee, and run this cloud environment. Furthermore, it can be situated either on the organization's premises or at an external location, as seen in Figure 1.9.

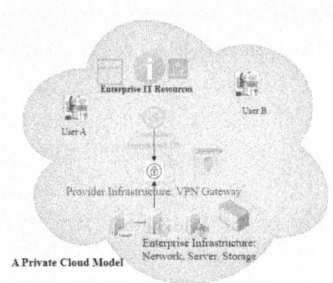

FIGURE 1.9 A Private Cloud.

In a private cloud, you can get all the public cloud features, such as the on-demand availability of all kinds of cloud services. Aside from that, a private cloud, like a public cloud, also has massive computing resources and storage available, making it easily scalable.

Security and control are the main advantages of a private cloud. For example, since a private cloud is behind a firewall, it makes it easier to restrict access to valuable assets. Regarding the control advantage of the private cloud, the absence of an external public cloud provider means there is no risk or single point of failure in the event of a problem with the public cloud provider. The private cloud controls all computing resources.

The private cloud also has a controlling advantage if regulatory needs are critical to controlling the environment.

Here are some examples of private clouds:

- Deutsche Bank employs a private cloud infrastructure to manage sensitive financial data and transactions. This model guarantees the highest level of security and control for their critical financial systems.
- To enable the secure testing and deployment of new technologies within their own environment, General Motors utilizes a private cloud for research and development activities.
- Johnson & Johnson utilizes a private cloud for internal applications and data analytics, which allows them to tightly regulate sensitive healthcare data.

Hybrid Cloud

A hybrid cloud infrastructure is constructed by combining two or more different cloud deployment models, for instance, a hybrid cloud consisting of private, public, or community types. The individual cloud sites are connected via either standardized or proprietary technology, which preserves their distinct identities. It is, therefore, possible to implement cloud bursting and load balancing between different cloud instances due to the connection of data and applications. A hybrid cloud is shown in Figure 1.10.

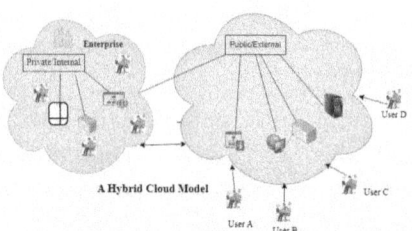

FIGURE 1.10 A Hybrid Cloud.

In simple words, it combines both public and private clouds. The key characteristic of a hybrid cloud is that it enables the seamless integration of public and private clouds for the different cloud solutions as per organizations' needs. For example, a public cloud can access the data and applications of a private cloud, and the converse is also possible.

A hybrid cloud's main benefit is that it allows us to leverage the best features of both types of clouds. For example, organizations can use private clouds to secure and regulate their data tightly. Furthermore, they can securely move them to public clouds such as AWS to leverage their analytical machine learning services to build actionable insight solutions with cost and time efficiency.

Regarding challenges, since there is integration involved between private and public clouds, this integration can cause potential performance issues because of network latency and security risks as data is shared between public and private clouds.

Here are some examples of a hybrid cloud:

- BMW uses a combination of AWS for its public-facing apps, such as its Web site and customer portal, and a private cloud for handling sensitive production data and manufacturing procedures. This hybrid approach balances scalability and security to meet unique requirements.
- Siemens uses a hybrid cloud to establish a connection between its on-premises infrastructure and Azure for IoT applications. This enables them to gather and analyze data from interconnected devices in real time while maintaining the security of confidential industrial information.
- Starbucks employs a hybrid cloud approach, utilizing AWS to operate its loyalty program and mobile app while safeguarding consumer financial data on a private cloud. This approach offers flexibility while ensuring the secure handling of sensitive information.

Community Cloud

A community cloud refers to a cloud infrastructure that is utilized by multiple organizations, catering to a particular community with common interests, such as shared missions, security needs, policies, and compliance requirements. Management responsibilities for this cloud environment can rest with the participating organizations or be delegated to a third party. Additionally, the community cloud can be located either on the premises of the organizations or externally, as seen in Figure 1.11.

FIGURE 1.11 A Community Cloud (AI-generated image).

Essentially, a community cloud is a private cloud; however, it functions as a public cloud. Community clouds are collaborative and multi-tenant in nature and usually cater to the same type of businesses or industries that share the exact requirements regarding security and compliance. Though community clouds are not commonly used, they are typically used by government, healthcare, financial, and other organizations.

Pros and Cons of Community Cloud

The community cloud's advantages are scalability and cost. They are more scalable compared to private clouds. Also, costs could be shared among the organizations using the community clouds. As well as advantages, community clouds have some significant drawbacks because of the sharing nature of this type of cloud. These concern data security, bandwidth, and resource utilization and prioritization.

DIFFERENT CLOUD DEPLOYMENT MODEL CHARACTERISTICS

The different cloud deployment models' characteristics are represented in Figure 1.12.

We can clearly see the characteristics of each model in this figure.

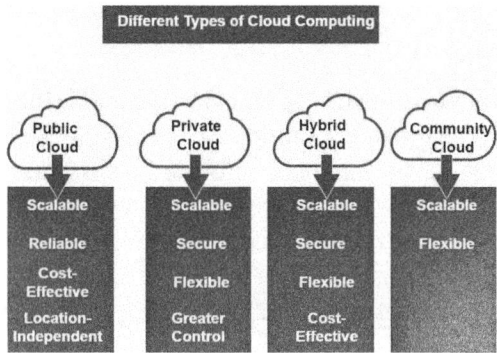

FIGURE 1.12 Different Types of Cloud Computing.

Here are some details about each model and what it can do:

1. Public cloud:
   - *Scalable*: It is able to grow quickly to meet customers' needs.
   - *Reliable*: It is always available.
   - *Cost-effective*: As resources are shared, it's cheap to use.
   - *Location-independent*: It can be reached online from anywhere.
2. Private cloud:
   - *Scalable*: It lets you make changes as your business grows.
   - *Secure*: It offers more protection for private information.
   - *Flexible*: It is able to be changed to fit the needs of each group.
   - *Greater control*: It gives you more power over facilities and supplies.
3. Hybrid cloud:
   - *Scalable*: It combines the ability to grow both public and private clouds.
   - *Secure*: It uses private cloud features for important processes to make security better.
   - *Flexible*: It combines resources to adapt to changing needs.
   - *Cost-effective*: It cuts costs by using the public cloud for jobs that aren't as important.
4. Community cloud:
   - *Scalable*: It meets the needs of a group or society as a whole.

- *Flexible*: Organizations can share resources to work toward common goals.

By organizing the above deployment models into well-defined categories, businesses can compare operational flexibility, security, compliance, scalability, and cost. Companies can make informed decisions and select the deployment model that best correlates with their strategic goals, technical requirements, and regulatory constraints by understanding all these differences.

THE FIVE CHARACTERISTICS OF CLOUD COMPUTING

The five essential characteristics of cloud computing according to NIST are:

1. On-demand self-service
2. Broad network access
3. Resource pooling
4. Rapid elasticity
5. Measured service

The five characteristics of cloud computing can be seen in Figure 1.13.

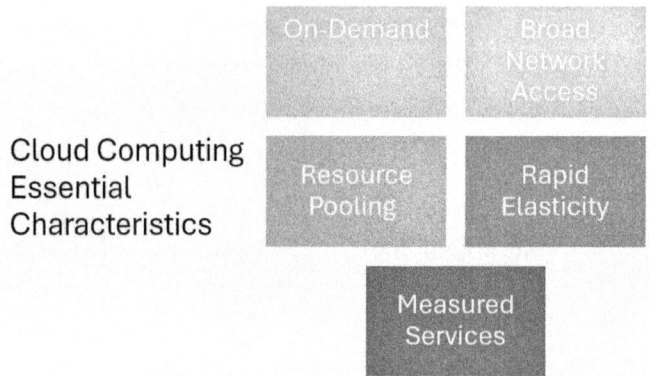

FIGURE 1.13 Essential Characteristics of Cloud Computing.

On-Demand Self-Service

As the name suggests, on-demand self-service allows users to provision different computing resources, such as virtual machines, storage, and applications, automatically without any human intervention from the service provider as per instant needs or demands. This enables users and organizations to quickly and easily access the resources they need for their business requirements.

Broad Network Access

This cloud computing characteristic assists users in accessing cloud computing resources over the Internet or other wide-area networks, using different available sources such as desktops, laptops, tablets, and smartphones. The key benefit of broad network access is that users can access computing resources from anywhere in the world with Internet facilities. Broad network access enables the cloud environment to be independent of location.

Multi-Tenancy and Resource Pooling

Utilization of existing computing resources effectively and efficiently is a very important factor in the IT world. By using resource pooling characteristics, cloud service providers can achieve better performance and usage of available resources. It also helps cloud providers serve multiple customers from a shared pool of computing resources. Providers can dynamically assign and reassign resources to customers as per their business requirements. In essence, by using this, providers can maximize the efficiency and utilization of their computing resources, while providing customers with high availability and scalability.

Rapid Elasticity and Scalability

By using rapid elasticity, users can quickly and easily scale their computing resources up or down, based on their business requirements. It is a JIT service and enables users to respond to changes in demand quickly, without incurring the costs and complexity of maintaining their own computing infrastructure. Hence, it removes the burden of the management of computing inventory and increases productivity.

Measured Service

In a traditional on-premises environment, we need to consider CapEx to set up the different services required to start and run the business successfully. In the case of cloud computing, all the resources are automatically available with the cloud service provider, and we can use them as per our requirements and pay for them based on usage. Most of the services and resources that are available in the cloud are on a pay-as-you-go basis. This means you only pay for what you use or how much you use. It is similar to electricity usage at home. Providers are responsible for monitoring and measuring resource usage, whereas users need to pay only for the resources they consume. These services avoid upfront costs and long-term commitments for organizations.

SUMMARY

Cloud computing is performed via a high-speed Internet connection, which offers scalable, cost-effective, flexible IT solutions to businesses. In this chapter, the essential concepts of cloud computing were introduced by comparing them with traditional on-premises infrastructure, which is often expensive and difficult to scale. The main advantages of cloud computing include lower costs, the ability to scale, fast and secure data transmission, and reliable performance. This chapter also investigated the 3-4-5 principles of cloud computing and described the three models of service (IaaS, PaaS, and SaaS), the four models of deployment (public, private, hybrid, and community), and the five characteristics of cloud computing (on-demand self-service, broad network access, resource pooling, rapid elasticity, and measured service). These notions are the foundation of the idea that cloud computing helps streamline and make organizations more innovative, thus being the preferred option for global businesses.

REFERENCES

[Amazon23] Amazon Web Services, "AWS Global Infrastructure Overview". Available online at: *https://aws.amazon.com/about-aws/global-infrastructure/*, 2023.

[Gartner23] Gartner, "Gartner Magic Quadrant & Critical Capabilities", Gartner Research, 2023. Available online at: *https://www.gartner.com/en/research/magic-quadrant*.

[Barr06] Barr, Jeff, "Our Origins", Amazon Web Services, 2006. Available online at: *https://aws.amazon.com/about-aws/our-origins/*.

[Lorenz21] Lorenz, Eric, "AWS Edge Locations: Enhancing Low-Latency Performance," AWS Architecture Blog, November 2021.

[Quinn19] Quinn, Michael, "What to Consider when Selecting a Region for your Workloads," AWS Architecture Blog, September 2019. Available online at: *https://aws.amazon.com/blogs/architecture/what-to-consider-when-selecting-a-region-for-your-workloads/*.

[NIST11] National Institute of Standards and Technology, "The NIST Definition of Cloud Computing", Special Publication 800-145, September 2011. Available online at: *https://csrc.nist.gov/publications/detail/sp/800-145/final*.

[Smith20] Smith, Karen, "Comprehensive Guide to AWS Compute Services", Addison-Wesley Publishing Co., 2020.

KNOWLEDGE CHECK: MULTIPLE-CHOICE Q&A

Question 1

What does the term "hybrid cloud" refer to?

A. Public cloud.

B. Private cloud.

C. Combination of public and private cloud.

D. None.

Question 2

Which of the following is a cloud platform by Amazon?

A. Azure.

B. Alibaba.

C. AWS.

D. Cloudera.

Question 3

In which cloud service model does the provider manage the infrastructure, operating system, and applications?

A. IaaS (Infrastructure as a Service).

B. PaaS (Platform as a Service).

C. SaaS (Software as a Service).

D. CaaS (Container as a Service).

Question 4

In which cloud deployment model can only internal users access the contents of the cloud?

A. Private cloud.

B. Public cloud.

C. Hybrid cloud.

D. Community cloud.

Question 5

IaaS provides access to which of the following?

A. Fully managed applications.

B. Operating system and applications.

C. Bare metal servers and networking resources.

D. Development tools and runtime environments.

CHAPTER 2

INTRODUCTION TO AMAZON WEB SERVICES (AWS)

OVERVIEW OF AMAZON WEB SERVICES (AWS)

AWS is a public cloud service provider, and its architectural foundation is based on the fundamentals of cloud computing. AWS is the world's most popular cloud services platform, and it is run from different data centers scattered all over the world. The AWS Global Cloud Infrastructure offers 200+ fully featured services in a secure, extensive, and reliable cloud platform.

AWS is used to procure, deploy, and manage IT infrastructure. Additionally, AWS is a secure modern platform to build, deploy, and run almost all kinds of software applications.

It provides a comprehensive range of computing, storage, database, analytics, application, and deployment services that assist enterprises in increasing their speed, reducing IT expenses, and expanding their applications. These services may be accessed whenever needed and are charged on either an hourly or monthly basis, ensuring that businesses only pay for what they use.

THE GARTNER MAGIC QUADRANT FOR STRATEGIC CLOUD PLATFORM SERVICES

The Gartner Magic Quadrant is a graphical representation of a company's ability to execute its vision and capabilities in comparison to other technologies and market standards in a particular market. It is a well-known evaluation tool for vendors in a specific market. By using the Gartner Magic Quadrant for Cloud Infrastructure and Platform Services (CIPS) graph, a company's potential can be understood, which means a company's ability to execute its vision in a specific market is represented by the degree to which it performs relative to other technologies and market standards.

The Magic Quadrant contains four quadrants:

- *Leaders*: Leaders are companies that are executing their current vision and are also in a better position for the coming days.
- *Visionaries*: Visionaries have an idea of where the market is heading or what changes will happen in the market, but they have not yet executed well enough.
- *Challengers*: These companies have a strong market presence and are doing well today, yet they may have some problems with innovation or face competition from new technologies.
- *Niche players*: Niche players either lack focus and fail to outperform or innovate others, or they successfully concentrate on a narrow market area.

In 2023, Gartner conducted a Magic Quadrant study to evaluate leaders in strategic cloud platform services, specifically within the CIPS market. According to this study, the key players are:

- AWS
- Microsoft
- Google

The 2023 Gartner Magic Quadrant for CIPS graph is shown in Figure 2.1.

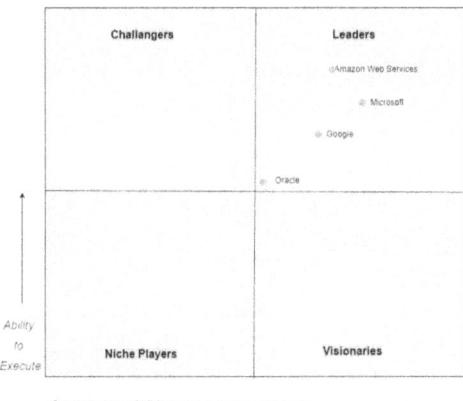

FIGURE 2.1 Gartner Magic Quadrant.

AWS is regarded as the market leader in terms of breadth and depth of capabilities and has contributed to the establishment of industry standards. Microsoft Azure stands out for its strong AI and developer services, while Google Cloud is highlighted for its data analytics and machine learning capabilities.

Nevertheless, AWS tends to prioritize short-term gains in its customer interactions, according to Gartner, which may result in lower brand loyalty.

AWS CLOUD HISTORY

In the early 2000s, Amazon engineers were looking for a way to make the company's infrastructure more efficient and scalable. This is where the idea of AWS came from. Amazon had a huge e-commerce business at the time, and it needed a better way to handle its infrastructure.

Amazon Simple Storage Service (S3) was the first major service that AWS offered in 2006. For organizations, S3 offered a scalable and reliable storage solution. Amazon Elastic Compute Cloud (EC2), which offered scalable computing resources in the cloud, was introduced by AWS in 2008.

AWS continued to grow quickly over the next few years. AWS opened its first cloud computing area outside of the US in 2013.

In 2014, AWS announced that it had passed $10 billion in revenue.

Currently, AWS is the world's leading cloud computing platform. It offers over 200 services to millions of customers worldwide. AWS is used by businesses of all sizes, from startups to Fortune 500 firms. Some of the key milestones in AWS history include:

- *2003*: Amazon begins to develop AWS internally.
- *2006*: AWS launches its first major service, Amazon S3.
- *2008*: AWS launches Amazon EC2.
- *2010*: Amazon moves its own e-commerce business to AWS.
- *2013*: AWS launches its first cloud computing region outside of the US.
- *2014*: AWS announces that it has passed $10 billion in revenue.
- *2015*: AWS launches the Amazon Elasticsearch service and Amazon Managed Services for Hadoop.
- *2016*: AWS launches AWS Lambda and Amazon SageMaker.

- *2017*: AWS launches Amazon Rekognition and Amazon Comprehend.
- *2018*: AWS launches Amazon SageMaker Neo and AWS Outposts.
- *2019*: AWS launches AWS Wavelength and Amazon Elastic Kubernetes Service (EKS).
- *2019*: AWS launches AWS Graviton2 processors and Amazon Quantum Ledger Database.
- *2021*: AWS launches Amazon Aurora Serverless v2 and Amazon SageMaker Canvas.
- *2022*: AWS launches Amazon Nimble Studio and Amazon CodeCatalyst.

The history of the AWS cloud can be seen in Figure 2.2.

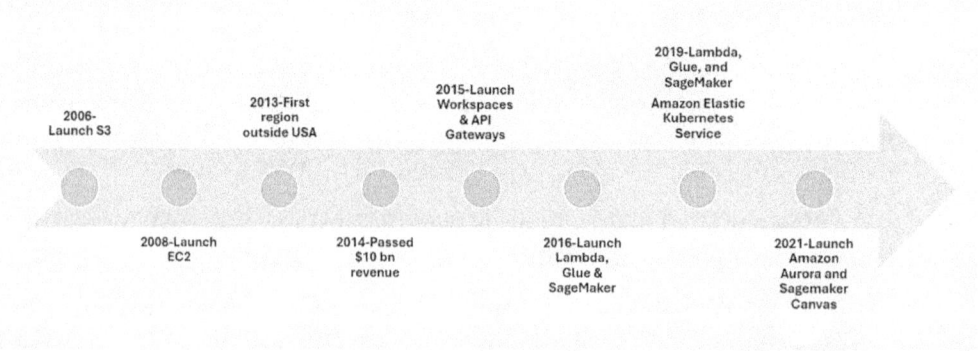

FIGURE 2.2 AWS Cloud History.

OVERVIEW OF AWS SERVICES AND KEY CHARACTERISTICS

AWS provides a wide range of cloud computing services. These services are constantly being expanded and added to the AWS service portfolio. They provide a wide variety of functions that can be utilized for creating, deploying, and managing workloads and applications in the cloud. You can find different AWS products and services at this link: *https://aws.amazon.com/products/*. We can see different key services in Figure 2.3.

AWS Products and Services

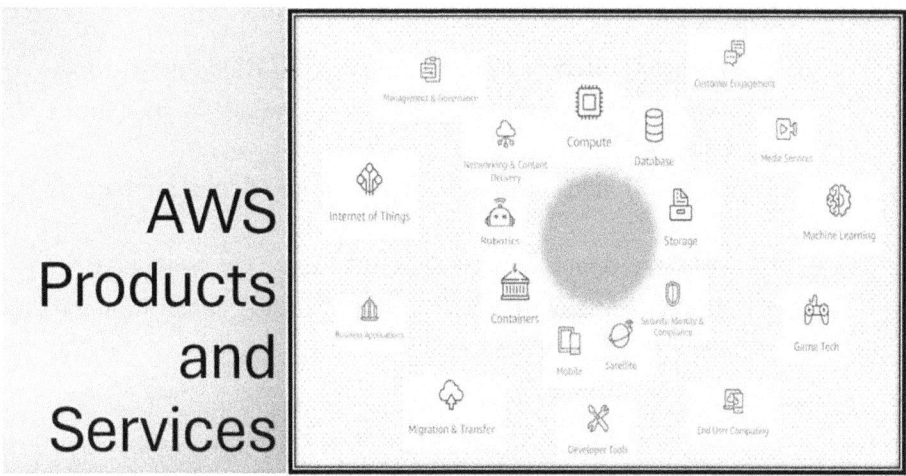

FIGURE 2.3 AWS Products and Services.

These AWS services span various categories and have different important services, as mentioned below:

- *Compute*:
    - Virtual servers for running applications (Amazon EC2)
    - Serverless functions for running code without managing infrastructure (AWS Lambda)
    - Container orchestration for managing and deploying containers (Amazon ECS and EKS)
    - Batch computing for running large-scale, high-performance workloads (AWS Batch)
- *Storage*:
    - Object storage for any type of data (Amazon S3)
    - Block storage for EC2 instances (Amazon EBS)
    - Managed file systems for EC2 instances (Amazon EFS)
    - Hybrid cloud storage for connecting on-premises data to AWS (Storage Gateway)
    - Low-cost archive storage for long-term data retention (Amazon S3 Glacier and S3 Glacier Deep Archive)

- *Database*:
  - Managed relational databases (Amazon RDS and Aurora)
  - NoSQL databases for high-performance applications (Amazon DynamoDB)
  - Managed data warehouses for large-scale data analysis (Amazon Redshift)
  - Managed document databases (Amazon DocumentDB)
  - Graph databases for storing and analyzing relationships (Amazon Neptune)
- *Networking*:
  - Private virtual networks (Amazon VPC)
  - Private connections between on-premises networks and AWS (AWS Direct Connect)
  - DNS services (Amazon Route 53)
  - Network traffic management (AWS Transit Gateway)
  - Load balancing for distributing traffic across multiple targets (AWS Application Load Balancer)
  - Managed firewalls (AWS Network Firewall)
- *Other notable categories*:
  - Security services for protecting applications and data
  - Analytics services for analyzing data and building machine learning models
  - AI services for developing and deploying AI applications
  - Application development services for building and deploying Web and mobile applications
  - Business productivity services for email, collaboration, and other office tasks
  - Internet of Things (IoT) services for connecting and managing devices
  - Game development services for building and hosting games
  - And many more

AWS KEY CHARACTERISTICS

AWS has some common characteristics across its whole portfolio:

- *On-demand:* AWS can be scaled up or down as needed. It helps organizations manage their infrastructure efficiently and save money.

- *Pay-as-you-go*: You only need to pay for the resources you consume for your business or other purposes.

- *Globally available*: AWS is available in multiple Regions and Availability Zones (AZs) around the world. As of the time of writing, it is available in 245 countries worldwide.

- *Secure and reliable*: AWS is one of the most secure and reliable cloud platforms available.

- *Innovative*: AWS is constantly adding new services and features to its portfolio, such as generative AI and machine learning.

To get a snapshot of current AWS services from the AWS Web site, follow these steps:

1. Log in to your AWS account at *https://console.aws.amazon.com/* by entering your username and password.

2. Click the All Services option in the top-left corner of the console. Refer to this link for the us-west-2 Region:

   https://us-west-2.console.aws.amazon.com/console/services?region=us-west-2

AWS GLOBAL INFRASTRUCTURE: A DIGITAL ECOSYSTEM

The AWS Global Infrastructure (*https://aws.amazon.com/about-aws/global-infrastructure/*) is the most extensive and reliable cloud platform in the world. There are several different components of the AWS Global Infrastructure, each with its own purpose and advantages. Regions, AZs, and edge locations are three of the most important components of the AWS Global Infrastructure. Let's briefly understand these concepts; we'll cover them in more detail in the following sections of this chapter. We can see the different components of the AWS Global Infrastructure in Figure 2.4 and in the following list:

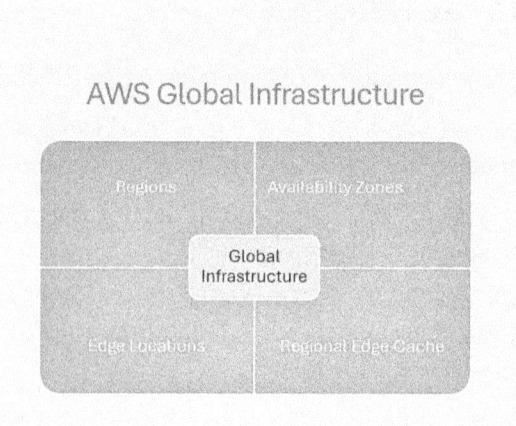

FIGURE 2.4 AWS Global Infrastructure.

- *Regions*: Regions are physical locations around the world, where data centers are available. Regions are isolated from each other, and each Region has its own power, cooling, and networking infrastructure. This helps ensure that AWS services are available even in the event of a major outage in one Region.
- *Availability Zones*: AZs are isolated within each Region. Each AZ has its own power, cooling, and networking infrastructure. This helps protect your applications from failures in a single AZ.
- *Edge locations (points of presence)*: Edge locations are located closer to end users than data centers, which reduces latency and improves performance. Edge locations are used to deliver content and services such as Amazon CloudFront, Amazon Route 53, and AWS Web Application Firewall (WAF).
- *Regional edge cache*: This is a technology used in Content Delivery Networks (CDNs) such as Amazon CloudFront to improve Web site and application performance for users around the world. It works by storing frequently accessed content on servers located closer to users than the origin server (where the content resides). This reduces the distance that data needs to travel, resulting in faster loading times and a more responsive user experience.

We can also consider some other resources with respect to infrastructure:

- *Local zones*: Local zones are located within metropolitan areas. They provide single-digit millisecond latency to applications that need to be close to end users, such as mobile and IoT applications.

- *Wavelength zones*: Wavelength zones are located within telecommunications providers' facilities. They provide single-digit millisecond latency to applications that need to be close to mobile networks.

- *Outposts*: Outposts bring AWS services, infrastructure, and APIs to your on-premises data center. This allows you to run AWS-native workloads on-premises while still benefiting from the scalability, reliability, and security of the AWS cloud.

We can explore more about AWS Global Infrastructure Regions and AZ services at this AWS Web site link: *https://infrastructure.aws/*.

Regions

An AWS Region is a physical location in the world where AWS has multiple AZs. Regions are isolated from each other so that if there is a disruption in one Region, the other Regions will continue to operate.

As of January 2025, AWS has 36 Regions encompassing 114 AZs around the world. There are three types of AWS accounts, and your account determines the Regions that are available to you.

An AWS account provides multiple Regions so that you can launch Amazon EC2 instances in locations that meet your requirements. For example, you might want to launch instances in Europe to be closer to your European customers or to meet legal requirements. Here are the main Regions:

- *North America*: US East (N. Virginia), US East (Ohio), US West (Oregon), US West (N. California), Canada (Central), Canada (East), AWS GovCloud (US-West), and AWS GovCloud (US-East)

- *South America*: São Paulo (Brazil)

- *Europe*: London (UK), Ireland, Frankfurt (Germany), Paris (France), Stockholm (Sweden), Milan (Italy), Madrid (Spain), and Athens (Greece)

- *Asia Pacific*: Tokyo (Japan), Seoul (South Korea), Singapore, Sydney (Australia), Osaka (Japan), Hong Kong, Mumbai (India), Jakarta (Indonesia), and New Delhi (India)

- *Middle East*: Bahrain
- *Africa*: Cape Town (South Africa)

Regions in AWS are marked with country-direction-number, for example, us-east-1 and us-west-2. Please bear the following points in mind:

- An *AWS GovCloud* account provides access to the AWS GovCloud (US-West) and AWS GovCloud (US-East) Regions. GovCloud can be used by the US federal government and private companies. It's operated by US employees on US soil, for US entities only.
- An *AWS (China)* account provides access to the Beijing and Ningxia Regions only. For more information, you can refer to *https://www.amazonaws.cn/en/about-aws/china/*.

Availability Zones

An AZ consists of one or more discrete data centers (buildings filled with servers). Each AZ has its own power, networking, and connectivity, housed in separate facilities. An AZ can consist of several data centers, but they share resources and are so close that they are counted as one AZ. AZs are denoted by an additional letter at the end of the region name, for example, us-east-1a, us-east-1b, and us-east-1c. Let's look at some more details:

- Each Region (such as Sydney-ap-southeast-2) has many AZs (usually 3; the minimum is 3 and the maximum is 6). For example:
  - ap-southeast-2a
  - ap-southeast-2b
  - ap-southeast-2c
- An AZ is a physically isolated location within an AWS Region.
- AZs are designed to be highly available and fault tolerant.
- Each AZ has its own power, cooling, and networking infrastructure.
- AWS places AZs within a Region far enough apart to minimize the impact of a physical disruption, such as a flood or earthquake, but close enough to provide low-latency network connectivity between them.

A sample AZ is shown in Figure 2.5.

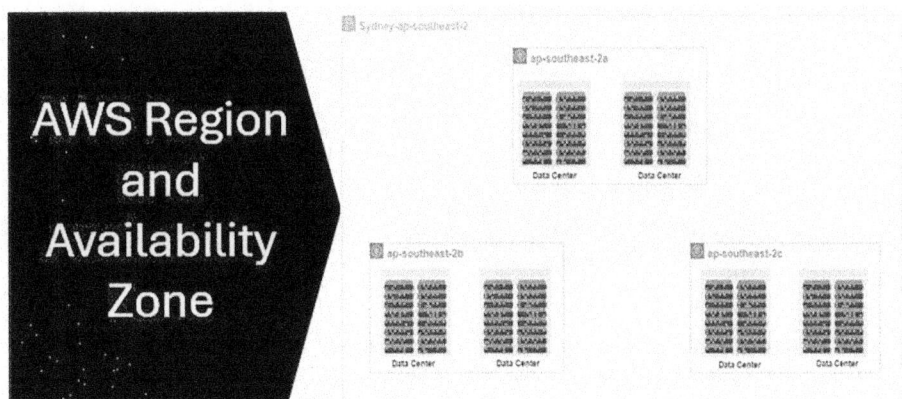

FIGURE 2.5 AWS Region and AZs.

Edge Locations

Edge locations are the endpoints for AWS that are used for caching content. An edge location is the nearest point to the consumer (user) who is consuming the AWS service. In these locations, the server is not present but there is a small setup there. Typically, this consists of CloudFront (Amazon's CDN), which we'll talk about more later in the book. Amazon CloudFront uses a global network of 550+ Points of Presence (PoPs) and 13 regional edge caches in 100+ cities across 50 countries. The Amazon CloudFront edge locations map is available at

https://aws.amazon.com/cloudfront/features/.

Edge locations and AZs are AWS data centers, but edge locations are primarily used for caching the data to provide a better user experience with low latency, whereas AZs are used for hosting servers, Web sites, applications, software, big data processing, analytics, and a wide variety of use cases.

Regional Edge Caches

As we know, edge locations are the endpoints for AWS that are used for caching content. Proximity is crucial for reducing latency. Regional edge caches are used in CDNs to enhance the performance of Web sites and applications globally and are directly related to Amazon CloudFront. Location and content storage are two important factors when working with regional edge caches:

- *Location*: We can think of PoPs as data centers located closer to users than the Web site's main server. These PoPs contain regional edge caches, which are larger storage areas for frequently accessed content.

- *Content storage*: Popular content such as images, videos, and static files get stored in these caches. When a user from that Region requests content, it is delivered directly from the regional edge cache instead of accessing it from the origin server.

From August 2024, AWS strategically distributed 13 regional edge caches across the globe to enhance performance, reduce latency, and improve the overall user experience by bringing content closer to end users in key geographical regions.

METHOD TO CHOOSE THE RIGHT AWS REGION

While provisioning the different services in AWS environments, choosing the right AWS Region is crucial for the availability of services, performance, and compliance with data storage regulations. Here is what you need to consider:

- *AWS services*: The availability of services varies across different Regions, so it is important to select the Region that offers services as per business requirements. The us-east-1 Region always has the most services available because it is the primary Region in which new features are released first.

- *Data sovereignty laws*: Data sovereignty means that data is governed by the laws of the country in which it is collected. Some countries require their data to stay within their borders, so you might be limited by geographic location. You can consider the example of GDPR related to the European Region. In this case, when handling the personal data of European Union (EU) citizens, you should select a Region within the EU (e.g., EU-Central (Frankfurt) or EU-West (Ireland)) to ensure compliance with GDPR.

- *Latency end users*: You need to consider the Regions where most of your end users are located so that you can avoid high latency.

DIFFERENT METHODS TO ACCESS OR CONNECT TO AWS

We have already discussed different aspects of AWS services and now we need to understand the different ways to access (as well as connect to) the AWS environment. There are different methods to access or connect to AWS, depending on your needs and preferences. Here are some of the most common methods.

AWS Management Console

The AWS Management Console is a Web-based interface that allows you to manage your AWS resources. To access the AWS Management Console, you will need to go to the AWS Web site and log in with your AWS account credentials.

To access or connect to AWS, you can use the following steps:

1. Go to the AWS Web site at *https://console.aws.amazon.com/*.
2. Enter your AWS account email address and password.
3. Click on the Sign in button.

If you are using Two-Factor Authentication (2FA), you will also need to enter your 2FA code. If you are successful, you will be logged in to the AWS Management Console.

AWS CLI

The AWS Command Line Interface (CLI) is a command-line tool that allows you to manage your AWS resources. The prerequisite to the usage of the AWS CLI is that you need to install the AWS CLI on your computer and configure it with your AWS account credentials.

AWS SDKs

AWS Software Development Kits (SDKs) are libraries that enable users to manage AWS resources directly from their own code. They are available in different programming languages, such as Python, Java, JavaScript, and C#.

AWS Mobile App

The AWS mobile app lets users manage AWS resources from their mobile devices. To use the AWS mobile app, download the app from the App Store or Google Play and log in with your AWS account credentials.

AWS SAML Provider

The AWS SAML provider connects users with an existing identity provider, such as Active Directory or Okta. This allows users to use their existing credentials to log in to AWS.

AWS SSO

AWS offers a Single Sign-On (SSO) experience to its users. With AWS SSO, users can log in to AWS using a single set of credentials, regardless of how they are accessing AWS.

The various methods to connect to AWS are shown in Figure 2.6.

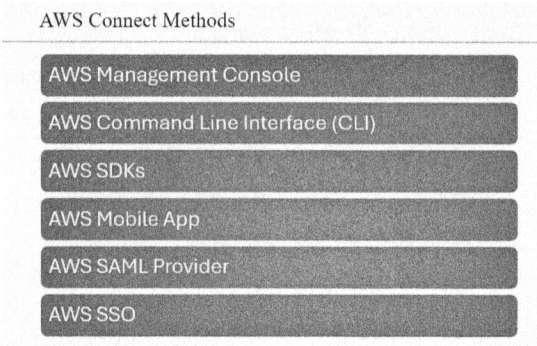

FIGURE 2.6 AWS Connection Methods.

LAB: CREATING AN AWS ACCOUNT USING THE AWS MANAGEMENT CONSOLE

Follow these steps to complete this lab:

1. Open the AWS home page at *https://signin.aws.amazon.com/*.

   Select the Sign in button. Choose Create an AWS account.

2. Enter your account information, then choose Verify email address. This action will transmit a verification code to the email address you have given.

3. Input your verification code and select the Verify option.

4. Input a strong password for your root user, verify it, and proceed by selecting Continue.

5. Choose Business or Personal. Both account kinds provide identical features and functionalities.

6. Enter your company or personal details.

7. Read and accept the AWS Customer Agreement. Ensure that you comprehend the phrases.

8. Select the option labeled Continue. An email will be sent to you to confirm that your AWS account is now operational.

9. Input your payment method details and then choose Verify and Continue. It is necessary to have a valid payment method in order to continue.

10. Choose your country or area code and enter a phone number where you can be contacted promptly.

11. Input the provided CAPTCHA code and proceed with submission.

12. Upon receiving a communication from the automated system, input the PIN provided and proceed with submission.

13. Choose one of the accessible AWS Support plans.

14. Select the option Complete sign up. Upon completion, a confirmation page will be displayed to indicate the activation of your account.

15. Check your email inbox and spam folder for a confirmation message indicating that your account has been enabled. The process of activation may require anything from a few minutes to a maximum of 24 hours.

SUMMARY

This chapter provided a clear explanation of AWS cloud services, their beginnings, and what these services are. The focus was on the variety of services that AWS offers (compute, storage, database, and network), as well as the AWS Global Infrastructure and the innovation of AWS. Techniques for choosing Regions and accessing the platform were among the highlights of the chapter. Additionally, we looked at the Gartner Magic Quadrant, which is one of the key factors that illustrate the dominance of AWS among cloud computing providers. The stability, scalability, and budget savings of the product make AWS the natural choice for businesses to spruce up and streamline their IT structure.

REFERENCES

[AWS06] Amazon Web Services, "*AWS Global Infrastructure*", AWS, 2006. Available online at: *https://aws.amazon.com/about-aws/global-infrastructure/*.

[Gartner23] Gartner, "*Magic Quadrant for Cloud Infrastructure & Platform Services (CIPS)*", Gartner Research, 2023. Available online at: *https://www.gartner.com/en/research/magic-quadrant* (subscription required).

[Jeff03] Barr, Jeff, "*Our Origins*", Amazon Web Services, 2003. Available online at: *https://aws.amazon.com/about-aws/our-origins/*.

[Quinn22] Quinn, Michael, "*What to Consider when Selecting a Region for your Workloads*", AWS Architecture Blog, September 2022. Available online at: *https://aws.amazon.com/blogs/architecture/what-to-consider-when-selecting-a-region-for-your-workloads/*.

[NIST11] National Institute of Standards and Technology, "*The NIST Definition of Cloud Computing*", Special Publication 800-145, September 2011. Available online at: *https://csrc.nist.gov/publications/detail/sp/800-145/final*.

[AWS24] Amazon Web Services, "*Edge Networking with AWS*", AWS, 2024. Available online at: *https://aws.amazon.com/products/networking/edge-networking/*.

[Turing24] "*Comprehensive Guide to AWS Service Portfolios*" does not appear to be an actual publication by Alan Turing. For AWS services, however, refer to: *https://aws.amazon.com/products/*.

KNOWLEDGE CHECK: MULTIPLE-CHOICE Q&A

Question 1

Which of the following is an advantage of AWS?

- **A.** Flexibility.
- **B.** Cost-effectiveness.
- **C.** Scalability.
- **D.** Security.
- **E.** All of the above.

Question 2

Which AWS service category encompasses tools for building and deploying applications?

- **A.** Compute.
- **B.** Storage.
- **C.** Database.
- **D.** Application services.

Question 3

What makes an AWS Region different from an Availability Zone?

- **A.** Regions are geographical locations, while Availability Zones are isolated locations within a region.
- **B.** Availability Zones are for storage, while Regions are for compute resources.
- **C.** Regions are for testing, while Availability Zones are for production environments.
- **D.** There is no difference between the two.

Question 4

Which of the following is NOT a frequent approach to accessing or connecting to AWS?

A. AWS Management Console.

B. AWS Command Line Interface (CLI).

C. AWS Software Development Kit (SDK).

D. On-premises data center connection.

Question 5

What of the following are AWS infrastructure components?

A. Edge locations.

B. Regions.

C. Availability Zones.

D. Regional edge caches.

E. All of the above.

Question 6

What is the definition of a Region in AWS?

A. A Region is a geographical area or collection of data centers.

B. A Region is an isolated logical data center.

C. A Region is the endpoint for AWS.

D. None of the above.

Question 7

What is an Availability Zone in AWS?

A. An Availability Zone is a geographical area or collection of data centers.

B. An Availability Zone is an isolated logical data center in a Region.

C. An Availability Zone is the endpoint for AWS.

D. None of the above.

CHAPTER 3

AWS IAM and *Compute Services*

This chapter provides an in-depth exploration of the fundamental elements of AWS, specifically regarding security and computing. It discusses the Identity and Access Management (IAM) service, which serves as a cloud security agent that controls users' entry into cloud resources by recognizing their identity, assigning roles, and providing audit facilities. IAM ensures that the right people have appropriate permissions, enhancing security, simplifying access management, and ensuring compliance with industry standards.

The chapter describes IAM's core components—users, groups, policies, and roles—giving real-world use cases and pointing out how IAM is very flexible in controlling permissions between teams and applications. It also emphasizes security best practices such as Multi-Factor Authentication (MFA), which adds an additional layer to the protection of AWS accounts.

Along with IAM, the chapter also discusses AWS compute services, which provide organizations with elastic and flexible infrastructure that allows running applications in the cloud. Cloud technologies such as Amazon Elastic Compute Cloud (EC2), AWS Lambda, and Amazon Elastic Kubernetes Service (EKS) are discussed, focusing on their potential to handle diverse workloads.

Using AWS compute services, companies can build their applications using serverless computing and container orchestration, so that the resources are managed in a scalable and secure way.

This chapter explains how AWS IAM and compute services virtually empower organizations to scale securely in the cloud while maintaining control over access and resource allocation.

IDENTITY AND ACCESS MANAGEMENT

IAM is a cloud security service that assists you in securely controlling access to cloud resources. It is one of the key services and is available from all major cloud providers, such as AWS, Microsoft Azure, and Google Cloud Platform (GCP).

IAM has the following functions:

- *Authentication*: By implementing authentication, IAM makes sure that users are verified. Users are granted access to resources through federated identities, passwords, or MFA.
- *Authorization*: IAM allows authenticated users to access and manage cloud resources by assigning roles to users. These define the permissions needed.
- *Auditing*: IAM enables customers to monitor who has accessed and performed actions on cloud resources.

We can see a high-level overview of how IAM works in Figure 3.1.

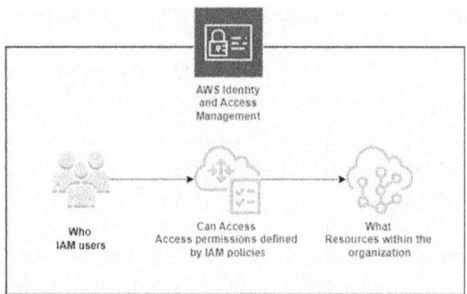

FIGURE 3.1 AWS Identity and Access Management.

Here are the steps:

1. An IAM principal (a user, group, or role) asks for permission to access AWS resources.
2. The first action the IAM takes to verify the principal's identity is authentication. IAM verifies that the principal holds the necessary resource access permissions.
3. If the principal has the requisite permissions, IAM proceeds with the request.

4. The request will be denied by IAM if the principal does not possess the necessary authorizations.

IAM is a policy for monitoring access to the system's infrastructure, helping organizations control access to devices.

IAM Benefits

IAM has numerous advantages, including the following:

- *Increased security*: IAM enhances the security of cloud resources by managing access and defining what users are allowed to do.
- *Simplified process*: By standardizing the granting of permissions, IAM simplifies the process of managing access to cloud resources, reducing unnecessary complexity.
- *Improved compliance*: IAM can help companies comply with different industry regulations, such as HIPAA, PCI DSS, and so on.

IAM: Users, Groups, and Roles

IAM has four key components, as shown in Figure 3.2 and the following list:

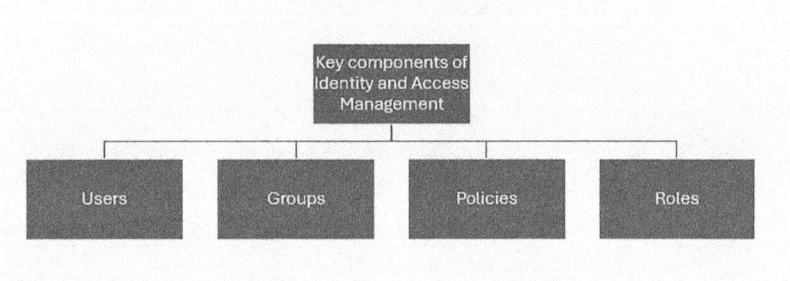

FIGURE 3.2 Key Components of IAM.

- Users
- Groups
- Policies
- Roles

What Is a User?

An IAM user is an essential identity in your AWS account with the authority to perform operations across AWS services and use AWS resources. An IAM user can be a human, a service, or an application that accesses AWS services on your behalf. Each IAM user has its own credentials (password or access keys) for signing in and permissions that define what actions it can perform. IAM users are not the same as the root user, who has full administrative access to the account.

These are the key characteristics of IAM users:

- *Credentials*: IAM users can have different types of credentials:
  - *Password*: For signing in to the AWS Management Console
  - *Access keys*: For programmatic access using the AWS CLI, SDKs, or APIs
- *Permissions*: IAM users are granted permission to perform the actions mentioned in the AWS resource policies.

Examples of users are:

Developer:
  - *Username: developer1*
  - *Permissions: Can create and manage EC2 instances, S3 buckets, and Lambda functions*

Data analyst:
  - *Username: analyst2*
  - *Permissions: Can access and analyze data in S3 and Redshift but cannot modify resources*

Application:
  - *Username: appserver1*
  - *Permissions: Can read and write data to a specific S3 bucket but cannot access other AWS services.*

Lab: AWS IAM User Creation

To create an IAM user, you need to do the following:

1. Log in to the AWS Management Console from the main AWS sign-in URL: *https://console.aws.amazon.com/*.

2. You must choose your user type, either Root user or IAM user.
3. Open the IAM console. Click on the Users link.
4. Click on the Create user button.
5. Enter the user's name: demouser.
6. Select the Provide user access to the AWS Management Console – optional option.
7. For User type, select I want to create an IAM user.
8. For Console password, select Custom Password and enter your password.
9. Add the user to one or more groups. You have three options:
    a. Add user to group
    b. Copy permissions
    c. Attach policies directly.
10. Click on the Create user button.
11. On the Retrieve password page, select Download .csv file to save a CSV file with the user's credential information (connection URL, username, and password).
12. You can find the `demouser.csv` file in your download directory. Keep this file in a secure place for future reference.

What Is a Group?

IAM groups in AWS work similarly to the teams for your IAM users. Directly granting access rights to users is not only impractical but it also forces users to work with permissions. IAM streamlines the process of managing access and guarantees that all personnel are equipped with the appropriate tools for their respective roles.

Consider the following scenario: You have a team of developers building a Web application on AWS. While access is required for the creation of EC2 instances, S3 buckets, and Lambda functions, the ability to delete resources or manage IAM users should be restricted.

Creating separate policies for every developer might be avoided by creating a group named *AppDev* to which a policy with the necessary rights can be added. All you need to do is add each of your developers to the group. They are given the access they require without having to handle managing specific policies.

Here are some key things to know about IAM groups:

- *Centralized permissions*: They simplify the process of adding, removing, and updating permissions for multiple users simultaneously.
- *Enhanced organizational capabilities*: Users are categorized according to their projects or responsibilities, thereby establishing a straightforward framework for managing access.
- *Streamlined administration*: Rather than administering individual policies, users can be added or removed from groups.
- *Granular control*: For more granular control, you can still designate individual policies to users within a group:

Group: Developers

Permissions:

- Create and manage EC2 instances
- Create and manage S3 buckets
- Create and manage Lambda functions
- View CloudWatch logs

Users:

- developer1
- developer2
- developer3

By adding these developers to the *Developers* group, they automatically inherit the group's permissions, allowing them to work on the Web application without needing individual policies.

Lab: AWS IAM Group Creation

1. Log in to the AWS Management Console from the main AWS sign-in URL: *https://console.aws.amazon.com/*.
2. You must choose your user type, either Root user or IAM user.
3. Open the IAM console. Click on the Groups link.

4. Click on the Create group button.
5. Enter a name for the group: demogroup.
6. Add one or more policies to the group. We are selecting the AdminstratorAccess policy. In AWS IAM, the AdministratorAccess policy is a managed policy that grants extensive, near-complete permissions to manage all aspects of your AWS account and its resources. This includes:
   - *Full access to IAM*: Create, modify, and delete users, groups, roles, and policies.
   - *Manage all AWS services*: Perform any action on any AWS service within your account, such as creating and deleting EC2 instances, S3 buckets, RDS databases, etc.
   - *View billing information and reports*: Access detailed information about your AWS usage and costs.
7. Click on the Create group button. This will create a group named demogroup.
8. This group has an AdminstratorAccess policy, as selected during group creation.

Lab: Adding a User to an Available Group

1. Log in to the AWS Management Console using the main AWS sign-in URL: *https://console.aws.amazon.com/*.
2. Sign in with your AWS administrator account credentials.
3. In the AWS Management Console, navigate to the IAM (Identity and Access Management) service.
4. Click on the Groups link in the left navigation pane.
5. Select the group to which you want to add the user (e.g., demogroup).
6. Navigate to the Users tab and click on the Add Users button.
7. Select the user (e.g., demouser) from the list and click Add Users.
8. Verify that demouser is now listed in the demogroup group

What Is a Role?

A role defines the permissions that can be granted to users or groups. Roles are versatile tools that can be changed easily. They can be assigned to users and groups in the long or short term so that they can get access to the necessary resources for a project.

Here are some important characteristics of IAM roles:

- *Temporary credentials*: Roles provide limited-duration credentials and help reduce the risk of unauthorized access.
- *Improved security*: Roles do not use long-term passwords or access keys, reducing vulnerability to unauthorized use.
- *Granular control*: You can strictly limit the actions a role can perform on specific resources.
- *Scalability*: Roles are best suited for either automated tasks or workloads that require user changes to be made frequently.

Here's an example of an IAM role in action:

Role: EC2TaskRole

- *Permissions*:
  - Start and stop EC2 instances
  - Read and write data to a specific S3 bucket
  - Execute a predefined Lambda function
- *Used by*:
  - Auto Scaling group for scaling the Web application
  - CI/CD pipeline for deploying new code versions

When the Auto Scaling group requires a new EC2 instance, it takes on the EC2TaskRole role. This role provides the instance with the required permissions to start up, access the S3 bucket for configuration files, and execute the deployment Lambda function. The role will expire upon the successful completion of work, and the access will be automatically revoked by the system.

AWS IAM Role Creation

A role can be created in three different steps. The first step is to select a trusted entity.

In AWS IAM role creation, a trusted entity refers to the entity that can assume the role and utilize its associated permissions. It's like granting someone a temporary security pass to access specific resources within your AWS account.

Here are the five main types of trusted entities:

- *AWS service*: Allows AWS services such as EC2, Lambda, or others to perform actions in this account.
- *AWS account*: Allows entities in other AWS accounts belonging to you or a third party to perform actions in this account.
- *Web identity*: Allows users federated by the specified external Web identity provider to assume this role to perform actions in this account.
- *SAML 2.0 federation*: Allows users federated with SAML 2.0 from a corporate directory to perform actions in this account.
- *Custom trust policy*: Create a custom trust policy to enable others to perform actions in this account.

The next step is to add permissions. AWS permission policies are essentially JSON documents that define the permissions associated with an IAM identity (user, group, or role) or a resource. These policies determine what actions the identity or resource can perform on specific AWS services and resources. At the time of writing, AWS has 914 permission policies.

The final step is to add a role name, review the role, and create it.

Lab: AWS IAM Role Creation

To create an IAM role, you need to do the following:

1. Log in to the AWS Management Console from the main AWS sign-in URL: *https://console.aws.amazon.com/*.
2. You must choose your user type, either Root user or IAM user.
3. Open the IAM console. Click on the Roles link.
4. Click on the Create role button.
5. Select the type of trusted entity (AWS Service and EC2 Service) for the role.
6. Choose the permissions that the role should have, such as AdministratorAccess.
7. Add tags to the role if needed.
8. Click on the "Create role" button to generate a role named "demorole," which will be available on the Roles page

What Is a Policy?

An IAM policy is a document that defines the permissions granted to an IAM user or group to access and use AWS resources. Policies may be associated with resources, users, or organizations and are expressed in JSON format.

To determine whether a request to access an AWS resource is granted or denied by an IAM user or group, the policies associated with that user or group are reviewed by IAM.

IAM policies implement the principle of least privilege, which states that users should only be granted the permissions that they need to perform their duties.

Here is an example of an IAM policy in JSON:

```
{
  "Version": "2012-10-17",
  "Statement": [
    {
      "Effect": "Allow",
      "Action": [
        "s3:ListBucket"
      ],
      "Resource": "arn:aws:s3:::my-bucket"
    }
  ]
}
```

The following table describes the main elements of an IAM policy:

TABLE 3.1 Main Elements of an IAM Policy.

Element	Description
Version	The version of the JSON policy document
Statement	An array of statements that define the permissions that the user or group has
Effect	Whether the statement allows or denies access to the specified resources
Action	The AWS actions that the user or group can or cannot perform
Resource	The AWS resources that the user or group can or cannot access

MFA in IAM

MFA in IAM is a security feature that adds an extra layer of protection to your AWS account by requiring users to provide two factors of authentication when signing in.

The first factor of authentication is typically a username and password. The second factor can be a variety of things, such as a One-Time Password (OTP) generated by an authenticator app, a code sent to your phone via SMS, or a hardware security key.

The MFA process can be seen in Figure 3.3.

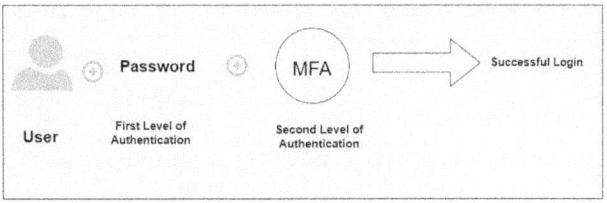

FIGURE 3.3 Multi-Factor Authentication Process.

MFA helps to protect your AWS account from unauthorized access, even if an attacker has your username and password.

Benefits of using MFA in IAM include:

- *Improved security*: MFA adds an extra layer of protection to your AWS account and makes it more difficult for attackers to gain access.
- *Reduced risk*: MFA can help reduce the risk of data breaches, compliance violations, and other security incidents.
- *Increased compliance*: MFA can help you comply with a variety of industry regulations, such as HIPAA and PCI DSS.

Use cases for MFA in IAM include:

- *Protecting your AWS root account*: You should enable MFA for your AWS root account to protect it from unauthorized access.
- *Protecting sensitive resources*: You should enable MFA for users who need access to sensitive resources, such as S3 buckets and RDS databases.
- *Complying with regulations*: If you are subject to industry regulations that require MFA, you should enable MFA for all users of your AWS account.

Lab: Enabling MFA in the IAM Console

1. Go to the IAM console.
2. Click Users or Groups.
3. Click the name of the user or group for which you want to enable MFA.
4. Click the Security credentials tab.
5. Click the Assign MFA Design tab in the Multi-factor authentication (MFA) section.
6. Choose a type of MFA and follow the on-screen instructions.

The key benefit of MFA is that if a password is stolen or hacked, the account is not compromised.

What Is an Access Key?

An access key is an authentication credential that allows users to access AWS resources using the AWS CLI, AWS SDKs, or AWS APIs. Access keys are composed of two parts: an access key ID and a secret access key.

Here is an example:

- Access key ID: `AKIAIOSFODNN7EXAMPLE`
- Secret access key: `wJalrXUtnFEMI/K7MDENG/bPxRfiCYEXAMPLEKEY`

Access keys can be used to perform a wide range of actions on AWS resources, such as creating and deleting resources, modifying permissions, and managing data.

Use cases for access keys include:

- *Automating tasks*: Access keys can be used to automate tasks on AWS, such as creating and deleting resources, modifying permissions, and managing data.
- *Creating IAM users and groups*: Access keys can be used to create IAM users and groups, which can then be assigned to specific roles and policies.
- *Accessing AWS resources from outside of the AWS Management Console*: Access keys can be used to access AWS resources from outside of the AWS Management Console, such as using the AWS CLI, AWS SDKs, or AWS APIs.

Security best practices for using access keys include:

- Only share access keys with authorized users.
- Rotate access keys regularly.
- Use strong passwords for access keys.
- Store access keys in a secure location.
- Use IAM policies to restrict the permissions that access keys have.

Access keys are generated through the AWS Management Console. Users manage their own access keys.

AWS COMPUTE SERVICES

AWS compute is a set of services that provide the resources needed by various workloads for cloud-based systems. It enables procedures and applications to run without physical hardware management, providing flexibility, scalability, and cost-effectiveness. The key services under AWS compute are the following:

- *Amazon Elastic Compute Cloud (EC2)*:
  - *Core compute service*: Provides instances, which are virtual servers with specific CPU, memory, storage, and networking configurations.
  - *On-demand scaling*: You only pay for the instances you have, turning them on/off as required.
  - *Instance types*: There are several instance types—general purpose, compute, memory, Graphics Processing Unit (GPU), and

storage-optimized instances. These are designed to focus on a specific type of work.
- *AWS Lambda*:
  - *Serverless*: The execution of this code is performed by a serverless compute service, without a server setup or management.
  - *Event-driven*: It is triggered automatically based on events such as HTTP requests, file uploads, and database changes.
  - *Pay-per-use*: The cost is measured on the number of code executions, in addition to their durations.
- *Amazon Elastic Container Service (ECS)*:
  - *Container orchestration service*: It manages a number of EC2 instances at scale.
  - *Task-based*: It assembles containers into tasks for scalability and deployment.
  - *Seamless integration with other AWS services*: It is compatible with load balancing, auto scaling, and monitoring, among others.
- *Amazon Elastic Kubernetes Service (EKS)*:
  - *Managed Kubernetes service*: This uses AWS to run Kubernetes clusters without human setup or management.
  - *Scalable and highly available*: It maintains Kubernetes master nodes automatically and offers high availability.
  - *Connecting to AWS services*: It integrates with other AWS services, such as security, networking, and storage.
- *AWS Fargate:*
  - *Container serverless computing engine: This manages containers without requiring cluster or server management.*
  - *Pay-per-use: Expenses are determined by the resources that containers consume.*

We can see the key AWS compute services in Figure 3.4.

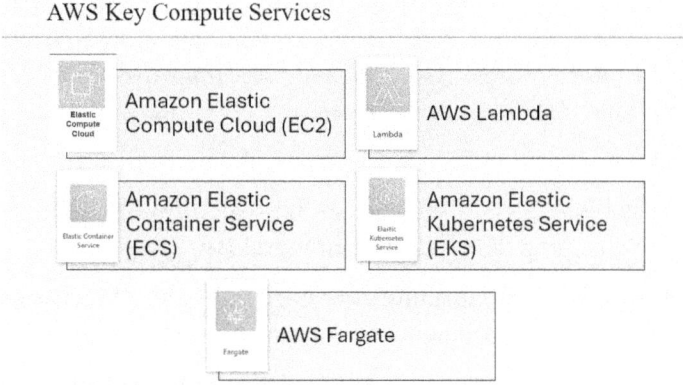

FIGURE 3.4 Different AWS Compute Services.

Amazon EC2

The first service on the list is Amazon EC2, which is a Web service running in the cloud that provides secure, resizable compute capacity. Running applications virtually is easier than on-premises, and AWS customers can select from various options for the processing of the main server, such as different languages and variations. EC2 instances have access to the AWS Global Infrastructure and are available in various types to meet the requirements of any workload.

Customers are billed by the hour and have two options to pay: On-Demand or Reserved Instances. On-Demand is good but is not the best choice for handling sudden automated cost increases. Reserved Instances offer the most significant savings to users who commit to at least one-year warranty periods. The main reason for this cost deduction is the high usage of CPU and/or memory for a long period. The more resources consumers allocate to manage capacity optimization, the more Availability Zones (AZs) they have to back up the reduced costs.

Customers can deploy computing resources quickly by using Amazon Machine Images (AMIs) that are pre-set for EC2 cloud instances. AMIs are preconfigured with everything from the root disk to the software, but customers can add their own configurations as required. AMIs are the master templates for your root computers, allowing you to launch pre-packaged software. Alternatively, customers can create a private AMI where they install their configurations and software on a copy of the original instance.

Amazon EC2 is designed so that you can launch anything from applications, databases, and Web servers to complex industrial software, based on the operators' tastes. Also, machine learning tasks and High-Performance Computing (HPC) experiments are closely connected to the daily use of EC2.

Here are some of the key features of Amazon EC2:

- Scalability: EC2 instances can be scaled up or down as needed to meet the changing demands of your workload.
- Reliability: EC2 instances are backed by the AWS Global Infrastructure, which is highly reliable and secure.
- Security: EC2 instances are protected by a variety of security features, including firewalls, intrusion detection systems, and encryption.
- Flexibility: EC2 instances offer a wide range of instance types to choose from, so you can find the right instance for your specific workload.
- Cost-effectiveness: EC2 instances are billed by the hour, so you only pay for the resources you use.

Amazon EC2 is a powerful and flexible computing platform that can be used to run a wide variety of workloads. It is a popular choice for businesses of all sizes, from startups to large enterprises.

Different Types of Amazon EC2 Instances

There are five types of Amazon EC2 instances:

- *General Purpose*: General Purpose instances are the most common type of EC2 instance. They provide a combination of computational power, memory, and networking resources, so these are suitable for a variety of workloads, such as Web servers, application servers, and databases. These instances include M5, T3, and T4g.
- *Compute Optimized*: Compute Optimized instances are designed to perform well in a very short time for large-scale operations such as HPC, machine learning, and batch processing. These instances include C5, C5n, and C5gd).
- *Memory Optimized*: Memory Optimized instances are designed to have large areas of memory allocated to them, as they will be needed for memory-based workloads such as in-memory databases and data analytics applications. These instances include R5, R5n, and R5ad.

- *Storage Optimized*: Storage Optimized instances deliver high-performance storage that reads and writes a huge amount of data quickly, and thus are best suited for workloads such as databases and big data applications. These instances include H1, H1e, and H1ad.
- *Accelerated Computing*: Accelerated Computing instances are built with hardware resources dedicated to workloads, primarily GPU-accelerated machine learning and video transcoding. These instances include P4d, P4, and G5.

We can see the different types of EC2 instances in Figure 3.5.

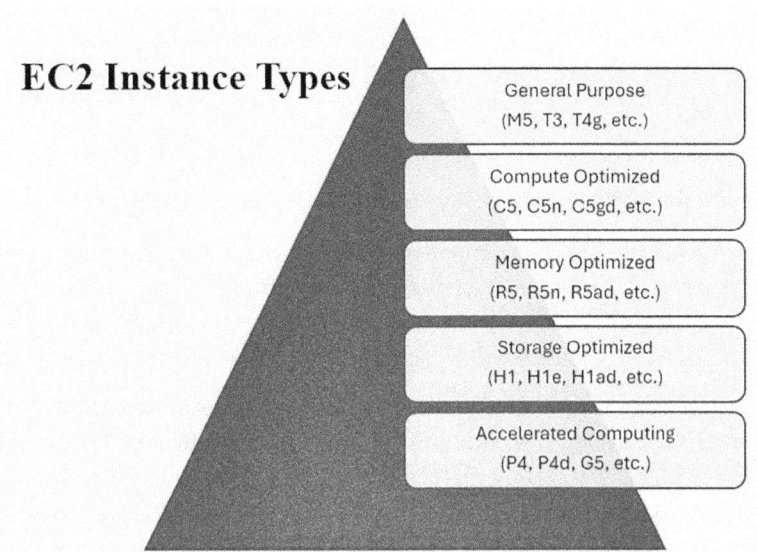

FIGURE 3.5 Different Types of EC2 Instances.

Each type of EC2 instance is available in a variety of different instance families, each with its own unique set of characteristics. For example, the M5 instance family is a General Purpose instance family that offers a wide range of instance types with different computing, memory, and networking resources.

When choosing an EC2 instance, it is important to consider the specific needs of your workload. For example, if you are running a Web server, you will need an instance with enough computing resources to handle the expected traffic load. If you are running a database, you will need an instance with enough memory and storage to store your data.

Here are the Amazon EC2 instances with their families for reference:

TABLE 3.2 Amazon EC2 Instances with Families.

Category	Family	Details
General Purpose	A1, T3, T3a, T2, M5, M5a, M4	General-purpose workloads with a balance of compute, memory, and storage
Compute Optimized	C5, C5n, C4	Compute-intensive workloads such as scientific computing, machine learning, and video encoding
Memory Optimized	R5, R5a, R4, X1e, X1, High Memory, z1d	Memory-intensive workloads such as database servers, in-memory caching, and analytics
Accelerated Computing	P3, P2, G4, G3, F1	Workloads that require hardware acceleration, such as machine learning, graphics rendering, and video transcoding
Storage Optimized	I3, I3en, D2, H1	Workloads that require high storage throughput or capacity, such as data warehousing, file servers, and media streaming

Different Pricing Models for Amazon EC2 Instances

There are primarily four pricing models for Amazon EC2 instances:

- *On-Demand*: On-Demand instances are the most flexible type of EC2 instance. They can be launched and terminated at any time, and you are only charged for the time that you use them; however, they are quite expensive.

- *Reserved Instances*: Reserved Instances are a great way to save money on your EC2 costs if you can commit to a certain amount of usage. Reserved Instances offer a significant discount over On-Demand instances. You are required to commit to a one-year or three-year term when you purchase a Reserved Instance.

- *Spot Instances*: Spot Instances are unused EC2 capacity that is available at a discounted price. They are great for cost saving, but they are not scheduled to always run, and the price is highly variable. You can request Spot Instances from Amazon EC2 Spot Fleet, which will automatically release and create them based on the workload and available budget.

- *Dedicated Hosts*: Dedicated Hosts are physical EC2 servers that are dedicated to your use. You can take advantage of Dedicated Hosts by using your current server-bound software licenses, thus decreasing costs; however, Dedicated Hosts are also the least flexible type of EC2 instance, and they can be more expensive than other types of instances.

Different pricing models for Amazon EC2 instances can be seen in Figure 3.6.

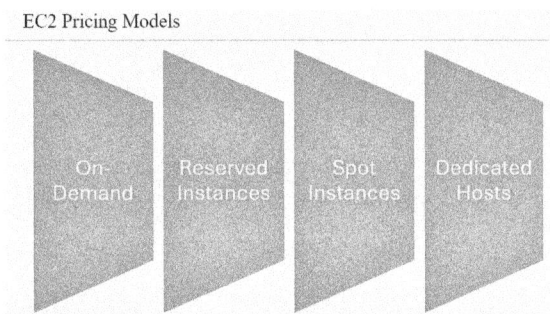

FIGURE 3.6 Different Pricing Models for Amazon EC2 Instances.

Which pricing model is right for you depends on your specific needs and requirements. If you want to have the most flexible option, you should opt for On-Demand instances. Reserved Instances can save you a lot of money if you commit to a certain amount. Cost is a major factor in your decision, so you should decide whether lower prices are provided by Spot Instances to meet your needs. If you want to utilize a physical node that is just available to you, then go for Dedicated Hosts.

Amazon Machine Image

An AMI is a template that contains the information required to launch an instance. It includes the operating system, applications, and settings that will be applied to the instance when it is launched. The key details regarding AMIs are:

- AMIs are the basic unit of deployment for Amazon EC2 instances.
- AMIs can be created and shared by AWS users.
- AMIs can be used to launch new instances, to replace existing instances, and to create backups of instances.

The main categories of AMIs can be seen in Figure 3.7.

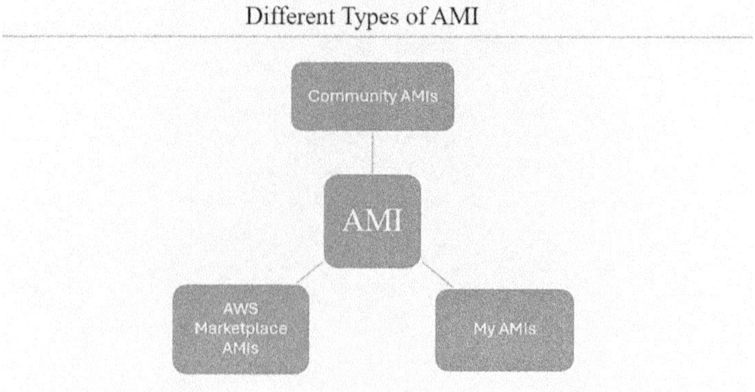

FIGURE 3.7 Different Types of AMI.

AMIs come in three main categories:

- *Community AMIs*: These AMIs are free to use and are generally packaged with the operating system of your choice.
- *AWS Marketplace AMIs*: These are pay-to-use AMIs and generally come packaged with additional, licensed software.
- *My AMIs*: These AMIs are created by you and are only available to your AWS account.

To launch an instance from an AMI, you select the AMI that you want to use and then specify the instance type, the number of instances that you want to launch, and the other configuration options for the instance. The instance will be launched with the same operating system, applications, and settings as the AMI after you have launched the instance.

Amazon Instance User Data and Instance Metadata

Amazon instance user data, also known as user data, is text data that you can add during your Amazon EC2 instance launch process. It allows you to configure the instance, install certain applications, or run scripts. User data is a string that has a limit of 16 KB and must be Base64-encoded.

Amazon instance metadata is the dynamic data related to your EC2 instance, and it is delivered by the AWS Instance Metadata Service (IMDS). Instance metadata is data relating to the actual instance, such as the type of instance, instance ID, AZ, etc. It also includes information about the instance's environment, such as the Region and AMI from which it was launched.

You can use instance user data to install the Apache Web server on an EC2 instance. The following user data script will install Apache and start the Web server:

```
#!/bin/bash
yum update -y
yum install -y httpd
systemctl start httpd
```

To specify this user data when launching your instance, you can use the AWS CLI or the Amazon EC2 console.

Once your instance is launched, you can retrieve instance metadata using the IMDS. For example, the following command will retrieve the instance ID:

```
curl http://169.254.169.254/latest/meta-data/instance-id
```

You can also use instance metadata to access user data that you specified when launching your instance. To do this, you can use the following URI:

```
http://169.254.169.254/latest/user-data
```

The following example shows how to retrieve user data from within a running instance:

```
curl http://169.254.169.254/latest/user-data > user-data
```

This will save the user data to a file called user-data. You can then view the user data using a text editor.

Instance metadata and user data can be useful for a variety of tasks, such as:

- Automating the configuration of EC2 instances
- Installing and configuring software on EC2 instances
- Running scripts on EC2 instances
- Troubleshooting EC2 instances
- Collecting information about EC2 instances

It is important to note that instance metadata and user data are not encrypted, so you should not store sensitive data in them.

Classic Port in Windows and Linux

In Linux and Windows servers, a classic port is another name for a well-known port that is used by a certain application or service. These ports are commonly used for simple tasks such as accessing Web sites, exchanging files, or logging in to a server network.

The classic ports that are listed are all important ports to know, especially if you are working with Linux or Windows servers. Here is a summary of some of the important classical ports:

- *Port 22*: Secure Shell (SSH) is a network protocol that offers a secure method to log in to a remote computer. It makes use of cryptography or encryption to safeguard the data from unauthorized access.

- *Port 21*: File Transfer Protocol (FTP) is a network protocol that permits the user to send a file from their computer to a remote server. It is a safe way to communicate that allows users to securely send or receive data on the network.

- *Port 22*: Secure File Transfer Protocol (SFTP) is a secure line of FTP that uses the SSH protocol to encrypt your data. It is the better way of data transfer between the computer and the server. This is the same port used by SSH, as SFTP is typically implemented as an extension of SSH for secure file transfer; however, it is possible to configure SFTP to use a different port if needed.

- *Port 80*: Hypertext Transfer Protocol (HTTP) is the protocol used to transfer Web pages and other resources over the Internet. It is not secure, so users should be directed to only visit Web sites that use the HTTPS protocol.

- *Port 443*: Hypertext Transfer Protocol Secure (HTTPS) is a safe version of HTTP using SSL/TLS, which encrypts the data. This is the primary method for users to access Web sites and other resources over the Internet.

- *Port 3389*: Remote Desktop Protocol (RDP) is the protocol that lets you monitor and manage a remote system as if you were there physically. Nevertheless, it is not secure, so ensuring that it is used only over a trusted network is crucial.

The classic ports we have listed are all important ports to know, especially if you are working with Linux or Windows servers. As well as these classic ports, there are numerous other ports available for different applications and services. It is essential to be aware of the open ports on your network and take the necessary measures to secure them.

What Is SSH?

SSH refers to Secure Shell. It is a network protocol that enables a secure way to log in to a remote computer. SSH is used for encrypting data to prevent your data from being intercepted.

SSH has many uses; however, the following ones are commonly cited:

- Logging in to a remote server
- Transferring files between computers
- Running commands on a remote server
- Creating a secure tunnel between two computers

SSH is a tool that can be employed in many different ways, and it is used by system administrators, developers, and other IT professionals in different parts of the world.

To connect to an EC2 instance using SSH, you will need to have an SSH client installed on your local computer.

On macOS or Linux:

1. Open a Terminal window.
2. Navigate to the directory where your EC2 private key is stored.
3. Run the following command:

   ```
   ssh -i [private_key_file] [ec2_username]@[ec2_public_ip_address]
   ```

   Replace the following values:

   - `[private_key_file]`: The path to your EC2 private key file
   - `[ec2_username]`: The username for your EC2 instance
   - `[ec2_public_ip_address]`: The public IP address of your EC2 instance

On Windows:

1. Install an SSH client such as PuTTY.
2. Open PuTTY and enter the following information:
   - *Host Name (or IP address)*: The public IP address of your EC2 instance
   - *Port*: 22
   - *Connection type*: SSH
3. Click Open.
4. When prompted, enter the username for your EC2 instance.
5. When prompted, enter the password for your EC2 instance.

Once you have successfully connected to your EC2 instance, you will be able to run commands on the instance as if you were sitting in front of it.

Here is an example of how to connect to an EC2 instance using SSH on macOS or Linux:

```
ssh -i ~/.ssh/my_key.pem ubuntu@10.10.10.10
```

Where:

- `~/.ssh/my_key.pem` is the path to the EC2 private key file.
- `ubuntu` is the username for the EC2 instance.
- `10.10.10.10` is the public IP address of the EC2 instance.

Here is an example of how to connect to an EC2 instance using SSH on Windows using PuTTY:

1. Open PuTTY.
2. Enter the public IP address of your EC2 instance in the Host Name (or IP address) field.
3. Click Open.
4. When prompted, enter the username for your EC2 instance.
5. When prompted, enter the password for your EC2 instance.

Once you have successfully connected to your EC2 instance, you can start running commands on it.

Preparation for the Use of Amazon EC2

First, we need to have a proper understanding of the following subjects and associated topics to complete the lab titled *Creation of an EC2 Instance in AWS* successfully.

- *EC2 instances*:
    - Understanding instance types and families
    - On-Demand, Reserved, and Spot Instances, and Dedicated Hosts
    - Pricing models
- *Amazon Machine Images (AMIs)*:
    - Understanding AMIs and their role in launching instances
- *Security*:
    - Security groups and their role in controlling access to instances
    - Key pairs and secure login
- *Storage*:
    - Elastic Block Store (EBS) volumes and their types
    - Attaching and detaching EBS volumes
    - Creating and managing EBS snapshots
- *Networking*:
    - VPCs, subnets, and security groups
    - Public and private IP addresses
    - Elastic IPs and their uses
- *Monitoring and management*:
    - CloudWatch for monitoring instance performance and health
    - Auto Scaling for automatically scaling instances based on demand

You can refer to the subsequent sections of this book to gain knowledge of these areas.

Some of the terminology is discussed next for quick reference.

Key Pairs

AWS provides a secure way to log in to the instance that you operate, during which the company uses public key cryptography. In the case of Linux, a password does not work in gaining access to your instance. This is where a key pair comes in handy, as it provides a secure login to your instance that will keep it and its contents safe from attacks or sabotage. When you are about to launch your instance, you need to specify the name of the key pair to enable you to log in using SSH functionalities to get your private key, which will allow you to access your instance. You need to protect your private key and not share it with anyone else, similar to the way you would keep your house keys or car keys safe, or keep any other piece of vital equipment or access cards private.

Security Groups

Security groups are extremely useful as they act as a firewall at an instance level and control the traffic you receive and send from your instance. Security groups are a great way to ensure that only the right people have access to your instance. If you want to connect to your instance from your home computer, be sure to add rules to the security group that will allow you to connect using the SSH protocol from your IP address. Likewise, you can also include rules to allow users or traffic to access your instance through HTTP or HTTPS for both sources and destinations. Consequently, if you want to develop or test an application before its official release, you can be confident that users only have access to the application that they need in order to improve the quality of the application as a whole.

When you launch your EC2 instance, you ensure its safety by specifying the key pair to be used (this is to prove you are the valid user) and the use of a security group (acting as a virtual firewall enabling the control of all traffic across the instance). It is important to note that accessing an instance through SSH requires you to provide the private key associated with the key pair you selected during instance creation. Additionally, the security policy you introduce in any security group is the only factor that allows you to reach a particular instance. Therefore, you can be sure that unauthorized people will not be able to access your computer, as only the right people have been granted access, making it almost impossible for them to steal anything from your machine.

Root Volume

On every EC2 instance, an instance uses a single root volume hosting the operating system and boot files. It can be described as the anchor of the instance that contains all the essential software tools. By default, the root volume is based on Amazon EBS, which implies that it is still available even after the EC2 instance has shut down.

Additional Volumes

To start with the base or root EBS volume, you can easily attach additional EBS volumes to your EC2 instance for wider storage options. In these cases, these additional volumes appear as separate and undistinguishable devices within the EC2 instance, enabling you to efficiently store a wide variety of files such as important databases, application files, log files, and many other types of data. These additional volumes may be easily and effectively managed in the same way as the base/root volume—you can resize the existing volumes up to the set limits, detach them from the EC2 instance without any issues, and take precise snapshots so that all your backup data is available.

The key components of an EC2 instance can be seen in Figure 3.8.

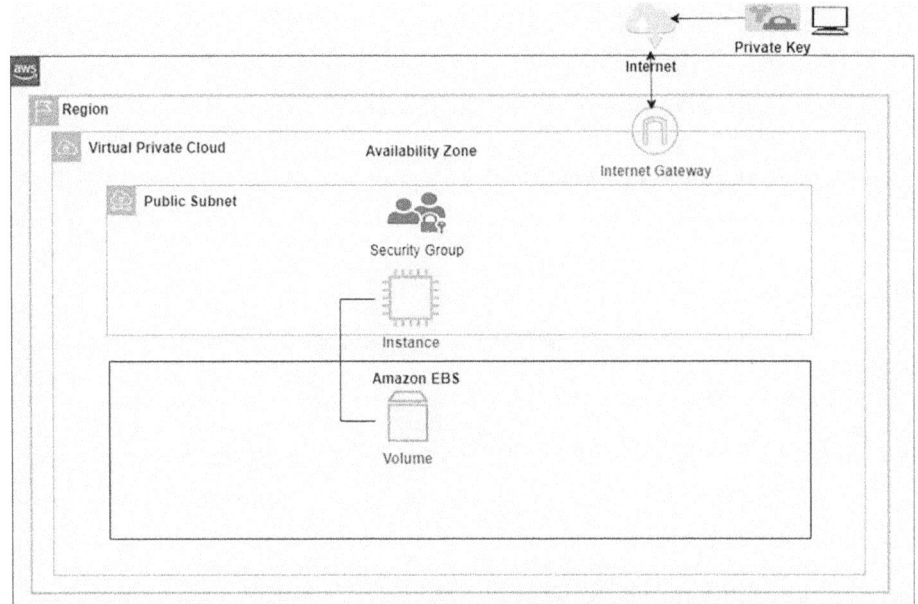

FIGURE 3.8 Overall Architecture of an EC2 Instance.

Volumes

An EBS volume is a highly durable, scalable, and high-performance block-level storage device provided by AWS. Users can easily attach them to any of their Amazon EC2 instances and thus enjoy the full power of elastic and scalable storage.

It is similar to connecting multiple solid-state drives designed to function inside a virtual machine, making it appear as more than just another set of external or rather local storage capabilities. Adding an EBS volume for use with specific applications offered by cloud computing providers is essential for efficiently storing data that must remain for some time, including database data, application files, and operating systems.

Lab: Creation of an EC2 Instance in AWS

We can create an EC2 instance using the following steps:

1. Sign up for an AWS account.
2. Create a key pair.
3. Create a security group.
4. Launch an instance.
5. Get information about the newly created instance.
6. Connect to the newly created instance.

Step 1: Sign Up for an AWS Account

Open the Amazon EC2 console at *https://console.aws.amazon.com/ec2/*.

Step 2: Create a Key Pair

1. In the navigation pane, choose Key Pairs.
2. Choose Create key pair.
3. For Name, enter a descriptive name for the key pair.
4. For Key pair type, choose either RSA or ED25519 (not supported for Windows).
5. For Private key file format, choose the format in which to save the private key.

For OpenSSH, you can select pem, whereas for PuTTY, choose the ppk extension.

6. Choose Create key pair.

7. The private key file *EC2-demo24-pk.pem* is automatically downloaded by your browser. Save the private key file in a safe place.

If you plan to use an SSH client on a macOS or Linux computer to connect to your Linux instance, use the following command to set the permissions of your private key file so that only you can read it:

```
chmod 400 EC2-demo24-pk.pem
```

Step 3: Create a Security Group

1. In the left navigation pane, choose Security Groups.

2. Choose Create security group.

3. For Basic details, do the following:

   a. Enter a name for the new security group: *EC2-demo24-SG*.

   b. In the VPC list, select your default VPC for the Region.

4. For Inbound rules, create rules that allow specific traffic to reach your instance. For example, use the following rules for a Web server that accepts HTTP, HTTPS, and SSH traffic:

   - Choose Add rule. For Type, choose HTTP. For Source, choose Anywhere.
   - Choose Add rule. For Type, choose HTTPS. For Source, choose Anywhere.
   - Choose Add rule. For Type, choose SSH. For Source, do one of the following: select a specific IP range, choose Anywhere (0.0.0.0/0), or select a security group.

5. Click on Create security group.

Step 4: Launch an Instance

1. From the EC2 console dashboard, in the Launch instance box, choose Launch instance.

2. Under Name and tags, for Name, enter the name *EC2-demo24*.

3. Under Application and OS Images (Amazon Machine Image), select Free Tier eligible Amazon Linux Machine Image. Under Instance type, choose the t2.micro instance type, which is selected by default.

4. Under Key pair (login), for Key pair name, select an existing key pair or create a new key pair if you don't have one.

5. Next to Network settings, choose Edit.

6. For Security group name, you'll see that the wizard created and selected a security group for you. You can use this security group, or you can select the security group that you created when getting set up using the following steps:

   a. Choose Select existing security group.

   b. In Common security groups, choose your security group from the list of existing security groups.

7. Keep the default selections for the other configuration settings for your instance.

8. Review a summary of your instance configuration in the Summary panel, and when you're ready, choose Launch instance.

9. A confirmation page lets you know that your instance is launching. Choose View all instances to close the confirmation page and return to the console.

10. On the Instances screen, you can view the status of the launch. It takes a short time for an instance to launch. When you launch an instance, its initial state is Pending. After the instance starts, its state changes to Running and it receives a public DNS name. If the Public IPv4 DNS column is hidden, choose the settings icon (⚙) in the top-right corner, toggle on Public IPv4 DNS, and choose Confirm.

    It can take a few minutes for the instance to be ready for you to connect to it.

11. Check that your instance has passed its status checks; you can view this information in the Status check column.

Step 5: Get Information About the Newly Created Instance

1. Navigate to the EC2 dashboard in the AWS console.

2. Select the Instances tab from the left-hand menu.

3. Click on the instance ID of the newly created instance.
4. In the Details tab, you will find information such as:
   - Public DNS Name: DNS name (if the instance has a public IP assigned)
   - Private IP DNS Name: Resolves the private IPv4 address of the instance
   - Private Resource DNS Name: Resolves the DNS records selected for the instance
   - Instance ID: Unique identifier for the instance
   - Instance Type: The type of hardware the instance is running on
   - Launch Time: When the instance was launched
   - Security Groups: The security groups associated with the instance
   - Tags: Any tags that have been applied to the instance

Step 6: Connect to the Newly Created EC2 Instance

There are several ways to connect to EC2 instances via the AWS Management Console, depending on your specific needs and the operating system of your instances.

EC2 Instance Connect (Recommended for Public Instances)

This method is the simplest and most secure for connecting to public instances with a Web browser:

- *Prerequisites*:
  - The instance must have a public IPv4 address.
  - You need a supported Web browser such as Chrome, Firefox, or Safari.
- *Steps*:
  1. Go to the EC2 dashboard in the AWS console.
  2. Select the Instances tab.
  3. Click on the instance ID of the instance you want to connect to.
  4. Click on Connect.
  5. Choose EC2 Instance Connect.
  6. Verify the username and click Connect. This will open a Web terminal in your browser where you can interact with the instance.

7. Press the Connect button and the final screen will appear, where you will receive a prompt. An example of this screen can be seen in Figure 3.9.

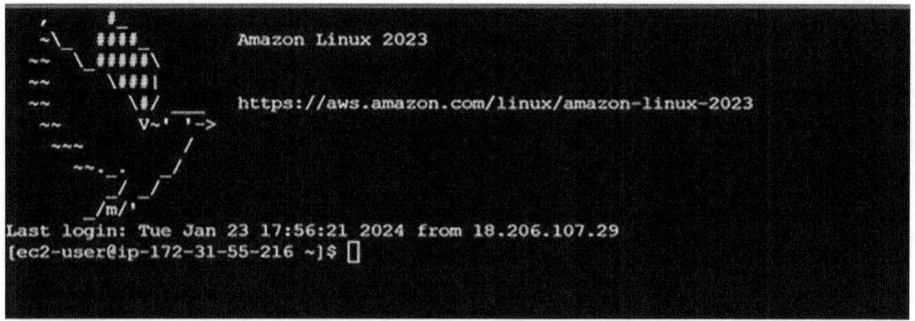

FIGURE 3.9 Example of Command Prompt.

Session Manager (Recommended for Both Public and Private Instances)

This method allows connecting to both public and private instances with a Web browser or SSH client:

- *Prerequisites*: The IAM user needs the SSM:StartSession permission.
- *Steps*:
    1. Go to the EC2 dashboard in the AWS console.
    2. Select the Instances tab.
    3. Click on the instance ID of the instance you want to connect to.
    4. Click on Connect.
    5. Choose Session Manager.
    6. Choose your preferred connection method (Web browser or SSH client).
    7. Click Connect.

    This will open a Terminal session where you can interact with the instance.

RDP (Windows Instances Only)

This method allows remote desktop connection to Windows instances:

- *Prerequisites*:
  - The instance must have a public IP address or be in a VPC with a NAT gateway.
  - You need an RDP client such as Microsoft Remote Desktop.
- *Steps*:
  1. Go to the EC2 dashboard in the AWS console.
  2. Select the Instances tab.
  3. Click on the instance ID of the instance you want to connect to.
  4. Click on Connect.
  5. Choose Connect using Remote Desktop.
  6. Enter the public IP address or DNS name of the instance.
  7. Click Connect.

This will open an RDP session where you can interact with the Windows desktop environment of your instance.

SSH (Linux and Windows Instances with SSH Enabled)

This method allows secure shell connection to both Linux and Windows instances with SSH enabled:

- *Prerequisites*:
  - The instance must have a public IP address or be in a VPC with a NAT gateway.
  - You need an SSH client such as PuTTY.
- *Steps*:
  1. Go to the EC2 dashboard in the AWS console.
  2. Select the Instances tab.
  3. Click on the instance ID of the instance you want to connect to.
  4. Click on Connect.
  5. Choose Connect using SSH client.
  6. Enter the public IP address or DNS name of the instance.

7. Enter your username and key pair information.
8. Click Connect.

This will open an SSH session where you can interact with the CLI of your instance.

Connecting to an EC2 Instance Using PuTTY

One of the most popular methods to connect to an EC2 instance is by using PuTTY. There is another piece of software named PuTTYgen that is used to convert PEM extension-based private keys to PPK extension-based private keys.

Note: Earlier, we only had a PEM-based file, but now, AWS gives us both options (i.e., PEM and PPK).

Step 1. Download and Install PuTTY

1. Visit the PuTTY Web site (*https://www.putty.org/*) and download the appropriate installer for your Windows operating system.
2. Run the installer to complete the installation process.

Step 2. Prepare Your Key Pair

1. If you don't have a key pair already, create one in the AWS Management Console when launching your EC2 instance.
2. Download the PEM key file and store it securely.

Step 3. Convert PEM to PPK (Optional)

PuTTY requires a PPK (PuTTY Private Key) file format. If you have a PEM file, use PuTTYgen to convert it:

1. Open PuTTYgen.
2. Click Load and select your PEM file.
3. Click Save private key and choose a location to save the PPK file.

Step 4. Open PuTTY

Launch the PuTTY application. You can see the PuTTY application in Figure 3.10.

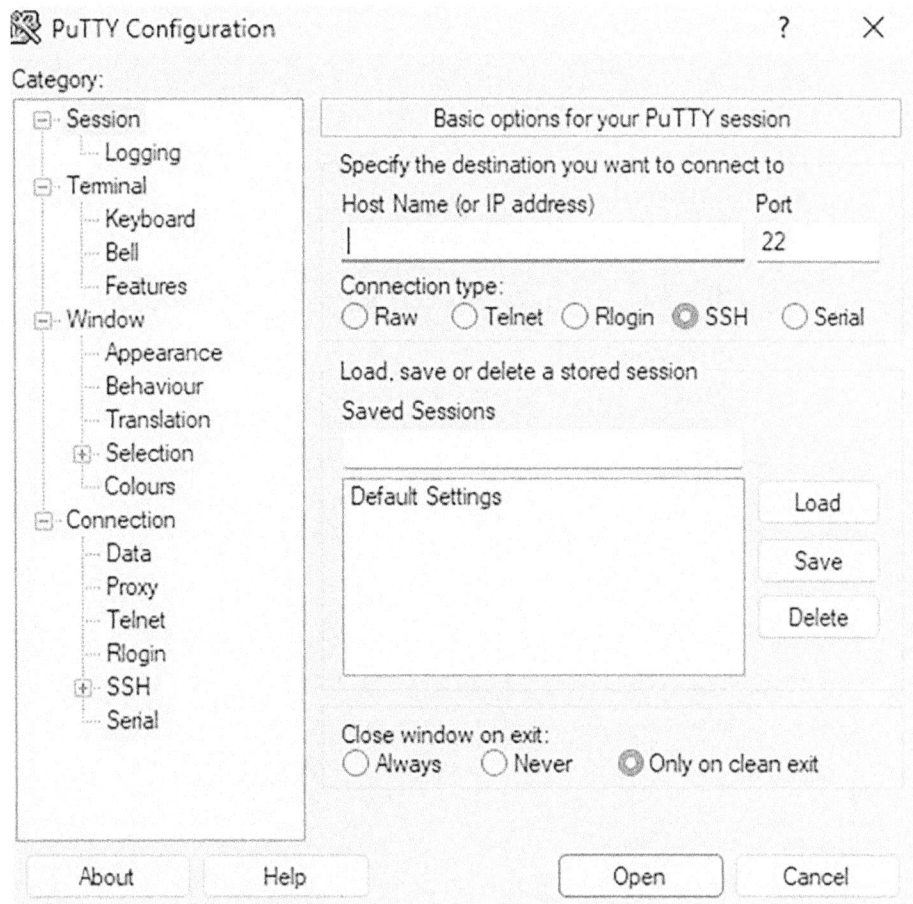

FIGURE 3.10 PuTTY Application Configuration.

Step 5. Configure the Connection Settings

- Host Name (or IP address): Enter the public IP address or hostname of your EC2 instance. You can find this information in the AWS Management Console.
- Port: Set the port to 22 (default for SSH).
- Connection type: Select SSH.

Once you enter all this information, your screen will look similar to Figure 3.11.

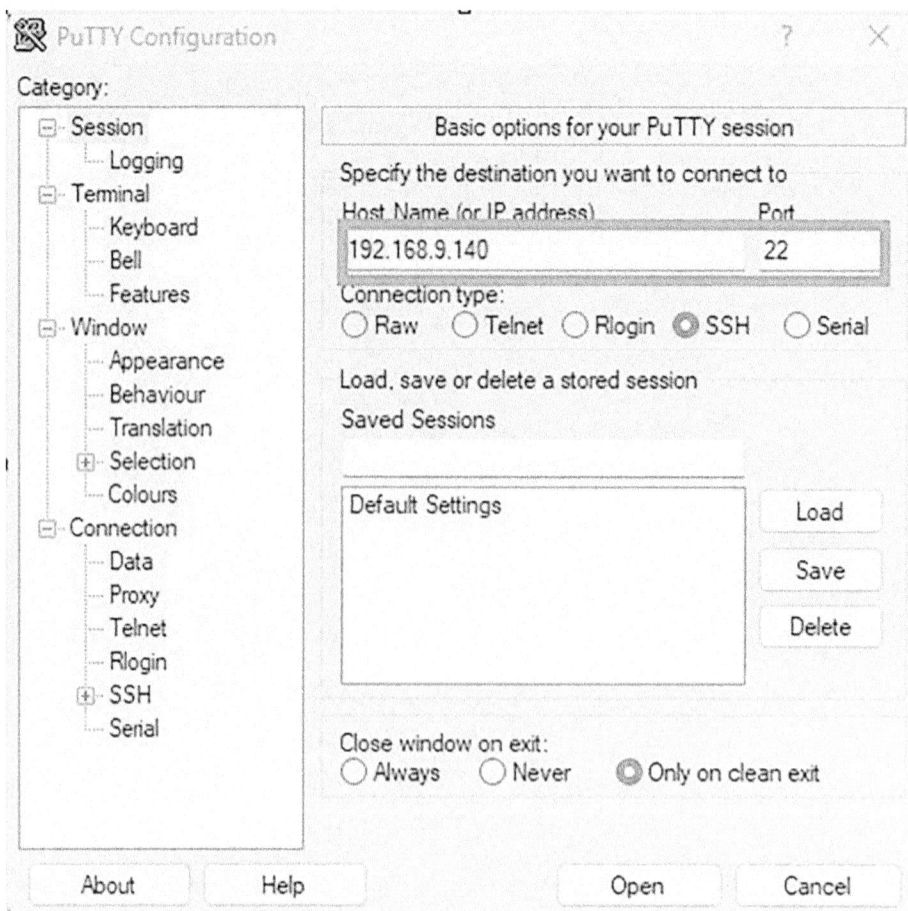

FIGURE 3.11 PuTTY Application and Configuration Settings 1.

You need to select the Auth option under SSH and select a private key file for authentication. Browse for and select your PPK file. Refer to Figure 3.12.

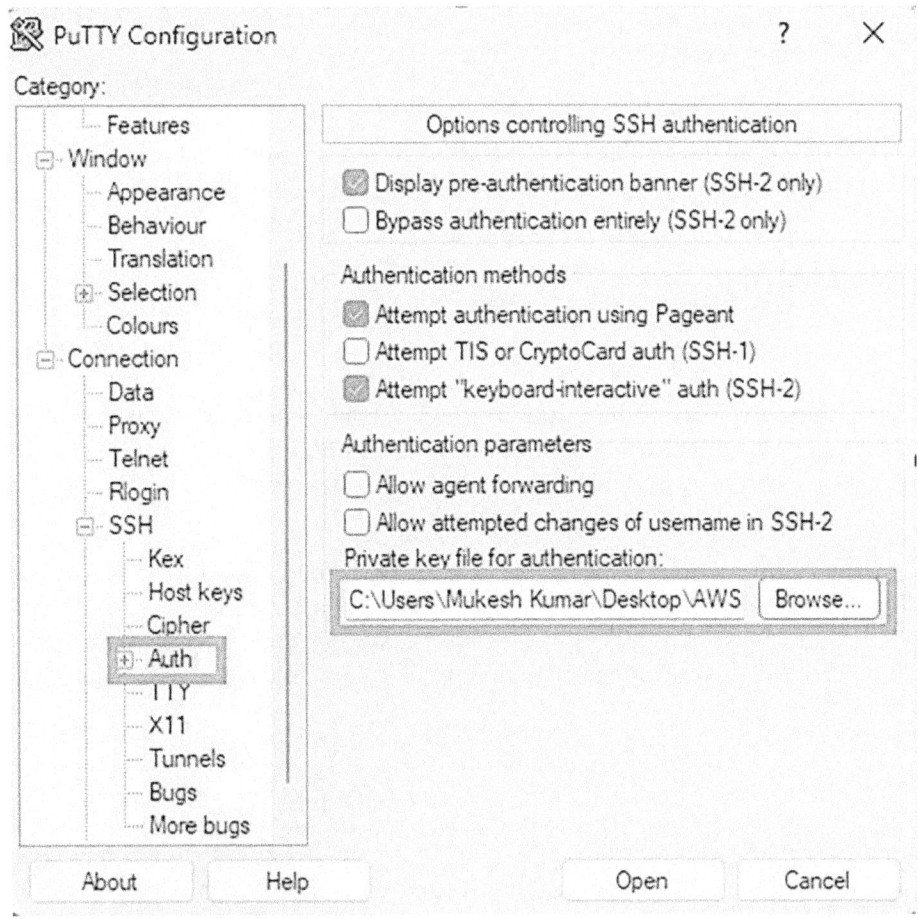

FIGURE 3.12 PuTTY Application and Configuration Settings 2.

Step 6. Start the Connection

Click Open to initiate the connection.

Step 7. Log In

- If prompted, accept the security certificate.
- Enter the username for your EC2 instance (usually, ec2-user for Amazon Linux or ubuntu for Ubuntu).

- You won't be prompted for a password if you've configured the key pair correctly.

Step 8. Interact with Your Instance

Once connected, you'll see a Terminal window where you can interact with your EC2 instance using command-line commands.

SUMMARY

This chapter provided a very detailed explanation of two core AWS components: Identity and Access Management (IAM) and compute services. IAM allows you to protect your resources from unauthorized users through the use of authentication, authorization, and auditing of every service. It plays a critical role in enhancing security, simplifying access control, and ensuring compliance with industry regulations.

AWS compute services such as EC2, Lambda, and ECS offer flexible, scalable, and cost-effective solutions for managing various workloads. From virtual server establishments to serverless computing, AWS-managed services help scale your organization's performance while ensuring a balance of safety and agility.

By successfully combining IAM and compute services, businesses can build secure, scalable cloud environments that meet their operational needs while minimizing risks and optimizing resource management.

REFERENCES

[AWS23a] AWS, *"AWS Identity and Access Management"*, Amazon Web Services, March 2023. Available online at: *https://aws.amazon.com/iam/*.

[AWS23b] AWS, *"Amazon EC2"*, Amazon Web Services, May 2023. Available online at: *https://aws.amazon.com/ec2/*.

[AWS23c] AWS, *"AWS Lambda"*, Amazon Web Services, April 2023. Available online at: *https://aws.amazon.com/lambda/*.

[AWS23d] AWS, *"Amazon Elastic Kubernetes Service"*, Amazon Web Services, February 2023. Available online at: *https://aws.amazon.com/eks/*.

[AWS23e] AWS, *"AWS Fargate"*, Amazon Web Services, June 2023. Available online at: *https://aws.amazon.com/fargate/.*

[AWS23f] AWS, *"Amazon Elastic Container Service"*, Amazon Web Services, July 2023. Available online at: *https://aws.amazon.com/ecs/.*

[AWS23g] AWS, *"Amazon Machine Images (AMI),"* Amazon Web Services, March 2023. Available online at: https://docs.aws.amazon.com/AWSEC2/latest/UserGuide/AMIs.html.

[AWS23h] AWS, *"Multi-Factor Authentication (MFA) for IAM,"* Amazon Web Services, August 2023. Available online at: https://aws.amazon.com/iam/features/mfa/

KNOWLEDGE CHECK: MULTIPLE-CHOICE Q&A

Question 1

What are the benefits of AWS IAM?

A. Increased security.

B. Simplified access management.

C. Improved compliance.

D. All of the above.

Question 2

What feature in AWS IAM allows you to group users with similar permissions?

A. Roles.

B. Policies.

C. Groups.

D. Users.

Question 3

Which AWS service is not based on AWS compute services?

A. Amazon S3.

B. AWS Lambda.

C. Amazon EC2.

D. Amazon Elastic Kubernetes Service (EKS).

Question 4

What is the most important benefit of IAM roles in AWS?

A. Storing data securely.

B. Providing temporary permissions to entities.

C. Managing container orchestration.

D. Configuring virtual private networks.

Question 5

Which feature of IAM is used to add an extra layer of authentication to users' accounts?

A. Bucket policies.

B. Multi-Factor Authentication (MFA).

C. Access keys.

D. Instance metadata.

Question 6

What is the cheapest pricing model for workloads that have steady and predictable usage in Amazon EC2?

A. On-Demand Instances.

B. Spot Instances.

C. Reserved Instances.

D. Dedicated Hosts.

Question 7

What are the three main categories of Amazon Machine Images (AMIs)?

A. Free, Paid, and Shared.

B. Community, AWS Marketplace, and My AMIs.

C. General Purpose, Compute Optimized, and Accelerated Computing.

D. Public, Private, and Encrypted.

Question 8

Which of the following is an advantage of AWS Lambda?

A. Pay-per-use pricing.

B. Manual server configuration.

C. Fixed scalability.

D. Long-term storage.

Question 9

What is the role of a security group in Amazon EC2?

A. Managing access keys for users.

B. Acting as a virtual firewall to control traffic.

C. Allocating resources for applications.

D. Setting up a pricing model.

CHAPTER 4

STORAGE SERVICES AND VIRTUAL PRIVATE CLOUD (VPC)

This chapter provides complete details about AWS storage services and Virtual Private Cloud (VPC). Initially, the chapter introduces various storage options such as Amazon Simple Storage Service (S3) for object storage, Elastic Block Store (EBS) for block storage, and Elastic File System (EFS) for file storage. All these services are designed to address different data storage needs, ranging from frequently accessed data to long-term archival solutions such as Amazon Glacier.

The chapter delves into the most important components, such as subnets, route tables, security groups, and Internet gateways, explaining how these features are used as a control to traffic routing, security, and Internet access, respectively. Also, it touches on advanced VPC features such as NAT gateways, VPC peering, and site-to-site VPNs, which are critical in establishing secure connections between on-premises networks and the cloud.

In general, this chapter emphasizes how AWS storage services and VPCs work together to provide scalable, secure, and efficient cloud solutions, enabling organizations to manage their data and networks with flexibility and control.

AWS STORAGE SYSTEMS

A storage system in AWS is a service that provides you with a place to store your data. AWS offers a variety of storage services, each with its own unique features and benefits. You can choose the storage service that best meets your specific needs, considering the following:

- The type of data you need to store
- How often you need to access it
- How much you are willing to pay

AWS storage services can be classified into three main categories:

- Object storage
- Block storage
- File storage

We can see the different types of AWS storage systems in Figure 4.1.

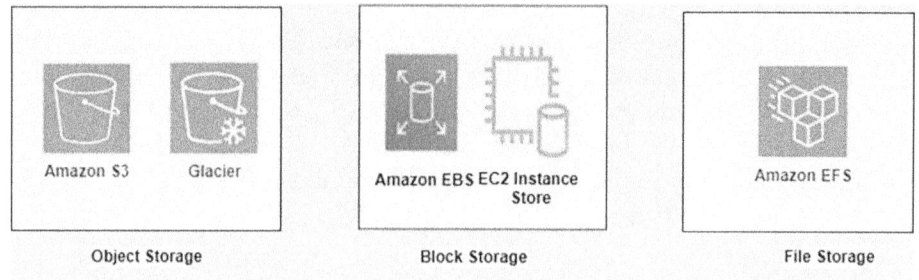

FIGURE 4.1 Different AWS Storage Systems.

Object Storage

Object storage is a storage type that stores data as separate objects. An object is a combination of the data itself, metadata that describes the data, and the identifier of the object, which ensures its uniqueness. Object storage is a very secure and flexible storage method, so it is considered a perfect solution for storing data such as data lakes, Web sites, and mobile applications. The most well-known example of object storage is Amazon S3. S3 is known for its scalability, data availability, security, and performance. It is a utility for storing and retrieving any data, regardless of the amount, time, or location, without consuming time and space.

Block Storage

Block storage is a type of storage that stores data in blocks, which comprise a fixed-size data unit. Block storage is great for storing data that needs to be read and written often, such as the files of a database and application logs. The most popular example of AWS block storage is Amazon EBS. EBS provides the capability of durable, block-level storage volumes to be associated with a running instance. EBS is even well suited for data that is frequently updated in a medium-grained manner, such as database files and application logs.

File Storage

File storage is a kind of hierarchical storage that keeps data in logically related files. File storage is the main method used to store data in a traditional file-based system, for instance, with user directories and folders. A well-known example of this type of storage is Amazon EFS. EFS is a fully managed, scalable file storage service for use with the AWS cloud. You can use EFS to share files between EC2 instances, on-premises servers, and other devices.

AWS also has other storage services such as Amazon Glacier (for long-term archival storage), Amazon Elastic Container Registry (ECR) (for container images), AWS Storage Gateway, and AWS Snow Family.

AWS Storage Gateway

Storage Gateway is a hybrid cloud storage service that provides you with an environment for data storage on-premises and in the AWS cloud.

Storage Gateway offers two types of gateways for use:

- S3 File Gateway
- Volume Gateway

S3 File Gateway connects an on-premises file server with Amazon S3, allowing you to cache some files locally and archive them to the cloud.

Volume Gateway connects an on-premises storage volume with Amazon EBS, allowing you to create cached or stored EBS volumes.

AWS Snow Family

AWS Snow Family is a group of small devices for storing and processing data at the edge and transferring large amounts of data to and from AWS. Snow Family includes three devices:

- Snowcone
- Snowball
- Snowmobile

Amazon Glacier

Amazon Glacier is a secure, low-cost storage option that will last for a very long time and can store data that you rarely access but that must be kept for compliance, regulatory, or other reasons. Cold data storage is for data that is rarely or never accessed. Amazon Glacier is also used for storing data such as medical images, financial records, and customer data. Amazon Glacier is designed to provide 99.999999999% (11 nines) of data durability. Once your data is in Amazon Glacier, it is not immediately accessible. You must first initiate a retrieval request. Retrieval requests can take several hours to complete, depending on the size of the data and the retrieval class you choose.

Amazon Glacier offers three retrieval classes:

- *Expedited*: These retrievals are typically completed within 1–5 minutes; however, expedited retrievals are more expensive than standard retrievals.
- *Standard*: These retrievals are typically completed within 3–5 hours.
- *Bulk*: These retrievals are typically completed within 5–12 hours. Bulk retrievals are the least expensive retrieval option.

Amazon Glacier is compliant with a variety of industry standards, including HIPAA, PCI DSS, and GDPR, and is one of the most affordable storage services available.

Amazon ECR

Amazon ECR is a fully managed container registry that makes it easy for developers to store, share, and deploy container images and artifacts. Amazon ECR is integrated with Amazon Elastic Container Service (Amazon ECS) and Amazon Elastic Kubernetes Service (Amazon EKS), simplifying your development-to-production workflow. Amazon ECR eliminates the need to operate your own container repositories or worry about scaling the underlying infrastructure.

Amazon S3

Amazon S3 is an object storage service that only exists as a data storage service. It provides scalability, data availability, security, and performance. S3 can accept files of any nature. S3 can provide 99.999999999% durability for files and 99.99% data availability. Organizations of different dimensions and domains can make use of S3 for their necessary data storage, such as:

- *Web sites and Web applications*: S3 is a popular storage option for Web site and Web application content such as images, videos, and HTML files. The reliability and ability to load even under intense traffic conditions are the main advantages of S3. It automatically and dynamically increases its capacity and can handle increased loads, even in the case of peak periods.

- *Mobile applications*: S3 can be employed to save mobile application data, for example, user profiles, game assets, and media files. S3 is the first choice for hosting mobile application backends.

- *Data lakes*: S3 is a competent storage option for data lakes, which are gigantic raw data repositories used in analytics and machine learning. S3 has the ability to reach the highest levels one can imagine in terms of capacity and is also a game-changer in the field of data lake handling.

- *Backup and restore*: S3 can be used to back up data from on-premises servers and applications. It is an excellent option to restore data from a backup file, as well.

- *Archive*: S3 can be utilized as an archive for data that needs to be kept for a long time but is not accessed frequently. It has the best data protection and archiving features with extremely high durability and is loss/garbage-proof.

In addition to these general use cases, S3 is also used for a variety of more specific applications, such as:

- *Streaming video and audio*: S3 can be used to store and deliver streamed video and audio content. It is highly scalable and can handle even the most demanding streaming workloads.

- *Internet of Things (IoT)*: S3 can be used to store and manage data from IoT devices. It is scalable and can handle even the largest IoT datasets.

- *Machine learning*: S3 can be used to store and manage data for machine learning applications. It is highly scalable and can handle even the largest machine learning datasets.

- *Gaming*: S3 can be used to store and manage game assets, such as textures, models, and code. S3 is highly scalable and can handle even the most demanding gaming workloads.

S3 is not only suitable for basic use cases but it can also be implemented for a lot of different applications. S3 is highly scalable, secure, and durable, and it provides many features for data management as well.

What Is a Bucket in S3?

A bucket in S3 is a logical container for your objects. It is like a folder on your computer, but it is designed to store objects of any size, type, and access pattern. You can store any number of objects in a bucket, and you can have up to 100 buckets in your account.

More precisely, files are kept in buckets and buckets are top-level folders. The size of stored files can be anywhere from 0 bytes to 5 TB. There is virtually unlimited storage available.

S3 is a global service so bucket names must be unique all over the world. You create your buckets in a Region. The correct way to have a good service is to place your buckets in the closest Region to your users to diminish latency. Objects stored in a bucket consist of:

- Key (name of the object)
- Value (data made up of a sequence of bytes)
- Version ID (used for versioning)
- Metadata (data about the data that is stored)

S3 Features

Amazon S3 has the following features:

- Different storage classes
- Data security using access control lists and bucket policies
- Lifecycle management of different storage classes
- Versioning
- Encryption

S3 Storage Classes

Amazon S3 offers multiple storage classes depending on your use case scenario and performance access requirements. These are classified as:

- Storage classes for frequently accessed objects
- A storage class for automatically optimizing data
- Storage classes for infrequently accessed objects
- Storage classes for archiving objects

S3 storage classes can be seen in Figure 4.2.

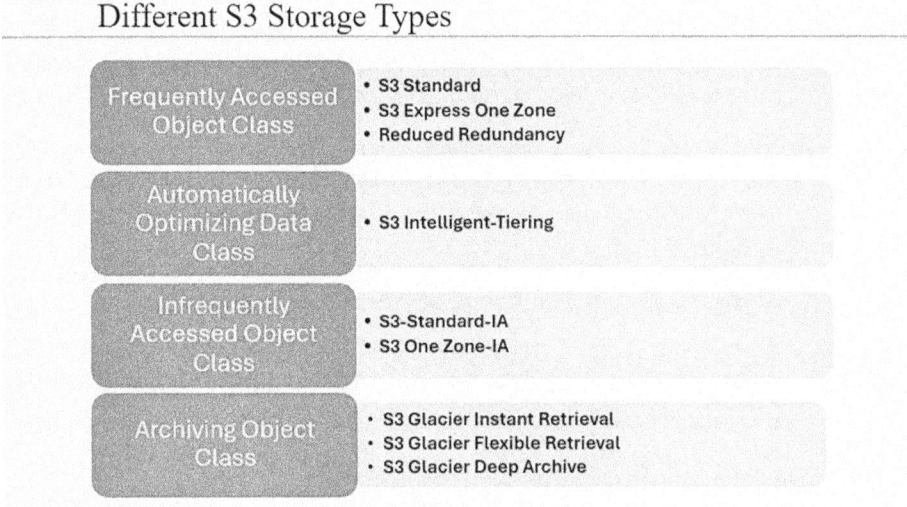

FIGURE 4.2 Different S3 Storage Types.

Storage classes for frequently accessed objects are as follows:

- *S3 Standard*: S3 Standard is the default storage class for S3. It is designed for frequently accessed data, such as Web site and Web application content, mobile application data, and streaming video and audio content. S3 Standard offers high availability and performance.

- *S3 Express One Zone*: Specifically designed to offer consistent, single-digit millisecond data access for your most critical applications, this is a high-performance, single-zone S3 storage class. It has data access speeds that are up to 10 times faster and request costs that are 50% lower than S3 Standard.

- *Reduced Redundancy Storage (RRS)*: Specifically designed for non-critical data that needs to be reproducible, the RRS storage class provides lower redundancy than the S3 Standard storage class.

The storage class for automatically optimizing data is called *S3 Intelligent-Tiering*. This storage class is specifically designed to optimize storage expenses through the automated movement of data to the most economical access tier while ensuring that there is no adverse influence on performance or operational burden. S3 Intelligent-Tiering is the only cloud storage class that automatically reduces costs when access patterns change by transferring data between access tiers on a granular object level.

Storage classes for infrequently accessed objects are as follows:

- *S3 Standard-IA*: This is designed for infrequently accessed data, such as backups, archives, and media files. It offers lower storage costs than S3 Standard, but it may take longer to access data stored in S3 Standard-IA.
- *S3 One Zone-IA*: This is a lower-cost alternative to S3 Standard-IA for infrequently accessed data. It stores data in a single Availability Zone (AZ), which makes it more cost-effective, but it also makes it less resilient to failures in that AZ.

Storage classes for archiving objects are as follows:

- *S3 Glacier Instant Retrieval*: This is a way of storing archive data that needs to be accessed instantly, such as medical images and financial records. S3 Glacier Instant Retrieval can deliver the high availability and performance of the other S3 storage classes but it costs more than the lower-speed alternatives.
- *S3 Glacier Flexible Retrieval*: This is a way of safely storing old data that does not need to be accessed immediately, such as historical data and compliance records. It has lower storage costs than S3 Glacier Instant Retrieval; even so, it might take longer to access data stored in S3 Glacier Flexible Retrieval.
- *S3 Glacier Deep Archive*: This is the ideal place to store long-term archive data because of activities such as digital preservation and disaster recovery. S3 Glacier Deep Archive is the cheapest of all the S3 storage classes; however, it may take a few hours to access the data stored here.

You can choose the S3 storage class that is best suited for your needs based on the frequency of access to the data and the required durability and availability.

TABLE 4.1 Comparison of Different S3 Storage Types.

Storage Class	Availability	Durability	Access Latency	Storage Cost	Use Cases
S3 Standard	99.99%	99.999999999% (11 nines)	Milliseconds	Highest	Web sites and Web applications, mobile applications, streaming video and audio content, and frequently accessed data
S3 Standard-IA	99.90%	99.999999999% (11 nines)	Minutes	Lower than S3 Standard	Infrequently accessed data, such as backups, archives, and media files
S3 One Zone-IA	99.90%	99.999999999% (11 nines)	Minutes	Lower than S3 Standard-IA	AZs, such as secondary backups and easily re-creatable data
S3 Glacier Instant Retrieval	99.90%	99.999999999% (11 nines)	Milliseconds to seconds	More expensive than S3 Standard-IA	Archive data that needs to be accessed quickly, such as medical images and financial records
S3 Glacier Flexible Retrieval	99.90%	99.999999999% (11 nines)	Minutes to hours	Lower than S3 Glacier Instant Retrieval	Archive data that does not need to be accessed immediately, such as historical data and compliance records
S3 Glacier Deep Archive	99.90%	99.999999999% (11 nines)	Hours to days	Lowest of all S3 storage classes	Long-term archive data, such as digital preservation and disaster recovery

Data Security Using Access Control Lists and Bucket Policies

Access Control Lists (ACLs)

ACLs are a great feature to use with Amazon S3 to provide more security for your data. These can be controlled at the object level and are safe to use; however, it is important to understand that ACLs are not the primary recommended method for managing access control in S3. AWS tells us to use an S3 bucket policy or an IAM policy for wider and finer control. Let's look at the use of ACLs in more detail:

- Grant granular permissions: ACLs make it feasible to issue specific permissions (read, write, delete, and full control) to AWS accounts, predefined groups, or the public. This procedure mainly helps when you need to give shared access to a particular object wherein the different access levels are clearly defined.

- Limit public access: As standard, S3 buckets are private, being accessible only to their owner; however, you can unknowingly allow the access of an object to the public through ACLs. To prevent this, ensure you avoid using the *public-read* or *public-read-write* canned ACLs. Additionally, consider using the S3 Block Public Access feature to prevent public access altogether.

- Monitor ACL changes: ACLs can be modified by anyone with write access to the object. To maintain control and detect potential security issues, enable CloudTrail logging for S3 and monitor for ACL changes.

- Use ACLs cautiously: Even though ACLs can have their advantages in specific cases, there are some limits to their usability. They can become complex to manage for a large number of objects, and they lack features such as centralized control and condition-based access. For broader and more secure access control, consider using S3 bucket policies or IAM policies.

S3 Bucket Policies

An S3 bucket policy is a JSON document that defines the permissions that users and applications must have to access your S3 bucket and its objects. Bucket policies can be used to grant or deny access to specific users or groups, specific objects or prefixes, or specific operations (such as reading, writing, or deleting objects).

Here is an example of a simple bucket policy (an S3 Lifecycle policy):

```
{
  "Version": "2012-10-17",
  "Statement": [
    {
      "Effect": "Allow",
      "Principal": "*",
      "Action": "s3:GetObject",
      "Resource": "arn:aws:s3:::my-bucket/*"
    }
  ]
}
```

This policy allows any user to read any object in the `my-bucket` bucket.

Here is an example of a more complex bucket policy:

```json
{
  "Version": "2012-10-17",
  "Statement": [
    {
      "Effect": "Allow",
      "Principal": "arn:aws:iam::123456789012:user/my-user",
      "Action": "s3:PutObject",
      "Resource": "arn:aws:s3:::my-bucket/private/*"
    },
    {
      "Effect": "Deny",
      "Principal": "*",
      "Action": "s3:GetObject",
      "Resource": "arn:aws:s3:::my-bucket/private/*"
    }
  ]
}
```

This policy allows the user `my-user` to upload objects to the `my-bucket/private` prefix, but it denies all users from reading objects from that prefix.

You can create and manage bucket policies using the AWS Management Console, the AWS CLI, or the AWS SDKs.

How Bucket Policies Work

One of the most important concepts that we need to understand is how to use an IAM role and an S3 bucket policy to allow users to access an S3 bucket. This is a common way to grant access to S3 buckets in a secure and controlled manner.

In a normal scenario, bucket policies are applied before IAM policies. This means that even if a user has permissions granted by an IAM policy, they will still be denied access if the bucket policy denies them access.

Here are some reasons why you might want to grant public access to your S3 bucket:

- To host a static Web site
- To share files with the public
- To use S3 as a Content Delivery Network (CDN)

It is important to note that granting public access to your S3 bucket can be a security risk. Anyone on the Internet will be able to access your bucket and its objects, even if they do not have an AWS account. You should only grant public access to your bucket if you are sure that you want to do so.

Here are some tips for granting public access to your S3 bucket securely:

- Use bucket policies to restrict access to specific objects or prefixes.
- Use encryption to protect your data.
- Use versioning to recover from accidental deletions or overwrites.
- Monitor your bucket activity for suspicious activity

Amazon S3 Versioning

Amazon S3 Versioning is a feature that allows you to keep multiple versions of an object in the same bucket. This can be useful for a variety of reasons, such as:

- To recover from accidental deletions or overwrites
- To track changes to objects over time
- To create and maintain backups of objects

S3 Versioning can be seen in Figure 4.3.

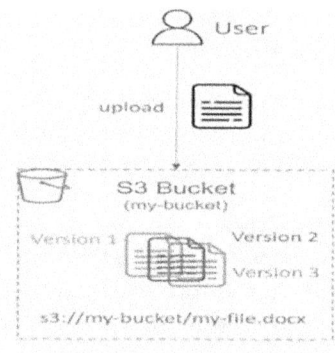

FIGURE 4.3 S3 Versioning.

When you enable S3 Versioning for a bucket, S3 will automatically create a new version of an object every time you modify it. Each version of an object has a unique version ID. You can access any version of an object by specifying its version ID.

S3 Versioning is a very powerful feature, but it is important to understand how it works and how to use it properly. Here are some important things to keep in mind:

- S3 Versioning does not protect your data from unauthorized access. You still need to use bucket policies to control who has access to your buckets and objects.
- S3 Versioning can increase your storage costs. Each version of an object counts as a separate object, so storing multiple versions of an object can increase your storage usage.
- S3 Versioning can be used to recover from accidental deletions or overwrites, but it is not a backup solution. You should still have a separate backup solution in place in case of a major disaster.

S3 Lifecycle Policies

An S3 Lifecycle policy is a set of rules that define actions that Amazon S3 applies to a group of objects. These actions can be:

- Transitioning objects to a different storage class
- Archiving objects
- Deleting objects

S3 Lifecycle policies can help you manage your storage costs and ensure that your objects are stored in the most appropriate storage class for their lifecycle.

S3 Lifecycle policies are a powerful tool that can help you manage your S3 objects more cost-effectively and efficiently. By automating the management of your S3 objects, you can save time and money and improve the security and compliance of your data.

A diagram of how an S3 Lifecycle policy works is shown in Figure 4.4.

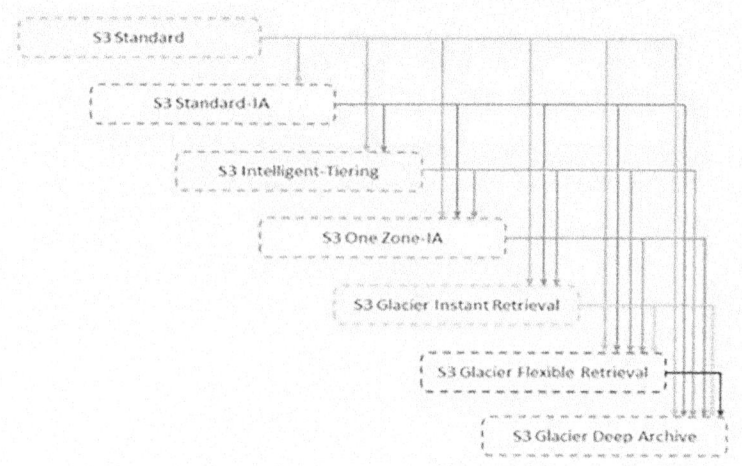

FIGURE 4.4 S3 Lifecycle Policy.

The diagram illustrates the Amazon S3 Storage Class hierarchy and how S3 Lifecycle Policies can transition objects between different classes over time. Each arrow in the diagram represents a possible transition path that a Lifecycle policy can implement.

Storage Classes (Top to Bottom Order in Diagram)

- S3 Standard – Default class for frequently accessed data.
- S3 Standard-IA – For infrequently accessed data, lower cost but with retrieval fee.
- S3 Intelligent-Tiering – Automatically moves data between frequent and infrequent tiers.
- S3 One Zone-IA – Lower cost, stored in a single AZ, less resilient.
- S3 Glacier Instant Retrieval – Archive class for millisecond access to rarely accessed data.
- S3 Glacier Flexible Retrieval – Archived data, minutes to hours access.
- S3 Glacier Deep Archive – Lowest cost, designed for data rarely accessed, hours access.

Step-by-Step Lifecycle Transition

1. Upload to S3 Standard
   - Objects typically start in the S3 Standard class.
2. Lifecycle Policy Applied
   - A defined S3 Lifecycle Policy checks object age, prefix, or tag.
3. Transitions Between Storage Classes
   - Based on rules (like "after 30 days"), objects move to:
   - Standard-IA (less frequent access)
   - Intelligent-Tiering (automatic movement based on usage)
   - One Zone-IA (for non-critical data)
   - Glacier Classes for archiving:
     - Instant Retrieval
     - Flexible Retrieval
     - Deep Archive

   Each arrow in the diagram shows a valid transition path, e.g.:
   - From S3 Standard → S3 Standard-IA
   - From S3 Standard-IA → S3 Glacier Flexible Retrieval
   - From Intelligent-Tiering → Glacier Deep Archive, etc.
4. Optional Expiry
   - After a certain time (e.g., 365 days), the policy can delete the object automatically.

Some examples of an S3 Lifecycle policy are given below:

- *Example 1*: Transition objects to S3 Standard-IA after 90 days and delete them after 1 year.
- *Example 2*: Archive objects to S3 Glacier after 1 year.
- *Example 3*: Delete objects after 30 days if they have not been accessed.

How to Create an S3 Lifecycle Policy

You can create an S3 Lifecycle policy using the AWS Management Console, AWS CLI, or AWS SDKs.

To create an S3 Lifecycle policy using the AWS Management Console:

1. Go to the Amazon S3 console and select the bucket for which you want to create the S3 Lifecycle policy.
2. Click the Management tab.
3. Click Create lifecycle rule.
4. Enter a name for the rule and specify the scope of the rule.
5. Click Add condition.
6. Select the condition that you want to use to filter the objects to which the lifecycle rule will apply.
7. Click Add action.
8. Select the action that you want Amazon S3 to take on the objects that match the condition.
9. Click Save.

Let's look at some sample S3 Lifecycle policies, covering all objects in a bucket and individual objects.

This S3 Lifecycle policy is for all objects in a bucket:

```
{
    "Rules": [
        {
            "ID": "Transition to Standard-IA after 30 days",
            "Prefix": "",   // Applies to all objects because of empty prefix
            "Status": "Enabled",
            "Transition": {
                "Days": 30,
                "StorageClass": "STANDARD_IA"
```

```
            }
        },
        {
            "ID": "Expire objects after 1 year",
            "Prefix": "",  // Applies to all objects
            "Status": "Enabled",
            "Expiration": {
                "Days": 365
            }
        }
    ]
}
```

This policy has two rules:

- The first rule transitions all objects to the Standard-IA storage class after 30 days, reducing storage costs for less frequently accessed data.
- The second rule makes all objects expire after 1 year, automatically deleting them to save space and costs.

This S3 Lifecycle policy is for individual objects:

```
{
    "Rules": [
        {
            "ID": "Transition images to Glacier after 90 days",
            "Prefix": "images/",  // Applies only to objects with the "images/" prefix
            "Status": "Enabled",
            "Transition": {
                "Days": 90,
                "StorageClass": "GLACIER"
```

```
            }
        },
        {
            "ID": "Expire logs after 30 days",
            "Prefix": "logs/",   // Applies only to objects with the "logs/" prefix
            "Status": "Enabled",
            "Expiration": {
                "Days": 30
            }
        }
    ]
}
```

This second S3 Lifecycle policy applies different rules to specific types of objects in the bucket based on their prefixes. Here's an explanation of each rule:

1. Transition images to Glacier after 90 days

    - This rule applies only to objects stored under the "images/" prefix (i.e., objects located in the "images/" folder within the bucket).
    - After 90 days, these objects are moved to the Glacier storage class, which is designed for long-term archival storage at a lower cost but with longer retrieval times.
    - This helps reduce storage costs for images that are not frequently accessed.

2. Expire logs after 30 days

    - This rule applies only to objects stored under the "logs/" prefix (i.e., objects located in the "logs/" folder).
    - After 30 days, these objects are automatically deleted from the bucket.
    - This is useful for log files that are only needed temporarily, helping to free up storage space and reduce costs.

Unlike the first policy, which applies to all objects in the bucket, this policy targets specific object types (images and logs) based on their prefixes. This allows for more granular lifecycle management, optimizing storage costs and retention based on usage patterns.

In the next exercise, we will perform the following steps:

1. Bucket creation
2. Viewing the properties of an S3 bucket
3. Uploading objects to the bucket
4. Emptying the bucket
5. Deleting the bucket

LAB: AMAZON S3 – BUCKET CREATION

We can use the Amazon S3 console, Amazon S3 APIs, AWS CLI, or AWS SDKs to create a bucket.

Here, we will use the Amazon S3 console for bucket creation.

Bucket Creation Using the S3 Console

1. Sign in to the AWS Management Console and open the Amazon S3 console at *https://console.aws.amazon.com/s3/*.
2. In the left navigation pane, choose Buckets.
3. Choose Create bucket. The Create bucket page will open.
4. For Bucket name, enter the name *project-s3bucket-demo24* for your bucket.
5. For Region, choose the AWS Region (US-EAST-1) where you want the bucket to reside.
6. Under Object Ownership, to disable or enable ACLs and control ownership of objects uploaded in your bucket, choose one of the following settings:
    - ACLs disabled
    - Bucket owner enforced (default) – ACLs enabled

- Bucket owner preferred – The bucket owner owns and has full control over new objects that other accounts write to the bucket with the *bucket-owner-full-control* canned ACL.

7. Under Block Public Access settings for this bucket, choose the Block Public Access settings that you want to apply to the bucket. By default, all four Block Public Access settings are enabled.

8. (Optional) Under Bucket Versioning, you can choose whether you wish to keep variants of objects in your bucket. To disable or enable versioning on your bucket, choose either Disable or Enable.

9. (Optional) Under Tags, you can choose to add tags to your bucket. Tags are key-value pairs used to categorize storage.

   To add a bucket tag, enter a key and, optionally, a value and choose Add Tag.

10. Under Default encryption, choose Edit.

11. To configure default encryption, under Encryption type, choose one of the following:
    - Amazon S3 managed key (SSE-S3)
    - AWS Key Management Service key (SSE-KMS)

    If you chose AWS Key Management Service key (SSE-KMS), do the following:
    - Under AWS KMS key, specify your KMS key.
    - To create a new customer-managed key in the AWS KMS console, choose Create a KMS key.

12. (Optional) If you want to enable S3 Object Lock, do the following:
    - Choose Advanced settings.
    - To enable Object Lock, choose Enable, read the warning that appears, and acknowledge it.

13. Choose Create bucket.

14. A bucket with the name *project-s3bucket-demo24* will be created and will be available in the Amazon S3 bucket section.

Key Points for Bucket Naming

For general-purpose buckets, the naming rules are as follows:

- Bucket names must be from 3 (min) to 63 (max) characters long and no more (or less) than this.

- Bucket names must consist of only lowercase letters, numbers, periods (.), and hyphens (-).
- Bucket names must begin and end with a letter or number.
- Bucket names must not contain two adjacent periods.
- Bucket names must not be formatted as an IP address (for example, 192.168.5.4).
- Bucket names must be unique across all AWS accounts in all the AWS Regions within a partition. A partition is a grouping of Regions. AWS currently has three partitions:

    `aws` (Standard Regions), `aws-cn` (Chinese Regions), and `aws-us-gov` (AWS GovCloud (US)). Allowing AWS accounts to share bucket names in the same partition is not valid until the bucket is deleted.

Viewing the Properties of an S3 Bucket

1. Sign in to the AWS Management Console and open the Amazon S3 console at *https://console.aws.amazon.com/s3/*.
2. In the Buckets list, choose the name of the bucket (*project-s3bucket-demo24*)

    that you want to view the properties for.
3. Choose Properties. On the Properties page, you can configure the following properties for the bucket:
    - Bucket Versioning
    - Tags
    - Default encryption
    - Server access logging
    - AWS CloudTrail data events
    - Event notifications
    - Transfer acceleration
    - Object Lock
    - Requester Pays
    - Static website hosting

Uploading Folders and Files to an S3 Bucket

When you upload a file to Amazon S3, it is stored as an S3 object. Objects consist of the file data and metadata that describes the object. You can have an unlimited number of objects in a bucket. Before you can upload files to an Amazon S3 bucket, you need write permissions for the bucket. You can upload any file type—images, backups, data, movies, and so on—into an S3 bucket. The maximum size of a file that you can upload by using the Amazon S3 console is 160 GB.

Follow these steps:

1. Sign in to the AWS Management Console and open the Amazon S3 console at *https://console.aws.amazon.com/s3/*.
2. In the left navigation pane, choose Buckets.
3. In the Buckets list, choose the name of the bucket (*project-s3bucket-demo24*) to which you want to upload your folders or files.
4. Click on it.
5. Choose Upload. In the Upload window, do one of the following:
   - Drag and drop files and folders to the Upload window.
   - Choose Add file or Add folder, choose the files or folders to upload, and choose Open.

   Select the file named AWS Logo, available in my desktop/Aws Beginners folder.
6. Once you select the file, you can click the Upload button to upload it to the given bucket, *project-s3bucket-demo24*.
7. To enable versioning, under Destination, choose Enable Bucket Versioning.
8. To upload the listed files and folders without configuring additional upload options, at the bottom of the page, choose Upload.

   Amazon S3 uploads your objects and folders. When the upload is finished, you see a success message on the Upload: Status page.

Emptying a Bucket

1. Sign in to the AWS Management Console and open the Amazon S3 console at *https://console.aws.amazon.com/s3/*.
2. In the Bucket name list, select the option next to the name of the bucket that you want to empty, and then choose Empty.
3. On the Empty bucket page, confirm that you want to empty the bucket by entering the bucket name into the text field, and then choose Empty.
4. Monitor the progress of the bucket emptying process on the Empty bucket: Status page.

Deleting an S3 Bucket

1. Sign in to the AWS Management Console and open the Amazon S3 console at *https://console.aws.amazon.com/s3/*.
2. In the Buckets list, select the option next to the name of the bucket that you want to delete, and then choose Delete at the top of the page.
3. On the Delete bucket page, confirm that you want to delete the bucket by entering the bucket name into the text field, and then choose Delete bucket.

    Here are some important points regarding deletion:

1. Make sure that your given bucket is empty; otherwise, you will get a warning to empty the bucket.
2. Delete any access points that are attached to the bucket before deleting the bucket.
3. A service control policy can deny the delete permission on a bucket.

AMAZON S3 TRANSFER ACCELERATION

Amazon S3 Transfer Acceleration stands out as one of the most robust and effective features available on AWS, capable of significantly shortening the duration of data transfers to and from S3 buckets when customers operate across large distances as well as close locations. When dealing with these outstanding features, transfer acceleration that can handle the high-speed transfer of big data through long distances on the Internet is the most important thing you should master.

Here's how it works:

- *Problem*: When transferring data over long distances, you often encounter issues such as:
  - *High latency*: Distance increases network latency, impacting upload and download speeds.
  - *Varying Internet speeds*: Unpredictable Internet routing and congestion can further slow down transfers.
  - *Distance to S3*: Applications far from the S3 bucket's Region experience slower transfers.
- *Solution*: S3 Transfer Acceleration tackles these challenges by:
  - *Routing through CloudFront*: Your data is routed through Amazon CloudFront edge locations that are well situated to your users or applications. This logically shortens the distance to S3, reducing latency.
  - *Faster network paths*: S3 Transfer Acceleration can use AWS's backbone network for quick data transfers.
  - *Efficiency in the network protocol*: S3 Transfer Acceleration makes use of advanced protocols as well as fast error correction mechanisms for reliable transfer.
- *Benefits*:
  - *Cost reduction*: S3 Transfer Acceleration is a method that reduces costs by accelerating long-distance data transfers to and from S3.
  - *Improved speed*: This can really improve transfer speed, lessen variability, as well as enhance the application's performance.
  - *Ease of use*: The process is easy, and you only need to pay for the services that you use.

You can compare upload speeds using the following link:

https://s3-accelerate-speedtest.s3-accelerate.amazonaws.com/en/accelerate-speed-comparsion.html.

Users can obtain 163% performance improvement related to the US Virginia Region after enabling Amazon S3 Transfer Acceleration.

LAB: ENABLE S3 TRANSFER ACCELERATION FOR A GIVEN BUCKET

1. Select the source target and go to the properties of the source bucket. You will find multiple options in the Source Bucket properties.

2. Scroll down the page and you will find the Transfer acceleration option. Click on Edit.

3. Select Enable and Save the change. You can now find the source endpoint:

    project-s3bucket-demo24.s3-accelerate.amazonaws.com.

4. Use the S3 Transfer Acceleration endpoint for transfers. Replace the regular S3 endpoint with the S3 Transfer Acceleration endpoint for your bucket.

5. Test and monitor. Use the provided speed comparison tool to assess the performance improvement and track transfer costs.

AMAZON VIRTUAL PRIVATE CLOUD (VPC)

Overview of Amazon VPC

A VPC can be seen as a virtual network in the AWS cloud and is different from a private network that is isolated from other networks within AWS in that it is a logically isolated section of AWS. It will be available to you in a similar way as when you establish and maintain a physical network within an on-premises data center.

VPCs cover all the Regions' AZs and thus you have full control over which entities are allowed to use the VPC resources.

By default, you can create up to five VPCs per Region. Each Region is assigned a default VPC, which includes a subnet in every AZ.

You must specify a range of IPv4 addresses for the VPC in the form of a Classless Inter-Domain Routing (CIDR) block when creating the VPC; for instance, 10.0.0.0/16. A simple diagram of a VPC can be seen in Figure 4.5.

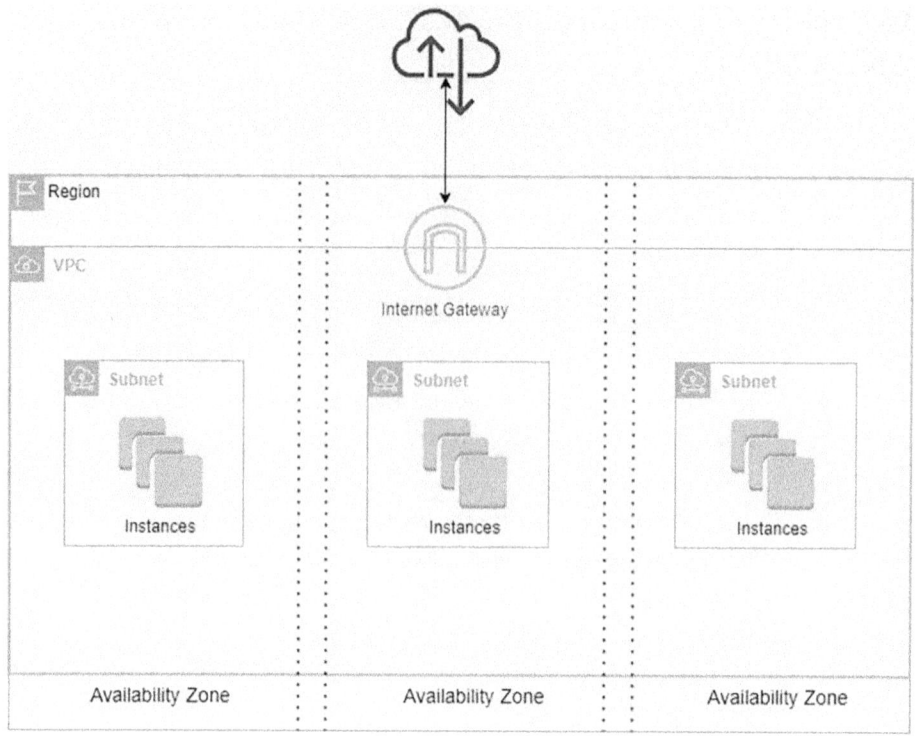

FIGURE 4.5 Simple VPC Diagram.

You can manage everything about your VPC, including the IP address range, subnets, and how the traffic is routed. You can also launch AWS resources, such as EC2 instances, into your VPC. We will go through subnets and routing in the next section.

Amazon VPC Components

Amazon VPC components are the building blocks that you use to create and manage your VPC. The below diagram (Figure 4.6) shows a VPC without any resources.

FIGURE 4.6 VPC Without Any Resources.

The following are some of the most common components.

Subnets

A subnet is a part of your VPC that is logically isolated from the rest of the VPC so that other users cannot interfere and cannot access its resources. If you need to group resources for specific reasons or security requirements, you can do so here. For instance, you can create a subnet for your Web servers as well as a subnet for your database servers. Whenever a client requests access to a Web page, it can serve the actual data and not the database required by the user. This type of server separation offers efficient performance and security. Each subnet has a different range of IP addresses, which ensures that there are no overlaps and there is no rate of duplicity in network connections.

Route Tables

VPC route tables manage the flow of traffic when utilizing your VPC or the Internet. These tables are used primarily to determine where traffic from your VPC should be directed. Using the destination IP address, route tables can identify the right directions for your incoming or outgoing traffic. For every subnet that you create, you can assign one or more route tables, and each route table can contain multiple routes defining destination, target, and other relevant parameters to ensure successful redirection of network traffic. Choosing the right route impacts the performance and availability of Web sites, which helps in conducting reliable e-commerce.

Security Groups

A security group can restrict the type of network traffic that is allowed into and out of your specified instances. These security measures define rules regarding which traffic can enter or leave specific VPC instances and when. When it comes to implementing a security policy, you can specify inbound and outbound rules to block or allow inbound or outbound traffic according to your application requirements. For example, if you have a Web server that is hosted on a public Internet IP address but must be protected from potential attacks, you might decide that it is important only to allow communication for a particular port or IP address. Security groups provide you with effective yet flexible security risk mitigation based on the application used on your servers.

Network ACLs

Network ACLs (NACLs) can be defined as a type of network security and are applied at the subnet level. They can either be stateful or stateless, wherein stateful checks recognize the type of packets and prevent repeat passes while stateless do not. It is worth noting that any such NACL or rule will apply to the entire subnet and not traffic that has been filtered. In this way, you can set rules for your flow of traffic and maintain operations in a specific direction. Although this is the security aspect of the public cloud, the NACLs are more rigid; they cannot change easily when the technology changes or when there is a need for change. Overall, NACLs act as supporting players to the more valuable and flexible security groups in situations with a greater need for control on the network level.

Internet Gateways

Internet gateways can be thought of as the bridge connecting all the resources hosted on AWS to the rest of the world on the Internet. These gateways act as routers, decryptors, and packet generators, creating an Internet space for your public resources while maintaining and defining the process of routing between the instances and the Internet. By including one gateway in your VPC, you can directly attach features provided by AWS and make cloud computing accessible to all people globally. While other instances are included within the private IP address, their update or interruption will now go unnoticed by their clients.

The remaining web traffic will be routed through AWS using your address while simultaneously transferring packets between your public instances and the public Web.

Elastic IP (EIP) Addresses

EIP addresses are publicly visible and these IP addresses can be used to further configure specific instances or other resources. It is worth remembering that IP addresses on the Internet can lead to visibility.

Different components of VPC can be seen in Figure 4.7.

Different Components of Virtual Private Cloud (VPC)

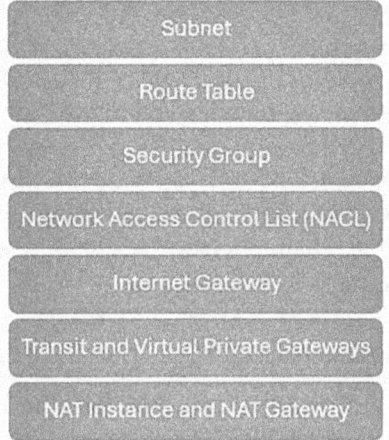

FIGURE 4.7 Different Components of VPC.

In addition to the components listed above, there are a few other VPC components that you can use to manage your network.

Endpoints

With the use of endpoints, it is possible for the instances in your VPC to connect to some AWS services without the need to make a connection to the Internet. The key AWS services that can be reached by endpoints are Amazon S3, which is an object storage service, and Amazon DynamoDB, which is a NoSQL database service. Endpoints can help in keeping communication between the instances and services more secure and make the network management processes easier and more efficient.

Peering Connections

Peering connections can allow users to join two separate VPCs into one single network. This establishes direct communication, which makes it easy to share resources such as EC2, RDS, and other AWS services between VPCs. Peering connections can also provide users with the ability to form a private network that combines VPCs at different locations that are geographically separate within a Region on the global system.

NAT Instances and NAT Gateways

Cloud users need to be assured that their instances can connect to the Internet. Doing this means that NAT instances and NAT gateways can connect to the Internet without compromising on the IP address of the instances. NAT instances serve to convey traffic between a private instance and an Internet address without revealing the identity details of the original request. NAT gateways, being a managed service like NAT instances, have easy setup and performance advantages over the former. NAT instances and NAT gateways serve to ensure that strong security and privacy demands remain necessary and that a high degree of availability and reliable performance with good speed must still be offered.

Virtual Private Gateways (VPGs)

For organizations that are interested in using the hybrid cloud to improve their IT systems, VPGs provide an excellent option for connecting a VPC with the on-premises environment through a VPN. By employing VPGs, organizations can configure secure tunnels capable of supporting various types of workloads and using instances and facilities of the cloud. They provide high-speed and reliable networks since organizations are not obligated to fully depend on public network resources. Thus, VPGs can allow organizations to experience the power of the cloud while staying connected to their on-the-ground IT structures.

We will describe some of the important components, known as the building blocks, of a VPN in more detail for better understanding.

VPC with All Components

You can easily customize the network configuration for your Amazon VPC. For example, you can create a public-facing subnet for your Web servers that has access to the Internet and place your backend systems such as databases or application servers in a private-facing subnet with no Internet access. You can leverage multiple layers of security, including security groups and NACLs, to help control access to Amazon EC2 instances in each subnet.

When you get started on Amazon VPC, you automatically establish a faultless VPC in every AWS Region. The main VPC incorporates a public subnet in each of the available AZs, as well as the Internet gateway, which enables communication with the Internet. The configuration that allows for DNS resolution enhances the flexibility of service usage within the environment; hence, initializing your network enables the launching of the required Amazon EC2 instances within the default VPC. You can also use Elastic Load Balancing, Amazon RDS, and Amazon EMR on a default VPC within your organization and provision pairs of these services, too, with minimal effort. Therefore, by using a default VPC and its resources effectively, you will be able to easily expand your use of AWS services.

The default VPC is recommended for quickly and easily starting the use of certain services, especially for publicly available instances, such as a blog or a simple Web site. The default VPC has adjustable components, and can be modified in case the application or Web site requires the alteration of any networking component. Hence, when developing the default VPC, some adjustments may be made based on the specific project requirements and performance needs; some parts may be modified for public access, while other parts of this system will remain secure and private under the obfuscating nature of the Internet.

The below diagram shows the VPC with all feasible components for better understanding. Here, the Web server is placed in a public subnet and has Internet access. Meanwhile, the database server is placed in a private subnet as per standard practice. You also have two layers of security known as a security group and NACL.

Please remember that the security group is applicable at the instance level while the NACL is applicable at the subnet level. A VPC with all its components can be seen in Figure 4.8.

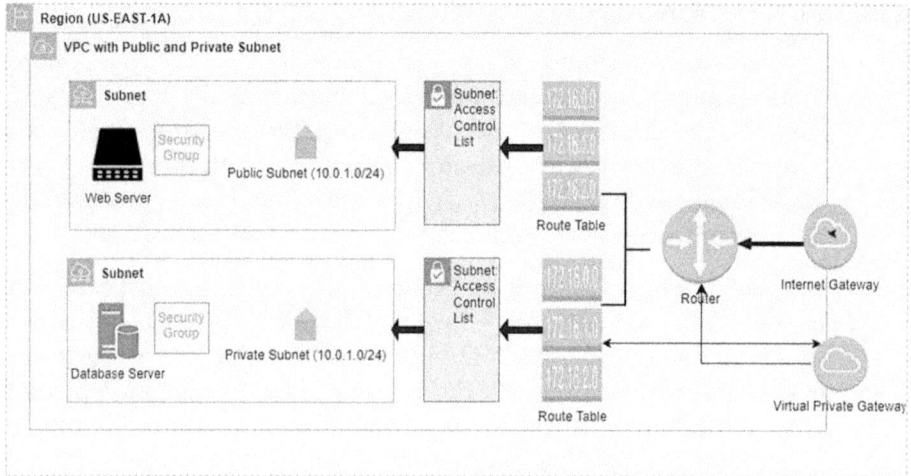

FIGURE 4.8 VPC with All Its Components.

This is what you can do with a VPC:

- Launch instances into a subnet of your choosing.
- Assign custom IP address ranges in each subnet.
- Configure route tables between subnets.
- Set up the Internet gateway and attach it to your VPC.
- Have much better security control over your AWS resource.
- Use instance security groups.
- Use subnet NACLS.

AWS Transit Gateway

AWS Transit Gateway is a powerful and flexible solution that connects VPCs to on-premises networks. It makes it possible to transfer data instantly between these environments, thus enabling smooth communication and free movement of information. As a result, businesses can streamline their operations and boost their network infrastructures by utilizing transit gateways.

AWS Transit Gateway can help you simplify your network topology and avoid complex peering relationships between large numbers of VPCs. You can create a Site-to-Site VPN connection as an attachment on a transit gateway.

AWS Transit Gateway supports many connection options that may be used based on an organization's needs for configuration, protection, and connectivity. Among the many connection options available is Site-to-Site VPN, a connection type that can offer an extensive, dedicated protection level across company networks. AWS Transit Gateway can be seen in Figure 4.9.

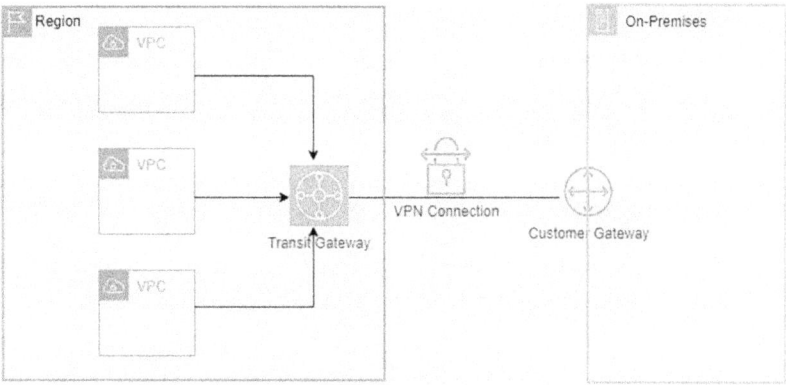

FIGURE 4.9 AWS Transit Gateway.

The following architecture diagram (Figure 4.10) shows a simplified representation of using Transit Gateway to connect your VPCs to those of a third-party provider. Each VPC connects to the transit gateway, and the gateway supports transitive routing between all the attached VPCs.

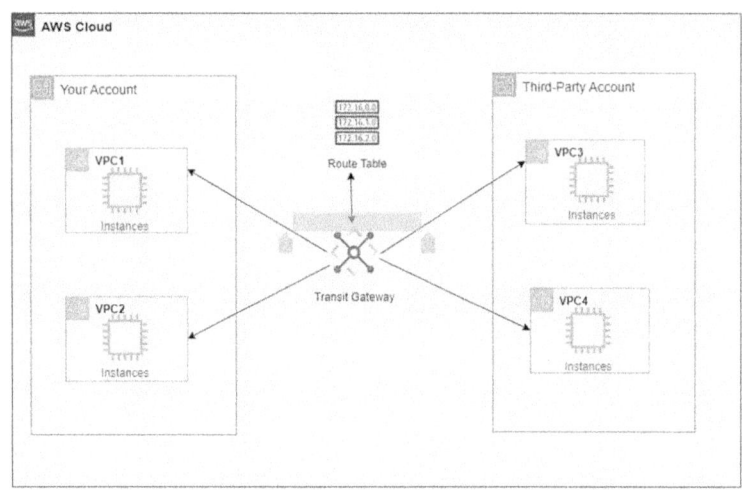

FIGURE 4.10 Transit Gateway to Third-Party Providers.

AWS Site-to-Site VPN

AWS Site-to-Site VPN is a managed service that is used for creating secure links between the local networks of organizations and Amazon VPC or AWS Transit Gateway via the Internet. It employs encrypted IPsec tunnels for safeguarding data transmission.

The key components are as follows:

1. *Customer gateway device*: A device (either a physical device or software that is located in your on-premises network) that creates and secures the VPN connection.

2. *Virtual Private Gateway (VGW) or transit gateway*: The AWS-managed VPN gateway at Amazon's end of the connection.

3. *VPN connection*: The new, secure connection between your customer gateway device and the VGW or transit gateway.

4. *VPN tunnels*: A VPN connection comprises two redundant tunnels for high availability of the service.

This is how it works:

1. Traffic from your on-premises network is encrypted and sent through the VPN tunnels to the VGW or transit gateway.

2. The VGW or transit gateway decrypts the traffic and routes it to the appropriate VPC or resources within AWS.

3. Traffic from AWS to your on-premises network flows in the reverse direction.

The AWS Site-to-Site VPN working mechanism can be seen in Figure 4.11.

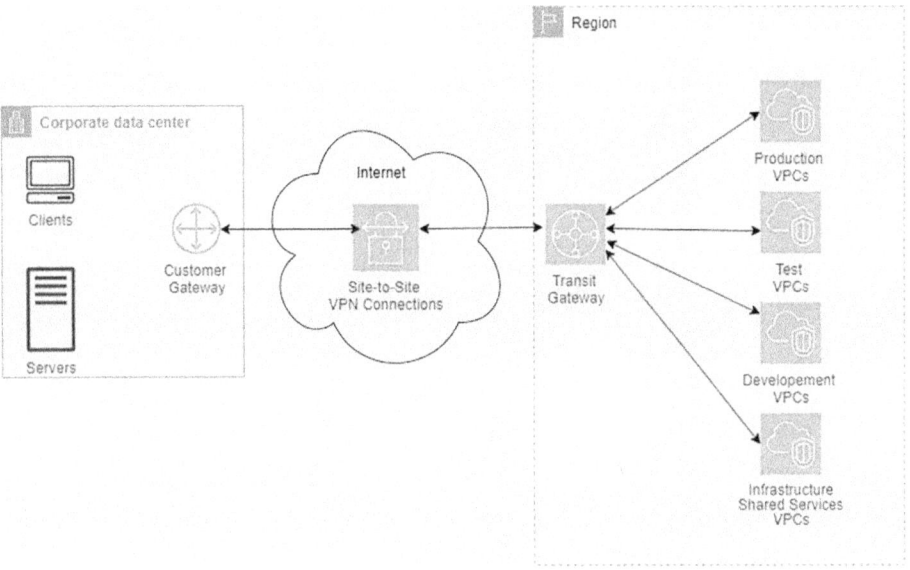

FIGURE 4.11 AWS Site-to-Site VPN Working Mechanism.

SUMMARY

This chapter went through AWS storage services and VPCs in detail. It started with an introduction to a range of AWS storage solutions, such as Amazon S3 for object storage, EBS for block storage, and EFS for file storage. Each of these fulfills a different data storage demand, such as accessing data continuously. In addition, Amazon Glacier is a long-term storage alternative. The storage methods used by an organization depend on, for instance, the type of data, how often it is accessed, and how much it costs.

Furthermore, the chapter discussed VPCs and how users could create isolated networks within AWS. With VPC elements such as subnets, security groups, and Internet gateways, companies can monitor and secure their network setup. The chapter also talked about advanced features such as NAT gateways, VPC peering, and site-to-site VPNs, which help the connectivity and security of hybrid cloud architectures.

With the use of AWS capabilities for storage and networking, organizations can handle their data efficiently and maximize network performance. This is the way that strong security can be achieved, the required cloud migrations can happen seamlessly, and work can be done at a higher level of efficiency.

REFERENCES

[AWS23a] Amazon Web Services, *"Amazon S3"*. Available online at: *https://aws.amazon.com/s3/*, 2023.

[AWS23b] Amazon Web Services, *"Amazon Elastic Block Store"*. Available online at: *https://aws.amazon.com/ebs/*, 2023.

[AWS23c] Amazon Web Services, *"Amazon Elastic File System"*. Available online at: *https://aws.amazon.com/efs/*, 2023.

[AWS23d] Amazon Web Services, *"Amazon S3 Glacier storage classes"*. Available online at: *https://aws.amazon.com/glacier/*, 2023.

[AWS23e] Amazon Web Services, *"Amazon Storage Gateway"*. Available online at: *https://aws.amazon.com/storagegateway/*, 2023.

[AWS23f] Amazon Web Services, *"AWS Snowball"*. Available online at: *https://aws.amazon.com/snow/*, 2023.

[AWS23g] Amazon Web Services, *"Amazon Virtual Private Cloud"*. Available online at: *https://aws.amazon.com/vpc/*, 2023.

[AWS20] Amazon Web Services, *"How Amazon VPC works"*. Available online at: *https://docs.aws.amazon.com/vpc/latest/userguide/VPC_Subnets.html*, 2020.

[Cloudflare21] Cloudflare, *"Cloudflare Peering Policy"*. Available online at: *https://www.cloudflare.com/peering-policy/*, 2021.

[AWS19] Amazon Web Services, *"NAT Gateways"*. Available online at: *https://docs.aws.amazon.com/vpc/latest/userguide/vpc-nat-gateway.html*, 2019.

KNOWLEDGE CHECK: MULTIPLE-CHOICE Q&A

Question 1

Which of the following does AWS NOT offer as one of its storage types?

A. Object storage.

B. Block storage.

C. File storage.

D. SQL storage.

Question 2

Which AWS storage service is the best for accessing data, Web sites, and mobile applications?

A. Amazon Glacier.

B. Amazon S3.

C. Amazon Elastic File System (EFS).

D. Amazon Elastic Block Store (EBS).

Question 3

Which Amazon S3 feature is capable of changing storage classes and transferring data aligned with defined lifecycle policies on its own?

A. S3 Intelligent-Tiering.

B. S3 Lifecycle policy.

C. S3 Versioning.

D. S3 bucket policy.

Question 4

Which functional element is dedicated to the management of traffic flow as well as routing in a VPC?

A. Subnet.

B. Internet gateway.

C. Route table.

D. Security group.

Question 5

What is Amazon Glacier mostly used for in storage?

A. Frequently accessed data.

B. Long-term archival storage.

C. Real-time analytics.

D. Streaming data.

Question 6

Which AWS service do enterprises primarily use for hybrid cloud storage and connecting on-premises environments to AWS?

A. AWS Snow Family.

B. Amazon Storage Gateway.

C. Amazon S3.

D. Elastic File System (EFS).

Question 7

What is the maximum number of S3 buckets an AWS account can have by default?

A. 10.

B. 50.

C. 100.

D. Unlimited.

Question 8

Which of the following VPC components is responsible for filtering traffic at the subnet level?

A. Security group.
B. Internet gateway.
C. Network Access Control List (NACL).
D. Elastic IP.

Question 9

What does S3 Intelligent-Tiering optimize?

A. Data encryption.
B. Data durability.
C. Storage costs based on access patterns.
D. Data transfer speeds.

Question 10

Which of the following is NOT a feature of Amazon S3?

A. Object versioning.
B. Lifecycle management.
C. SQL query processing.
D. Bucket policy.

CHAPTER 5

*AWS D*ATABASE *S*ERVICES

This chapter centers around the AWS database services, giving a broader overview of how various database solutions in the AWS ecosystem are designed to fit different workload requirements. Four main database types are explained at the beginning of the chapter: *relational*, *non-relational*, *data warehouse*, and *memory-based* databases. Each type is further subdivided into several categories by creating different structures for different use cases and benefits. For example, relational databases, such as Amazon Relational Database Service (RDS) and Aurora, offer structured data storage and are well suited for applications requiring complex queries, whereas non-relational databases, such as DynamoDB, which are examples of data warehouse technology, are considered unstructured databases due to their general flexibility for storing non-standard data.

In addition to this, Amazon Redshift, a data warehousing solution intended for large-scale data analytics, is introduced in this chapter, along with Amazon ElastiCache, which is classified as a memory-based data storage service that will guarantee high-speed access to frequently accessed data. The chapter also looks at the key considerations for choosing a database service, such as performance, scalability, and cost, guiding organizations in their decision-making process.

Furthermore, the chapter outlines the differences between EC2 database models, where users have full control over the infrastructure, and AWS-managed databases, which automate tasks such as backup and performance tuning, allowing users to focus on application development.

By the end of this chapter, you will be able to understand the types of AWS database services, the situations they are most suited for, and how to select the most appropriate solution for your specific needs.

OVERVIEW OF AWS DATABASES

Storing data on disk (EFS, EBS, EC2 instance store, and S3) can have its limits; hence, sometimes, users want to store data in a database. AWS offers a wide range of database services that are designed to meet the needs of a variety of workloads. These services can be broadly categorized into four types, as shown below in Figure 5.1.

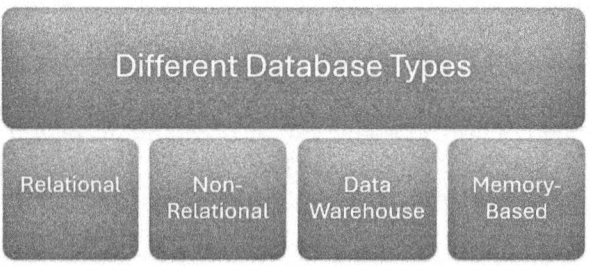

FIGURE 5.1 Different Database Types.

- *Relational databases*: Relational databases store data in tables with rows and columns. They are suitable for structured data that needs to be accessed and manipulated in a predictable way. Examples of relational databases on AWS are Amazon RDS and Amazon Aurora. Relational databases get their name from the fact that they help maintain a relationship between the stored data. Every table column contains one type of unit that is referenced by columns in another table. Data in relational databases can be thought of as the set of all real-world instances defined by the data model.

- *Non-relational databases*: Non-relational databases store data in various formats such as key-value pairs, documents, and graphs. They are good for storing data that is unstructured and flexible for interpretation and manipulation. Examples of non-relational databases on AWS are Amazon DynamoDB, Amazon DocumentDB, and Amazon Neptune. Still, users have noted a limitation in scaling graph databases. These are single-server databases that can't handle millions of requests at a time.

- *Data warehouse databases*: A data warehouse database is a central repository that gathers data from various sources for analysis and reporting, enabling businesses to gain insights and make informed decisions. It's like a giant historical record, combining information from different systems to understand trends and optimize operations. Redshift is a well-known AWS data warehouse database.
- *Memory-based databases*: Memory-based databases such as AWS ElastiCache store data in RAM for ultra-fast access at the expense of limited persistence. They act as a performance booster for frequently accessed data, reducing the load on slower disk-based systems.

RELATIONAL DATABASES

A relational database is a type of database that stores data in tables with rows and columns. The data in each row is related to the data in other rows using keys. Keys are unique identifiers that are used to link related data together.

A Customer table contains data about the customer:

- Customer ID (primary key)
- Customer name
- Billing address
- Shipping address

In the Customer table, the customer ID is a primary key that uniquely identifies who the customer is in the relational database. No other customer would have the same customer ID.

An Order table contains transactional information about an order:

- Order ID (primary key)
- Customer ID (foreign key)
- Order date
- Shipping date
- Order status

Here, the primary key used to identify a specific order is the order ID. You can connect a customer with an order by using a foreign key to link the customer ID from the Customer table. This relationship can be shown below in Figure 5.2.

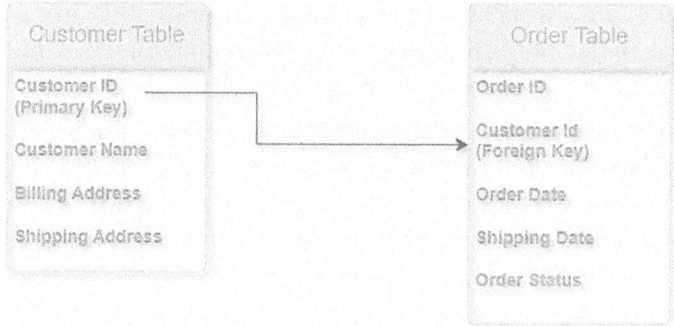

FIGURE 5.2 Entity Relationship Diagram.

NON-RELATIONAL DATABASES

A non-relational database, also known as a NoSQL database, is a type of database that stores data in a non-tabular format. This means that data is not stored in rows and columns like in a relational database. Instead, data is stored in a variety of formats, such as key-value pairs, documents, or graphs. Overall, non-relational databases are categorized into four different types:

- Key-value stores
- Document stores
- Column-family stores
- Graph-based

The above-defined non-relational database types can be seen below in Figure 5.3.

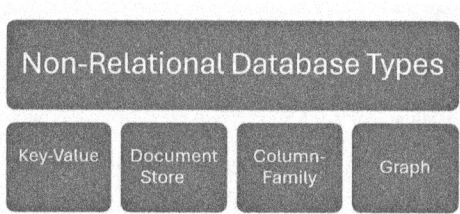

FIGURE 5.3 Non-Relational Database Types.

Key-Value Stores

Key-value stores store data as a collection of key-value pairs. The key is a unique identifier for the data, and the value is the data itself. Key-value stores are simple and fast, and they are well suited for storing small amounts of data.

Examples include Redis, Riak, and Amazon DynamoDB. We can consider the following phone directory and MAC table as an example having keys and corresponding values.

TABLE 5.1 Example of Key-Value Store.

Phone Directory

Key	Value
Paul	(091) 9786453778
Mary	(091) 9686154559
David	(091) 9868564334

MAC Table

Key	Value
10.94.214.172	3c:22:fb:86:c1:b1
10.94.214.173	00:0a:95:9d:68:16
10.94.214.174	3c:1b:fb:45:c4:b1

Document Stores

Document stores store data as documents. A document is a collection of key-value pairs, but it can also include other types of data, such as arrays and objects. Document stores are flexible and can be used to store a variety of different types of data. Documents can be stored in formats such as JSON and XML.

Examples include Amazon DocumentDB, MongoDB, and Azure Cosmos DB.

Below is a JSON document that stores information about a user named John Doe:

```json
{
  "_id": 12345,  // Unique document ID
  "name": "John Doe",
  "age": 30,
  "address": {
    "street": "123 Main St",
```

```
    "city": "Anytown",
    "state": "CA"
  },
  "interests": ["music", "movies", "sports"]
}
```

Column-Family Stores

Column-family stores store data as columns. A column family is a collection of columns that are related to each other. Column-family stores are well suited for storing large amounts of data that is frequently accessed by columns.

Here's a closer look at a column family:

TABLE 5.2 Example of a Column Family.

John	Email Address	Gender	Age
	John@example.com	M	47
Mary	Email Address	Gender	
	Mary@example.com	F	
David	Email Address	Country	Height
	David@example.com	USA	5'9"

This shows a column family containing three rows. Each row contains its own set of columns.

As the above diagram shows:

- A *column-family store* consists of multiple rows.

- Each *row* can contain a different number of columns to the other rows and the columns don't have to match the columns in the other rows (i.e., they can have different column names, data types, etc.).

- Each *column* is contained in its own row. It doesn't span all rows like in a relational database. Each column contains a name/value pair, along with a timestamp. Note that this example uses Unix/Epoch time for the timestamp.

Here's how each row is constructed:

TABLE 5.3 Example of a Column Store.

ROW →	Row Key	Column		Column		Column
		Name		Name		Name
		Value		Value		Value
		Timestamp		Timestamp		Timestamp

Here's a breakdown of each element in the row:

- Row Key: Each row has a unique key, which is a unique identifier for that row.
- Column: Each column contains a name, a value, and a timestamp.
- Name: This is the name of the name/value pair.
- Value: This is the value of the name/value pair.
- Timestamp: This provides the date and time that the data was inserted. This can be used to determine the most recent version of data.

Examples of column-family store databases include:

- *Bigtable*: *https://cloud.google.com/bigtable/*
- *Cassandra*: *https://cassandra.apache.org/*
- *HBase*: *https://hbase.apache.org/*

Graph Databases

Graph databases store data in the form of a graph. A graph is a set of nodes and edges. Each node signifies an entity, while a relationship between two entities is depicted by an edge. Graph databases are good for representing how two entities relate to one another, especially for strongly associated data that requires a low amount of data storage.

A graph database has three key elements, as given below:

- *Nodes*: These represent entities such as people, products, places, or events.
- *Edges*: These associate one node with another or the edge from one node to another. You may use directed or undirected edges—directed edges may have a direction, and undirected edges may be bidirectional.
- *Properties*: These are used for additional information about nodes and edges, such as names, attributes, timestamps, etc.

Data can be stored in both a node and an edge in a graph database.

DIFFERENT AWS DATABASES

Amazon provides different kinds of databases to customers to perform their day-to-day work.

A list of all these key database services is given here for reference:

- *Amazon Relational Database Service (RDS)*: A fully managed service that makes it easy to set up, operate, and scale relational databases in the cloud.
- *Amazon Aurora*: A MySQL- and PostgreSQL-compatible relational database that combines the performance and availability of traditional enterprise databases with the simplicity and cost-effectiveness of open-source databases.
- *Amazon Redshift*: A fully managed, petabyte-scale data warehouse service that makes it simple and cost-effective to analyze large datasets.
- *Amazon DynamoDB*: A fully managed document database service that is compatible with MongoDB.
- *Amazon DocumentDB*: A fully managed document database service that is compatible with MongoDB.
- *Amazon Neptune*: A fully managed graph database service that makes it easy to build and run applications that work with highly connected datasets.
- *Amazon ElastiCache*: A fully managed in-memory cache service that makes it easy to deploy, operate, and scale in-memory data stores.
- *Amazon MemoryDB for Redis*: A fully managed, in-memory database service that delivers ultra-fast performance for real-time applications.

- *Amazon Quantum Ledger Database (QLDB)*: A fully managed ledger database that provides a transparent, tamper-proof, and auditable record of transactions.

CHOOSING THE RIGHT AWS DATABASE

The most appropriate AWS database for your needs will be determined by the specific requirements of your workload. The best AWS database for your needs requires a design that considers the set of requirements and the job structure. The following will help you decide on a database and develop your knowledge of different databases:

- *Data structure*: What is the structure of your data? Does it demonstrate a structured, unstructured, or hybrid nature?
- *Utilization patterns*: In what manner will your data be accessed? Will the work involve executing complicated queries, or will it be limited to data viewing and writing?
- *Performance requirements*: What are your performance requirements? Do you require high throughput or minimal latency?
- *Scalability prerequisites*: To what extent must your database be scalable?
- *Cost*: What is your database expenditure budget?

AWS employs two distinct methodologies when it comes to utilizing databases:

- EC2-hosted databases
- AWS-managed databases

EC2-Hosted Databases

EC2-hosted databases are databases that are deployed and managed on Amazon Elastic Compute Cloud (EC2) instances. You control the basic infrastructure, the database software, OS, and database configuration when you use EC2-hosted databases. This allows you to mold your database setting to correspond to your specific needs. It is your job to manage the database, such as making backups, providing security updates, and performance optimization, among other things. Different types of EC2-hosted databases can be seen below in Figure 5.4.

FIGURE 5.4 Different Types of EC2-Hosted Databases.

Examples of EC2-hosted databases are given below:

- MySQL on Amazon EC2
- PostgreSQL on Amazon EC2
- Oracle Database on Amazon EC2
- Microsoft SQL Server on Amazon EC2

AWS-Managed Databases

AWS-managed databases are cloud-based services that handle the entire lifecycle of your database, from provisioning and setup to patching, upgrades, and backups. You choose the database engine you need (such as MySQL, PostgreSQL, or Aurora) and let AWS handle the rest. Hence, the end-to-end responsibility lies with AWS.

Examples of AWS-managed databases are given below:

- Amazon RDS
- Amazon Aurora
- Amazon Redshift
- Amazon DynamoDB
- Amazon DocumentDB

Different types of AWS-managed databases can be seen below in Figure 5.5.

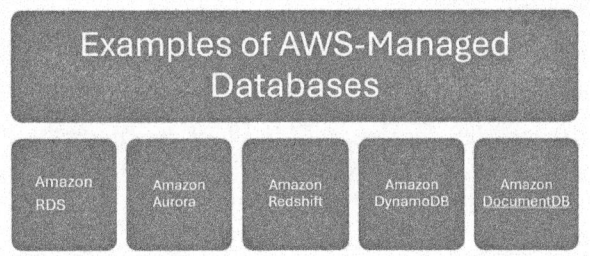

FIGURE 5.5 Different Types of AWS-Managed Databases.

AWS-managed databases are databases that are managed by AWS. With AWS-managed databases, you do not need to worry about managing the underlying infrastructure. AWS takes care of all the database administration tasks, such as backups, security patches, and performance tuning. This allows you to focus on developing and deploying your applications.

Deciding When to Use EC2-Hosted Databases or AWS-Managed Databases

The best type of database for you will depend on your specific needs. If you need full control over your database environment, then EC2-hosted databases may be the right choice for you. If you want to avoid the hassle of managing a database, however, then AWS-managed databases may be a better option. Refer to the below table:

TABLE 5.4 EC2 vs. AWS-Managed Databases.

Feature	EC2-Hosted Databases	AWS-Managed Databases
Control over infrastructure	Full control	Limited control
Responsibility for database administration	You are responsible	AWS is responsible
Flexibility	High	Low
Cost	Can be lower	Can be higher

AMAZON RDS

Amazon RDS is a cloud-based Web service that simplifies the configuration, management, and expansion of relational databases. It provides resizable capacity at a reasonable cost for an industry-standard relational database and handles routine database administration responsibilities.

Features of Amazon RDS

- *Managed services*: RDS is a managed service that uses SQL as its query language.

- *Different RDS databases*: This allows you to create databases in the cloud that are managed by AWS. The different RDS databases available in AWS are given below:
    - PostgreSQL
    - MySQL
    - MariaDB
    - Oracle
    - Microsoft SQL Server
    - Aurora (Amazon proprietary database)

- *Multi-AZ deployments*: Multi-AZ deployments are supported by RDS, ensuring durability and high availability. RDS generates one primary database instance in one AZ and a standby instance in another when a multi-AZ deployment is created. In the event of a failure in the primary instance, the reserve instance is promoted automatically to the status of the primary instance.

- *Read replicas*: Employing the read replicas that RDS provides can enhance the efficiency of applications that rely heavily on reading. Read replicas function as duplicates of the principal database instance, providing access to fulfill read requests.

- *Point-in-time recovery*: RDS supports point-in-time recovery, which allows you to restore your database to a specific point in time. This can be useful if you need to recover from data corruption or other problems.

- *Automated backups*: RDS automatically backs up your database instances on a daily basis. These backups can be used to restore your database to a previous point in time.

- *Performance insights*: RDS offers performance insights that can be utilized to detect and resolve performance issues. Metrics including CPU utilization, memory usage, and database connections are encompassed within these insights.

Advantages of RDS over Deploying a Database on EC2

Amazon RDS is a fully managed database service that provides a reliable and secure method of deploying, managing, and scaling relational databases in the cloud. Launching a database on your own with Amazon EC2 gives you the advantage of handling the infrastructure it runs on but also imposes the responsibility to manage the database yourself along with such tasks as backups, security patching, and performance tuning.

The advantages of using RDS instead of starting a database on EC2 are:

- *Managed service*: Since RDS is a managed service, AWS takes care of all the database management jobs, such as making backups, installing security patches, and fine-tuning performance. This gives you more time to work on creating and launching your applications.

- *Automated provisioning, OS patching, and continuous backups*: Database instances are automatically provisioned by RDS, and OS patching and continuous backups are automatically performed. This way, your databases are always kept up to date, and the possibility of your data being lost is minimized.

- *Point-in-time restore*: RDS supports point-in-time restore, which allows you to restore your database to a specific point in time. This can be useful if you need to recover from data corruption or other problems.

- *Monitoring dashboards*: RDS provides monitoring dashboards that give you insights into the performance of your databases. Thereby, it is possible to draw conclusions and make correct analyses in case of overloads or slow performance.

- *Read replicas for improved read performance*: RDS supports read replicas, which can be used to improve the performance of read-heavy applications. Read replicas are copies of the primary database instance that can be used to serve read requests.

- *Multi-AZ setup for disaster recovery*: RDS supports multi-AZ deployments, which support high availability and durability. When you create a multi-AZ deployment, RDS creates a primary database instance in one AZ and a standby instance in another. In the case of failure of the primary instance, the standby instance is automatically promoted to become the primary instance.

- *Maintenance windows for upgrades*: RDS provides maintenance windows for upgrades. This allows you to schedule upgrades for a time when they will have the least impact on your applications.
- *Scaling capability (vertical and horizontal)*: RDS supports both vertical and horizontal scaling. Vertical scaling enables you to increase the resources allocated to a database instance. Horizontal scaling allows you to add additional read replicas to a database instance.
- *Storage backed by EBS (gp2 or io1)*: RDS instances are backed by Amazon Elastic Block Store (EBS) volumes. EBS volumes provide high performance and durability.

AMAZON AURORA

Amazon Aurora is a fully managed relational database where the user can experience both the ease of using open-source databases and the low cost of owning them. They can also benefit from the high performance and reliability of expensive commercial databases. Aurora customers have the advantage that it is both MySQL- and PostgreSQL-compatible, so they will be able to use existing applications and databases without changing them.

Amazon Aurora is also equipped with a storage system that is fault-tolerant, self-healing, and distributed, and it can automatically grow up to 64 terabytes for each database instance.

RDS SOLUTION ARCHITECTURE

Several different RDS solution architectures can be used to meet the needs of different applications. Some of the most common RDS solution architectures are discussed next.

Single-AZ RDS Deployment

In a single-AZ RDS deployment, your database instance is deployed in a single AZ. This is the simplest and most cost-effective RDS deployment option; however, single-AZ deployments do not provide high availability. If the AZ in which your database instance is deployed becomes unavailable, your database will also be unavailable.

The architecture of a single-AZ RDS deployment can be seen below in Figure 5.6.

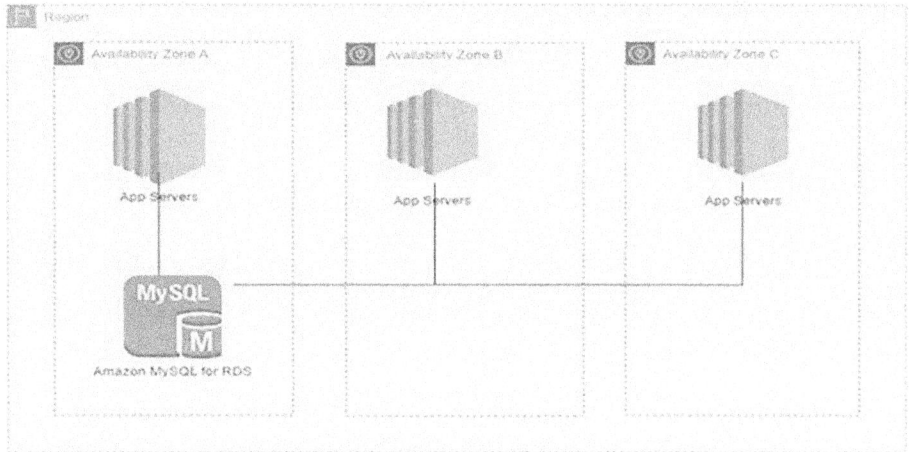

FIGURE 5.6 Architecture of Single-AZ RDS Deployment.

Multi-AZ RDS Deployment

In a multi-AZ RDS deployment, your database instance is deployed in two or more AZs. This provides high availability. If the AZ in which your primary database instance is deployed becomes unavailable, your database will automatically failover to a replica in another AZ.

The architecture of a multi-AZ RDS deployment can be seen below in Figure 5.7.

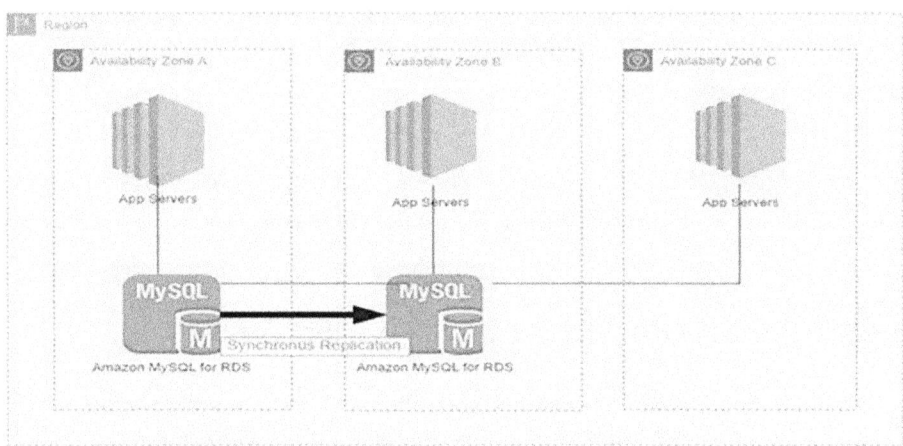

FIGURE 5.7 Architecture of Multi-AZ RDS Deployment.

RDS Deployment with Read Replicas

In an RDS deployment with read replicas, you have one primary database instance and one or more read replicas. Read replicas are copies of the primary database instance that can be used for read-only operations. Using read replicas can improve the performance of your database by offloading read-only operations from the primary database instance.

The architecture of RDS with read replicas can be seen below in Figure 5.8.

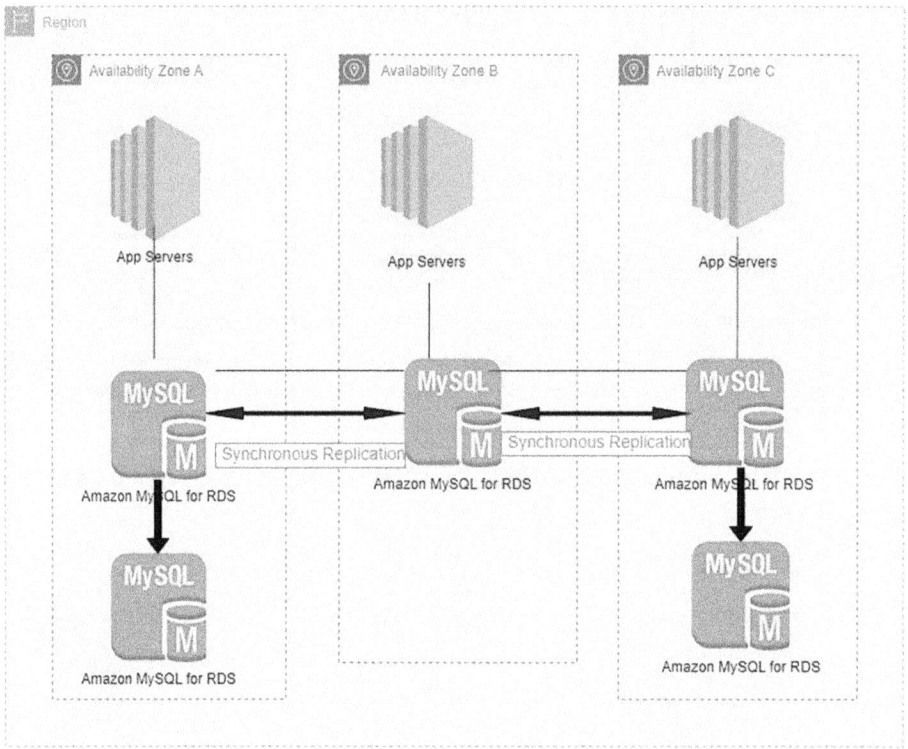

FIGURE 5.8 Architecture of RDS Deployment with Read Replicas.

LAB: CREATING AN RDS DATABASE INSTANCE

1. Log in to the Amazon RDS console at *https://console.aws.amazon.com/rds/*. Click Create database to start the configuration process. We also have the option Restore Multi-AZ DB Cluster from Snapshot, which we can ignore now.

2. In the Choose a database creation method section, ensure the Standard Create option is selected. Next, in the Engine options section, choose the MySQL engine type and the MySQL 8.0.35 version.

3. In the Templates section, select Production. In the Availability and Durability section, select the Single DB instance option. We also have two other options:

   - Multi-AZ DB Instance (Read Replica): Used to improve performance by enabling read replicas.
   - Multi-AZ DB Instance (Disaster Recovery): Provides multi-AZ support for enhanced availability and disaster recovery.

   You can select the Free Tier or Dev/Test option as per your business needs. In the case of Free Tier, you will not get different Availability and Durability options.

4. In the Settings section, set the DB instance identifier to database-demo-24. Configure the name and password of the master database user, with the most elevated permissions in the database.

5. In the DB instance size section, select Burstable classes, and choose t3.medium in the Size dropdown. In the Storage section, select Provisioned IOPS under Storage Type, and set 100 as Allocated Storage. Select 1000 under Provisioned IOPS. Uncheck the Enable storage autoscaling box.

6. In the Database Authentication section, select Password and IAM database authentication.

7. Finally, click on Create Database.

8. While the database creation is in progress, the screen will display a status such as "Creating database".

9. Finally, you will receive a screen saying that the database is available.

10. The MySQL database instance may take several minutes to provision. In order to connect to the database instance and start using it, you need to retrieve the database instance endpoint.

11. The Endpoint & port section in the Connectivity and security tab of the details page displays the endpoint. Note this value down, as you will use it later.

LAB: DELETING AN RDS DATABASE

Here are the steps to delete an RDS database in AWS:

1. Access the RDS console:
   - Log in to the AWS Management Console and navigate to the Amazon RDS service.
2. Locate the database instance:
   - Find the target database instance you want to delete from the list of instances. If needed, utilize filters or the search bar to locate it.
3. Initiate the deletion:
   - Click on the Actions button associated with the instance.
   - Select Delete from the drop-down menu.
4. Confirm the deletion:
   - A pop-up window will appear requesting confirmation.
   - Type delete me in the text box to verify your intent.
   - Click on the Delete button to proceed.
5. Monitor the progress:
   - The instance status will change to Deleting.
   - Track the deletion progress in the RDS console.
   - Deletion typically takes a few minutes, but it may vary depending on database size and complexity.

Here are some important considerations when deleting a database:

- *Data loss*: Deleting a database instance permanently erases all its data, including automated backups.
- *Snapshot retention*: If you want to preserve a snapshot of the database before deletion, you need to manually create one.
- *Associated resources*: Deletion terminates the database instance but not other related resources such as snapshots, parameter groups, or database security groups. You can manage those separately.
- *Final snapshot*: AWS automatically creates a final snapshot before deletion. You can choose to create manual snapshots as well.

- *Deletion protection*: Ensure the instance doesn't have deletion protection enabled, as this will prevent deletion.
- *Additional costs*: Snapshots incur storage costs. Monitor and manage them accordingly.
- *Caution*: Exercise care when deleting RDS instances as the process is irreversible. Ensure you have backups or snapshots if data preservation is crucial.

LAB: MODIFYING AN RDS DATABASE

While you cannot directly modify an existing RDS database instance, you can achieve modifications through these methods:

1. Modifying the instance class:
   - To adjust compute resources:
     - Navigate to the RDS console.
     - Select the target instance.
     - Click Modify under Instance Actions.
     - Choose the desired DB instance class.
     - Apply modifications.
- *Impact*: Brief outage for the instance.
2. Scaling storage:
   - To increase storage capacity:
     - Follow similar steps to the above.
     - Modify the allocated storage size.
   - *Impact*: Typically, no downtime but I/O might be affected during resizing.
3. Updating parameters:
   - To change database configuration settings:
     - Edit the associated DB parameter group. Changes usually take effect within a few minutes.
   - *Caution*: Some parameters require an instance reboot.

4. Restoring from a snapshot:
   - To revert to a previous state or create a modified copy:
     - Restore a snapshot to a new instance.
     - Configure the desired changes during the restoration process.

Other modifications include:

- *Changing the DB engine version*: Create a new instance with the desired version and migrate data.
- *Modifying security group rules*: Edit the associated DB security group.
- *Enabling/disabling deletion protection*: Toggle the setting on/off.

SUMMARY

This chapter provided a detailed overview of AWS database services, including the various kinds of databases that AWS has in its portfolio to cater to different data management requirements. It talked about the different database types: relational, non-relational, data warehouses, and memory-based databases, and pointed out their individual structures and use cases. Services such as Amazon RDS, Aurora, DynamoDB, and Redshift were examined, with a focus on their characteristics for processing structured, unstructured, large-scale, and real-time data.

The chapter also covered the difference between EC2-hosted databases and AWS-managed databases, where you are in control of the infrastructure but also handle the automation of tasks such as backup, patching, and scaling. This contrast allowed you to grasp why it is better to use fully managed services to simplify database management rather than holding full control with EC2-hosted databases.

Finally, the chapter provided the tools to choose the best database service for performance, scalability, and cost, helping organizations enhance their storage strategies within AWS.

REFERENCES

[AWS20] Amazon Web Services, *"Amazon Relational Database Service"*. Available online at: *https://aws.amazon.com/rds/*, 2020.

[AWS21a] Amazon Web Services, *"Amazon DynamoDB"*. Available online at: *https://aws.amazon.com/dynamodb/*, 2021.

[AWS21b] Amazon Web Services, *"Amazon Redshift"*. Available online at: *https://aws.amazon.com/redshift/*, 2021.

[AWS21c] Amazon Web Services, *"Amazon ElastiCache"*. Available online at: *https://aws.amazon.com/elasticache/*, 2021.

[AWS22] Amazon Web Services, *"Amazon Aurora"*. Available online at: *https://aws.amazon.com/rds/aurora/*, 2022.

[AWS23] Amazon Web Services, *"Amazon Neptune"*. Available online at: *https://aws.amazon.com/neptune/*, 2023.

[Bigtable15] Google Cloud, *"Bigtable: Scale your latency-sensitive applications with the NoSQL pioneer"*. Available online at: *https://cloud.google.com/bigtable/*, 2015.

[HBase13] Apache Software Foundation, *"Welcome to Apache HBase"*. Available online at: *https://hbase.apache.org/*, 2013.

[MongoDB19] MongoDB Inc., *"MongoDB"*. Available online at: *https://www.mongodb.com/*, 2019.

[QLDB21] Amazon Web Services, *"Amazon Quantum Ledger Database"*. Available online at: *https://aws.amazon.com/qldb/*, 2021.

KNOWLEDGE CHECK: MULTIPLE-CHOICE Q&A

Question 1

What kind of databases does AWS support?

A. Relational databases.

B. Non-relational databases.

C. Data warehouse databases.

D. Memory-based databases.

E. All of the above.

Question 2

What is the main feature of Amazon ElastiCache?

A. In-memory data storage for ultra-fast access.

B. Document-based data storage.

C. Column-family data structure.

D. Graph-based data relationships.

Question 3

Which AWS service is ideally suited for analyzing large-scale datasets?

A. Amazon DynamoDB.

B. Amazon ElastiCache.

C. Amazon Redshift.

D. Amazon Neptune.

Question 4

Which of the following database engines are also present in Amazon Aurora?

A. MySQL.

B. PostgreSQL.

C. Oracle.

D. Both A and B.

Question 5

Which of the following is most suitable for databases with a lot of connections between them?

A. Amazon Neptune.

B. Amazon RDS.

C. Amazon DynamoDB.

D. Amazon ElastiCache.

Question 6

What are the advantages of having databases that are managed by AWS over ones that are hosted by EC2?

A. Automated backups.

B. Security patching.

C. Performance tuning.

D. All the above.

Question 7

Which database system uses JSON or XML to store data as records?

A. Key-value stores.

B. Document stores.

C. Column-family stores.

D. Graph databases.

Question 8

What does multi-AZ deployment in Amazon RDS provide?

A. High availability and durability.

B. Data analytics.

C. In-memory data storage.

D. None of the above.

Question 9

Which AWS service provides a tamper-proof and auditable record of transactions?

A. Amazon DynamoDB.

B. Amazon Quantum Ledger Database (QLDB).

C. Amazon Redshift.

D. Amazon ElastiCache.

CHAPTER 6

MISCELLANEOUS AWS SERVICES (AMAZON CLOUDWATCH, AMAZON CLOUDFRONT, AWS CLOUDTRAIL, AND AWS SYSTEMS MANAGER)

This chapter explores various miscellaneous AWS services that provide essential functions for monitoring, content delivery, and operational management in cloud environments. It covers key services such as *Amazon CloudFront*, *Amazon CloudWatch*, *AWS CloudTrail*, and *AWS Systems Manager*, each of which plays a unique role in optimizing cloud performance and security.

AMAZON CLOUDFRONT

Amazon CloudFront is a highly efficient Content Delivery Network (CDN) service that helps to speed up the delivery process of your Web content to users all over the world, regardless of whether it is static or dynamic. It achieves this by caching your content at edge locations in the AWS Global Infrastructure (geographically distributed data centers that are close to the origin server) to the maximum.

A CDN is a globally distributed network of servers that work together to quickly and reliably deliver Internet content, such as Web pages, images, videos, and other static assets, to users.

How Does CloudFront Work?

When a user requests content to be delivered by CloudFront, the request gets sent to the closest edge location to that user. If the content resides in the cache of that edge location, it is delivered rapidly. If the content is not yet cached, CloudFront retrieves it from the origin server (this may be an Amazon S3 storage bucket, an EC2 instance, or an already existing Web server) and then it caches it at the edge location (the network). The content also goes through a final check at the regional edge cache. Regional edge caches are located between the origin Web servers and the global edge.

CloudFront's working mechanism can be seen in Figure 6.1.

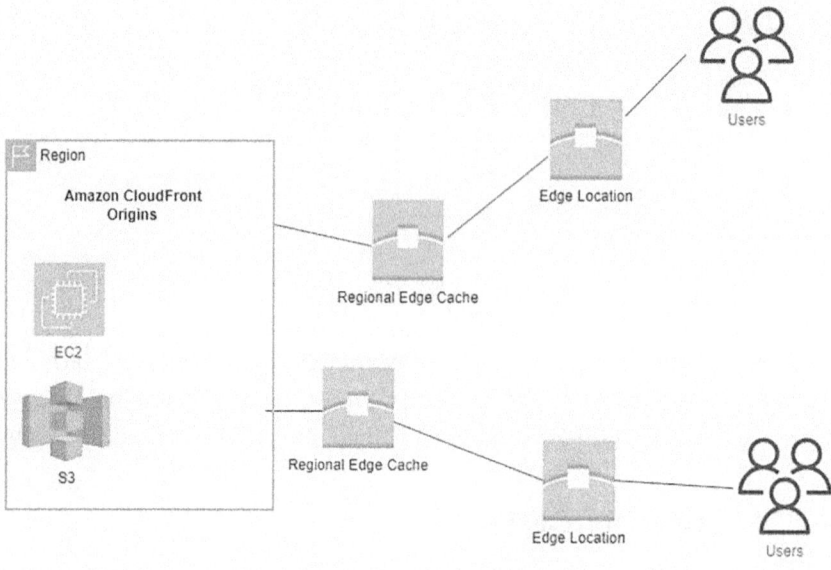

FIGURE 6.1 How CloudFront Works.

Benefits of Using CloudFront

There are numerous advantages of CloudFront, including:

- *Decreased latency*: By caching your content at edge locations that are nearer to your users, CloudFront significantly reduces the latency of your Web site or application.

- *Increased availability and reliability*: CloudFront's global network has a high level of redundancy and robustness, which is why your content will remain available for users even if your origin server goes down.
- *Lower costs*: CloudFront can help you reduce your bandwidth expenses by transferring part of the traffic from the main server.
- *Improved security*: CloudFront has many security mechanisms, such as field-level encryption and access controls, which can help you protect your content.

Origins are the source of the files that the CDN will distribute. The source may be anything from an S3 bucket, an Elastic Load Balancer, Route 53, or an EC2 instance. It can also be an external (non-AWS) device. To use CloudFront, you must have a *distribution*.

An *edge location* is a location where content is cached (separate from AWS Regions/AZs). Requests are automatically routed to the nearest edge location.

Regional edge caches are located between the *origin* Web servers and global edge locations, and thus the goal of network edge caches is to enhance content delivery by providing a larger regional edge cache capability.

In essence, the content delivery process involves establishing a CloudFront distribution, which specifies the desired origin and the necessary parameters for managing and tracking content delivery. From there, CloudFront efficiently delivers the requested content to users or viewers by utilizing edge servers, which are computers located near the users.

AMAZON CLOUDWATCH

Amazon CloudWatch is a service that handles the monitoring of AWS cloud resources and the applications that you deploy on AWS. CloudWatch is for performance monitoring (whereas CloudTrail is for auditing) and it is a regional service.

CloudWatch alarms can be set to react to changes in your resources. CloudWatch Events generates events when resource states change and delivers them to targets for processing.

Here is a breakdown of what CloudWatch does:

- Collects data
- Analyzes and visualizes
- Automates actions

Let us discuss each of these in more detail:

- *Collects data*:
  - Metrics: These are numerical values that measure things such as CPU usage, disk space, and API calls. CloudWatch automatically collects metrics from most AWS services, and you can also define custom metrics for your own applications.
  - Logs: These are textual records of events that happen within your resources and applications. CloudWatch can collect logs from AWS CloudTrail, Amazon S3, Amazon EC2, and other services, as well as your own custom logs.
  - Events: These are notifications about specific events that occur, such as an EC2 instance launching or an S3 bucket being created. CloudWatch can integrate with various AWS services and applications to capture these events.
- *Analyzes and visualizes*:
  - Dashboards: You can create custom dashboards to visualize the data CloudWatch collects. These dashboards can include charts, graphs, and tables, allowing you to quickly identify trends and patterns.
  - Alarms: You can set alarms on metrics, logs, and events to trigger notifications when certain thresholds are met. This allows you to proactively address potential issues before they become major problems.
  - Insights: CloudWatch provides built-in analytics that can help you identify anomalies, uncover root causes of issues, and optimize your resource utilization.
- *Automates actions*:
  - Auto-scaling: You can use CloudWatch alarms to automatically trigger auto-scaling actions, such as launching new EC2 instances or scaling down an ECS cluster. This helps you maintain performance and optimize costs based on real-time demand.

- CloudWatch Events: You can use CloudWatch to trigger Lambda functions or send notifications to other AWS services based on alarms or events. This allows you to automate responses to changes in your environment.

Amazon CloudWatch Metrics

Amazon CloudWatch metrics are Key Performance Indicators (KPIs) for monitoring critical resources. CloudWatch provides a comprehensive monitoring service for various AWS resources, enabling you to gain insights into their performance, health, and utilization. Here is a breakdown of the key metrics you should consider tracking:

- *EC2 instances*:
  - *CPU utilization*: This measures the percentage of CPU capacity in use.
  - *Status checks*: These indicate the instance's overall health and functionality.
  - *Network in/out (excluding RAM)*: This tracks incoming and outgoing network traffic.
  - *Default monitoring*: Metrics are collected every 5 minutes at no additional cost.
  - *Detailed monitoring (enhanced)*: This offers 1-minute granularity for deeper insights, incurring additional charges.
- *EBS volumes*:
  - Disk Read/Write Bytes measures the volume of data read from or written to the disk.
  - Disk Read/Write Operations tracks the number of read/write operations performed on the disk.
- *S3 buckets*:
  - BucketSizeBytes tracks the total size of all objects stored in the bucket.
  - NumberOfObjects indicates the total number of objects within the bucket.
  - AllRequests monitors the total number of requests made to the bucket.
- *Billing*:
  - Total Estimated Charge (us-east-1 only) provides an estimate of your current AWS charges within the us-east-1 Region.

- *Service limits*:
  - Monitored metrics track your API usage for individual AWS services, helping you identify potential throttling issues.
- *Custom metrics*:
  - *Provision*: CloudWatch allows you to define and push your own custom metrics for specific applications or resources.
- *Additional notes*:
  - Enhanced monitoring for EC2 instances incurs additional charges.
  - Total Estimated Charge metrics are currently limited to the us-east-1 Region.

Amazon CloudWatch Alarms

Amazon CloudWatch alarms are proactive response mechanisms for automated actions. They are a crucial tool that assists with automated responses that are triggered in the case of events or conditions being detected within the AWS environment.

Below is a detailed analysis of their features and functions.

The main features include:

- *Trigger notifications*: Alarms can be programmed to report any of the metrics being monitored and thus the timely detection of potential problems or the appearance of irregularities is ensured.
- *Automatic actions*: CloudWatch alarms have a variety of automated actions that contribute to the optimization of response and remediation processes.
- *Auto-scaling*: This feature allows you to adjust the number of EC2 instances based on alarm thresholds, thus improving efficiency and enabling the smooth deployment of new resources.
- *EC2 actions*: You can directly launch operations on EC2 machines as necessary, such as adding, removing, restoring, or stopping.
- *SNS notifications*: It is now possible to send alerts as dedicated SNS topics through email or their API functionalities, just like alerts from other services do.

Configuration options include:

- *Customizable thresholds and sampling*: Fine-tune alarm triggers through different configurations and the use of sampling rates, percentages, maximum and minimum values, and statistical functions.

- *Evaluation periods*: Pick out specific time spans over which to evaluate alarm conditions, providing flexibility for short-term or long-term analysis.

For example, you can set a CloudWatch billing alarm using a metric that will notify you when total estimated charges exceed a previously defined threshold, making cost management proactive.

Benefits of CloudWatch alarms include:

- *Proactive response*: Automate actions required to resolve potential issues or optimize resource usage before they impact system performance or cause excessive cost.

- *Enhanced visibility*: Receive immediate information on the state of your AWS resources by means of timely notifications and automated actions.

- *Streamlined operations*: Reduce manual intervention and improve operational efficiency by employing automated actions.

By making use of the Amazon CloudWatch alarms system, you can create a more responsive and cost-effective AWS environment, ensuring optimal performance and resource utilization.

Amazon CloudWatch Logs

The key function of Amazon CloudWatch Logs is efficient log aggregation and resource monitoring in the AWS cloud environment. This tool serves as a central part of the AWS ecosystem, enabling comprehensive collection, storage, and analysis of log data from diverse sources. Among other things, it can deliver the following:

- *Full log ingestion*: CloudWatch Logs seamlessly collects logs of many services of AWS smoothly, including:
  - *Elastic Beanstalk*: Check application performance within the managed environments.
  - *Amazon ECS*: View the statistics of workloads in containers shared by your ECS clusters.

- *AWS Lambda*: Gather and examine logs of function invocations to identify issues and optimize operations.
- *CloudTrail (with filtering)*: Maintain granular control over event history tracking.
- *CloudWatch Logs agents*: Share logs from EC2 instances and on-premises servers through inclusive log streaming.
- *Route 53*: Explore DNS query records for more efficient domain management.
* *Real-time monitoring*: Employ real-time log streams to detect and solve issues instantly, making the whole process proactive.
* *Flexible retention*: Determine the appropriate log retention period so that it complies with your compliance and auditing needs. This ensures data availability as needed while optimizing storage costs.

CloudWatch Logs for EC2

Here are some things to consider for EC2:

* By default, no logs from your EC2 instance will go to CloudWatch.
* You need to run a CloudWatch agent on EC2 to push the log files you want.
* Make sure IAM permissions are correct.
* The CloudWatch Logs agent can be set up on-premises too.

Monitoring with Amazon CloudWatch can be seen in Figure 6.2.

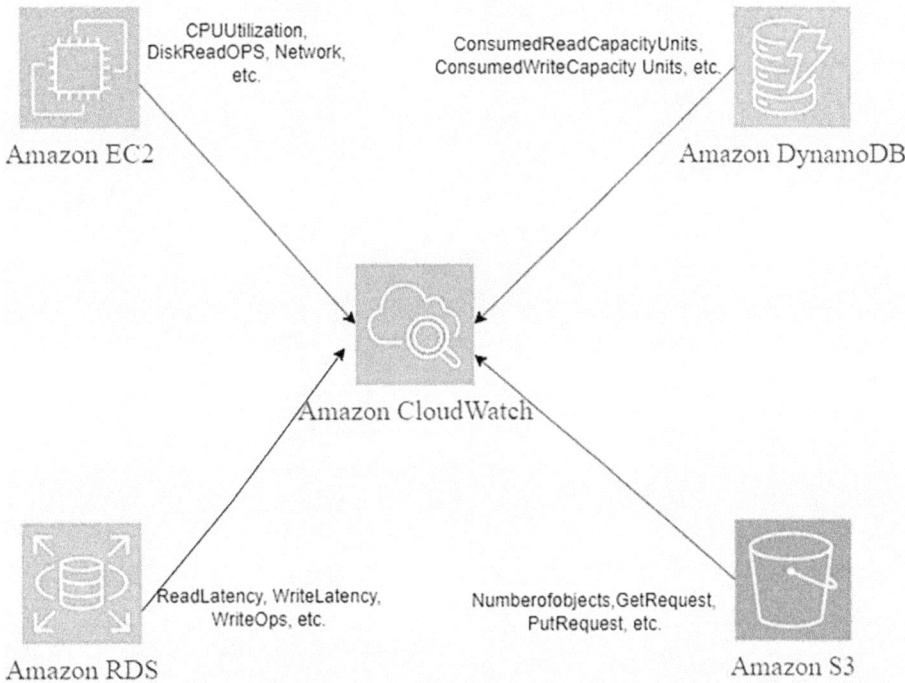

FIGURE 6.2 Monitoring with Amazon CloudWatch.

AWS CLOUDTRAIL

AWS CloudTrail is a service that is primarily used for auditing and monitoring purposes. This service can monitor what is happening in your AWS account and track all user activity and calls to APIs. This comprises actions executed through the AWS Management Console, CLI, SDKs, or APIs. In effect, it creates a record of all actions made against the account, including the user, action type, time, and location.

AWS CloudTrail can be seen in Figure 6.3.

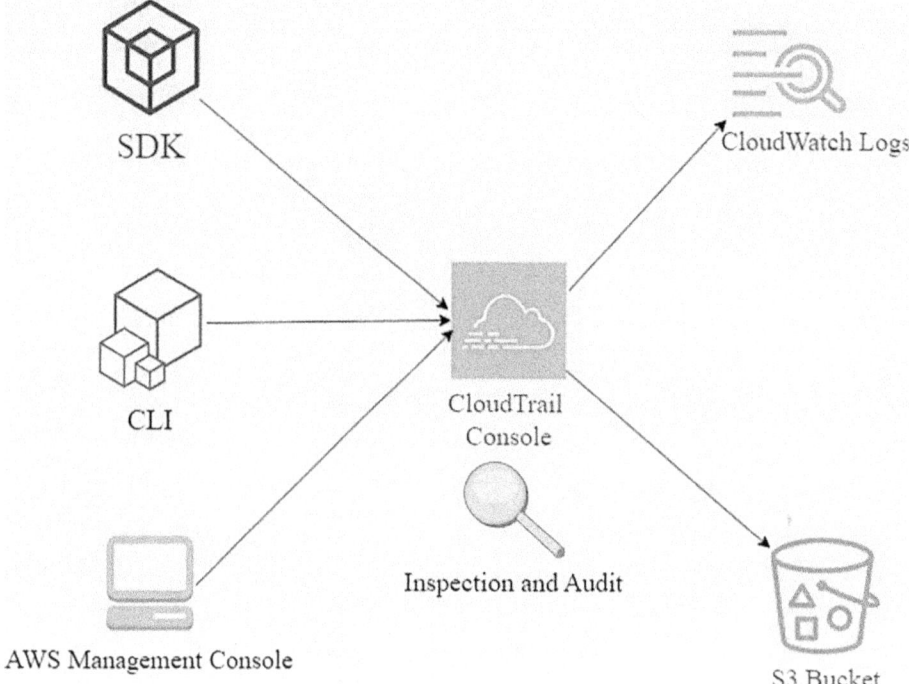

FIGURE 6.3 AWS CloudTrail.

In an AWS environment, CloudTrail is enabled by default. You can move logs from CloudTrail into CloudWatch Logs or S3. A trail can be applied to all Regions (default) or a single Region. If a resource is deleted in AWS, we can investigate this action in CloudTrail.

CloudTrail Working Methodology

CloudTrail categorizes activities into four different methods:

- *Capture*: Record activity in AWS services as AWS CloudTrail events.
- *Store*: AWS CloudTrail delivers events to the AWS CloudTrail console, Amazon S3 buckets, and, optionally, Amazon CloudWatch Logs.
- *Act*: Use Amazon CloudWatch alarms and events to take action when important events are detected.

- *Review*: View recent events in the AWS CloudTrail console, or analyze log files with Amazon Athena.

Auditing with AWS CloudTrail, AWS Audit Manager, and AWS Config

AWS CloudTrail serves as an auditing and monitoring tool, as stated previously. This service keeps a complete record of all user actions and API calls that take place in your AWS account, including those conducted using the AWS Management Console, CLI, SDKs, or APIs. Essentially, it records the "who", "what", "when", and "where" of every action taken in your account.

AWS Audit Manager is a service that allows you to verify that your AWS account meets best practices and security standards, such as PCI DSS and HIPAA. The tools offered by AWS Audit Manager include a variety of predefined audit rules.

AWS Config is a service that maintains the history of your AWS resource configurations and any changes made to them. The tool not only logs the date and time of the change but also the source of the change as well as the resources that were affected.

AWS CloudTrail, AWS Audit Manager, and AWS Config can be used in conjunction with one another to form an all-encompassing audit solution for your AWS environment. Start by using CloudTrail to collect a record of all activity in your AWS account, then use AWS Audit Manager to see whether your AWS environment conforms to the best practices and security standards, and lastly, use AWS Config to be aware of the changes made to the configuration of your AWS resources.

AWS SYSTEMS MANAGER

AWS Systems Manager is a comprehensive management service designed to help users manage their AWS resources effectively. It provides a centralized interface for viewing, managing, and automating operational tasks across various environments, including AWS, on-premises servers, and multi-cloud setups. By utilizing the AWS Systems Manager, organizations can enhance operational efficiency and streamline resource management.

What Is AWS Systems Manager?

AWS Systems Manager is a secure end-to-end management solution for hybrid cloud environments. It speeds up the process of identifying and fixing operational issues and streamlines resource and application management. Additionally, it facilitates the safe, scalable operation and management of your AWS infrastructure. By monitoring your managed instances and reporting (or taking remedial action on) any policy breaches it finds, AWS Systems Manager assists you in maintaining security and compliance.

You may automate operational processes across your AWS resources, including the following service instances, and see operational data from different AWS services using the Systems Manager console:

- Amazon EC2
- Amazon RDS
- Amazon ECS
- Amazon EKS

You can combine operational data from many AWS services and handle tasks across all of your AWS resources with Systems Manager. You can put resources into groups that make sense, such as applications, different levels of an application stack, or production environments along with testing environments. In Systems Manager, you can choose a resource group and see the most recent API activity, changes to the resource setup, operational alarms, software inventory, and the patch compliance state for that group. Depending on your requirements, you can also perform an action with each resource group. Systems Manager gives you a central location to see and handle all of our AWS tools, giving you full control and visibility over your processes.

AWS Systems Manager's supporting areas can be seen in Figure 6.4.

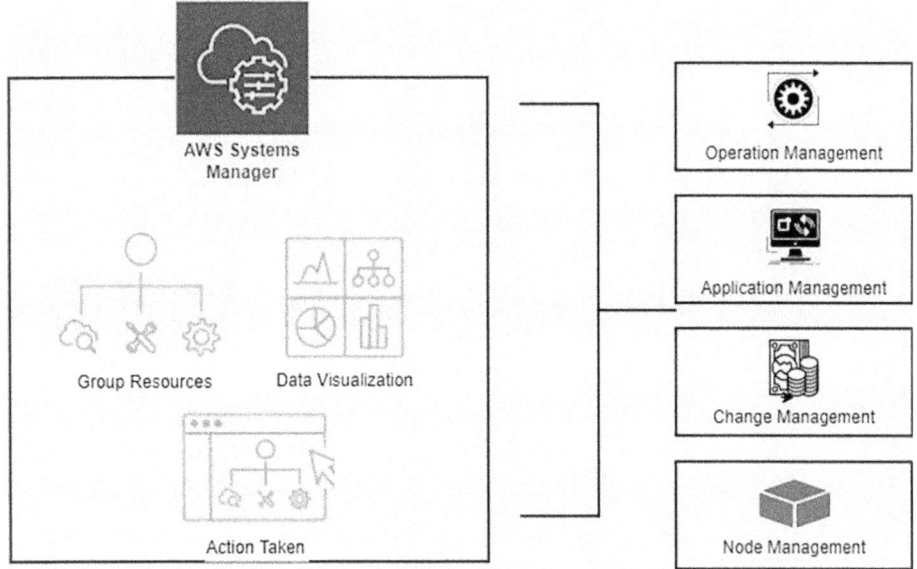

FIGURE 6.4 AWS Systems Manager Supporting Areas.

We can clearly understand, as per the above figure, that AWS Systems Manager can assist in the following areas:

- *Operations management*: Enables you to efficiently manage your AWS resources
- *Application management*: Assists in managing your applications running in AWS
- *Change management*: Facilitates safe and auditable actions or changes to your AWS resources
- *Node management*: Helps manage EC2 instances, on-premises servers, Virtual Machines (VMs) in hybrid environments, and other AWS resources (nodes)

AWS Systems Manager offers a robust set of tools and features to streamline operational tasks.

Let us explore its core capabilities next.

Capabilities of AWS Systems Manager

- Resource grouping: Organize AWS resources by purpose or activity, such as applications, environments, AWS Regions, projects, campaigns, business units, or software lifecycles.

- Centralized configuration: Define and enforce configuration options and policies for managed instances. Monitor and resolve operational issues across AWS resources from a single interface.

- Task automation: Automate and schedule maintenance or deployment tasks. Leverage Systems Manager documents as runbooks to define actions for managed instances.

- Service integration management: Execute commands across an entire fleet of managed instances with error and rate controls. Securely connect to instances without opening inbound ports or managing SSH keys.

- Secure data handling: Keep secrets and configuration data separate from your code. Use encrypted or unencrypted parameters to integrate securely with other AWS services.

- Metadata management: Automatically collect metadata from EC2 instances and on-premises managed instances, including application details, network configurations, and more.

- Unified inventory view: Access consolidated inventory data across multiple AWS Regions and accounts for streamlined resource tracking.

- Compliance monitoring: Identify non-compliant resources and take corrective actions via a centralized dashboard. View real-time metrics and alarms for AWS resources to ensure compliance.

KEY BENEFITS OF AWS SYSTEMS MANAGER

AWS Systems Manager delivers a rich array of features that simplify and enhance the management of your AWS environment.

The benefits of AWS Systems Manager can be seen in Figure 6.5.

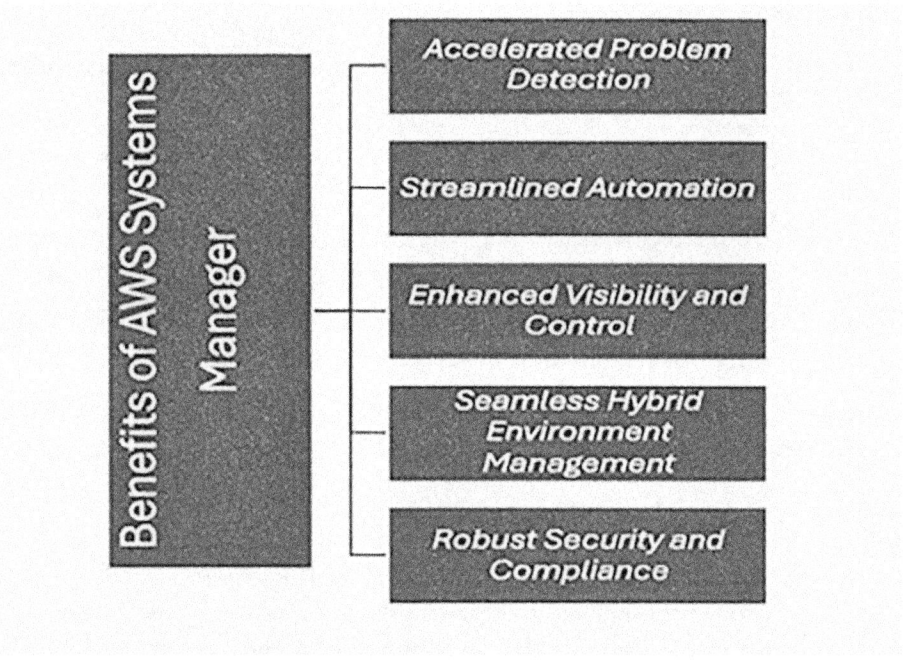

FIGURE 6.5 Benefits of AWS Systems Manager.

Accelerated Problem Detection

AWS Systems Manager brings together operational data of resource groups to speed up the process of identifying and correcting problems:

- Group resources by applications, environments, or other criteria.
- Monitor resources such as Amazon EC2, Amazon S3, and Amazon RDS from one consolidated dashboard.
- Get actionable insights such as figuring out which database instances were shut down or which S3 changes were made without switching between multiple AWS consoles.

Example: Create a resource group for the app to see installed software, recent changes, and instance health via one interface, thus reducing the time used for troubleshooting.

Streamlined Automation

Automate routine operational tasks to minimize the manual process and, hence, the likelihood of human error:

- Use the standard playbooks or design your own process automation to perform actions such as restarting instances or patching systems.
- Utilize the security checks involved to pause or revert changes during incremental rolling-out processes in case of any issues.
- Facilitate the efforts of your team with detailed text playbook descriptions and the capability to repeat the process in the future.

Example: Automate nightly backups for EC2 instances or schedule patch updates with minimum downtime.

Enhanced Visibility and Control

Gain deeper insights and manage the state of your AWS resources with ease:

- From a centralized dashboard, access the setup for system configurations, the patch levels for the operating system, the software inventory, and the application settings.
- Utilizing the AWS Config integration, observe any changes happening in your environment in real time.
- Utilize the Systems Manager Explorer and Inventory tools to maintain full surveillance over your infrastructure.

Example: Monitor the software patch levels on all EC2 instances and ensure that they remain compliant with organizational standards

Seamless Hybrid Environment Management

The process of managing resources across a variety of environments, such as on-premises servers and other cloud providers, is made simple by AWS Systems Manager:

- Use managed nodes such as Amazon EC2 instances, edge devices, and VMs in hybrid or multi-cloud setups.
- On both Windows and Linux operating systems, utilize Systems Manager Agent to perform management tasks securely.

- Connect to on-premises resources or any third-party cloud environment effortlessly, just as you do with AWS resources.

    Example: Under the same interface, control on-premises Windows servers and AWS EC2 Linux instances, thus unifying the hybrid cloud operations.

Robust Security and Compliance

Ensure security and compliance within your environment:

- Check the instances against patch definitions, configuration policies, and personalized compliance regulations.
- Automatically create rules about keeping antivirus definitions up to date and enforcing firewall policies.
- Sensitive configuration data such as database passwords or API keys should be centrally stored and managed in a fully secure manner.

Core Technical Concepts of AWS Systems Manager

Managed Nodes

The term *managed nodes* is used to describe any machine, whether real or virtual, that is set up for Systems Manager use. These nodes include Amazon EC2 instances running on Linux or Windows, servers located on-premises, or VMs in a hybrid or multi-cloud environment. To handle such nodes efficiently, you first need to install and configure Systems Manager Agent (SSM Agent) on the node, which is the resource, and attach the necessary AWS Identity and Access Management (IAM) roles or permissions to enable communication with Systems Manager. For instance, you can automate the central management of software patches, updates, and setup configurations for a fleet of EC2 instances throughout various Regions.

Systems Manager Agent (SSM Agent)

SSM Agent is the software that facilitates communication between Systems Manager and managed nodes. It makes it possible to carry out responsibilities such as patching, configuration management, and running commands on specified instances. AWS resources and hybrid environments are where SSM Agent works best. It is also open source, thus allowing for customization and flexibility. Although SSM Agent is usually pre-installed in AMIs, it is sometimes necessary to install it manually on on-premises servers or custom VMs.

For example, SSM Agent can automate the security update of Linux servers and streamline maintenance efforts.

Resource Groups

Resource groups in AWS are the means by which resources can be collected into groups that are defined by the criteria that you specify, including examples, applications, environments (e.g., production or development), Regions, or projects. Tags are used for the dynamic allocation of resources to these groups. Resource groups simplify activities such as monitoring, configuration management, inventory checks, and compliance. You can, for example, group all the resources related to a Web application such as EC2 instances, RDS databases, and S3 buckets to manage these resources from a single dashboard at the same time.

Systems Manager Documents

Systems Manager documents outline the actions that Systems Manager performs on the resources. Many types of documents are included—command documents for executing commands such as `AWS-RunShellScript`, automation runbooks for workflows such as backups or patching, and session documents for establishing secure connections to managed nodes for troubleshooting purposes.

AWS offers over 450 pre-built documents that users can choose from, but they can also create custom JSON/YAML documents. More specifically, a custom automation document can be used to deploy the application updates.

Parameters and Parameter Store

The main idea of Parameter Store is to securely manage configuration data and secrets. Hence, they can be maintained as plaintext values (for instance, application settings or identifiers) or as encrypted values (e.g., passwords or API keys) using the AWS Key Management Service (KMS). The single source of truth, which is represented by Parameter Store, supports improved database connection string security and automation by keeping it separate from the code.

Patch Manager and Baselines

Patch Manager provides automation functionalities to automatically download and apply security patches to the VMs. The patch baselines help to define the rules for automatically approving patches based on severity, classification, or operating system type. AWS offers predefined baselines, but you can create customized ones that are better suited to your company. You can set rules to patch systems during maintenance windows and generate compliance reports so that you can identify which systems are not patched. For example, a custom patch baseline can apply critical patches on Windows servers while delaying the non-critical ones for further testing to have better outcomes.

Compliance and Configuration Management

AWS Systems Manager takes care of compliance and configuration management to ensure that resources meet the required standards. Tools such as State Manager perform configuration tasks automatically, Inventory captures data of independent software and network configurations, and the Compliance dashboard helps monitor the non-compliance resources and take corrective actions.

The connection with AWS Config adds capabilities, including checking resource configuration changes and the launch of remediation workflows for non-compliant resources. For instance, firewall policies can be enforced automatically, and compliance can be verified across all the controlled nodes.

Key Use Cases of AWS Systems Manager

AWS Systems Manager offers complete solutions that will simplify the operations of AWS resources, hybrid environments, and on-premises infrastructure. Here, we analyze four key scenarios that illustrate its strong capabilities:

- Patch management
- Session management
- Operations management
- Configuration management

The use cases of AWS Systems Manager can be seen in Figure 6.6.

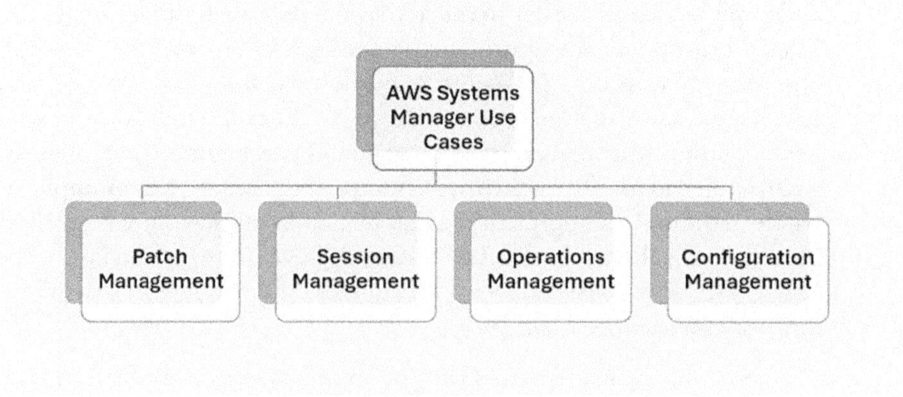

FIGURE 6.6 Use cases of AWS Systems Manager.

Patch Management

One of the most significant use cases is patch management. Patch Manager, a part of Systems Manager, optimizes the long-lasting and dynamic approach to patching the instances to keep them current with the newest and most vital patches. It is also a great alternative for patching both the operating system and application at the same time, though application patching is limited to only Microsoft software on Windows. Patch Manager allows you to install service packs on Windows servers, perform minor version upgrades on Linux instances, and patch fleets of EC2 instances, on-premises servers, and VMs, including those in hybrid clouds. Admins can configure Patch Manager to scan instances for missing patches and generate reports or to automatically install patches across their infrastructure, resulting in fast and secure processes and all regulations will be followed.

Session Management

Session management is another important area where you can securely and seamlessly connect to computers. Session Manager is such a tool, allowing users to log in and work with their EC2 servers, local machines, or hybrid cloud VMs through an interactive, browser-based shell or the AWS CLI. This absence of inbound ports being opened, bastion hosts, and any security keys being managed are some of the advantages of this tool. Furthermore, Session

Manager also meets the organization's policy for enforcing high security, as it ensures an entirely encrypted session and keeps a record of all access events.

Operations Management

Systems Manager excels in operations management by providing integrated tools for monitoring, diagnosing, and resolving operational issues. Systems Manager Explorer has a unified dashboard that collects and displays operational data from different AWS accounts and Regions, and it uses the data to inform about services such as AWS Config, AWS Trusted Advisor, and CloudWatch. OpsCenter, a feature of the system, is a tool that collects, stores, and provides tools for the investigation and resolution of incidents by utilizing automation runbooks generated from various sources such as AWS Config or CloudTrail. Incident Manager provides an innovative solution to critical application issues with automated plans for declaring, tracking, and resolving incidents, and Change Manager fosters controlled, auditable infrastructure changes. These characteristics result in organizations being able to resolve complex operational workflows and maintain a healthy, resilient infrastructure.

Configuration Management

State Manager is a robust tool designed to enable the automation and maintenance of configurations across managed nodes and AWS resources. State Manager gives admins the ability to specify and enforce resource states such as bootstrapping instances with required software, joining them to Microsoft Active Directory domains, or making sure that they have compliance in place using third-party tools such as Ansible or Chef. It also supports actions such as instance restarting or permissions management within S3 buckets, which aim to maintain operational consistency, and security areas across all environments. This allows organizations to reach their goals faster by effectively managing infrastructures, increasing security, and remaining compliant without high operating costs.

How AWS Systems Manager Facilitates AWS Cloud Migration

AWS Systems Manager is a critical component for businesses migrating to the cloud as it allows for the comprehensive control of all activities from the preliminary work to post-migration. It ensures that all migration operations are carried out efficiently, securely, and in compliance with regulations while significantly reducing the operational complexities normally attached to the process of migrating workloads to the cloud.

AWS Systems Manager's association with cloud migration can be seen in Figure 6.7.

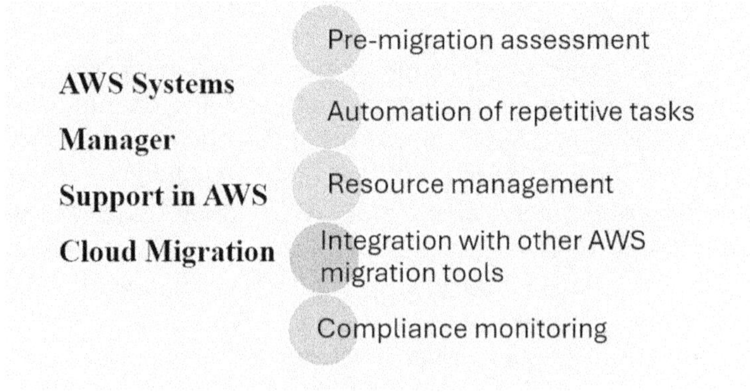

AWS Systems Manager Support in AWS Cloud Migration
- Pre-migration assessment
- Automation of repetitive tasks
- Resource management
- Integration with other AWS migration tools
- Compliance monitoring

FIGURE 6.7 AWS Systems Manager's Association with Cloud Migration.

Pre-Migration Assessment

One of the essential methods by which AWS Systems Manager supports migration is through pre-migration assessment. Through the collection of extensive inventory data on existing on-premises resources, Systems Manager gives a full understanding of resource dependencies, configurations, and utilization patterns. This knowledge is key in formulating a successful migration strategy, as it allows organizations to recognize potential obstacles, set workload priorities, and manage compatibility issues before the cloud transition.

Automation of Repetitive Tasks

As part of the migration process, Systems Manager also provides automation for repetitive tasks, which is another key advantage. With the help of the tool, tasks such as configuration updates, patch applications, and software compatibility checks with the cloud environment are automated. By eliminating manual interventions, this automation reduces the likelihood of errors, accelerates the migration process, and ensures a consistent deployment of workloads across the new environment.

Resource Management

After resources are migrated, Systems Manager then proceeds with the process of handling resources post-migration, which contributes to the complete management of the same. It automates operational tasks such as system performance, managing configurations, and performing compliance checks. The main challenge that IT infrastructure faces is the slow responsiveness of IT assets to changes in the environment; however, with the help of such features as State Manager and Patch Manager, organizations can keep the health and security of their cloud infrastructure intact without the need for extensive manual oversight.

Integration with other AWS Migration Tools

Systems Manager improves the migration process by integrating with other AWS migration tools, such as AWS Application Migration Service, AWS Database Migration Service, and AWS Migration Hub. This integration provides a consistent and methodical way of migrating workloads, ensuring that dependencies are addressed, resources are tracked, and the transition is smooth.

Compliance Monitoring

After migration, the need for continuous compliance monitoring becomes crucial. AWS Systems Manager assists in the enforcement of organizational policies and regulatory requirements for the migrated resources. Through automated checks, detailed reporting, and real-time alerts, Systems Manager enables organizations to stay in control and rapidly deal with compliance deviations.

By utilizing these capabilities, AWS Systems Manager reduces the complexity of cloud migration, minimizes downtime, and permits organizations to create a secure, optimized, and compliant cloud environment. Its extensive collection of tools and integrations guarantees that cloud migrations are not only safe and successful but also advantageous in the long run as they support equally efficient resource management and ongoing compliance.

SUMMARY

This chapter covered Amazon CloudFront, Amazon CloudWatch, AWS CloudTrail, and AWS Systems Manager in terms of effectiveness, security, and operational efficiency. These services streamline content delivery, monitor AWS resources, ensure auditing and compliance, and automate management tasks. Together, they provide essential tools for the improvement of cloud operations, user experience, and security in the AWS environment.

REFERENCES

[AmazonCF23] Amazon Web Services, *"Amazon CloudFront"*. Available online at: *https://aws.amazon.com/cloudfront/*, 2023.

[AmazonCW23] Amazon Web Services, *"What Is Amazon CloudWatch?"*. Available online at: *https://docs.aws.amazon.com/AmazonCloudWatch/latest/monitoring/WhatIsCloudWatch.html*, 2023.

[AmazonCT23] Amazon Web Services, *"What is AWS CloudTrail?"*. Available online at: *https://docs.aws.amazon.com/awscloudtrail/latest/userguide/cloudtrail-user-guide.html*, 2023.

[SkillBuilder23] AWS Skill Builder, *"AWS Skill Builder"*. Available online at: *https://explore.skillbuilder.aws*, 2023

KNOWLEDGE CHECK: MULTIPLE-CHOICE Q&A

Question 1

How does Amazon CloudFront help reduce latency?

A. Using a single centralized data center.

B. Caching content at edge locations closer to users.

C. Eliminating the need for a content delivery network.

D. Directly connecting users to the origin server.

Question 2

Which of the following is NOT a feature of Amazon CloudWatch?

A. Collecting and analyzing metrics.

B. Automatically caching content at edge locations.

C. Setting alarms for specific thresholds.

D. Automating responses to metric changes.

Question 3

What does AWS CloudTrail primarily help with?

A. Performance monitoring.

B. Content delivery optimization.

C. Auditing and tracking API activity.

D. Automated scaling of EC2 instances.

Question 4

What is the primary purpose of AWS Systems Manager?

A. To deliver content faster to global users.

B. To monitor and visualize application performance.

C. To manage AWS resources and automate operational tasks.

D. To provide compliance reports for AWS billing.

Question 5

Which AWS service provides a unified dashboard for operational data across multiple accounts and Regions?

A. AWS Config.

B. AWS Systems Manager Explorer.

C. Amazon CloudWatch Logs.

D. AWS CloudTrail.

Question 6

What is a key feature of Amazon CloudWatch alarms?

A. Automatically caching user content at the edge.

B. Automatically triggering actions based on metric thresholds.

C. Collecting logs from EC2 instances by default.

D. Tracking API usage in different AWS services.

Question 7

What is AWS Systems Manager Agent (SSM Agent) required for?

A. Managing and automating operational tasks on managed nodes.

B. Delivering cached content from edge locations.

C. Auditing API activities in AWS accounts.

D. Visualizing resource metrics in custom dashboards.

CHAPTER 7

Cloud Migration and Strategies

This chapter covers cloud migration planning and execution in detail. When it comes to cloud migration, there is a lot to take into consideration to achieve a good result. The first thing you must do is look for all the workloads that need to migrate from on-premises environments to the cloud, such as applications, databases, and virtual machines. The next step is to pick the migration strategy that best suits you from options such as rehosting (lift and shift), reformatting, or re-platforming.

After the strategy has been selected, you can make use of frameworks such as the AWS Cloud Adoption Framework to drive the migration process in an organized manner. The first step is to complete the migration in smaller phases, including assessment, planning, execution, testing, optimization, and ongoing management. Specific tools are required for each phase, and these are provided by cloud service providers. For instance, AWS Application Discovery Service and AWS Migration Service (MGN) are the tools you need to capture and execute these phases, ensuring that migration to the cloud is smooth, reliable, and efficient.

CLOUD MIGRATION WORKLOADS

The first step in any migration is to assess what you have in your environment. You need to determine how many servers you have, how much storage you use, and what the components of your network are, such as load balancers. In service management, these items are known as *configuration items* or *workloads*. Most professional organizations have a Configuration Management Database (CMDB) that contains all these configuration items. In the absence of a CMDB, we need to identify these items either manually or by using some tools in our environment. This identification process is known as *discovery*.

This allows you to assess costs, create a business justification, and conduct migration planning. You cannot plan and budget for servers and applications that you do not know about.

Cloud migration components can vary, depending on the specific migration strategy being used.

The different cloud migration components can be seen in Figure 7.1. Common key components of AWS cloud migration include the infrastructure, application, data, configuration, and database.

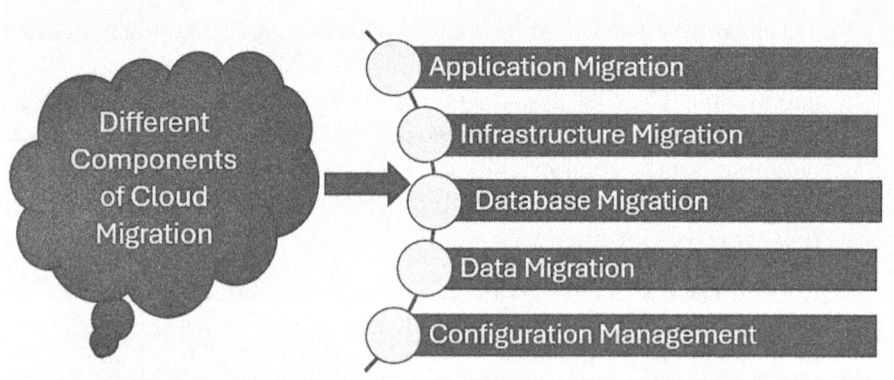

FIGURE 7.1 Different Components of Cloud Migration.

Data Migration

This involves moving data from the source to the target environment. Depending on the volume and kind of data being moved, this might be a complicated procedure.

Application Migration

This entails relocating applications from the source to the target environment. Depending on the size and complexity of the apps being migrated, this might also be a difficult procedure.

Database Migration

This is the process of transporting data from a local database to a cloud database. Although it may be a difficult and time-consuming task, it opens the door to advantages such as better performance, scalability, or cost savings, among others. There are different ways of migrating an on-premises database to the cloud.

The most effective solution is to use a database migration tool. Migration tools can be automated to execute the migration process and to handle complicated databases. Another method is manual data migration. This consists of first exporting data from the source database and then importing it into the target database.

Infrastructure Migration

This is the movement of infrastructure resources, such as servers, storage, and networks, from the original source environment to the target destination environment. In the case of cloud migration, the destination environment must be cloud-based. This can be a complex process, depending on the amount and complexity of the infrastructure being moved.

Configuration Management

Configuring the migrated environment to meet the needs of the organization is one of the most critical parts of the process. It is necessary to configure applications, infrastructure, and security settings.

In addition to these core components, there are a number of other factors that need to be considered when planning and executing a cloud migration, as we will see in the following subsections.

Testing

This involves testing applications, infrastructure, and security before deployment. Feedback should also be gathered. In doing so, the final version of the product can be shaped properly, and the right adjustments can be made. The cloud provider is a key partner for the organization.

Change Management

The process of preparing the organization's employees and other stakeholders for the changes associated with cloud migration usually has a strong element of change management. This includes clear communication with users, stakeholders, and management regarding the migration process to the new environment.

This might include establishing new security controls or moving current security controls to the cloud.

Compliance

The biggest concern for an organization when migrating to the cloud is compliance. The organization must ensure that the original data is not modified. Environmental compliance data and certifications should be prioritized at the highest level.

Cost Management

Cloud migration helps organizations discover the processes involved in moving their operations to the cloud. Controlling the costs of cloud migration and ensuring high business value are crucial factors. This includes business analysis tools for the cloud as well as corporate cloud cost management tools.

TRADITIONAL APPROACH TO CLOUD MIGRATION

Digital transformation and cloud adoption make IT infrastructure migration an important topic for organizations of all sizes. Managing cloud migration can be confusing and challenging due to the variety of strategies, making the process seem difficult. One simple solution, however, is the traditional migration approach to the cloud. We will look at this approach in this section, showing the detailed process to ensure an easy migration to the cloud.

In the standard or traditional cloud migration strategy, three main operations are always performed, namely, data collection and analysis, planning and assessment, and execution and migration. Every stage of the process adopted by the provider is crucial, even in the boot phase, effectively covering all IT infrastructure aspects that need to be investigated during the migration. We will now look at each of these phases in more depth.

Data Collection and Analysis

The foundation of any successful migration requires a thorough examination of data collection and analysis. This phase includes creating detailed inventories of all IT assets that will be migrated. Let us look at the key components in the subsequent subsections.

Servers

This involves both physical and virtual machines that serve as the host for core processes and services. Servers are the main part of the company's IT infrastructure, which includes the provision of core services such as application hosting. They can be off-the-shelf computers such as the ones hosted on-site, systems that run in the cloud, or something in between. For any organization, performing a detailed analysis is the only way to fully understand the significance of each server, the load on it, and the way it collaborates with other elements in the environment. Gaining a precise sense of how the server environment operates allows companies to make intelligent and timely decisions regarding the maintenance, upgrades, and planning of the capacities to ensure effectiveness and reliability for their IT systems. An updated server inventory brings vital knowledge to disaster recovery discussions and helps guarantee business continuity when difficulties occur due to server outages or malfunctions. To put it briefly, servers are a vital part of the model on which modern businesses run, and hence companies cannot afford to be unclear about the full range of their server infrastructure.

Application

Identifying business software that is essential for the operation of any business is also very important. Certain applications can help you accelerate internal processes, increase proficiency, and maximize total productivity.

Such applications can cover a wide range from internal tools that serve employees in their daily work, such as project management tools, to customer-facing interfaces that ensure smooth experiences, such as e-commerce platforms, customer relationship management software, and mobile applications. Ensuring that applications are up-to-date, user-friendly, and integrated with other systems is necessary so that your business operations run seamlessly. By purchasing applications that can add value to their business and regularly updating them to meet the changing demands of the market as well as the employees and customers, they can stay ahead of their competitors in today's competitive environment.

Software

This involves all components of software together with tools such as middleware, databases, and systems management tools. Understanding software dependencies is very important for maintaining application performance post-migration.

Software is a critical success factor in the migration of any system, ensuring smooth operation. This includes all software components, such as middleware, databases, and systems management tools. To determine how application performance can be maintained following migration, it is important to understand software dependencies clearly. Identifying and documenting these dependencies will prevent any potential issues as well as disruptions during the migration process. Furthermore, an understanding of the software landscape will allow more efficient and effective migration planning. A careful evaluation of each software component and its compatibility with the new environment ensures a successful transition without any issues. Careful planning with attention to detail is essential for a smooth migration process, ensuring that the system functions properly in the new environment.

Mappings and Dependencies

Once inventories are established, the next step involves identifying the mappings and dependencies of these components in the existing IT infrastructure. Let us look at the key components in the subsequent subsections.

Network Dependencies

Identifying other components in a software development process reveals how their functions are interdependent and how they can be modified for a smooth transition to the cloud. Before migrating to a new cloud environment, network dependencies must be analyzed to ensure a seamless transition. This involves understanding the interactions and connections between various components to determine whether they will remain intact in the new environment. By understanding the different elements and how they interact, organizations can prevent any disruptions or network failures during or after migration. It is crucial to examine these dependencies and make necessary changes to maintain their relationships in the cloud. This strategy will reduce any potential issues and make the migration process a smooth one. Additionally, efficient management of network dependencies will help organizations optimize their cloud performance and increase operational efficiency.

Application Mappings

Understanding the relationships between applications and how much they depend on each other is vital for a successful migration.

Application mappings are the most important step in making the migration process as smooth as possible. They provide useful insights into the interconnection of various applications and dependencies that may exist. By understanding these interconnections, organizations can better decide their migration strategy to minimize the risk of disruption in service delivery. Application mapping is critical in discovering potential barriers and is also a platform for testing and validation before migration begins. It also helps you anticipate problems that can arise from migration, thus allowing for proactive actions to be taken. Application mappings are a clear path to a successful migration process because they provide a detailed assessment of how interdependent the various applications are and guarantee a smooth transition.

This comprehensive mapping process results in the visibility of the entire system architecture, enabling the creation of a clear and efficient migration roadmap.

Planning and Assessment

In the planning and assessment phase, organizations begin to map out a strategy for the actual migration. This phase is critical as it establishes the framework within which migration will occur.

Application Sizing

By studying the available information, organizations can gauge the applications' adaptability in cloud situations. This helps in resource estimation and the selection of cloud services.

Application sizing is an essential process for organizations planning to be cloud-based. Infrastructure as a Service (IaaS) analysis enables organizations to calculate the scalability of the application on the cloud, assess resource requirements, and make informed decisions on cloud service selection. This process allows organizations to effectively plan for the capacity that is needed to support their application in the cloud environment. By properly sizing their applications, organizations can avoid the risk of over- or under-provisioning resources, ensuring optimal performance and cost-effectiveness. It also provides insight into the order of migrating services to the cloud based on the resources required and the predicted impact on other applications. Application sizing is at the forefront of a cloud migration strategy and can be leveraged by all organizations for optimal cloud resources.

Total Cost of Ownership (TCO) Reports

Preparing TCO reports provides good insights into how migration will affect the finances of the organization, including long-term operating expenses and possible savings.

TCO reports are crucial for any type of migration project. These reports include the initial costs of migration as well as the long-term operational costs and their possible returns. By fully analyzing all the financial implications of migration, businesses are in a better position to determine whether migration will be worth it in the long run. TCO reports analyze various project components, such as hardware and software costs, maintenance and support costs, and potential savings from increased efficiency or reduced downtime. TCO knowledge provides businesses with an opportunity to effectively plan their budgets and allocate resources for a successful migration project.

Wave Plans

Migration can be achieved by utilizing either a phase-based or wave-based method. Designing a clear migration plan that enables a gradual transition with continuous assessment at all stages helps mitigate risks.

Although migration can seem daunting and complicated, a wave plan can be an opportunity to divide the process into small, manageable tasks. By converting the migration into phases, companies can ensure a gradual transition for their clients without interrupting their work. This approach allows for prompt modifications at every stage, helping to eliminate risks and prevent potential disruptions to operations. Once solid plans are in place, managers can apply their judgment to prioritize tasks, set start-up schedules, and allocate resources, leading to an effective and efficient migration process. By applying a methodical and organized approach to migration, companies can reduce downtime, save money, and make a smooth transition to their new IT environment.

Migration Project Plans

A comprehensive project plan detailing timelines, responsibilities, and milestones will guide the migration process, helping all stakeholders stay aligned.

Migration project plans play a critical role in the successful migration to new cloud environments. These plans guide the entire migration process by allocating resources, scheduling timelines, assigning responsibilities, and setting milestones.

This ensures that the project stays on schedule and that all stakeholders are aligned with the same objectives. To migrate effectively, the motivation and management arrangement must be correct, and a good project plan can help to achieve that. A thorough migration plan defines the tasks and roles, such as who will do what in the transition project, the duration of the project, the assignment of tasks to people, and the monitoring of their execution. Furthermore, it allows team members to complete the project efficiently, leading to a successful outcome. Therefore, putting together a detailed project plan is a prerequisite for the effectual migration of a system, ensuring that all stakeholders are satisfied with the transition.

Execution and Migration

The execution and migration phase is the final phase of cloud migration. During this phase, the actual migration occurs, and a structured approach ensures minimal disruption to operations.

Migration Execution

The migration process is executed based on the project plan. It might involve transferring data, reconfiguring systems, and modifying support for cloud-native operations.

Migration execution is a very important phase in the migration process because it involves putting the carefully laid out project plan into action. During this step, large amounts of data are transferred from on-premises servers to the cloud, which can be a complex and time-consuming task. Sometimes, associated systems need to be reconfigured to ensure compatibility with the new cloud environment, and adjustments may need to be made to enable cloud-native operations. This phase of migration requires different teams and stakeholders to have close coordination to ensure a smooth transition and minimize any potential disruptions to business operations. Organizations can benefit from improved scalability, flexibility, and cost-efficiency by following the established project plan and executing the migration effectively.

Each stage is interlinked, and effective communication throughout the entire process is an important factor for successful migration. Organizations should conduct regular meetings with stakeholders at all levels, from IT to CEO, to ensure a smooth transition and avoid problems.

COMMON CLOUD MIGRATION STRATEGIES

What Is a Migration Strategy?

A migration strategy is a plan for moving data, applications, or other IT resources from one environment to another. It should identify the goals of migration, the scope of work, the resources that will be needed, and the potential risks involved. A successful migration strategy should also feature a blueprint for testing and validating the new environment as well as a guide to managing the change process that comes with the migration.

The diagram in Figure 7.2 depicts the whole migration strategy for AWS cloud migration.

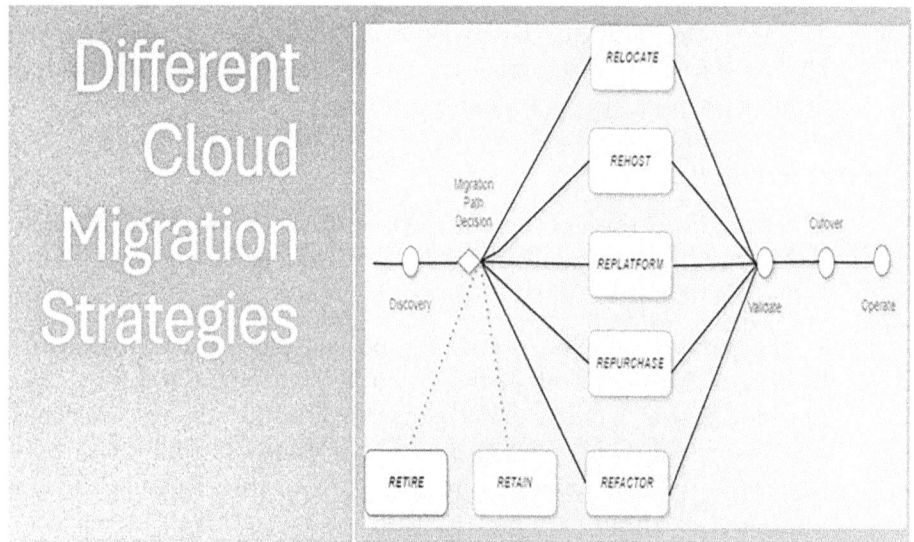

FIGURE 7.2 Different Cloud Migration Strategies.

Here is a step-by-step description of each component shown in the above figure.

Discovery

This is the initial phase where the current system and applications are assessed to understand different factors such as configurations, dependencies, and requirements.

Migration Path Decision

Following the discovery phase, decisions are made regarding the most suitable migration path for each application or system. This decision can be one of seven potential paths:

- *Relocate*: Moving applications without making changes
- *Rehost*: Also known as *lift and shift*, where applications are moved to the cloud with minimal or no modifications
- *Replatform*: Making a few cloud optimizations without changing the core architecture
- *Repurchase*: Moving to a different product, typically a Software as a Service (SaaS) solution
- *Refactor*: Redesigning and rewriting the application, typically to take full advantage of cloud-native features
- *Retire*: Decommissioning the application if it is no longer needed
- *Retain*: Keeping a few applications on-premises or in their current environment for security or compliance

Validation

When the migration path is chosen and executed, applications or systems are then tested to confirm that they are functioning properly in the new cloud environment. This involves the use of testing and verification processes to make sure that everything operating correctly, as intended.

Cutover

After successful validation, the cutover phase is the transfer from the old environment to the new cloud environment. This can be a progressive move or a one-time switch, depending on the strategy and importance of the operation.

Operate

In this final phase, the focus shifts to the ongoing management and optimization of the newly migrated applications or systems in the cloud environment. This includes monitoring performance, ensuring security and compliance, managing costs, performing regular updates, and leveraging cloud-native tools to enhance efficiency. The goal of the Operate phase is to ensure long-term stability, scalability, and continuous improvement in the cloud.

Each of these steps represents a critical phase in the cloud migration strategy, ensuring a smooth transition from on-premises infrastructure to a cloud environment. Cloud migration has seven different strategies, known as the 7 Rs. These strategies are:

1. Rehost (lift and shift)
2. Relocate
3. Replatform (lift and reshape)
4. Refactor (re-architect)
5. Repurchase (drop and shop)
6. Retire
7. Retain (revisit)

The 7 Rs of cloud migration strategies can be seen in Figure 7.3.

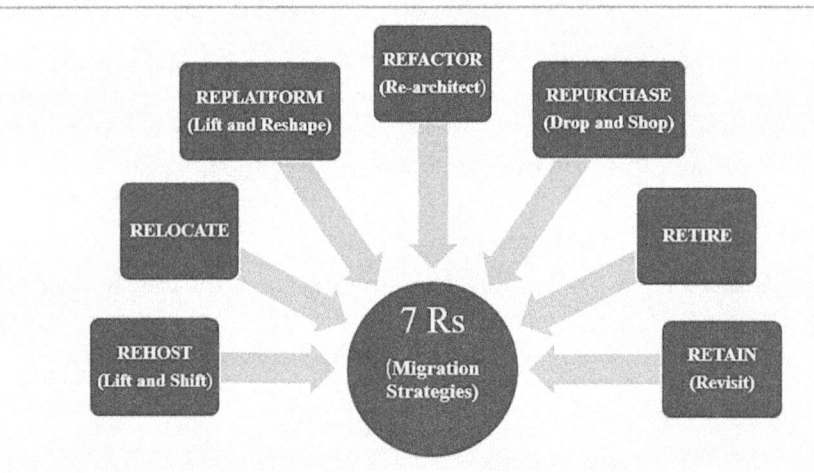

FIGURE 7.3 The 7 Rs of Cloud Migration Strategies.

Let us discuss the different cloud migration strategies in detail in the subsequent sections.

Rehost (Lift and Shift)

This involves shifting applications and current data to the cloud without making any changes to it. This is a good option for applications that are already running well on-premises and that do not require any special modifications to take advantage of the cloud.

The Rehost cloud migration strategy can be seen in Figure 7.4.

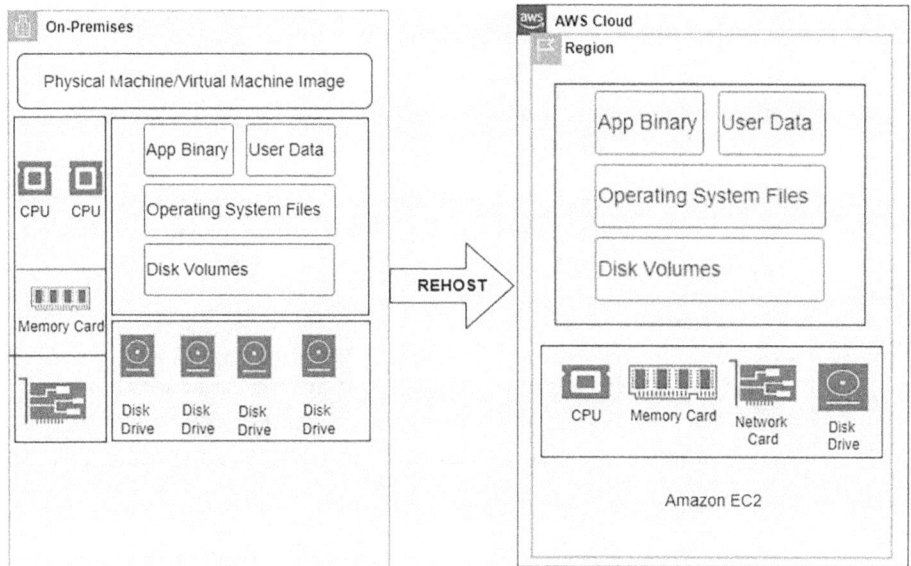

FIGURE 7.4 Rehost Cloud Migration Strategy.

The benefits of rehosting are as follows:

- By rehosting, organizations can improve system resilience and service availability and perform other metric-based testing without expensive system upgrades.
- This strategy is suitable for migrating entire legacy systems.
- This is generally the first step to moving on-premises operations without risking users or teams.

- It reduces migration time and costs by half.
- It can be used by organizations to quickly transition to the cloud, such as switching contacts without returning to leased space.
- It requires no extra skills or processes, saving time and money on staff training.

The disadvantages of rehosting are as follows:

- Rehosting a project in a new environment might result in issues in compatibility, performance, security, and other operational gaps that may negatively impact the end user.
- Onboarding to the cloud can cause inefficiencies in the cloud environment.
- By rehosting, an application becomes cloud-enabled and cloud-based, not cloud-native. As a result, the workload is still restricted in the cloud-native capabilities it can utilize.
- In a cloud context, safeguarding secret data is extremely challenging; therefore, ongoing costs are significantly lower than full data protection procedures.

Relocate

This involves moving data centers (or large portions of them) to an equivalent cloud infrastructure. This may be necessary for data that is subject to compliance regulations or needs to be stored in a specific geographic location.

The benefits of relocating are as follows:

- Supported workloads continue to operate in the normal way.
- The migration can be done quickly because it requires minimal modification, resulting in fewer errors in existing applications.
- Retraining employees is not necessary due to no major significant changes being made.
- Costs are more predictable since they limit scaling up and down.

The disadvantages of relocating are as follows:

- As the bulk of operations are still managed by the organization, relocation shifts less responsibility to the cloud provider, saving time, effort, and talent search.
- VMware licenses might be costly to keep up with.

The Relocate cloud migration strategy can be seen in Figure 7.5.

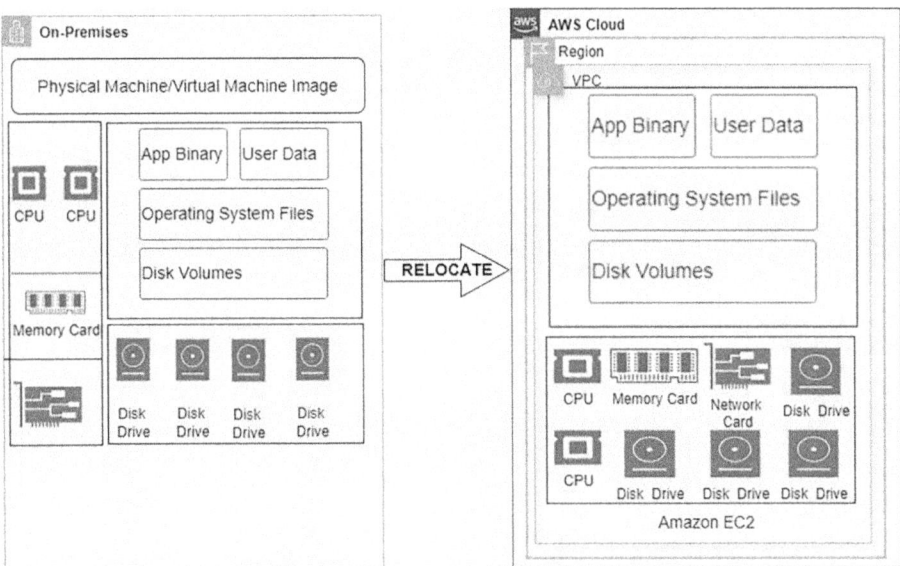

FIGURE 7.5 Relocate Cloud Migration Strategy.

Replatform (Lift and Reshape)

This involves moving applications to a new platform in the cloud, such as a different operating system or database, and installing applications on VMs in the data center. The applications are redeployed in a new cloud platform, for example, by installing a different operating system or a different version or distribution of the database.

Companies frequently need to modify their infrastructure, particularly when migrating to the cloud. In this instance, the new version of an application is involved.

The Replatform cloud migration strategy can be seen in Figure 7.6.

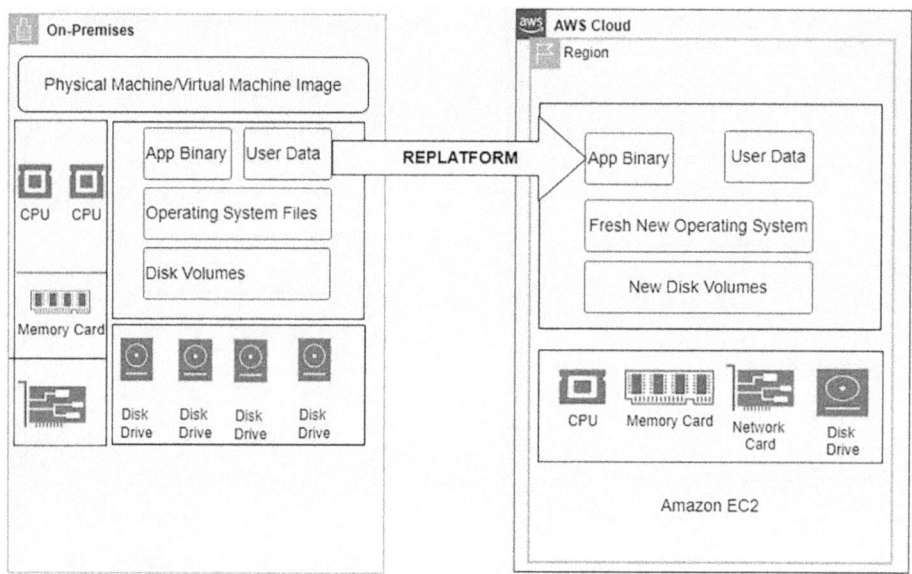

FIGURE 7.6 Replatform Cloud Migration Strategy.

The benefits of replatforming are as follows:

- *Improved performance and scalability*: Cloud platforms provide a broad range of functions and services that can be utilized to enhance application performance and scalability. For example, cloud platforms offer elastic computing, allowing you to expand or reduce your resources at any time.

- *Reduced costs*: Cloud platforms can help reduce your IT costs by getting rid of the requirement of buying and maintaining hardware and software. Cloud platforms also have pay-as-you-go pricing, which means you pay only for the resources you use.

- *Increased speed and innovation*: Cloud platforms can also make you more innovative by producing applications in a cheaper, faster, and more efficient way. Cloud platforms additionally provide numerous tools and services that can be used to both build and innovate new products and services.

- *Improved security*: Cloud platforms offer many security features and services that help you protect your applications and data. For example, cloud platforms provide encryption, access control, and intrusion detection systems.

The disadvantages of replatforming are as follows:

- *Increased complexity*: Replatforming can be a difficult process, especially when you are dealing with a large or complex application. It is essential to have a clear plan and acquire the correct capabilities and resources needed to carry out the plan.
- *Increased costs*: Replatforming can be costly, especially if you want to make big changes to your application. It is important to estimate the costs involved before starting the replatforming process.
- *Downtime*: Replatforming can cause downtime in your application. This will severely affect your business; hence, it is crucial to carefully plan and execute the migration.
- *Vendor lock-in*: Replatforming can be a source of the lock-in of the vendor, particularly if your application is very closely associated with a specific cloud provider. It is crucial to select a cloud platform that has a range of features and services and to limit the coupling of your application with the platform.

Refactor (Re-architect)

This involves modifying existing applications to make them more efficient and cloud-friendly. This may involve things such as changing the codebase, using different technologies, or optimizing the application for the cloud environment. Refactoring can be a more complex and time-consuming process than lift and shift, but it can offer significant performance and cost benefits.

The Refactor cloud migration strategy can be seen in Figure 7.7.

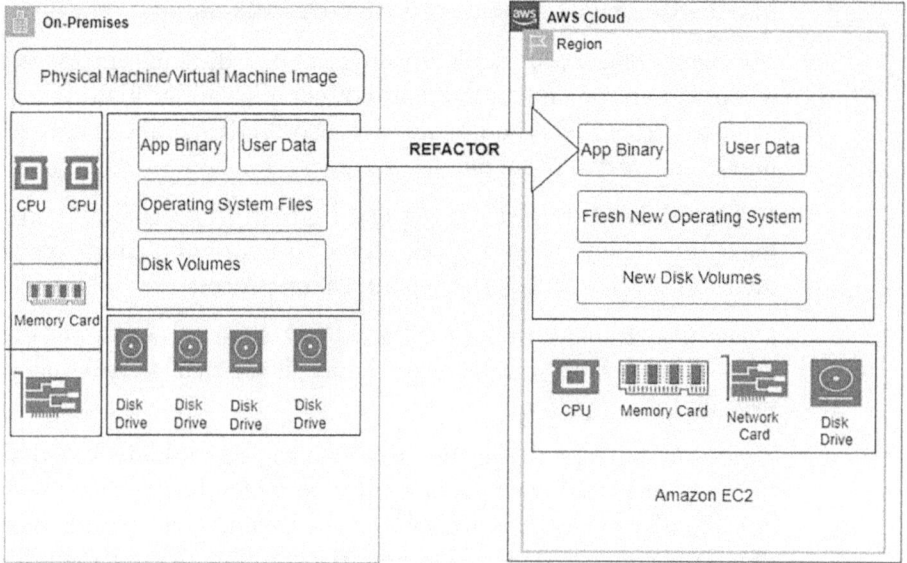

FIGURE 7.7 Refactor Cloud Migration Strategy.

The advantages of refactoring are as follows:

- The refactoring process can give you a competitive edge by enhancing the performance of your applications and automation processes, which cannot be achieved in an on-premises environment.
- Refactoring guarantees that business operations can continue without any disruptions, whether the on-premises environment exists or not.
- It provides a simple and low-cost solution to different markets by repurposing resources.
- It ensures the full utilization of cloud resources while providing long-term savings through cloud architecture.

The disadvantages of refactoring are as follows:

- Thorough planning, execution, and testing are required to prevent mistakes that could lead to cloud security, performance, and cost issues.
- Carrying out the work in question is time-, effort-, and cost-intensive.
- It entails redesigning how legacy workloads interact with cloud architecture, which necessitates extensive cloud knowledge and staff training.
- To enhance performance and minimize costs, cloud-native apps require continual monitoring.

Repurchase (Drop and Shop)

This involves replacing existing applications with cloud-based or cloud-native applications. Cloud-native applications are designed to run in the cloud and take advantage of its unique capabilities. Repurchasing can be a good option for applications that are difficult or expensive to refactor, or for applications that need to take advantage of the unique capabilities of the cloud.

The Repurchase cloud migration strategy can be seen in Figure 7.8.

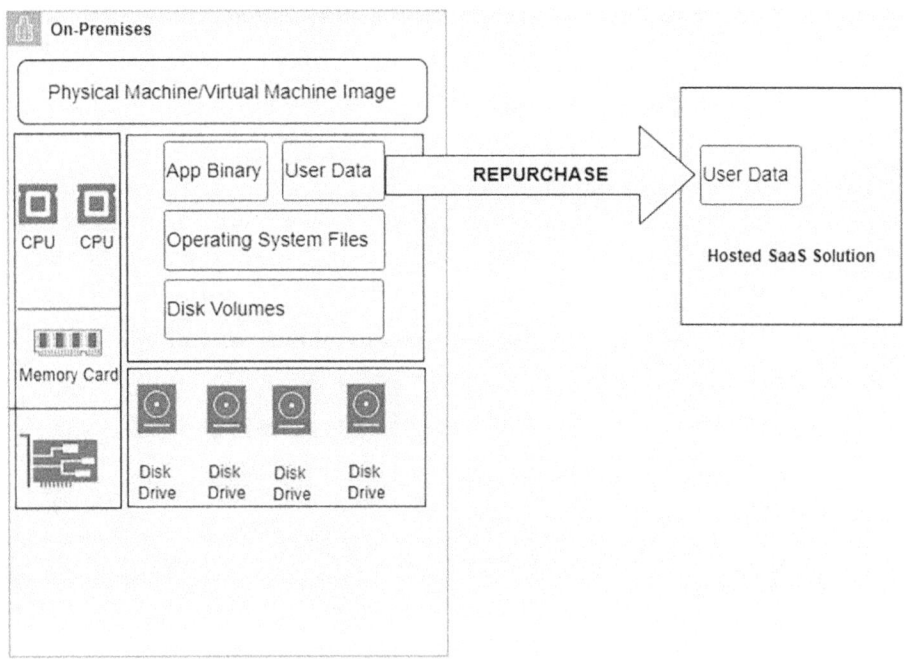

FIGURE 7.8 Repurchase Cloud Migration Strategy.

The benefits of repurchasing are as follows:

- You can implement a cloud-optimized solution as soon as possible.
- They dramatically cut migration costs.
- They allow you to utilize more cloud-native features than rehosting.
- It replaces the old licensing model with a flexible subscription-based approach, which offers cost allocation and tax benefits.
- It may offer feature set improvements that improve the user experience, application performance, and cost-effectiveness.

The disadvantages of repurchasing are as follows:

- Your team may have to undergo some new training to be familiar with the new configuration.
- Sometimes, you cannot make any significant changes to the platform because it belongs to someone else.
- Many companies are skeptical about business data passing through another system.
- There is nothing you can do about service outages other than wait for a fix.
- Likewise, you must wait for the SaaS provider to release updates at their own pace to fix security, compatibility, and performance issues.

Retire

This involves discontinuing the use of applications or data that are no longer needed by the organization. This can help to reduce costs and improve security.

The Retire cloud migration strategy can be seen in Figure 7.9.

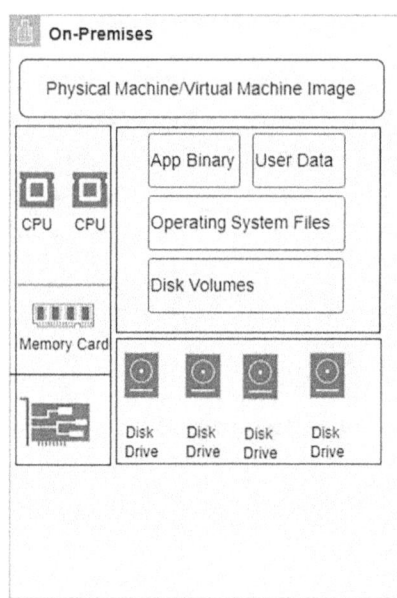

- Mergers and Acquisitions (M&A)

  Duplicate systems often exist due to past mergers, which can be retired during migration.

- Clustered Hosts

  On-Premises clusters may have excess nodes no longer needed in the cloud environment.

- High-Availability Hosts

  Traditional HA setups can be retired as cloud-native HA features replace them.

FIGURE 7.9 Retire Cloud Migration Strategy.

The benefits of retiring are as follows:

- Software that uses the retiring method for passive migration needs less money, time, specialized knowledge, and effort than any other alternative.
- By disabling unnecessary workloads, you can potentially eliminate performance, financial, and security burdens on your IT resources.
- The reallocation of resources toward more beneficial workloads and processes can heighten their performance at no additional expense.

What Are the Risks of Retiring?

Unsupported workloads that are archived might give rise to compatibility or performance issues in the long run, which could be expensive to fix later. We can prevent this potential error by carrying out a cloud suitability assessment right at the initial planning stage.

When to Retire Applications

The first task to be completed after migration to the cloud is to identify any redundant workloads, procedures, and tools along with backup solutions that you will no longer require, as disabling them can result in immediate cost savings. If not implemented, it could result in duplicate workloads in the cloud, and eventually increase cloud costs.

Retain (Revisit)

This involves keeping applications and data on-premises. This may be necessary for applications that are not compatible with the cloud, or for applications that need to be kept on-premises for security or compliance reasons.

The Retain cloud migration strategy can be seen in Figure 7.10.

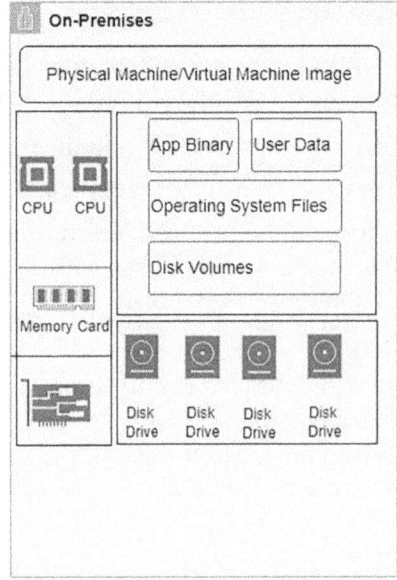

- Operating systems and applications that are not supported
- Applications that do not need to migrate to the cloud
- Outdated applications (update them and then migrate them to the cloud)

FIGURE 7.10 Retain Cloud Migration Strategy.

The benefits of retaining are as follows:

- It is a chance to determine which workloads should not be moved to the cloud.
- Keeping on-premises inefficiencies out of the cloud helps reduce cloud waste.
- It acts as the base that designers work with to efficiently build new and improved applications before they need upgrades or become obsolete.

The disadvantages of retaining are as follows:

- The more time the work remains on-premises, the more resources you may spend managing it.
- Maintaining the status quo could mean not using newer, safer, more cost-effective, and more productive procedures.

Migrating all IT operations from on-premises sources to the cloud is the best way to move forward with your digital transformation. It is important to carefully assess the organization's current IT environment and develop a migration plan that is tailored to the organization's specific goals.

Here are some additional considerations when choosing a migration strategy:

- *The source environment*: What type of environment are you migrating from (e.g., on-premises, cloud, or hybrid)?
- *The destination environment*: What type of environment are you migrating to (e.g., cloud or hybrid)?
- *The data and applications*: What type of data and applications are you migrating? What are their dependencies?
- *The business requirements*: What are the business requirements for migration (e.g., downtime, budget, and timeline)?
- *The technical constraints*: What are the technical constraints of migration (e.g., bandwidth, storage capacity, and processing power)?
- *The risks*: What are the potential risks associated with migration? How will you mitigate those risks?
- *Minimum effort*: The effort level is minimal in the Retire strategy and increases to maximum effort in the Refactor strategy.

Once you have considered all these factors, you can begin to develop a migration strategy that is tailored to your specific needs. Here are some tips for successfully migrating to the cloud:

- *Plan carefully*: Spend time developing the plan to make it more detailed. The plan should include the identification of the applications and data to be migrated, the timeline for migration, and the resources needed.
- *Test thoroughly before migration*: Before migrating any applications or data to production, be sure to test them thoroughly in a staging environment. This will help to identify and resolve any potential issues.
- *Communicate with stakeholders*: Keep stakeholders informed of the migration plan and timeline. This will help to minimize disruption to business operations.
- *Have a rollback plan in place*: In case something goes wrong with the migration, be sure to have a rollback plan in place. This will allow you to revert to your previous environment if necessary.

- *Validate*: Once you have migrated your applications to the AWS cloud, you need to test them thoroughly to ensure that they are working as expected. This may involve running functional and performance tests.
- *Cutover*: This is the process of switching traffic from your on-premises applications to the new applications running in the AWS cloud. There are a few different cutover strategies that you can use, such as a blue/green deployment or a rolling cutover.
- *Operate*: Once your applications have been cut over to the AWS cloud, you need to monitor and manage them on an ongoing basis. This includes tasks such as patching the applications, scaling the infrastructure, and backing up your data.

IDENTIFYING THE RIGHT MIGRATION STRATEGY

When migrating to the cloud, it is important to find the right strategy. You need to understand the specific needs of the application plus the overall business objectives before the migration to the cloud. Here are the strategies along with guidance on when to use each one:

- *Relocate*:
    - *When to use*: This is for moving the entire data center or physical servers to the cloud without changing their functionality.
    - *Business needs*: It is mostly used when a data center needs to be closed down or when there is a merger or an acquisition.
- *Rehost (lift and shift)*:
    - *When to use*: This is most suitable for applications that can be moved effortlessly without making changes.
    - *Business needs*: It is perfect for cost management, scalability, and faster migration with existing applications that do not require modifications.
- *Replatform (lift, tinker, and shift)*:
    - *When to use*: This works well when small changes can improve performance in the cloud.

- *Business needs*: It balances the need for rapid migration with the desire to leverage some cloud benefits such as improved scalability or managed services.
- *Repurchase*:
  - *When to use*: This is ideal when switching to a SaaS solution that can meet business requirements better than existing applications.
  - *Business needs*: It is usually driven by the need to replace outdated applications, reduce management overhead, or improve functionality.
- *Refactor (re-architect)*:
  - *When to use*: This is best suited for applications that would be substantially enhanced by means of the cloud-native architecture.
  - *Business needs*: It can be used when performance, scalability, and agility are a matter of crucial importance or to take full advantage of cloud capabilities.
- *Retire*:
  - *When to use*: This is suitable for applications that are obsolete or redundant.
  - *Business needs*: It helps reduce costs and makes the IT landscape less complicated by decommissioning outdated applications.
- *Retain*:
  - *When to use*: This is best for applications that need to remain in their current environment.
  - *Business needs*: It identifies the applications that are crucial to business operations but cannot be migrated due to compliance, security, or technical constraints.

TABLE 7.1 Identification of the Right Migration Strategy.

Strategy	When to Use	Business Needs
Relocate	Suitable for moving entire data centers or physical servers to the cloud without changing their functionality	Typically used when there is a need to vacate a data center or during a merger/acquisition
Rehost (Lift and Shift)	Best for applications that need to move quickly to the cloud with minimal changes	Ideal for cost reduction, scalability, and faster migration with existing applications that don't require modifications
Replatform (Lift, Tinker, and Shift)	Suitable when minor adjustments can improve performance in the cloud	Balances the need for rapid migration with the desire to leverage some cloud benefits such as improved scalability or managed services
Repurchase	Ideal when switching to a SaaS solution that can meet business requirements better than existing applications	Usually driven by the need to replace outdated applications, reduce management overhead, or improve functionality
Refactor (Re-architect)	Best for applications that would benefit significantly from a cloud-native architecture	Used when there is a need for significant improvements in performance, scalability, and agility, or to take full advantage of cloud capabilities
Retire	Suitable for applications that are no longer needed or are redundant	Helps in reducing costs and simplifying the IT landscape by decommissioning outdated applications
Retain	Appropriate for applications that are better off remaining in their current environment	Used when applications are critical to business operations and face challenges in migration due to compliance, security, or technical constraints

SUMMARY

This chapter provided a clear understanding of cloud migration. It covered the major strategies, planning, as well as execution routes in transferring workloads from on-premises environments to the cloud. It investigated the necessity of workload assessment, choosing the most suitable migration strategy, the 7 Rs of cloud migration (Rehost, Relocate, Replatform, Refactor, Repurchase, Retire, and Retain), and the use of different tools such as the AWS Cloud Adoption Framework, AWS Migration Service (MGN), and AWS Application Discovery Service. It provided a list of different migration parts (data, application, database, and infrastructure) to help you understand important aspects such as testing, compliance, and cost management. Moreover, it identified various migration types—traditional, phased, and wave-based—to avoid technical issues during the migration process and keep the process running smoothly and efficiently with less risk and disruption.

REFERENCES

[AWSCF20] AWS, *"AWS Cloud Adoption Framework (AWS CAF)"*. Available online at: *https://aws.amazon.com/cloud-adoption-framework/*, 2020.

[Sharma22] Sharma, N., *"Cloud Migration Strategies: A Practical Guide"*, Packt Publishing, 2022.

[Berman18] Berman, S., *"The Migration Playbook: IT Strategies for Cloud Adoption"*, Wiley, 2018.

[Smith19] Smith, J., *"Optimizing Application Migration: Lessons from Enterprise Case Studies,"* Journal of Cloud Computing (March 2019): pp. 45-60.

[AzureCAF20] Microsoft, *"Microsoft Cloud Adoption Framework for Azure"*. Available online at: *https://learn.microsoft.com/en-us/azure/cloud-adoption-framework/*, 2020.

[Anderson21] Anderson, R., *"7Rs of Cloud Migration Strategies: A Comparative Analysis,"* TechInsights Magazine (July 2021): pp. 23-29.

[Amazon23] Amazon Web Services, *"What is AWS Database Migration Service?"*. Available online at: *https://docs.aws.amazon.com/dms/latest/userguide/Welcome.html*, 2023.

[Lohar20] Lohar, P., *"Mastering Cloud Security and Compliance for Migration"*, Apress, 2020.

KNOWLEDGE CHECK: MULTIPLE-CHOICE Q&A

Question 1

What is the first step in the cloud migration process?

A. Testing the target environment.

B. Assessing workloads and configurations.

C. Selecting the cloud provider.

D. Executing migration directly.

Question 2

Which of the following is a core component of cloud migration?

A. Refactoring.

B. Configuration management.

C. Cost optimization.

D. All of the above.

Question 3

The Rehost migration strategy is also referred to as what?

A. Lift and shift.

B. Retain.

C. Refactor.

D. Relocate.

Question 4

What is the main advantage of replatforming during cloud migration?

A. Minimal downtime.

B. Improved performance and scalability.

C. No configuration changes.

D. Reduced training requirements.

Question 5

Which cloud migration strategy involves moving applications to a SaaS-based solution?

A. Retire.

B. Repurchase.

C. Relocate.

D. Retain.

Question 6

What is the purpose of creating Total Cost of Ownership (TCO) reports during cloud migration?

A. To identify redundant applications.

B. To calculate long-term operational costs and savings.

C. To create a migration roadmap.

D. To allocate roles and responsibilities.

Question 7

Which phase in the migration process involves testing and validating applications in the target environment?

A. Planning and assessment.

B. Validation.

C. Cutover.

D. Operate.

Question 8

Which of the following is NOT one of the 7 Rs of cloud migration strategies?

A. Rehost.

B. Retain.

C. Reassess.

D. Relocate.

Question 9

What is one disadvantage of the Retain strategy in cloud migration?

A. Increased downtime.

B. Resource expenditure on managing on-premises systems.

C. Lack of scalability in applications.

D. Complex compliance requirements.

Question 10

Which tool is used in the discovery phase of AWS cloud migration?

A. AWS Database Migration Service (DMS).

B. AWS Application Discovery Service.

C. AWS Auto Scaling.

D. AWS Elastic Load Balancing.

CHAPTER 8

Cloud Migration Framework and Different Phases

The process of moving to the cloud is complex and has many aspects, so it needs a well-thought-out and systematic approach to succeed. Two key frameworks that guide organizations through this process are the cloud adoption framework and the well-architected framework.

While the cloud adoption framework emphasizes the full cloud adoption process, the well-architected framework particularly deals with the design and implementation of cloud solutions. Mastering both frameworks can significantly boost the success of your cloud migration and cloud management operations. As an introduction to the various migration phases of AWS, it is important to grasp the different frameworks that affect the success of each phase.

WHAT IS A CLOUD ADOPTION FRAMEWORK?

A cloud adoption framework provides a structured approach for organizations to prepare, enforce, and supervise their transition to cloud computing. It is a complete set of policies, best practices, tools, and methodologies that companies can use to navigate the cloud service adoption obstacles. It aims to ensure a smooth, secure, and highly effective migration to the cloud without burning any resources. The strategy is to minimize the risks and maximize the benefits of the cloud.

Key Components of a Cloud Adoption Framework

A cloud adoption framework is an essential tool for organizations looking to traverse the digital landscape by migrating to the cloud or making the most of their current cloud infrastructure. It can be divided into strategy and planning, governance, technology, people and processes, adoption and migration, and optimization and innovation. Let's discuss each of them one by one.

Strategy and Planning

The following three important processes are the strategy and planning components of the cloud adoption framework:

- *Business goal*: Cloud adoption begins by first aligning cloud solutions with the business goals of the organization. This alignment makes sure that the investments in the cloud have a positive impact, for example, higher customer service, faster operations, and a better position in the market.

- *Cloud readiness assessment*: A cloud readiness assessment is a way of evaluating the organization's performance, applications, and workforce skill level. This research is effective in detecting the areas to be taken care of for the seamless transition to the cloud.

- *Cost management*: Strong cost management is a necessity. Organizations must come up with a detailed budgeting plan that will include the initial costs of setup, continuous operational expenses, and potential opportunities to reduce costs. Some of the important costs to consider:

  - *Initial setup costs*: These are the initial costs associated with migrating applications and data to the cloud.
  - *Operational expenses*: These include day-to-day ongoing work costs such as data storage, compute, power, and so on.
  - *Cost optimization*: This involves implementing best practices for improving resource utilization and minimizing redundant expenses.

Governance

Effective governance is the basis of responsible cloud adoption. Clearly established rules and standards make sure that data access, cloud service usage, and industry regulations are followed in the right way. The following governance factors need to be considered in the cloud adoption framework:

- *Policies and standards*: Establishing clear policies and standards is essential for ensuring responsible cloud use. Organizations should introduce policies on data access, cloud service usage, and compliance with industry standards as a way of protecting sensitive information.

- *Risk management*: Cloud adoption introduces new risks such as potential data breaches and service disruptions. A robust risk management framework is effective in allowing organizations to participate in analytics and identify and mitigate threats in the cloud infrastructure promptly before they impact a service.

- *Compliance*: This refers to compliance with regulatory and industry requirements. In the location where data is to be secured, organizations have to meet the relevant regulatory frameworks such as GDPR, HIPAA, or PCI-DSS to supervise data security and privacy.

Technology

The technological dimension of cloud adoption concentrates on creating a robust cloud architecture tailored to the enterprise's specific needs. Key aspects that come under the technology area are architecture, tooling and automation, and security:

- *Architecture*: A robust cloud architecture tailored to the organization's specific needs is essential. The architecture has to encompass scalability, performance, and resilience to ensure continuous service delivery.

- *Tooling and automation*: The use of cloud management tools and automation systems leads to improved operational efficiency. Automation helps reduce human error. Processes are streamlined, creating real-time visibility to cloud resources.

- *Security*: Besides moving data to the cloud, ensuring robust security measures is essential. This involves the use of encryption, access control, and constant security audits to protect applications and data effectively.

People and Processes

Success in cloud adoption depends heavily on workforce development and process transformation. By developing skills and training human capital, employees are given the tools they need to regulate cloud services efficiently. This category in the cloud adoption framework includes the following:

- *Skills and training*: Cloud adoption is the process of converting traditional working environments to the cloud. Integrating skill-building programs is a key element of this process. Organizations should adjust training courses according to the training that employees need to give them cloud skills and knowledge so that they can be able to work on the cloud servers.

- *Change management*: Transitioning to the cloud can cause a significant culture change among organizations. A change management strategy should be employed to ease the transitions so that all stakeholders fully comprehend and accept the new processes and technologies.

- *Operational model*: A clearly defined operational model for cloud services is the best way to ensure a smooth transition. In this model, responsibilities, processes, and performance benchmarks are put forth for control and continual improvement.

Adoption and Migration

A well-executed cloud migration plan is a necessary part of a company's smooth transition. This plan should detail the step-by-step approach for migrating applications and data while accounting for the infrastructure, resources, timeline, and potential disruptions that might occur. The components of this category are as follows:

- *Cloud migration plan*: The migration plan can determine whether the migration succeeds or results in a loss of profit. While this plan is in action, it must consider resources, timelines, and potential disruptions.

- *Workload prioritization*: Not all workloads are the same. The organization has to decide which applications and data to migrate first, considering factors such as their importance to the business, complexity, and cloud alignment.

- *Testing and validation*: Once the migration is complete, thorough testing and validation are necessary to ensure that every single system operates efficiently in the cloud environment. Problems are solved sooner and more efficiently thanks to the validation process, which is carried out before the actual complete cloud deployment.

Optimization and Innovation

The final phase of cloud adoption concerns continuous improvement and innovation:

- *Continuous improvement*:
  - *Monitor performance*: Organizations should regularly monitor performance and ask for feedback to identify areas of improvement. This is because cloud solutions are designed in such a way that they evolve together with the business objectives of organizations.
- *Innovation*: The cloud provides opportunities for innovation, using technologies such as AI, machine learning, and big data analytics. Organizations can use these to improve their offerings and, thus, they gain an advantage in the competitive market.

DIFFERENT CLOUD ADOPTION FRAMEWORKS

As we already know, there are three major cloud service providers—namely, AWS, Azure, and GCP—and all of them have cloud adoption frameworks. Each cloud platform has its own set of best practices and tools. They are all grounded in the same principles and goals but differ in implementation.

The popular cloud adoption frameworks are:

- AWS Cloud Adoption Framework (AWS CAF):

    https://aws.amazon.com/cloud-adoption-framework/

- Microsoft Cloud Adoption Framework for Azure:

    https://azure.microsoft.com/en-in/solutions/cloud-enablement/cloud-adoption-framework

- Google Cloud Adoption Framework:

    https://cloud.google.com/adoption-framework

The popular cloud adoption frameworks can be seen in Figure 8.1.

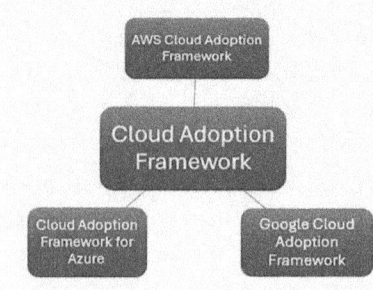

FIGURE 8.1 The Popular Cloud Adoption Frameworks.

AWS CAF

A cloud adoption framework is an essential guide for enterprises entering into the cloud business. It provides an organized method with best practices, relevant tools, and guidance for the whole cloud adoption process. This framework is the key for the organization to successfully transition to the cloud.

During cloud transformation, business outcomes are accelerated through cloud-driven organizational change, enabled by a set of foundational capabilities. The transformation domains represent a value chain where technological transformation enables process transformation, which enables organizational and, in turn, product transformation. Reduced business risk, increased revenue, operational efficiency, and enhanced Environmental, Social, and Governance (ESG) performance are the main objectives of businesses.

AWS CAF begins by identifying business stakeholders who are critical to cloud adoption. It divides stakeholders into six perspectives. This enables organizations to understand cloud adoption from the perspective of each stakeholder separately. In essence, it is the standard that defines the safety and cost-effectiveness of migrating to the AWS cloud.

These six perspectives can be seen in Figure 8.2.

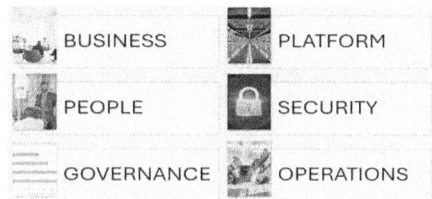

FIGURE 8.2 The Six Perspectives of AWS CAF.

We will discuss the six AWS CAF perspectives in detail next.

Business Perspective

By defining clear strategies that translate into concrete company-wide goals, AWS CAF enables the establishment of a global business model that is future-oriented and flexible, based on the changing demands of the market. The provision of this perspective could assist managers and business owners in the following:

- Providing great planning opportunities
- Maximizing satisfaction of the end-user needs
- Optimization of financial distribution
- End-to-end control of business risks, both external and strategic

Governance Perspective

This perspective helps in organizing and coordinating software and business processes outside of IT. It is helpful for IT managers, architects, and business analysts for the following:

- Scheduling cloud workloads and properly prioritizing services
- Choosing the right cloud migration methodologies
- Cost optimization
- License management

Operations Perspective

This perspective helps in managing workloads based on existing and future business needs. This enables a fast and low-risk implementation of a new business strategy. This phase is crucial for tech support operators who benefit from the following:

- Service monitoring for assessing the level of efficiency of IT operations and providing compliance with corporate requirements for operating software in the cloud
- Resource inventory management to rationalize the use of virtual IT assets
- Release/change management for intelligent selection of Continuous Integration/Continuous Delivery (CI/CD) methods
- Reporting and analytics for performance monitoring
- Creating backups and downtime assessments for continuous business processes

Security Perspective

The security perspective provides recommendations for the right structure for management points and helps reduce IT workloads for the network security team. The security advantages are as follows:

- *Identity and Access Management (IAM)*: Gives overall guidance for the integration of AWS to the user authentication and authorization process until its completion
- *Detective control*: Responsible for detecting suspicious network activity
- *Infrastructure security*: Responsible for drafting regulations and security requirements
- *Data protection*: Gives necessary guidelines to help in defining the right strategies for protecting data during the transfer and storing processes
- *Incident response service*: Helps you instantly respond to abnormal network activity

People Perspective

This perspective helps HR specialists prepare the staff for the journey to the cloud. In particular, HR specialists receive the following:

- The ability to predict new vacancies due to the modernized network architecture
- A common list of skills for cloud migration
- A training plan for employees to carry out their usual tasks in an updated environment

Platform Perspective

This perspective is a principle to serve the network infrastructure built with AWS. It plays a key role for network architects, CTOs, and project managers of the IT team. Here are the benefits related to the platform perspective:

- Knowledge of what requirements the design of the future system should meet
- Prospects for scaling and building new workflows in the cloud
- New business goals that are in line with the new computing power offered by the cloud

WELL-ARCHITECTED FRAMEWORKS

A set of guidelines and best practices that a cloud architect must adhere to in order to design, build, and manage cloud-based systems can be referred to as a cloud well-architected framework. These frameworks provide a template that gives both a structured and consistent approach to the realization of usability, effectiveness, and cost-effectiveness while also considering and meeting the particular needs of a business. The structured methods ensure that systems are secure, scalable, reliable, cost-effective, and meet the specific needs of a business. There are many cloud well-architected frameworks available, but the most popular ones are:

- *AWS Well-Architected Framework*: This AWS framework focuses on six key pillars—operational excellence, security, reliability, performance efficiency, cost optimization, and sustainability (*https://aws.amazon.com/architecture/well-architected/*).
- *Google Cloud Well-Architected Framework*: This GCP framework is a one-stop shop for valuable cloud architecture strategies. It is conceptually divided into defining architecture, deployment, and management,

security, resilience design, and optimization (*https://cloud.google.com/architecture/framework*).

- *Azure Well-Architected Framework*: This Microsoft Azure framework is a set of best practices for creating secure, high-performing, resilient, and cost-effective solutions on Azure. It is a critical tool that assists solution architects in determining the best cloud deployment strategies (*https://learn.microsoft.com/en-us/azure/well-architected/*).

These frameworks are not mutually exclusive. Each has its own pros and cons, and the choice depends on the cloud platform in use and project requirements.

AWS Well-Architected Framework

Amazon created the AWS Well-Architected Framework as a set of best practices to assist in the design and operation of secure, reliable, efficient, and cost-effective systems in the AWS cloud. It is a plan for the development of a high-quality cloud infrastructure. The two main advantages of the AWS Well-Architected Framework are:

- *Strong cloud foundations guidance*: The process of cloud migration is quite complex; however, with a well-designed plan, anyone can make the right decisions from the very beginning. Following these guidelines enables you to build secure systems that can handle increased workloads without generating unnecessary costs.

- *Continuous improvement*: The AWS Well-Architected Framework can help you identify areas for improvement and show you how to reconfigure your already existing architecture in terms of functions, safety, and cost-effectiveness for better results.

AWS Well-Architected Framework for Migration

When you migrate your IT infrastructure to the cloud via AWS, you will need the AWS Well-Architected Framework for your target site, ensuring smooth migrations and maximizing the benefits of cloud computing.

The AWS Well-Architected Framework is a complete guide that takes you through every step, from assessing existing settings to updating apps in the cloud. It is designed as a flexible tool. You can move back and forth within these phases, tweak your solutions, and step back to reflect on your progress.

The AWS Well-Architected Framework is your guiding star to build a cloud environment.

The AWS Well-Architected Framework is based on six pillars, each one focusing on the design and operation of cloud workloads on AWS.

These six pillars can be seen in Figure 8.3.

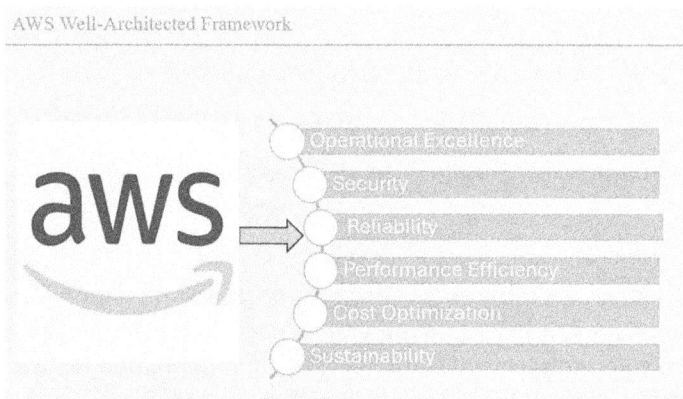

FIGURE 8.3 Six Pillars of the AWS Well-Architected Framework.

The following is a detailed explanation of each of these six pillars.

Operational Excellence

This pillar focuses on continuously improving processes and procedures for running and monitoring your cloud infrastructure. The key aspects include implementing automation, bringing effective change management, and providing the end-user with reliable resources. These are the benefits:

- Automated infrastructure provisioning and deployment
- Monitoring and logging for proactive issue identification
- Clear incident response procedures
- Continuous review and improvement of operational processes

Security

This pillar ensures that the data, applications, and cloud systems are secure (or security is provided). It includes the best methods to safeguard your organization by implementing strong access and identity management controls and granting the least privileges for your services. Some of the major activities of this pillar are as follows:

- IAM-based least-privilege access control implementation
- Securely encrypts both transitory and static data
- Regularly patches and updates your systems
- Continuously monitors for security threats

Reliability

This pillar focuses on building fault-tolerant systems that can withstand failures and recover quickly with minimal downtime. The main focus is on designing architectural structures with redundancy, scalability, and disaster recovery capabilities. The key activities include:

- Designing systems with redundancy built in
- Implementing automated recovery mechanisms
- Performing regular testing of disaster recovery plans
- Monitoring system health and performance metrics

Performance Efficiency

It is important for your infrastructure to be responsive and scalable to meet changing workloads and clients' needs. Choosing the right resources, managing performance, and correctly planning scalability are the main tasks under this pillar. In a nutshell, it is responsible for the performance, reliability, and scalability of the platform. Essential key activities to include are:

- Monitoring resource utilization and application performance
- Implementing auto-scaling to handle peak loads
- Optimizing resources for cost-efficiency

Cost Optimization

This pillar focuses on effectively managing your cloud expenditure by selecting the right AWS services for your needs. It involves optimizing resource usage, leveraging the available cost-saving options, and avoiding unnecessary expenses. Key activities include:

- Right-sizing your resources based on workload requirements
- Utilizing AWS services with pay-as-you-go pricing models
- Taking advantage of Reserved Instances or Savings Plans for predictable workloads
- Monitoring and analyzing your cloud expenditure

Sustainability

This pillar focuses on reducing the environmental impact of your cloud footprint by promoting energy-saving practices and building a sustainable cloud environment. The key activities include:

- Choosing energy-efficient AWS services
- Utilizing right-sizing and auto-scaling to optimize resource usage
- Implementing code optimization techniques for serverless functions
- Tracking and reporting on your cloud carbon footprint

DIFFERENT PHASES OF AWS CLOUD MIGRATION

The AWS Well-Architected Framework describes three phases of AWS cloud migration:

- Assess
- Mobilize
- Migrate and modernize

Migrate and *modernize* work simultaneously, hence they are treated as one phase.

The different phases of AWS cloud migration can be seen in Figure 8.4.

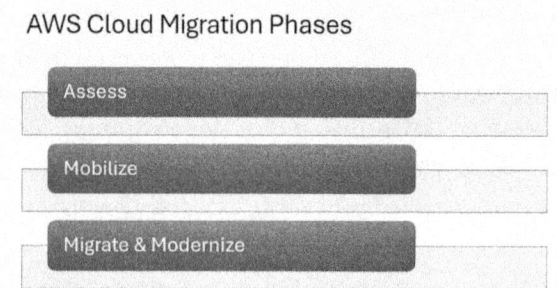

FIGURE 8.4 Different Phases of AWS Cloud Migration.

AWS WELL-ARCHITECTED FRAMEWORK WITH AWS MIGRATION PHASES

This outlines a methodical approach to transforming legacy applications to function within the AWS cloud environment according to the AWS Well-Architected Framework.

The AWS migration phases with the AWS Well-Architected Framework can be seen in Figure 8.5.

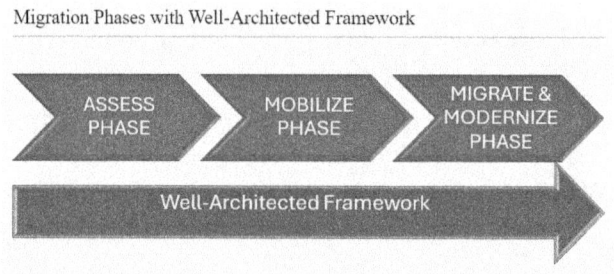

FIGURE 8.5 AWS Migration Phases with the AWS Well-Architected Framework.

Overall, the above diagram highlights the importance of the Well-Architected Framework throughout the migration process. This framework, along with AWS CAF, provides advice and best practices for the migration and the effective use of the AWS cloud.

To fully utilize the advantages of cloud adoption during migration, start by analyzing the readiness of your organization. This will ensure a smooth, large-scale migration and provide practical experience through the initial phase of application migration.

AWS migration consists of three distinct phases, each with corresponding activities, and each activity has specific tools to facilitate its completion.

AWS Migration Key Activities by Phase

Figure 8.6 shows the key activities associated with the three phases necessary for the successful completion of an AWS migration.

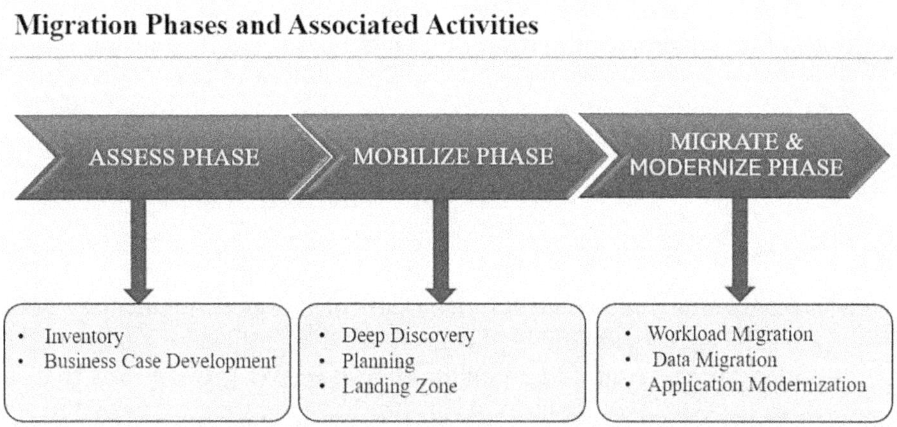

Migration Phases and Associated Activities

```
┌──────────────┐  ┌──────────────┐  ┌──────────────────┐
│ ASSESS PHASE │→ │ MOBILIZE     │→ │ MIGRATE &        │
│              │  │ PHASE        │  │ MODERNIZE PHASE  │
└──────┬───────┘  └──────┬───────┘  └────────┬─────────┘
       ↓                 ↓                   ↓
┌──────────────┐  ┌──────────────┐  ┌──────────────────┐
│ • Inventory  │  │ • Deep       │  │ • Workload       │
│ • Business   │  │   Discovery  │  │   Migration      │
│   Case       │  │ • Planning   │  │ • Data Migration │
│   Development│  │ • Landing    │  │ • Application    │
│              │  │   Zone       │  │   Modernization  │
└──────────────┘  └──────────────┘  └──────────────────┘
```

FIGURE 8.6 AWS Migration Key Activities in Different Phases.

Each phase includes key activities that are designed to address specific challenges in the migration process, supported by different tools and best practices.

The three different phases and their respective activities are as follows:

- *Assess phase*: The main activities of this phase are identifying the existing inventory and developing a business case.
- *Mobilize phase*: The main activities of this phase are deep discovery, detailed planning, and setting up a landing zone.
- *Migrate and modernize phase*: In this phase, the whole workload migration and data migration are accomplished, followed by application modernization.

By following these phases and activities, businesses can adequately plan, execute, and optimize their migration to AWS, ensuring minimal disruption, and maximizing the benefits of the cloud.

Here is a breakdown of the phases and the key activities involved in each of the phases.

Assess Phase

Successful migration often depends on careful planning and assessment. This phase constitutes a critical component of the AWS migration strategy, emphasizing the necessity of understanding the existing environment and laying a solid foundation for the rest of the migration steps. The major objectives and activities of this phase are based on two primary aspects:

- Inventory
- Business case

Understanding Inventory

The inventory process is a crucial part of the assessment phase. It involves identifying and categorizing IT assets, such as applications, servers, databases, and data. An accurate and comprehensive inventory ensures that organizations have a clear picture of what they are migrating to the AWS cloud. The main functions are:

- *Asset identification*: The primary goal is to compile a list of all the technology assets that exist within the current environment, including comprehensive evaluations of all hardware, software, and services, with a focus on key applications and the database architecture that supports them. Organizations can utilize AWS discovery tools such as AWS Application Discovery Service to streamline the inventory process, automate discovery, reduce manual workload, and increase accuracy in asset identification.
- *Dependencies mapping*: This involves understanding how various systems interact to identify dependencies requiring attention during migration, mapping out interactions between systems and applications, and creating a visual representation of the infrastructure to reveal critical interdependencies and workflows.

Creating a detailed inventory sets the stage for informed decision-making during the migration process. It minimizes risks by ensuring that all aspects of the current environment are considered as they transition to the cloud.

Developing a Business Case

In the assessment phase, a business case is an essential element to support the migration. The business case is developed in such a way that it directly pertains to the company's objectives and highlights the strategic benefits of the AWS cloud. The fundamental objectives of this phase are as follows:

- *Justify the migration*: The justification for the migration must be clear and concise to the stakeholders, supported by communication of the event. A complete overview of the benefits and costs of this transition will provide an analytical perspective and help inform decision-making.

- *Outline benefits and costs*: This can be done by comparing current expenditures with prospective cloud ones, and the benefits the change might bring to the transition.

While creating the business case for cloud migration, the following activities must be completed:

- *Evaluate costs*: Compare the initial IT costs with the predicted cloud operating expenses, as well as the costs of hardware, software, and maintenance overhead. Also compare costs such as maintenance, infrastructure upgrades, and additional costs for software upgrades.

- *Detailed financial assessment*: Perform a detailed financial assessment, comparing various expenses such as support, infrastructure upgrades, and software upgrades. You can use the AWS pricing calculator (available at *https://calculator.aws/#/*) for this purpose. Factor in a range of costs, including maintenance, infrastructure upgrades, and administrative overhead.

- *Identify potential benefits*: Highlight the advanced functions of AWS, such as increased scalability, better performance, and enhanced security measures. Demonstrate how migration can reduce downtime and improve the disaster recovery process.

    Develop presentations that clearly convey the financial impact, growth opportunities, and risk reduction associated with cloud migration. Emphasize how the move aligns with the organization's broader strategic vision and long-term goals.

The business case serves as a foundation for subsequent steps that will be taken in the migration process. By conducting a comprehensive analysis of the IT assets and preparing a solid business case, enterprises can clearly define the path of their migration efforts.

Mobilize Phase

This phase is crucial for planning and preparation. It focuses on laying the foundation for a successful migration and reducing risks by ensuring a smooth transition for the organization.

The essential components of this phase are deep discovery, comprehensive planning, and setting up a secure landing zone, all of which will be explored in subsequent sections.

Deep Discovery: Understanding the Existing Environment

In the mobilization phase, the first step in the cloud migration process is deep discovery. Understanding the current environment is an essential step for creating a tailored migration strategy and this assists an organization's migration requirements. It includes the following activities:

- *Detailed analysis of workloads, applications, and data*:
    - Perform thorough existing workload assessments to understand utilization patterns of the resources.
    - Analyze whether applications are adaptable to the AWS environment by studying their compatibility and performance requirements.
    - Review data management practices to establish data integrity and security during migration.
- *Identifying performance baselines and application dependencies*:
    - Enhance the performance of applications to better understand and assess the model's performance pre- and post-migration.
    - Identify application dependencies to understand the relationship between various components and the effects of the related applications on migration.
- *Utilizing AWS Migration Hub*:
    - AWS migration can easily be done by integrating AWS Migration Hub, which is the leading cloud migration tool to centralize and automate the process.
    - Gather essential metrics and observations of the current infrastructure or environment; this will help shape strategies and guide the decision-making process.

Planning: Developing a Comprehensive Migration Strategy

Once an in-depth understanding of the existing environment has been completed, the focus can move to the planning phase of migration. This task consists of making a detailed migration strategy and a roadmap that shows the way for the transition to the AWS cloud. Main activities include:

- *Building a migration strategy and roadmap*:
    - Define the migration approach (e.g., rehost, refactor, or rearchitect) in line with business objectives.
    - Develop a step-by-step roadmap to outline milestones and deliverables, ensuring a successful completion of the migration journey.
- *Defining timelines, resources, and roles*:
    - Allocate appropriate resources, including personnel and budget, to support the migration efforts.
    - Define a clear timeline for each phase of the migration and ensure that all of them are executed on time as per the stakeholders' expectations.
- *Developing a risk management plan*:
    - Identify potential risks associated with migration, including technical, operational, and security risks.
    - Define migration strategies to mitigate these risks proactively rather than reactively.

Landing Zone: Establishing a Secure AWS Environment

A well-architected landing zone is vital for companies that are in transition. It provides the platform on which the programs can be developed, deployed, and managed securely and efficiently. Essential activities include:

- *Establishing governance, security, and compliance frameworks*:
    - Establish governance structures to ensure compliance with organizational policies and industry regulations.
    - Develop security practices that ensure data and applications are safe in the AWS environment.
- *Setting up AWS accounts and networking*:
    - Set up AWS accounts based on different business units to enhance management and cost control. Setting up AWS Organizations can be useful here.

- Establish robust networking configurations that will improve both data and resource sharing and will enable seamless connectivity.
- *Deploying IAM*:
  - Create IAM policies to restrict access to AWS resources.
  - Ensure that only authorized people can access sensitive data and critical applications by using MFA for those sensitive applications and services.
- *Using AWS Control Tower*:
  - Leverage AWS Control Tower to automate a multi-account AWS environment configuration.
  - Benefit from pre-configured security and compliance controls to simplify governance across the organization.

Migrate and Modernize Phase

Organizations that want to migrate their workloads and business applications to the AWS cloud understand that this phase is crucial not only for data and workload transfer but also for the optimization of applications for cloud-centric deployment. The subsequent sections will explore the key components of this phase, including workload migration, data migration, and application modernization.

Understanding Workload Migration

The primary objective of workload migration is to move applications and workloads to AWS with minimal disruption to business operations, ensuring that businesses can continue their daily work without interruptions during the migration process. For a smooth workload migration, organizations must undertake several critical activities:

1. *Select the appropriate migration strategy*: Depending on the specific needs of the applications, organizations can choose from various strategies:
   - *Rehost (lift and shift)*:
     This is useful in cases where organizations are moving applications and data to the cloud without making any changes to them. This is a good option for applications that are already running well on-premises

and that do not require any special modifications to take advantage of the cloud.

- *Relocate*:

   This involves moving data centers (or large portions of them) to an equivalent cloud infrastructure. It is good for existing data that is subject to compliance regulations, or for data that needs to be stored in a specific geographic location.

- *Refactor*:

   This is useful when one needs to make some alterations to applications to enjoy the benefits of cloud functionality, thus improving performance without impacting the compatibility of the application with the cloud.

- *Replatform*:

   This is good when adapting applications to benefit from cloud-native features, often resulting in reduced costs and improved scalability.

- *Retire*:

   This is used when an organization wants to discontinue the use of applications or data that are no longer needed. This can help to reduce costs and improve security.

- *Retain (revisit)*:

   This is used for applications that are not compatible with the cloud or need to be kept on-premises for security or compliance reasons.

- *Repurchase*:

   This is helpful in cases where organizations want to transition to a fully managed service and use all cloud-native features, eliminating the need for in-house infrastructure and support.

2. *Execute the migration*: Services such as AWS Server Migration Service (SMS) and AWS Application Migration Service can be used to complete the migration process. These tools help automate and streamline the movement of applications.

3. *Perform testing and validation*: After migration, it is important to check and validate that migrated applications are functioning as per expectations in the new AWS cloud environment. This step ensures that any potential problems are solved before the applications go live.

Effective Data Migration

The process of migrating data from various systems to AWS is very important. Data migration must prioritize data integrity and security, with minimal downtime being an essential factor during this process. The key elements of a successful data migration are:

1. *Utilize migratory tools*: Use AWS Database Migration Service (DMS). This first creates a copy of your original database, and then migrates the data from the original instance to the copy while ensuring minimal downtime.

2. *Implement data transfer methods*: For large-scale data transfers, organizations can employ the following solutions:
   - *AWS Snowball*: A petabyte-scale data transport solution that helps physically move huge amounts of data
   - *AWS DataSync*: A service that facilitates rapid and secure data transfer between AWS and on-premises environments

3. *Validate post-migration data*: After the data is transferred, it is paramount to verify and check its accuracy and consistency. This ensures that the migrated data is correct and accurate and prevents any kind of data corruption or loss.

Application Modernization

After migrating the applications and data, organizations should focus on the modernization of applications to maximize their utilization of AWS services. This means they should improve the application architecture in such a way that it becomes more scalable, performs better, and is more cost-effective. The following actions are needed to discover the full capabilities of the cloud:

1. *Refactor applications*: Adjust existing applications to utilize AWS-native services. These include:
   - *AWS Lambda*: Utilizes serverless computing and streamlines operations
   - *Amazon RDS*: Manages and scales databases effortlessly
   - *Amazon S3*: Provides reliable and scalable storage that allows you to pay for what you use

2. *Enhance application architecture*: The prime focus of the application improvement process should be the application architecture. Major changes include modifying components to ensure they are cloud-compliant as well as cloud-scalable.

3. *Implement DevOps practices*: Leverage AWS DevOps tools such as AWS CodePipeline, AWS CodeBuild, and AWS CodeDeploy to facilitate (CI/CD. DevOps practices lead to faster deployment cycles and innovations with the use of cloud technology.

MIGRATION PHASES AND ASSOCIATED TOOLS

We have seen that migration and modernization constitute the most important phase in migration, where the actual migration work is done. Migration and modernization work in tandem, integrating seamlessly to deliver optimal results during the migration process. The adoption of the Well-Architected Framework is not limited to certain phases of migration only; it can apply to all of the phases.

Different tools associated with AWS migration can be seen in Figure 8.7.

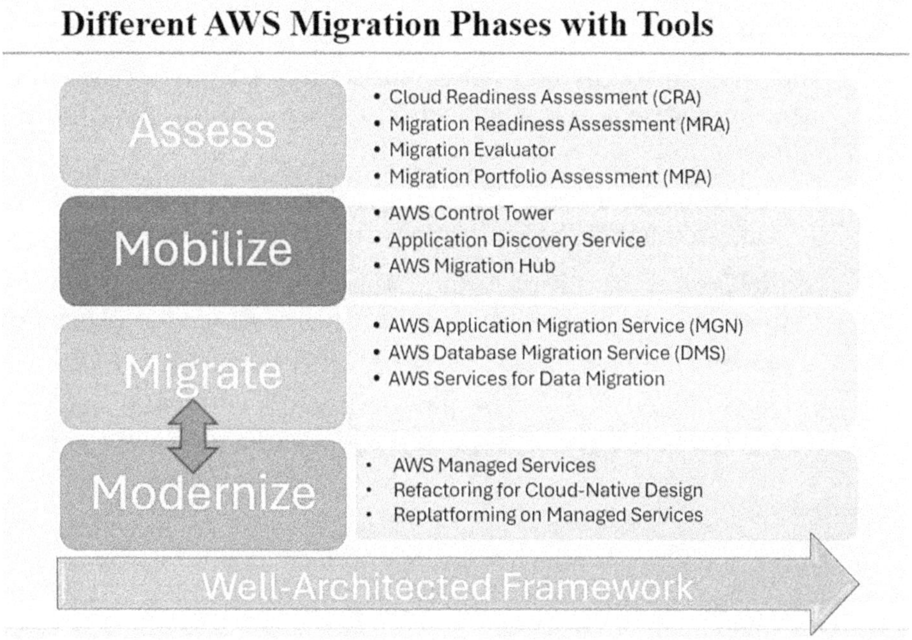

Different AWS Migration Phases with Tools

Assess
- Cloud Readiness Assessment (CRA)
- Migration Readiness Assessment (MRA)
- Migration Evaluator
- Migration Portfolio Assessment (MPA)

Mobilize
- AWS Control Tower
- Application Discovery Service
- AWS Migration Hub

Migrate
- AWS Application Migration Service (MGN)
- AWS Database Migration Service (DMS)
- AWS Services for Data Migration

Modernize
- AWS Managed Services
- Refactoring for Cloud-Native Design
- Replatforming on Managed Services

Well-Architected Framework →

FIGURE 8.7 Different AWS Migration Phases with Tools.

A brief overview of the phases and the associated tools is provided next.

Assess Phase

This phase involves evaluating your current on-premises environment to identify what can be moved to the cloud, as well as its readiness for migration. The tools in this phase help analyze and assess your infrastructure for migration feasibility. AWS provides some important tools during this phase, as follows:

- *Cloud Readiness Assessment (CRA)*: This determines whether your company is prepared for the cloud. It is used to identify necessary changes in the processes, skills, and tools.
- *Migration Readiness Assessment (MRA)*: This involves a structured approach to check whether workloads are ready for migration. It involves the identification of gaps in your migration capabilities.
- *Migration Evaluator*: This service offers insights into the cost of migration and helps in creating a data-driven business case for cloud migration.
- *Migration Portfolio Assessment (MPA)*: This aids in the assessment and categorization of your current application portfolio for migration according to business and technical requirements.

Mobilize Phase

After assessment, the next phase of this process is preparing your environment for migration. Planning and organizing migration activities are easier with the use of the following tools:

- *AWS Control Tower*: This is the easiest means to run a set of secure, multi-account AWS cloud settings in compliance with AWS best practices.
- *Application Discovery Service*: This collects substantial data about on-premises applications, which, in turn, helps in migration planning through a better understanding of application dependencies.
- *AWS Migration Hub*: This provides centralized tracking and monitoring of the migration progress across multiple AWS tools and services.

Migrate Phase

This is the phase in which the workload migration takes place. The following tools enable the efficient migration of applications, databases, and other resources to the AWS cloud:

- *AWS Application Migration Service (MGN)*: This automates the conversion of physical and virtual workloads to cloud-based workloads, ensuring minimal downtime.
- *AWS Database Migration Service (DMS)*: This simplifies the migration of on-premises databases to AWS. It supports homogeneous and heterogeneous migrations.
- *AWS services for data migration*: These are services that help with migrating large datasets, and they include AWS Snowball and AWS DataSync.

Modernize Phase

Once the migration is completed and workloads have been successfully migrated, the next focus area is the optimization and modernization of applications for cloud-native functionality with the help of the following tools:

- *AWS Managed Services*: This manages the AWS infrastructure, ensuring security, cost-efficiency, and operational reliability.
- *Refactoring for cloud-native design*: Re-architect the migrated applications to take full advantage of AWS cloud capabilities such as scalability and resilience.
- *Replatforming on Managed Services*: Meaningful application modifications can be made with cloud-native services, without requiring a complete refactor.

WELL-ARCHITECTED FRAMEWORK

The Well-Architected Framework serves as a guiding principle in all these phases, ensuring that applications are developed keeping best practices in mind. It concentrates on operational excellence, security, reliability, performance efficiency, sustainability, and cost optimization.

The Well-Architected Framework follows a structured migration approach and helps organizations move seamlessly to the AWS cloud, with tools designed to ease every stage of the migration journey.

The AWS Well-Architected Framework can be seen in Figure 8.8.

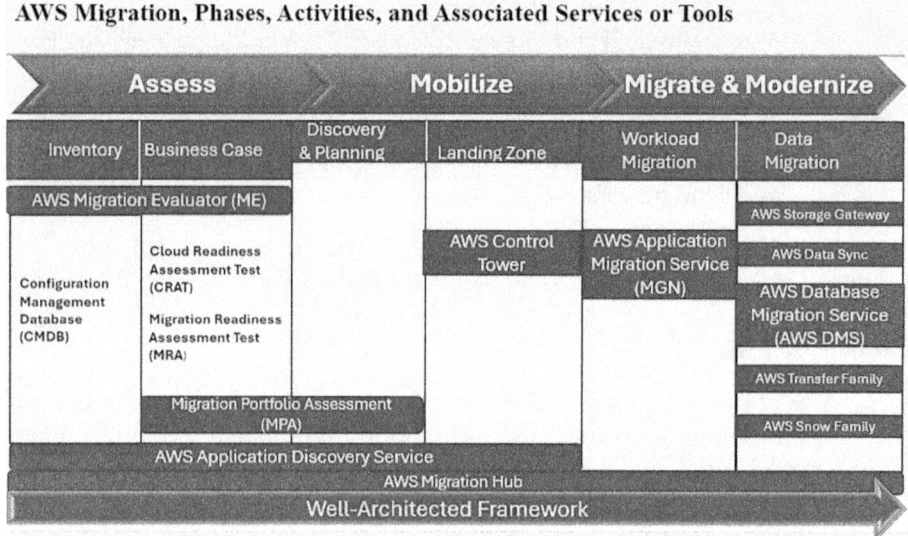

FIGURE 8.8 AWS Well-Architected Framework with Phases, Activities, and Tools.

CLOUD MIGRATION SUCCESS MANTRA: PEOPLE, PROCESS, AND TECHNOLOGY

A successful cloud migration depends on the execution of a well-planned strategy, skilled people, and up-to-date technology. By concentrating on these three crucial elements, businesses can guarantee a smooth transition to the cloud and take full advantage of cloud computing.

A successful migration does not only depend on technology—it's about navigating the human element, establishing efficient workflows, and leveraging the right tools.

The important factors of cloud migration success can be seen in Figure 8.9.

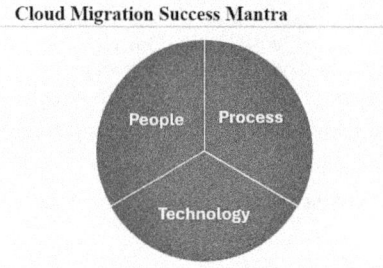

FIGURE 8.9 Cloud Migration Success Mantra.

People: Building Trust and Equipping Your Team

Nowadays, virtually every organization that wants to be relevant in the digital era is turning to cloud solutions to maximize efficiency, scalability, and the potential for collaboration; however, the path to the cloud is not only about technology. The success of cloud migration is also highly dependent on the people and their processes, which cannot be ignored. This section focuses on the *people* dimension of cloud migration.

Understanding Change Management

Cloud migration significantly impacts organizational behavior, requiring the organization to have a revolutionized approach to change management. As changes that people bring into organizations are often seen as a threat, the success of the migration will depend on well-thought-out, creative, and meaningful management during the transition. The key strategies of change management are:

- *Communication*: Clearly explain the main reasons for the migration. Employees must understand the "how" and the "why." For instance, employers could tell their employees how the new method will make accessing data easier, expand the possibilities of collaboration, and help them complete tasks more efficiently. Organizations should encourage employees to participate in new methods; they need to see the employees' reactions first and judge whether the methods are going to be useful.

- *Training*: Invest in technical or technological courses that will familiarize employees with the new cloud environment. This new training program should focus on the proper utilization of new cloud-based applications, security protocols, and collaboration tools. Employees will then feel equipped to navigate this new landscape confidently.

- *Addressing concerns*: Keep lines of communication open among the different stakeholders involved. Organizations should actively consider and respond to employees' worries in the transition process. This builds trust and reduces resistance, ensuring a smooth transition.

Skills and Expertise

Even with a strong management strategy, it is critical to find out whether the staff has sufficient cloud knowledge. The expertise and knowledge of the team members are crucial in making a cloud migration successful:

- *Upskilling*: One of the most effective methods is to reskill existing staff members. Offer training to employees in strategic cloud skills to engage the existing workforce in gaining practical knowledge, reducing redundancy in the organization.

- *Hiring cloud professionals*: For complex migrations, particularly those related to enterprise-level infrastructure, recruiting experts in this domain (e.g., cloud architects, engineers, and security professionals) could increase the capabilities of the team. These technologists can guarantee that your migration operation is deployed successfully and complies with the standards of the industry.

The Role of Leadership

Leadership is a key factor that influences the success of the migration process. Leaders must be involved as the main supporters of the change, creating an environment that encourages learning and adaptation. Leadership strategies are as follows:

- *Championing the migration*: Managers must not only support the migration but also lead the project, speaking out on the benefits and promising to invest time and money in training employees so they gain maximum benefits and rewards.

- *Creating a supportive culture*: The cultivation of a culture of continuous learning will enable employees to embrace new tools and methodologies willingly. As well as migration training, it will also create an innovative environment.

- *Recognizing efforts*: Recognition and the celebration of small successes during the migration process serve as good motivating forces for team members and result in a positive perspective on the transition.

Process: Charting a Clear Path with Flexibility

Migration Strategy

Develop and communicate a migration strategy that includes the 7 Rs (Rehost, Refactor, Replatform, Retire, Replace, Relocate, and Repurchase). This will help you understand how to plan and execute the migration of applications and data.

Phased Approach

Break down the migration process into different manageable phases, starting with the least important applications and data to identify and solve any issues before migrating core systems. For optimal results, always split the migration into phases and implementing the following strategies:

- *Start small*: Start by migrating low-priority applications and data. This allows you to identify and solve problems before migrating core systems.
- *Create momentum*: As teams progress through each phase of the migration process, they build confidence and expertise, creating the perfect environment for a smooth migration.
- *Iterate and adapt*: To ensure valid information, you should be ready to change your method as you progress. Lessons learned from earlier phases can guide improvements in later stages.

Technology: Choosing the Right Tools and Prioritizing Security

Cloud Assessment Tools

Evaluate your current infrastructure and applications with cloud assessment tools. These tools can also give relevant insights about:

- *Cloud readiness*: Identify the applications that are mostly cloud-friendly but might need some modifications.
- *Performance optimization*: Understand the behavior of the applications in a cloud environment and learn how to allocate resources optimally.
- *Security posture*: Evaluate possible security issues related to migration to the cloud.

Migration Tools

Do not reinvent the wheel. Use cloud migration tools from your cloud provider or third-party vendors. These tools can automate tasks such as:

- *Data transfer*: Accelerate the transfer of large volumes of data to the cloud, which will result in lower downtime and safer data transfer.
- *Workload management*: Resources are automatically prepared and configured by an automated system, moving from the source (on-premises or any cloud) to the target cloud environment.

Security Measures

Security is a vital aspect that needs to be considered in the cloud environment. We need to consider the following important factors:

- *Provider security*: Identify a cloud service provider and review all their security services, ensuring they have a strong security track record and comply with all security-related best practices as per industry standards.
- *Access controls*: Utilize strong access controls to restrict access to sensitive data and resources within the cloud environment so that they are only accessible to authorized individuals.
- *Encryption*: To prevent unauthorized access, be sure to encrypt data both at rest and in transit, even in the event of a security breach.

By focusing on the key areas of people, process, and technology, organizations can ensure a smooth and successful cloud migration.

SUMMARY

This chapter introduced a systematic approach to cloud migration by referring to the AWS CAF and the Well-Architected Framework WAF. It explained the three key phases of AWS migration—assess, mobilize, and migrate and modernize—with an overview of the most important activities, such as workload discovery, risk assessment, security implementation, and optimization. The chapter also presented the applications of AWS tools such as AWS Migration Hub, AWS Application Migration Service (MGN), and AWS Database Migration Service (DMS), which are responsible for smooth migration. It also focused on monitoring cloud usage conditions, ensuring adherence to security standards, and cost-efficient design to ensure a smooth, secure, and efficient cloud transition while maximizing business value.

REFERENCES

[AWSCAF21] Amazon Web Services, *"AWS Cloud Adoption Framework (AWS CAF)"*. Available online at: *https://aws.amazon.com/cloud-adoption-framework*, 2021.

[AWSWAF22] Amazon Web Services, *"AWS Well-Architected"*. Available online at: *https://aws.amazon.com/architecture/well-architected*, 2022.

[AzureCAF21] Microsoft, *"Microsoft Cloud Adoption Framework for Azure"*. Available online at: *https://azure.microsoft.com/en-us/solutions/cloud-enablement/cloud-adoption-framework*, 2021.

[GCPCAF21] Google Cloud, *"Google Cloud Adoption Framework"*. Available online at: *https://cloud.google.com/adoption-framework*, 2021.

[Snowball22] Amazon Web Services, *"AWS Snowball"*. Available online at: *https://aws.amazon.com/snowball*, 2022.

[DataSync21] Amazon Web Services, *"AWS DataSync"*. Available online at: *https://aws.amazon.com/datasync*, 2021.

[ControlTower20] Amazon Web Services, *"AWS Control Tower"*. Available online at: *https://aws.amazon.com/controltower*, 2020.

[Discovery22] Amazon Web Services, *"AWS Application Discovery Service"*. Available online at: *https://aws.amazon.com/application-discovery*, 2022.

[MGN22] Amazon Web Services, *"AWS Application Migration Service"*. Available online at: *https://aws.amazon.com/application-migration-service*, 2022.

[DMS22] Amazon Web Services, *"AWS Database Migration Service"*. Available online at: *https://aws.amazon.com/dms*, 2022.

KNOWLEDGE CHECK: MULTIPLE-CHOICE Q&A

Question 1

What is the primary purpose of AWS Cloud Adoption Framework (AWS CAF)?

- A. Define cloud architecture models.
- B. Provide a structured approach to cloud adoption.
- C. Migrate data without preparation.
- D. Eliminate the need for governance.

Question 2

Which of the following is NOT a key component of AWS CAF?

- A. Strategy and planning.
- B. Governance.
- C. Application deployment.
- D. Technology.

Question 3

What is the first step in the Assess phase of AWS migration?

- A. Deep discovery of the environment.
- B. Developing a business case.
- C. Establishing a secure landing zone.
- D. Performing workload migration.

Question 4

Which tool is used to automate the migration of on-premises databases to AWS?

- A. AWS Database Migration Service (DMS).
- B. AWS DataSync.
- C. AWS Snowball.
- D. AWS Control Tower.

Question 5

In the Mobilize phase, what does setting up a secure AWS landing zone involve?

A. Designing application architectures.

B. Establishing governance and security frameworks.

C. Testing and validating workloads.

D. Automating DevOps pipelines.

Question 6

What are the six perspectives of AWS CAF?

A. Strategy, Governance, Operations, Security, People, and Processes.

B. Business, Governance, Operations, Security, People, and Platform.

C. Innovation, Scalability, Cost Management, Governance, Security, and People.

D. Operations, Governance, Innovation, Security, Platform, and Technology.

Question 7

What is the main objective of the Optimize and Innovate phase in cloud migration?

A. Migrating applications to the cloud.

B. Conducting a readiness assessment.

C. Continuous improvement and innovation.

D. Managing cloud costs.

Question 8

Which AWS service is best suited for transferring large amounts of on-premises data to AWS?

A. AWS Application Migration Service.

B. AWS Database Migration Service.

C. AWS Snowball.

D. AWS Control Tower.

Question 9

The AWS Well-Architected Framework is based on how many pillars?

A. Four
B. Five
C. Six
D. Seven

Question 10

What is the primary goal of refactoring applications during the Modernize phase?

A. To rehost applications without modification.
B. To align applications with cloud-native capabilities.
C. To retire outdated systems.
D. To relocate workloads to a new data center.

CHAPTER 9

ASSESS PHASE OF AWS MIGRATION

OVERVIEW OF THE ASSESS PHASE

The Assess phase of cloud migration helps determine which operations will be migrated. It also provides a business case and a Total Cost of Ownership (TCO) analysis. This phase is critical as it involves understanding the current state of your IT landscape, also known as a "snapshot."

This snapshot includes all the assets your enterprise holds, such as hardware, software, applications, configuration data, and service levels. The Assess phase is important to a successful cloud migration because understanding everything that exists in the customers' infrastructure is critical to all subsequent steps in the cloud migration process.

The key factors to consider regarding cloud migration can be summarized as follows:

- Why we are migrating to the cloud
- What we want to migrate
- Cloud migration readiness
- The current state of migration

Why We Are Migrating to the Cloud

Some of the reasons for migrating to the cloud will be discussed next.

Business Needs

Business requirements can vary widely, including reducing expenditure on products and services, enhancing the organization's flexibility and agility, and learning how to use cloud services for recovery. The cloud model allows you to save money by providing on-demand access to computer resources without having to buy them upfront like traditional large companies. Resource utilization is improved through scalability, by provisioning or de-provisioning those resources as needed. Disaster recovery is enhanced by the cloud providers' ability to replicate data in different locations, ensuring redundancy in case one of them goes down.

Current IT Snapshot

To successfully determine what can be moved to the cloud, it is important to have a good understanding of the company's existing information system, including the inventory of its applications, types of data and storage needs, IT hardware, licenses, and their interdependencies, and the topology of the network.

Performance Information

Analyzing current performance metrics helps us unddrstand how the cloud can improve our IT operations. Metrics to consider include server CPU utilization, storage capacity, network bandwidth usage, and application response times.

What We Want to Migrate

We need to identify what we want to migrate to the cloud. Some important aspects that need to considered are mentioned below:

- Asset *inventory*: This involves checking the existing stock of your IT assets, and includes:
  - *Current infrastructure*: What does the current infrastructure look like? For example, types of servers and applications, source platform and environment types, network topology, and so on.
  - *Rightsizing*: Which compute, storage, and network configuration is best for each workload?
  - *Licensing*: Which applications will be able to operate workloads in the cloud with licenses?

- *Networking*: What devices/ports are needed for workload migration connection?
- *Shared services*: Which shared services does the workload depend on?
- *Application configuration and dependency mapping*: This involves understanding the requirements for configuring your applications and the data they use. Some applications may need to be refactored or re-architected to function correctly in the cloud environment. Dependency mapping helps us identify which applications should be migrated together.
- *Data and storage*: Data that will be stored in the cloud may require additional processing, such as formatting and converting it into the specific types or formats accepted by cloud storage providers.
- *Service-Level Agreements (SLAs)*: You must review existing SLAs with vendors and the cloud environment. If none are in place, we can establish SLAs with our cloud provider to cover service quality, uptime, and security.

How Ready We Are for Migration

Here are some factors that need to be considered when assessing your cloud migration readiness:

- Application *a*rchitecture: Understanding the architecture of your applications is critical to determining their cloud compatibility. Cloud-native applications are designed specifically for the cloud and are generally easier to migrate than traditional on-premises applications.
- *Configuration Management Database (CMDB)*: A robust CMDB gives a complete and accurate inventory of your IT assets and their configurations. This information is essential for planning and executing a successful cloud migration.

Where We Stand Currently

Understanding where we are on the cloud migration journey is crucial in determining the specific activities that will be going on in the assessment phase. An organization that is only just beginning to think about cloud migration will have different assessment needs from one that is already in the planning stage of the cloud migration project.

This assessment is based on the AWS Cloud Adoption Framework (AWS CAF) and its six perspectives: business, people, governance, technology, security, and operations. This framework helps us assess the phase by providing a holistic view of the cloud transformation initiative, ensuring its effectiveness.

The Assess phase involves a comprehensive high-level TCO assessment, in addition to some other assessment tools. These steps will help secure stakeholder commitment and funding for the bigger projects that will follow.

DIFFERENT TOOLS USED IN THE ASSESS PHASE

Before we set off on a cloud migration journey through AWS, it is crucial to thoroughly assess your source environment. This important step enables us to gather essential information to support decision-making, ensuring that migration goals are met. Conducting proper investigations in advance helps identify potential issues, understand the needs of applications or systems, and ensure that the testing and approval stages are properly handled to ensure a seamless transition to AWS.

Some of the key tools that need to be understood in each corresponding domain during the cloud migration assessment phase are:

- *Well-Architected Framework*: This is a framework, not a tool.
- *Cloud Adoption Readiness Tool (CART)*: This tool is available to everyone free of charge.
- *Migration Readiness Assessment (MRA)*: This tool is not free, and it is only available for client partners.
- *AWS Migration Evaluator*: This is a permissioned tool from AWS.
- *Migration Portfolio Assessment (MPA)*: This tool is not free, and it is only available for client partners.

We have already talked about the Well-Architected Framework in the previous chapter. Now, we will introduce the four tools that can fit into the "Customer Cloud Readiness" and "Business Case Development" segments:

- MPA
- CART
- MRA
- AWS Migration Evaluator

The different tools used in the AWS migration assessment phase can be seen in Figure 9.1.

Assessment Phase Tools

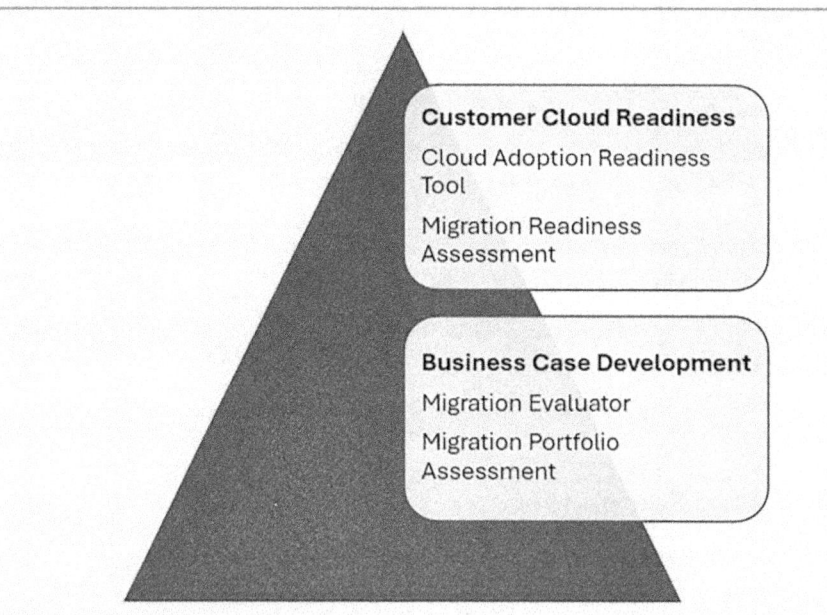

FIGURE 9.1 AWS Migration Assessment Phase Tools.

Let us evaluate all these tools one by one. CART shows us where we are and whether we are ready for migration to the cloud. It is a general good practice to conduct a CART assessment first. The MRA takes a narrower scope and focuses on the workload level. It is performed after the CART assessment. It goes deeper into the technical matters of moving the existing workloads to the AWS cloud, and everything gets explained in a much more detailed and explicit way. Think of the CART assessment as a general health check-up for your organization. It assesses your overall readiness for cloud adoption.

Assess phase activities and their associated AWS migration tools can be seen in Figure 9.2.

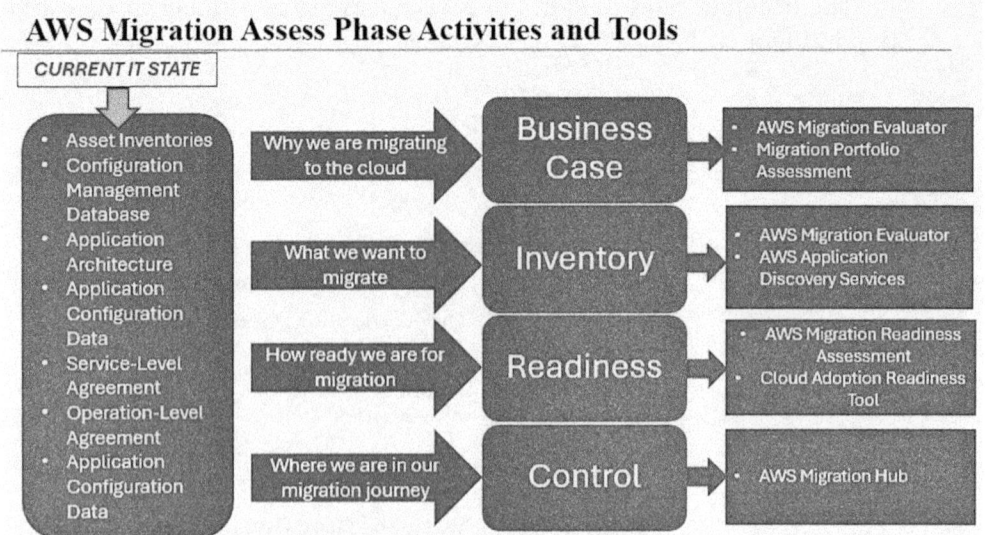

FIGURE 9.2 AWS Migration Assess Phase Activities with Tools.

Cloud Adoption Readiness Tool

Organizations can analyze their overall cloud readiness in the AWS environment by using the CART. This tool investigates the main domain and determines whether the organization is prepared to migrate to the AWS cloud environment, not just the people in the organization but also the processes and tools.

The CART can be utilized by anyone, including partners, individuals, businesses, and enterprises.

The CART is available at *https://cloudreadiness.amazonaws.com/*.

It is a specific assessment designed for AWS customers and AWS Partners containing 47 questions. It evaluates the extent to which your organization is ready to adopt the cloud through five key areas:

- *Business*: Are your business goals aligned with the potential benefits of cloud adoption (increased agility, scalability, etc.)?
- *Skills*: Does your IT team possess the necessary skills and qualifications for managing cloud technologies?

- *Process*: Are you able to use self-service and on-demand services of the IT cloud for your once-existing processes?

- *Technology*: Does your company's current IT infrastructure and applications work with AWS services?

- *Security*: Does your organization have a strong security system that can be adapted to the cloud computing model?

The CART is basically the launchpad for AWS success. By utilizing the CART, we are given legitimate insights into the areas that might need additional focus before migration. The initial CART can be seen in Figure 9.3.

FIGURE 9.3 Cloud Adoption Readiness Tool.

When we have answered all 47 questions, the CART provides the AWS Cloud Readiness Assessment Summary Report, which has the following important components:

- *Score chart*: This chart provides a quick snapshot of how ready your organization is across the six assessed categories. Each category is scored based on your responses, helping you identify areas that are ready and areas that need work.

- *Radar chart*: This chart provides a more detailed visualization of your strengths and weaknesses. It helps you quickly identify which areas are most critical to address before moving forward with migration.

- *Heatmap*: This map uses colors to indicate your readiness levels in each category, making it easy to see where your organization stands at a glance.

- *Summary report*: This report consolidates all the findings from the assessment and provides recommendations for the next steps, helping you develop a high-level action plan.

The AWS Cloud Readiness Assessment Summary Report can be seen in Figure 9.4.

FIGURE 9.4 AWS Cloud Readiness Assessment Summary Report.

The Cloud Readiness Heatmap report can be seen in Figure 9.5.

FIGURE 9.5 Cloud Readiness Heatmap Report.

The Cloud Readiness Radar Chart report can be seen in Figure 9.6.

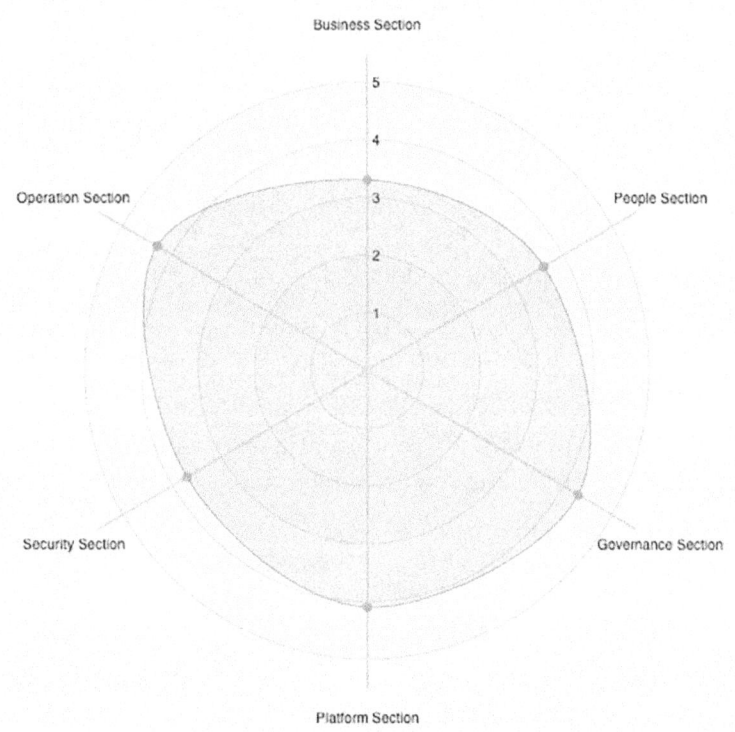

FIGURE 9.6 Cloud Readiness Radar Chart Report.

The CART can be a really useful tool in the early stages of checking for cloud adoption readiness.

To deeply engage and create an actionable migration strategy, we can use the Migration Readiness Assessment (MRA) tool.

MIGRATION READINESS ASSESSMENT

The MRA tool is more comprehensive and thus gives a more focused look at each of the performance areas. MRA is a wide-ranging process, like a detailed architectural review, and serves as an assurance that your migration is properly planned and carried out. The following is the breakdown of the main steps of the process:

1. *IT landscape inventory*: Create a list of all your on-premises applications and infrastructure components (servers, databases, and storage).
2. *Evaluating application suitability*: Analyze each application to determine the best migration approach (rehosting the application as-is, refactoring for cloud optimization, or rebuilding from scratch).
3. *Cost analysis*: Estimate the potential cost savings and TCO benefits of migrating to AWS. This involves analyzing factors such as resource utilization and the pricing models of different AWS services.
4. *Risk identification*: Proactively identify potential challenges that might arise during the migration process and develop mitigation strategies to address them.

MRA is a tool that helps prevent unexpected issues, ensuring a smooth migration by producing reports similar to those produced by the CART:

- Assessment Summary
- Cloud Readiness Heatmap
- Cloud Readiness Radar Chart

Please note that MRA is only available for AWS teams and AWS Partners and is not freely accessible to everyone.

Comparison Between CART and MRA

The CART is designed as a self-service tool that any AWS customer can use at no cost to assess their overall cloud adoption readiness. MRA, on the other hand, is a more in-depth assessment that is typically conducted by AWS professionals. It is designed to help customers develop a concrete plan for migrating their workloads to the AWS cloud. It is not available for everyone.

TABLE 9.1 CART vs. MRA.

Category	Cloud Adoption Readiness Tool (CART)	Migration Readiness Assessment (MRA)
Access	Available for all AWS customers	Available for AWS Professional Services, AWS solutions architects, and AWS Partners
Assessment Type	Perform initial stages to check cloud adoption readiness	To deepen engagement and create an actionable migration strategy
Engagement Level	Customers can self-assess and control assessment duration	Workshop/interview style engagement; typically, a 1-day face-to-face engagement
Content	Uses the six perspectives of the AWS CAF, with 47 questions spanning 6 categories: - Business - People - Governance - Platform - Security - Operations	Uses the six perspectives of the AWS CAF, with 80+ questions spanning 8 categories: - Business Case - Customer Migration Project Plan - Skills and COE - Landing Zone - Application Portfolio Discovery and Planning - Migration Process and Experience - Operating Model - Security and Compliance
Output	Score summary, radar chart, heatmap, and summary report	Score summary, radar chart, heatmap, and PowerPoint assessment review presentation
Web site	*cloudreadiness.amazonaws.com*	*https://accelerate.amazonaws.com/*

Migration Evaluator

AWS Migration Evaluator is a tool that evaluates your current on-premises workloads and their suitability for migrations to AWS. This involves cost and risk analyses, which are the primary driving factors associated with migration.

AWS Migration Evaluator simplifies on-premises analyses of compute, local storage, memory, and Microsoft licenses:

- *Overall portfolio*: It checks your portfolio for existing costs and utilization
- *Operating system*: It identifies whether the current versions of the operating systems are compatible with AWS services so that they can be migrated to the AWS cloud.
- *Database platform*: It determines whether the migration of the database systems is possible.

- *Middleware*: It checks for the compatibility of middleware used in your applications.
- *Comprehensive approach*: It takes a comprehensive approach to aligning your workloads with the provisioned servers in a cloud system as required.

AWS Migration Evaluator was previously called TSO Logic, and it is the product of a company acquisition from AWS. Even though the basic idea, UI, email address, and console may still be recognizable, it is now offered and managed within the AWS ecosystem.

Obtaining Access

You may not have immediate access to Migration Evaluator. To gain access, please reach out to your AWS support or migration team. They can assist you in obtaining the necessary permissions or setting up a demo environment for you to explore the tool's functionalities.

Please note that Migration Evaluator is not part of the AWS ecosystem, but it is available. You can request this tool by filling out the following form: *https://pages.awscloud.com/global-acq-ln-aws-migration-assessment-interest.html*.

Using Migration Evaluator

Once you have access, log in using the provided credentials. Upon successful login, you can view an evaluation (also referred to as an engagement) created by the AWS team for you. This engagement serves as your personalized migration assessment project within Migration Evaluator.

Use this link to sign in: *https://console.tsologic.com*.

AWS Migration Evaluator, while retaining some aspects of its former iteration (TSO Logic), empowers you to plan your migration to the AWS cloud effectively. By working with your AWS support or migration team, you can leverage this valuable tool to assess your on-premises environment and make informed cloud migration decisions. AWS Migration Evaluator provides recommendations for migrating your workloads to the most suitable AWS services.

Workflow of AWS Migration Evaluator

Migration Evaluator collects data from on-premises servers to help you assess your environment for cloud migration. Here is a breakdown of how Migration Evaluator works:

1. *Setting up*:
   - Windows *s*erver *s*etup: A Windows server will be provisioned to serve as the data collection platform.
   - Migration Evaluator *i*nstallation: Migration Evaluator, which can only be installed on Windows machines, will be deployed on the server.
   - Environment *d*iscovery: Migration Evaluator will be configured to discover your on-premises infrastructure, including physical servers, VMware servers, Hyper-V servers, and SQL servers.

2. Data *c*ollection:
   - Migration Evaluator will actively collect data about your on-premises environment.
   - This data will be stored locally within Migration Evaluator's internal database.

3. *Data export and analysis*:
   - Data *e*xport: The collected data can be exported from Migration Evaluator's local database.
   - Data *u*pload to Amazon S3: The exported data will be uploaded to a designated Amazon S3 bucket for further analysis. Uploading data to S3 provides the following benefits:
     i. Secure and scalable storage for large datasets
     ii. Access to data by authorized personnel for analysis

4. *Reporting and migration planning*:
   - Insights generation: Data stored within the S3 bucket can be used to generate migration insights reports.
   - Migration *p*ortfolio *a*ssessment: These reports can be utilized by your solution architect or AWS Partner to feed into the Migration Portfolio Assessment tool.
   - *Usage of Migration Hub*: Quick insight data is also stored in AWS Migration Hub, which is a centralized repository for the overall migration process.

The benefits of using Migration Evaluator include:

- It helps identify potential issues early in the migration process.
- It provides insights into cost optimization opportunities.
- It offers recommendations for improving performance in the cloud.

Overall, Migration Evaluator is a valuable tool that can help assess your on-premises environment and plan your AWS cloud migration more effectively.

Some organizations have a CMDB in place, which can be directly imported into Migration Evaluator.

AWS Migration Evaluator Reports

AWS Migration Evaluator offers two types of reports:

- Quick Insights *report*: This is a one-page summary and is ideal for business stakeholders. It provides:
  - Projected costs for rehosting your workload on AWS based on usage patterns
  - A breakdown of infrastructure and software license costs post-migration
- *Migration details reports*: These are downloadable reports with a more technical focus. They combine:
  - On-premises data (server hardware, software configuration, and resource utilization)
  - Recommendations for migrating to specific AWS services (e.g., Amazon EC2, EBS, etc.)

AWS Migration Quick Insights Sample Report

An AWS Migration Quick Insights sample report can be seen in Figure 9.7.

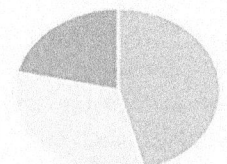

Quick Insights
Generated: 2022-09-15

Right sizing workloads on AWS would result in an estimated annual cost of **$1,107,195 USD** * for Amazon Elastic Cloud Compute (EC2) and Elastic Block Storage (EBS).

Based on your reported CPU and memory utilization, you could realize a **20% savings** ** compared to directly mapping your on-premises servers and storage. With AWS, you have access to more instances in every imaginable shape and size than you'll find elsewhere and we continue to add more so you can always find the right size based on your current needs.

Electing to repurchase non-optimized operating system licensing from AWS would add **$303,991 USD** * to the Amazon EC2 and EBS costs shown above.

If you would like to learn more about migrating workloads to AWS including software license optimization and exploring managed services, please contact your **AWS account team** or email migration-evaluator@amazon.com.

- Amazon EC2 : 46%
- Amazon EBS: 32%
- OS Licenses : 22%

About this report

The analysis is based on infrastructure, software licenses and utilization discovered from 2022-01-24 to 2022-02-02.

Servers
- 585 virtual machines
- 20 physical servers

Licensing
- 605 servers (Linux: 202, Windows: 197, RHEL: 110, SUSE: 96)
- 19 servers running SQL Server (Standard: 7, Enterprise: 12)

Storage
- 849 TB of attached block storage

Utilization
- 52.2% peak CPU utilization***
- 83.3% peak memory utilization***

* Projected AWS costs based on public standard reserved - no upfront - 1 year Instance Savings Plan USD pricing for Amazon EC2 and Amazon EBS running in US East (N. Virginia) with bring your own SQL Server licenses with active Software Assurance. This report provides an estimate of fees and savings based on certain information you provide. Fee estimates do not include any taxes that might apply. Your actual fees and savings depend on a variety of factors, including your actual usage of AWS services, which may vary from the estimates provided in this report. Additional configurations are available on request.

** Projected savings based on utilization data available to date compared to a like-for-like match of on-premises CPU and RAM specifications. A longer collection period will improve right sizing confidence.

*** The average P95 utilization value from all servers.

Engagement: example corp - phase 2

FIGURE 9.7 AWS Migration Quick Insights Sample Report.

AWS Migration Details Sample Report

This subsection shows a more detailed report, as follows.

✦✦

Executive Summary

The AWS Migration Evaluator Business Case for Example Corp provides a comprehensive analysis and strategic roadmap for transitioning from on-premises infrastructure to AWS cloud services. The evaluation includes a detailed assessment of Example Corp's existing infrastructure, financial implications, business value, and deployment strategies.

On-Premises Overview

Example Corp's current on-premises environment consists of 651 total instances, including 172 Windows servers and 373 Linux servers, with a provisioned storage capacity of 741 TB. The assessment revealed significant inefficiencies, such as 54 zombie machines and 49% of servers being utilized less than 20% of the time. The overall environment is primarily composed of VMware and bare metal servers, with a small percentage of RHEL and SQL servers.

Scoping Insights

- *Data Collection*: Conducted over 18 days, identifying 8% zombie machines.
- *Server Utilization*: 92% of servers were right-sized; however, a notable portion was underutilized.
- *AWS Annualized Spend*: Estimated at $1,020,763.
- *Additional Evaluations*: Included server dependency mapping, storage assessment, and licensing health checks.

Financial Summary

Four migration options were modeled with varying tenancy and licensing scenarios:

1. *Option 1*: Shared tenancy, On-Demand Instances with included licenses
2. *Option 2*: Reserved Instances (RIs) with included licenses
3. *Option 3*: Reserved Instances with Bring Your Own License (BYOL) for SQL Server
4. *Option 4*: Mixed tenancy, combining dedicated hosts and shared tenancy based on cost-effectiveness

The recommended mixed tenancy model (*Option 4*) offers significant cost savings, with an annual spend of $950,620 compared to the highest cost model of $1,287,113. This model optimizes licensing and storage utilization, enhancing overall cost efficiency.

Business Value

Migration to AWS is projected to deliver substantial business value across three key areas:

1. *Staff Productivity*:
   - 116% increase in VM management efficiency
   - 139% increase in storage management efficiency
2. *Operational Resilience*:
   - 52% reduction in unplanned downtime
   - 32% reduction in monthly critical incidents
3. *Business Agility*:
   - 40% improvement in developer efficiency, facilitating innovation and faster time-to-market

Deployment Summary

Example Corp's deployment strategy emphasizes the importance of accurate server dependency mapping, using AWS Migration Hub to visualize and tag servers. The plan includes:

1. *Account Setup*: Initiating AWS Migration Hub and deploying the Migration Evaluator Collector.
2. *Visualization*: Utilizing AWS Migration Hub for server dependencies.
3. *Storage Assessment*: Engaging AWS account teams for a detailed storage assessment to identify potential cost savings of up to 67%.

Storage Assessment

The storage assessment model assumes 50% utilization of provisioned storage, with costs modeled based on Amazon EBS volumes. The estimated monthly TCO for AWS storage is $67,105, leading to an annual consumption of $805,255. This assessment highlights significant opportunities for optimizing storage costs by leveraging AWS's scalable and efficient storage solutions.

Supplementary AWS Services

To support the migration, AWS recommends several supplementary services:

- *AWS Training & Certification*: Enhancing staff skills for cloud operations
- *Migration Readiness Assessment (MRA)*: Evaluating the organization's preparedness for migration
- *Immersion Days*: Hands-on workshops to familiarize teams with AWS services
- *Data Center Divestment*: Strategizing the phased closure of on-premises data centers

Next Steps

The migration plan outlines critical next steps to ensure a smooth transition to AWS:

1. *Executive Engagement*: Identifying and engaging an executive champion to sponsor the migration
2. *Migration Acceleration Program (MAP)*: Leveraging AWS's methodology and partner network to accelerate cloud adoption
3. *Licensing Health Check*: Conducting an AWS-funded assessment to optimize licensing strategies for Windows and SQL Server
4. *POC Implementation*: Planning a Proof of Concept (POC) for a sample workload to validate the migration strategy

By following these steps, Example Corp can achieve a successful migration to AWS, realizing significant cost savings, operational efficiencies, and enhanced business agility.

* * *

AWS Migration Evaluator data can be transferred to MPA as well as to Migration Hub.

MIGRATION PORTFOLIO ASSESSMENT

The AWS Migration Portfolio Assessment (MPA) is a powerful tool that makes the cloud migration process more efficient and less complex, integrating the best approaches for success. It serves as a central hub that covers two key aspects of migration: planning and reviewing. Let us now take a closer look at the MPA components and see how their synergy ensures the best possible migration:

- Data inventory
- Data collection
- Portfolio analysis
- Migration planning
- Business case development

Data Inventory

MPA provides a summary of your entire IT portfolio through a single portal, eliminating the need for manual data collection. It offers complete information for analysis, including information about your applications, databases, servers, and other resources.

Data Collection

MPA offers two methods for data collection:

- *Automated discovery*: MPA can automatically scan your on-premises environment to discover and collect data about your IT assets. This eliminates the need for manual data entry, saving valuable time and effort.
- *Manual upload*: You can also manually upload existing data or utilize flat files to populate the inventory within MPA.

Portfolio Analysis

Once the data is collected, MPA performs a comprehensive analysis of your IT portfolio. This analysis provides valuable insights into:

- *Application suitability for cloud migration*: MPA identifies applications that are well-suited for migration to AWS based on factors such as architecture and dependencies.
- *Potential migration challenges*: The analysis can uncover potential roadblocks such as security considerations or complex dependencies that might need to be addressed before migration.

- *Cost optimization opportunities*: MPA can estimate the potential cost savings associated with migrating your workloads to AWS. This helps build a compelling business case for cloud adoption.

Migration Planning

MPA empowers you to create a well-defined migration plan. It allows you to:

- *Prioritize workloads*: MPA helps prioritize which applications to migrate first, based on the analysis and your business objectives.
- *Select migration strategies*: MPA enables you to make informed decisions on the most appropriate migration strategy (rehosting, refactoring, etc.) for each workload.
- *Create migration waves*: MPA facilitates the creation of migration waves, which group related applications for a phased migration approach. This ensures a smooth and controlled transition to the cloud.

Business Case Development

MPA plays a crucial role in building a business case by curating data that helps demonstrate the advantages of migration. These advantages include the following:

- *Cost savings*: You will be able to accurately estimate the cost savings resulting from migrating to AWS.
- *Improved performance*: You will be able to demonstrate the potential performance improvements achieved through the use of cloud-based infrastructure.
- *Increased agility*: You will be able to highlight the improved scalability and mobility offered by the AWS cloud.

With instant data mining through MPA, the right data, insights, and strategies for cloud migration are readily available. This reduces data management complexity, streamlines migration planning, and strengthens the pathway for cloud adoption.

The benefits of MPA include:

- It provides a comprehensive view of your migration landscape.
- It enables informed decision-making regarding cloud migration strategies.

COMPARISON BETWEEN MIGRATION EVALUATOR AND MPA

Let us compare these two tools.

TABLE 9.2 Migration Evaluator vs. MPA

Category	Migration Evaluator	MPA
Engagement model	Open to all AWS customers and Partners	- Available to AWS Partners and AWS Professional Services - Self-service through AWS accelerate: *https://accelerate.amazonaws.com/*
Data collection	- Offline manual data transformation and upload by Migration Evaluator data analyst - Agentless method	- Guided/self-service process to import discovery results - CMDB or manually gathered data
Right-sizing with licensing analysis	- Right-sizing includes Operation System (OS) licensing analysis support - CPU and memory utilization considering the age of the processor	- Right size recommendation does not include OS licensing analysis support - CPU and memory utilization considering the age of the processor
Network and labor cost analysis	Not supported	On-premises and AWS estimate analysis for shared storage, network, and labor costs

SUMMARY

The Assess phase is the first step in AWS cloud migration, where the organization evaluates its current IT environment to determine what should be moved and understand the reasons for migration. This phase consists of a business case analysis, TCO assessment, and migration readiness evaluation. Companies review and verify the information received, the products ordered, delivery conditions, service quality, storage capacity, data processing, response time, disk I/O, and SLA to ensure a smooth migration. AWS provides tools such as the Cloud Adoption Readiness Tool (CART), Migration Readiness Assessment (MRA), AWS Migration Evaluator, and Migration Portfolio Assessment (MPA) to help companies select, assess, and refine their migration planning. These tools enable enterprises to make informed decisions with minimal disruptions and establish a migration strategy that aligns with AWS best practices.

REFERENCES

[AWSCAF22] Amazon Web Services, "*AWS Cloud Adoption Framework (AWS CAF)*", AWS Whitepaper, 2022. Available online at: *https://aws.amazon.com/professional-services/CAF/*

[AWSMRA23] Amazon Web Services, "*Evaluating Migration Readiness,*" AWS Prescriptive Guidance, August 2019. Available online at: *https://docs.aws.amazon.com/prescriptive-guidance/latest/migration-readiness/welcome.html*

[TSOLogic19] Amazon Web Services, "*Migration Evaluator*", AWS Whitepaper, 2019. Available online at: *https://aws.amazon.com/migration-evaluator/*

[CART20] Amazon Web Services, "*AWS Self Assessments*", AWS Whitepaper, 2020. Available online at: *https://cloudreadiness.amazonaws.com/*

KNOWLEDGE CHECK: MULTIPLE-CHOICE Q&A

Question 1

Which of the following is a key component of the Assess phase in AWS cloud migration?

A. Migrating workloads to AWS.

B. Determining what to migrate and performing TCO analysis.

C. Automating infrastructure deployment.

D. Configuring AWS security policies.

Question 2

What does the AWS Cloud Adoption Framework (CAF) help organizations assess?

A. Cost optimization strategies for AWS migration.

B. Readiness for cloud adoption across multiple perspectives.

C. The best AWS services for building a cloud-native application.

D. How to automate cloud infrastructure deployment.

Question 3

Which tool provides an initial assessment of an organization's cloud adoption readiness?

A. AWS Migration Evaluator.

B. Cloud Adoption Readiness Tool (CART).

C. AWS Well-Architected Framework.

D. Amazon QuickSight.

Question 4

Which of the following statements about AWS Migration Evaluator is true?

A. It provides licensing recommendations for AWS databases only.

B. It is a free tool available to all AWS customers.

C. It evaluates on-premises workloads and provides migration cost analysis.

D. It is used to automate the migration of virtual machines to AWS.

Question 5

What is the primary difference between the Cloud Adoption Readiness Tool (CART) and Migration Readiness Assessment (MRA)?

A. CART is used for self-service readiness assessment, while MRA is a deeper evaluation conducted by AWS professionals.

B. CART is only available to AWS Partners, while MRA is accessible to all AWS customers.

C. MRA focuses on storage migration only, while CART assesses applications and infrastructure.

D. CART provides detailed licensing insights but MRA does not.

Question 6

Which AWS tool helps analyze an organization's IT landscape for cloud migration and includes business case development?

A. AWS Migration Evaluator.

B. AWS Config.

C. Migration Portfolio Assessment (MPA).

D. AWS CloudTrail.

Question 7

What is the key benefit of the AWS Migration Evaluator tool?

A. It automates cloud migration with zero manual effort.

B. It provides insights into cost optimization and right-sizing workloads for AWS.

C. It allows organizations to deploy cloud-native applications automatically.

D. It replaces all manual workload migration assessments.

CHAPTER 10

AWS Migration Mobilize Phase

OVERVIEW OF THE MOBILIZE PHASE

The goal of the AWS cloud migration mobilization phase is to prepare your resources and organization for an efficient migration. This phase follows the development of your business case during the assessment phase. It is recommended to execute several workstreams during this phase, which can be carried out simultaneously after the assessment phase is completed.

The Mobilize phase involves discovering the current source environment through a data-gathering process that includes all information relating to the business, applications, infrastructure (devices), shared services, users, database, middleware, network, stakeholders, and the relationships between these elements. This process is part of the client migration activities.

The objectives of the Mobilize phase can be seen in Figure 10.1.

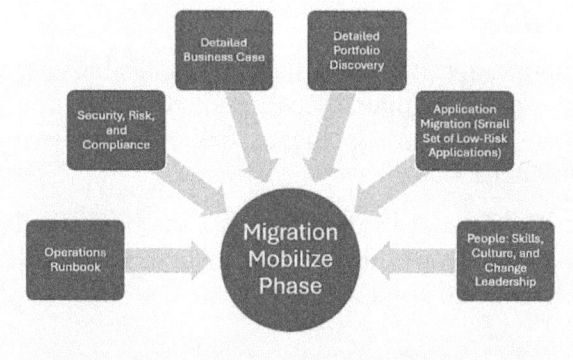

FIGURE 10.1 The Objectives of the Mobilize Phase.

The objectives of discovery/planning during this phase are:

- *Detailed business case*: The business case for migrating to AWS must be further defined. This involves thoroughly analyzing and identifying the main reasons for migration, such as cost savings, agility, and scalability.
- *Detailed portfolio discovery*: This involves a thorough examination of your application portfolio to determine its suitability for migration to AWS. It includes factors such as the application's dependencies, technical complexity, and business criticality.
- *Application migration*: A small set of low-risk applications are migrated to AWS during this phase. Participating in the actual migration process enables you to predict potential issues that may arise in larger migrations.
- *Operations runbook*: This is a comprehensive guide to the administrative operations of your applications in the AWS cloud. It is created during the Mobilize phase to ensure that the operational team has detailed instructions for managing ongoing operations.
- *Security, risk, and compliance*: Security is a key area of concern throughout the migration process. During the Mobilize phase, you will evaluate the security of your operation and check that your landing zone meets all the relevant compliance requirements.
- *People—skills, culture, and change leadership*: Migrating to AWS is a cultural transformation within your organization. The Mobilize phase focuses on educating your team about AWS, covering in-depth AWS concepts and techniques, and preparing them to work effectively in a cloud environment.

Two other factors are also considered, namely, migration governance and the landing zone:

- *Migration governance*: This involves establishing standards and procedures for the proper execution of the migration process. It addresses several key issues, including risk management, change control, and communication.
- *Landing Zone*: A landing zone is a safe and standardized AWS environment where your migrated applications will reside. The landing zone is developed and implemented during the Mobilize phase.

The Mobilize phase lays the foundation for a successful large-scale migration to AWS. It helps develop the necessary skills and processes to ensure that existing applications are migrated securely and efficiently.

DIFFERENT AWS CLOUD MIGRATION MOBILIZE TOOLS

AWS offers a variety of tools exclusively designed to handle the Mobilize phase of the cloud migration process:

- *AWS Control Tower*: This is used to set up the environment, which includes the landing zone as part of a secure, scalable, and well-architected multi-account AWS ecosystem.
- *Application Discovery Service (ADS)*: This helps gather information about on-premises data centers to prepare for migration. It automates the collection of application inventory, dependencies, and resource utilization data, enabling the creation of an effective migration strategy.
- *AWS Migration Hub*: This is an AWS service that provides a centralized migration dashboard to manage the migration of applications across all AWS and partner migration tools. It offers insights into the status and progress of migrations, ensuring better coordination and control throughout the process.

The different tools used in the AWS Mobilize phase can be seen in Figure 10.2.

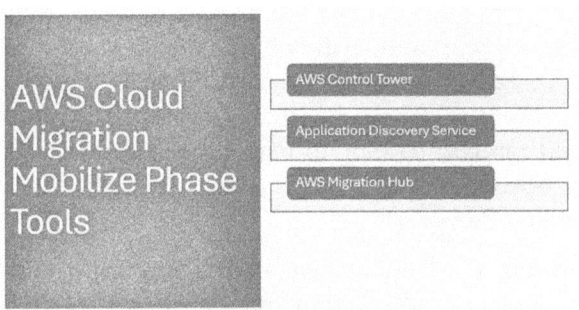

FIGURE 10.2 Different Tools Used in the AWS Mobilize Phase.

INTRODUCTION TO AWS CONTROL TOWER

AWS Control Tower is primarily used to set up the landing zone, which is a secure, scalable, and well-architected multi-account AWS environment. It utilizes tools such as Guardrails, Account Factory, and a centralized dashboard to support best practices in managing your AWS environment.

AWS Control Tower's role can be seen in Figure 10.3.

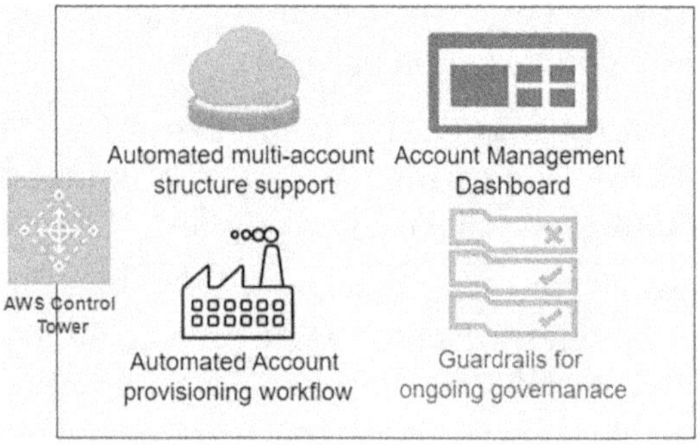

FIGURE 10.3 How AWS Control Tower Works.

Understanding the Landing Zone

The term "landing zone" is derived from military language and is usually used to refer to a designated area where helicopters can safely land. In action movies or games, you might have seen soldiers carefully guarding these zones to ensure the safe arrival of troops, evacuation of the wounded, or delivery of supplies.

In cloud computing, it functions similarly as the place where your workloads will "land" when you migrate to AWS. This includes setting up the account structure, creating Virtual Private Clouds (VPCs), granting permissions, and configuring monitoring and policies.

Building a Landing Zone

When setting up a landing zone, both the technical and business aspects need to be addressed. This could include business decisions on account organization (such as whether accounts will be set up per department or project), billing management, and determining who has access to which accounts. From the technical perspective, it includes how to connect services, how to deal with consolidated billing, and how to deal with security and access management.

A landing zone is not only a structure but also a concept that enables your organization to start and deploy applications quickly, securely, and at scale. It is designed for when your organization grows, enabling you to add more accounts, VPCs, and workloads according to your needs.

How to Build a Landing Zone

There are two options for building a landing zone. You can use AWS white papers alongside the Well-Architected Framework, which can be a lengthy and complex process. Alternatively, you can use AWS Control Tower, which is a wizard-driven process that can set up a landing zone in about 60 to 90 minutes. The process involves answering some questions to configure a well-governed, secure, and scalable environment.

Greenfield vs. Brownfield Deployments

There's a common misconception that AWS Control Tower is only suitable for greenfield deployments, where you start fresh without any existing AWS resources; however, Control Tower is equally effective in brownfield deployments, where you work with existing AWS accounts and resources. In brownfield scenarios, you can migrate existing accounts into a new landing zone, consolidating your infrastructure under a single, well-governed environment.

Key components of AWS Control Tower are:

- *Guardrails*: These are predefined policies that assist you in following the compliance and security measures of AWS throughout the whole environment. They function as boundaries that secure the AWS environment while allowing flexibility in operations.

- *Account Factory*: This is a method to automatically create new AWS accounts based on your company's specifications. Think of it as a vending machine for AWS accounts where new accounts are created automatically along with the required configurations and policies.

- *Dashboard*: Control Tower provides a centralized dashboard where you can see the compliance status of all your AWS accounts. The dashboard presents a visual summary of the progress of your landing zone and also helps you manage your AWS environment efficiently.

Key components of Control Tower can be seen in Figure 10.4.

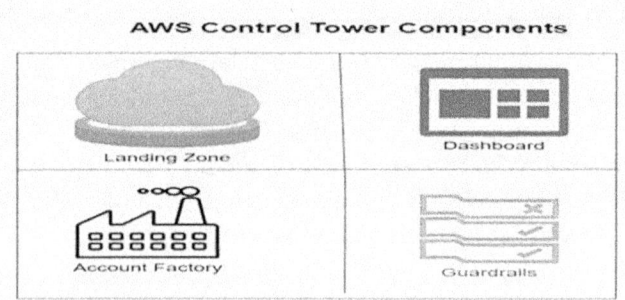

FIGURE 10.4 Key Components of AWS Control Tower.

Setting Up a Landing Zone with AWS Control Tower

AWS Control Tower is a governance solution that streamlines the management of a multi-account AWS environment through the AWS platform. At its core, a landing zone managed by Control Tower enables organizations to enforce consistent security, operational governance, and compliance frameworks across their AWS accounts. Let us look at a brief overview of the process.

Establishing the AWS Organization

The starting point of setting up a landing zone is to create an AWS organization. This organization involves multiple accounts with a simplified management structure. The important components are:

- *Management account*: This account is designed as the root of the organization and is only intended for administrative use. It is not a production or workload account.
- *Organizational Units (OUs)*: OUs represent the logical grouping of accounts with a similar purpose, such as development, testing (QA), and production environments. The hierarchical model makes it easier to apply policies and governance across teams and functions.

AWS Control Tower ensures that organizations are well-defined and clear and make use of resource management and access control with the defined organizational structures.

Creating AWS Accounts and Deploying Resources

Once the foundational organization has been established, the next step is to create individual accounts within each OU. This step enables teams to work independently but simultaneously enjoy the benefits of centralized governance. Key actions in this process include:

- *Account creation*: The AWS CLI or AWS Management Console can be used to create a new account, depending on the specific requirements of different domains such as testing, development, and production.

- *Resource deployment*: You can then deploy your resources and accounts on EC2, RDS, or Lambda, providing the teams with everything they need to run the applications.

This arrangement not only optimizes the use of resources for regional development but also reinforces security, mainly by compartmentalizing permissions and access.

Consolidated Management and Governance

A major benefit of AWS Control Tower deployment is the consolidated viewpoint achieved through the management account. This account serves the following functions:

- *Monitoring compliance and security*: Take advantage of AWS's pre-installed security services and compliance features, applying policy guardrails that restrict certain actions within the accounts.

- *Access to centralized logging and reporting*: Log all your account logs and reports, providing insights into resource usage, compliance status, and operational oversight.

With every account being securely monitored and governed from one management account, organizations can not only reduce risks but also considerably improve their security posture.

Optional Components

Control Tower also assists in configuring the AWS IAM Identity Center (formerly known as Single Sign-On or SSO), enabling you to manage access to different AWS accounts from a single portal. You can also configure AWS CloudTrail to monitor and record every activity on the account to ensure that a centralized logging mechanism is in place.

AWS Control Tower simplifies the process of setting up a secure, scalable, and well-governed AWS environment through its landing zone feature. Whether you're starting fresh or managing an existing infrastructure, Control Tower provides the tools and features you need to manage your AWS accounts effectively.

Benefits of Using AWS Control Tower

Introducing a landing zone using AWS Control Tower provides numerous benefits:

- *Speed and simplicity*: Speed up the process by deploying a multi-account environment with pre-configured best practices.
- *Enhanced security and compliance*: Set up automated governance and compliance tools to maintain consistency across different accounts.
- *Cost-efficiency*: Consolidated billing and management leads to reduced costs as well as the reduction of administrative overheads.
- *Scalability*: Businesses can add new accounts and services when needed, without impacting governance.

AWS APPLICATION DISCOVERY SERVICE

By now, you should have a foundational understanding of the cloud migration process, which comprises several crucial phases. We previously discussed tools such as Migration Evaluator and Cloud Adoption Readiness Tool (CART), which are part of the Assess phase. Now, our focus shifts to AWS Application Discovery Service (ADS), an essential component in the cloud migration journey.

ADS is pivotal during both the Migrate and Mobilize phases of cloud migration. Understanding ADS and its operation is crucial for a successful migration, and this section will provide an in-depth look at how ADS functions and why it is important.

What Is Application Discovery Service?

ADS is a service designed to collect detailed server and database configuration information. When managing a large inventory of on-premises resources such as databases and servers, accurate data collection is essential for effective migration planning. Key data points collected by ADS include:

- *Server information*: Hostnames, IP addresses, and MAC addresses
- *Resource utilization*: CPU usage (average and peak), memory, and disk utilization
- *Database information*: Database versions and engine types

This information is crucial for creating an accurate migration plan. AWS ADS helps to plan migration projects by gathering information about on-premises data centers. It facilitates the discovery of applications, servers, and dependencies within an organization's network, which is essential for a successful transition to the AWS cloud.

Key features of AWS ADS include:

- *Automated discovery:* It automatically identifies servers, storage, and networking equipment to map dependencies and performance metrics.
- *Data collection and analysis*: It collects and presents detailed data about applications and resources, aiding in the analysis of migration planning.
- *Secure data handling*: It ensures that collected data is handled securely, maintaining confidentiality and integrity.
- *Integration with migration tools*: It seamlessly integrates with other AWS services and third-party tools to facilitate a smoother migration process.
- *Customizable data collection*: It offers flexibility in terms of the depth and breadth of data collection, depending on the specific needs of the migration project.

AWS ADS Process

Planning data center migrations can involve thousands of workloads that are often highly interdependent. Server utilization data and dependency mapping are important early first steps in the migration process. AWS ADS helps collect usage and configuration data about on-premises servers. This data aids in planning the migration to AWS. ADS is integrated with AWS Migration Hub, which simplifies your migration tracking as it aggregates your migration status information into a single console.

The collected data is retained in encrypted format in an AWS ADS data store. You can export this data as a CSV file into Amazon Athena, Amazon Quicksight, and third-party visualization tools. These can be used to estimate the Total Cost of Ownership (TCO) of running on AWS and to plan your migration to AWS.

In addition, this data is also available in AWS Migration Hub, where you can migrate the discovered servers and track their progress during their migration to AWS.

AWS ADS operates from an AWS Region, necessitating connectivity to an ADS endpoint. There are three primary methods for data collection, including manual import.

Agent-Based Application Discovery Process

Agent-based discovery can be performed by deploying the AWS Application Discovery Agent on each of your VMs and physical servers. The agent installer is available for Windows and Linux operating systems. It collects static configuration data and detailed information on time-series system performance, inbound and outbound network connections, and processes that are running.

Agentless Application Discovery Process

Ideal for VMware vSphere or vCenter environments, this method uses a virtual appliance called the Application Discovery Service Agentless Collector, which communicates with vCenter. Agentless Collector collects static configuration data regarding server hostnames, IP addresses, MAC addresses, and disk resource allocations. Additionally, it collects the utilization data for each VM and computes average and peak utilization for metrics such as CPU, RAM, and disk I/O. This can be combined with the agent-based method, using the Agentless Collector for broad data collection and agents for specific machines when needed.

Manual Import

For existing server configuration and utilization data, you can leverage the manual import option. This allows you to upload data directly into the service, providing a way to integrate information that might not be obtainable through other methods.

Overall ADS Architecture

AWS ADS offers a robust architecture that supports detailed data collection, secure storage, and insightful analysis. It empowers organizations to streamline migration planning by providing a comprehensive view of their on-premises infrastructure. Whether leveraging agent-based, agentless, or pre-existing inventory data, ADS ensures that businesses can plan migrations confidently while optimizing costs, resources, and security.

The Application Discovery Service architecture can be seen in Figure 10.5.

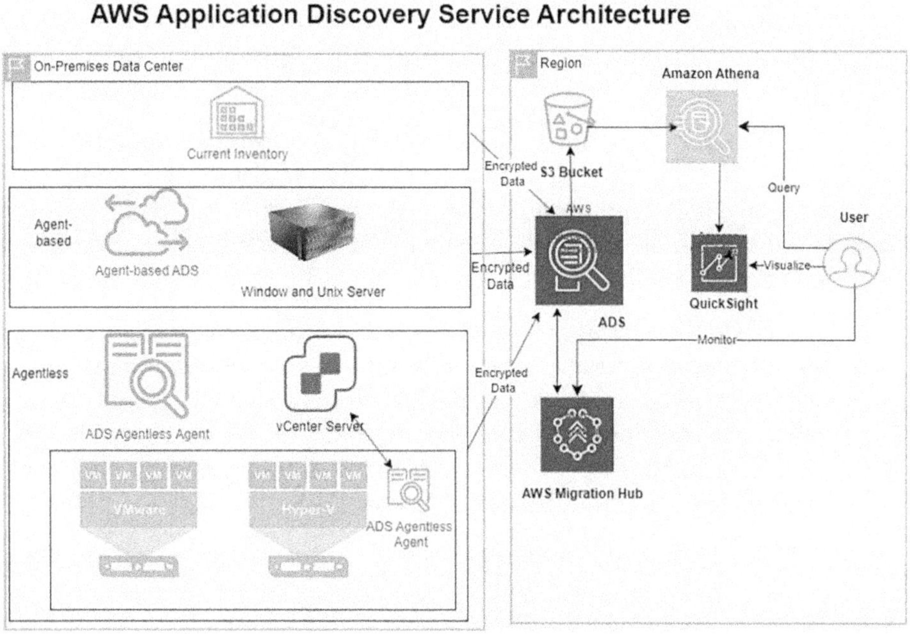

FIGURE 10.5 Application Discovery Service Architecture.

The AWS ADS architecture enables the collection, storage, and analysis of detailed on-premises application and infrastructure data to facilitate migration planning. Below is a breakdown of its architecture based on the details provided:

- Data collection
- Data storage and processing
- Data analysis and visualization

Data Collection

AWS ADS offers three approaches to gather data from on-premises environments, ensuring flexibility and adaptability to diverse infrastructure setups:

- Agent-based data collection
- Agentless data collection (VMware-based)
- Existing inventory data import

Agent-Based Data Collection

Agent-based data collection requires the deployment of the AWS Application Discovery Agent on each of your VMs and physical servers. The agent is available for both Windows and Linux operating systems and can be installed on physical on-premises servers, Amazon EC2 instances, and VMs.

The Discovery Agent captures detailed system configuration data, time-series system performance information, inbound and outbound network connections, and running processes. This comprehensive data collection helps you map your IT assets and their network dependencies, providing insights that are crucial for detailed cost analysis and migration planning.

When the Discovery Agent is started, it registers with the ADS endpoint and pings the service at 15-minute intervals for configuration updates. The agent then begins collecting data, including system specifications, performance metrics, network connections, and process data. This information is vital for grouping servers into applications and determining the cost implications of migrating your infrastructure to AWS.

The ADS agent-based data collection process can be seen in Figure 10.6.

AWS Application Discovery Service Agent-Based Collection Process

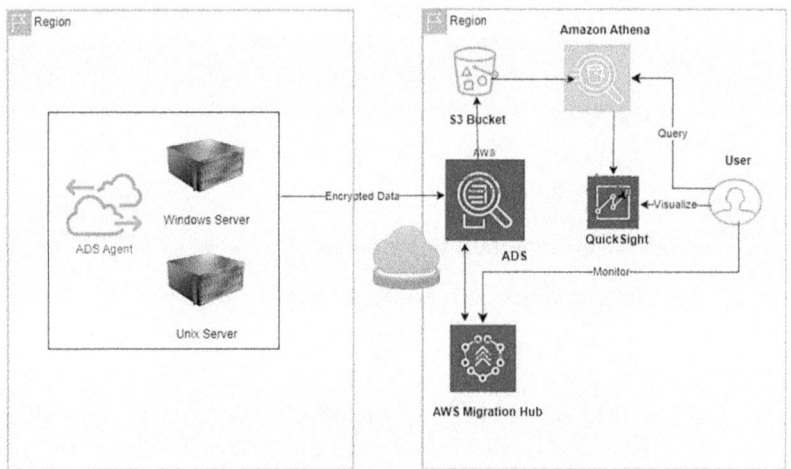

FIGURE 10.6 AWS Application Discovery Service Agent-Based Data Collection Process.

Agentless Data Collection (VMware-Based)

A virtual appliance, known as the Agentless Collector, is deployed within a VMware vSphere environment on a host running ESXi or vSphere. This collector interacts directly with the vCenter server, enabling it to gather data from virtualized resources without the need to install software on individual VMs. The data collected includes inventory information such as VM configurations, resource utilization, installed software, application dependencies, and metadata such as database types, which are essential for migration planning. Once gathered, this data is securely transmitted to the ADS endpoint in AWS for processing and analysis.

Existing Inventory Data Import

Pre-existing inventory data can be imported into AWS ADS as an alternative to using agents or agentless collectors. This data can come from various sources, including CSV files generated by third-party tools, AWS services such as CloudWatch, or manual data collection efforts. This approach is particularly useful when detailed infrastructure information has already been compiled and requires centralization within ADS for further analysis and migration planning.

Data Storage and Processing

The data collected through AWS ADS is securely stored and processed to support migration planning and analysis. The ADS endpoint serves as the primary gateway for receiving data from agent-based collection, agentless collection, or imported inventory files. This endpoint ensures that all incoming data is encrypted both in transit and at rest, adhering to AWS's stringent security standards to maintain confidentiality, integrity, and compliance with industry regulations.

Once received, the data is transferred to AWS Migration Hub, which acts as the central repository for all collected information. Migration Hub organizes and consolidates data from various sources, enabling seamless integration and a unified view of the infrastructure. Within Migration Hub, the data is processed to identify critical elements such as application dependencies, resource utilization patterns, and configuration details. This centralized processing facilitates comprehensive analysis, which is essential for planning migration workflows, optimizing resource allocation, and ensuring compatibility with cloud services.

AWS Migration Hub requires users to configure a home Region where the collected data is securely stored and processed. This ensures that organizations maintain control over the geographic location of their data, aligning with compliance and governance requirements. The combination of secure data storage, centralized processing, and Region-specific configuration makes AWS ADS an essential tool for building a detailed understanding of on-premises environments and creating effective migration strategies. Through these features, organizations can streamline their migration processes, mitigate risks, and maximize the benefits of transitioning to the AWS cloud.

Data Analysis and Visualization

Once the data is collected and securely stored, AWS equips users with robust tools to analyze and visualize the information, enabling actionable insights for migration planning. Amazon Athena serves as a powerful querying tool, allowing users to run SQL-like queries on data stored in S3 buckets. This functionality simplifies the extraction of detailed information, such as system configurations, application dependencies, resource utilization patterns, and other critical metrics needed for decision-making. With Athena's ease of use and flexibility, users can efficiently pinpoint specific details and trends within their infrastructure.

To further enhance understanding, Amazon QuickSight provides an intuitive platform for data visualization. By leveraging the results from Amazon Athena, QuickSight enables the creation of rich, interactive dashboards, charts, and reports that present complex data in a user-friendly format. These visualizations offer a comprehensive view of the on-premises environment, helping users identify hidden application dependencies, evaluate current resource utilization, and explore optimization opportunities. QuickSight's visual insights empower organizations to not only assess their infrastructure but also develop well-informed cloud migration strategies, ensuring smoother transitions to AWS while minimizing risks and costs. Together, Athena and QuickSight deliver a complete solution for analyzing and visualizing data collected by AWS ADS.

Key Features and Considerations

AWS ADS incorporates key features and considerations that make it a robust and flexible solution for migration planning.

Data Security

Data security is a cornerstone of the service, ensuring that all data collected, whether through agents, agentless collectors, or imported files, is encrypted end to end. This includes encryption during transmission to the AWS cloud and while the data is at rest in AWS services, aligning with strict security and compliance standards. Organizations can trust that sensitive infrastructure details, application dependencies, and utilization of metrics are protected throughout the entire data lifecycle.

Region Selection

Region selection plays a critical role in data storage and processing, as Migration Hub requires the designation of a home Region. This ensures that organizations have control over where their collected data is stored and processed, enabling them to meet regional compliance requirements and governance policies. The choice of a home Region allows organizations to optimize performance and maintain data residency in line with operational priorities.

Integration with Migration Tools

The data collected by ADS integrates seamlessly with other AWS services that aid in the migration process:

- *AWS Migration Hub*: This service acts as a central console for managing and tracking your entire application migration journey. The data from ADS helps populate Migration Hub with details about your discovered servers and their dependencies. You can then group these servers into applications and track the migration status of each application within the Migration Hub console.
- *AWS Database Migration Service Fleet Advisor*: This service analyzes the data from ADS to provide recommendations and optimize the migration process for your databases.

Agent-Based vs. Agentless Collection

Having options to use agent-based or agentless collection offers organizations the flexibility to adapt to diverse infrastructure needs. For environments requiring granular insights, the agent-based approach provides detailed data directly from Windows and Linux servers, including software inventory, resource utilization, and application dependencies. In contrast, the agentless method is ideal for VMware environments, gathering data efficiently without the need for deployment on individual VMs. For complex environments, a hybrid approach that combines both methods allows organizations to balance the depth of data collection with operational efficiency, ensuring comprehensive coverage across all systems.

These features, combined with the secure data processing and centralized analysis capabilities of AWS Migration Hub, make ADS a highly adaptable tool for organizations planning cloud migrations. By addressing key security concerns, enabling regional customization, and supporting versatile data collection methods, ADS empowers businesses to streamline their migration journeys while maintaining control and compliance.

Let's explore some key differences between agent-based and agentless collections in ADS:

- *Agent-based collection*:
  - *Data collection frequency*: Every 15 minutes
  - *Network information*: Captures network connections (TCP/UDP) and running processes
  - *Suitability*: Works for both physical and virtual servers running Windows and Linux
- *Agentless collection*:
  - *Data collection frequency*: Every 60 minutes
  - *Limitations*: Cannot capture network connections or running processes within VMs
  - *Suitability*: Designed for VMware vCenter server environments

BENEFITS OF ADS

The benefits of AWS ADS include:

- *Comprehensive data collection*: ADS provides detailed insights into server and database configurations, enabling precise migration planning.
- *Flexible deployment options*: Whether using agent-based or agentless methods, ADS adapts to various environments, making it versatile and user-friendly.
- *Free core service*: The core features of ADS are free, offering cost-effective data collection for migration planning.

- *Centralized data management*: With integration with AWS Migration Hub, ADS centralizes data storage and migration management, simplifying the migration process.
- *Enhanced security*: All data collected is encrypted, ensuring that sensitive information remains secure during the migration process.

These benefits make ADS an invaluable tool in the cloud migration journey, streamlining the discovery and planning phases, and setting the stage for a successful migration.

By providing a secure and reliable method to discover and document your on-premises server environment, AWS ADS helps streamline the migration planning process for moving your applications to the AWS cloud.

LAB: AWS APPLICATION DISCOVERY SERVICE TUTORIAL

Before you use AWS ADS for the first time, complete the following tasks.

1. Sign in to the AWS console at *https://console.aws.amazon.com*.
2. Create an IAM user with the username AWS-ADS.
3. Select the AWS access type.

   You need to select both AWS Management Console access and Programmatic access.

4. Select the AWS credential type:
   - For Programmatic access, select Access key. This enables an access key ID and secret access key for the AWS API, CLI, SDK, and other development tools.
   - For AWS Management Console access, select Password. This enables a password that allows users to sign in to the AWS Management Console.
5. For Console password, select Custom password.
6. For Require password reset, select User must create a new password at next sign-in.

   Users are automatically granted the IAMUserChangePassword permission to allow them to change their own password.

7. Select the following roles:
   - AWSApplicationDiscoveryServiceFullAccess
   - AWSApplicationDiscoveryAgentlessCollectorAccess
   - AWSApplicationDiscoveryAgentAccess
   - AWSAgentlessDiscoveryService
   - AWSMigrationHubFullAccess
8. Using the above user credentials, log in to the AWS console and navigate to Migration Hub.
9. Sign in to Migration Hub and choose a home Region.
10. In the Migration Hub console navigation pane, choose Settings and then choose the home Region US_EAST_1A.

    Migration Hub data is stored in your home Region for the purposes of discovery, planning, and migration tracking.

    Once you have completed the above user creation process with the provided credentials, you will have two different scenarios to perform the discovery process:

- Agent-based application discovery process
- Agentless application discovery process

LAB: AGENT-BASED APPLICATION DISCOVERY TUTORIAL

1. Set the home Region in AWS Migration Hub.
   - If the 1.X version agent is present, uninstall it before installing the latest version.
   - All Linux hosts support the Intel i686 CPU architecture (also known as the P6 microarchitecture).
   - Agents require access to the arsenal over TCP port 443. Outbound access is required. If the home Region is us-east-1, use *https://arsenal-discovery.us-east-1.amazonaws.com:443*.
   - Access to Amazon S3 in your home Region is required for auto-upgrade to work.
2. Create an IAM user (add the one created earlier).

3. Check the time skew from your Network Time Protocol (NTP) servers and amend as necessary. Incorrect time synchronization causes the agent registration call to fail.

4. Verify that your Operating System (OS) environment is supported:
   - *Linux*:
     - Amazon Linux 2012.03 and 2015.03
     - Amazon Linux 2 (9/25/2018 update and later)
     - Ubuntu 12.04, 14.04, 16.04, 18.04, and 20.04
     - Red Hat Enterprise Linux 5.11, 6.10, 7.3, 7.7, and 8.1
     - CentOS 5.11, 6.9, and 7.3
     - SUSE 11 SP4 and 12 SP5
   - *Windows*:
     - Windows Server 2003 R2 SP2
     - Windows Server 2008 R1 SP2 and 2008 R2 SP1
     - Windows Server 2012 R1 and 2012 R2
     - Windows Server 2016
     - Windows Server 2019

5. Now, we need to install Discovery Agent on Linux. To initiate this exercise, we need to install the Discovery agent on an Amazon EC2 instance using the following steps:
   i. Sign in to your Linux-based server or VM and create a new directory to contain your agent components.
   ii. Switch to the new directory and download the installation script.
   iii. To download from the command line, run the following command:
   ```
   curl -o ./aws-discovery-agent.tar.gz https://s3-us-west-2.amazonaws.com/aws-discovery-agent.us-west-2/linux/latest/aws-discovery-agent.tar.gz
   ```
   iv. To download from the Migration Hub console, do the following:
      a. Sign in to the AWS Management Console and open the Migration Hub console at *https://console.aws.amazon.com/migrationhub/*.
      b. In the left navigation page, under Discover, choose Tools.

    c. In the AWS Discovery Agent box, choose Download agents, then choose Download for Linux. Your download will begin immediately. Verify the cryptographic signature of the installation package with the following three commands:

- `curl -o ./agent.sig https://s3.us-west-2.amazonaws.com/aws-discovery-agent.us-west-2/linux/latest/aws-discovery-agent.tar.gz.sig`

- `curl -o ./discovery.gpg https://s3.us-west-2.amazonaws.com/aws-discovery-agent.us-west-2/linux/latest/discovery.gpg`

- `gpg --no-default-keyring --keyring ./discovery.gpg --verify agent.sig aws-discovery-agent.tar.gz`

    v. Extract from the tarball, as shown below:

```
tar -xzf aws-discovery-agent.tar.gz
```

    vi. To install the agent, use the following command:

```
sudo bash install -r your-home-region -k aws-access-key-id -s aws-secret-access-key
```

    The Linux server will show up in the Servers - Discovery section under Migration Hub.

6. After installing the agent, the Discovery Agent automatically collects system configuration, time-series utilization or performance data, process data, and Transmission Control Protocol (TCP) network connections. In Migration Hub, navigate to Data collectors, then select Discovery agents. The server will be visible. The status will be Collecting.

7. The next step is managing the Discovery Agent process.

    In Unix, you can manage the behavior of the Discovery Agent at the system level using the systemd, Upstart, or System V init tools. The following tabs outline the commands for the supported tasks in each of the respective tools.

TABLE 10.1 Different Unix commands as per given tasks.

SN	Task	Command
1	Verify that an agent is running.	`sudo systemctl status aws-discovery-daemon.service`
2	Start an agent.	`sudo systemctl start aws-discovery-daemon.service`
3	Stop an agent.	`sudo systemctl stop aws-discovery-daemon.service`
4	Restart an agent.	`sudo systemctl restart aws-discovery-daemon.service`

In Windows:

TABLE 10.2 Different Windows services as per given tasks.

SN	Task	Service Name	Service Status/Action
1	Verify that an agent is running.	AWS Discovery Agent	Started
		AWS Discovery Updater	
2	Start an agent.	AWS Discovery Agent	Choose Start
		AWS Discovery Updater	
3	Stop an agent.	AWS Discovery Agent	Choose Stop
		AWS Discovery Updater	
4	Restart an agent.	AWS Discovery Agent	Choose Restart
		AWS Discovery Updater	

These data collection tools store their data in the Application Discovery Service repository, providing details about each server and the processes running on them. When either of these tools is deployed, you can start, stop, and view the collected data from the AWS Migration Hub console.

To start or stop data collection tools:

1. Using your AWS account, sign in to the AWS Management Console and open the Migration Hub console at *https://console.aws.amazon.com/migrationhub/*.
2. In the Migration Hub console navigation pane, under Discover, choose Data collectors.
3. Choose the Agents tab.
4. Select the checkbox of the collection tool you want to start or stop.
5. Choose Start data collection or Stop data collection.

APPLICATION DISCOVERY SERVICE AGENTLESS COLLECTOR

Application Discovery Service Agentless Collector is an on-premises application that collects information through agentless methods about your on-premises environment, including server profile information (for example, OS, number of CPUs, and amount of RAM), and server utilization metrics. You install the Agentless Collector as a VM in your VMware vCenter server environment using an Open Virtualization Archive (OVA) file.

Agentless Collector has a modular architecture, which allows for the use of multiple agentless collection methods. Agentless Collector currently supports one-module collection from VMware VMs.

AWS MIGRATION HUB

AWS Migration Hub provides a centralized place to discover your existing servers, plan migrations, and track the status of each application migration. AWS Migration Hub provides visibility into your application portfolio and streamlines planning and tracking. You can see the status of the servers and databases that make up each of the applications you are migrating, regardless of which migration tool you are using.

Migration Hub gives you the choice to start migrating right away and group servers while migration is underway, or to first discover servers and then group them into applications. Either way, you can migrate each server in an application and track progress from each tool in AWS Migration Hub.

Migration Hub supports migration status updates from the following tools:

- *AWS Application Migration Service*: This is the primary migration service recommended for lift-and-shift migrations to AWS.
- *AWS Database Migration Service (AWS DMS)*: This simplifies and automates database migrations to AWS with minimal downtime, supporting homogenous and heterogeneous migrations. It enables seamless migration of databases to Amazon RDS, Aurora, or other AWS database services while maintaining data integrity and security.

Benefits of Cloud Migration with AWS Migration Hub

Migrating to the cloud offers numerous benefits, including increased scalability, cost savings, and improved security; however, the migration process itself can be challenging and time-consuming. AWS Migration Hub aims to simplify this process and provide organizations with a seamless migration experience. Here are some of the key benefits of using AWS Migration Hub for your cloud migration:

- Centralized visibility: AWS Migration Hub provides a centralized dashboard that allows organizations to track the progress of their migration projects. This visibility into every stage of the migration process enables teams to easily identify any roadblocks or bottlenecks and take necessary actions to address them. With a holistic view of the migration, teams can make informed decisions and ensure a smoother and more efficient migration experience.

- Comprehensive solution: AWS Migration Hub integrates with a range of other AWS services, making it a comprehensive solution for managing the entire migration lifecycle. It allows organizations to invent their on-premises applications, assess their cloud-readiness, create a migration plan, and execute it seamlessly. With AWS Migration Hub, organizations can avoid the hassle of using multiple tools and simplify their migration process.

- *Faster and more secure migration*: AWS Migration Hub provides organizations with the tools and resources they need to accelerate their migration to the cloud. It offers best practices and guidance to help organizations plan and execute their migration effectively. AWS Migration Hub ensures the security of your data throughout the migration process, helping you mitigate risks and protect your sensitive information.

Understanding the Migration Process with AWS Migration Hub

Before starting your cloud migration journey with AWS Migration Hub, it's important to understand the different stages of the migration process. Here is a brief overview of the migration process with AWS Migration Hub:

- *Discovery and assessment*: In this stage, organizations make an inventory of their on-premises applications and assess their cloud readiness. AWS Migration Hub helps organizations discover their applications, dependencies, and requirements, providing valuable insights for the migration planning process.

- *Planning and design*: Once the applications have been discovered and assessed, organizations can create a migration plan. AWS Migration Hub allows organizations to define the target architecture, identify migration waves, and estimate the cost and timeline of the migration.

- *Execution and validation*: After the migration plan has been created, organizations can start executing the migration. AWS Migration Hub provides tools and resources to help organizations execute migration effectively, ensuring minimal disruption to the business operations. Once the migration is complete, organizations can validate the migrated workloads to ensure everything is functioning as expected.

Preparing for Cloud Migration with AWS Migration Hub

Preparing for a cloud migration requires careful planning and preparation. Here are some key steps to consider when preparing for a cloud migration with AWS Migration Hub:

- Identify your migration goals: Before starting the migration process, it's important to identify your goals and objectives. This will help you prioritize your migration efforts and ensure a successful migration.
- Assess your applications: Use AWS Migration Hub to assess the cloud readiness of your applications. This will help you understand the dependencies and requirements of each application and make informed decisions during the migration process.
- Define your migration plan: Create a migration plan that outlines the steps and timeline for migrating your applications to the cloud. AWS Migration Hub provides tools and resources to help you create a comprehensive migration plan.
- Allocate resources: Ensure that you have the necessary resources, both human and technical, to support your migration process. This may include training your team on cloud migration best practices and allocating sufficient compute and storage resources in the cloud.

Managing and Tracking Your Migration with AWS Migration Hub

One of the key advantages of using AWS Migration Hub is the ability to manage and track your migration projects from a centralized dashboard. Here are some tips for effectively managing and tracking your migration with AWS Migration Hub:

- *Monitor the progress*: Regularly monitor the progress of your migration projects using the AWS Migration Hub dashboard. This will help you identify any issues or bottlenecks and take necessary actions to address them.

- *Communicate and collaborate*: Use the collaboration features of AWS Migration Hub to facilitate communication and collaboration among your migration team. This will help ensure that everyone is on the same page and working toward a common goal.
- *Leverage automation*: AWS Migration Hub offers automation capabilities that can help streamline your migration process. Automate repetitive tasks and leverage AWS services such as AWS Database Migration Service and AWS Server Migration Service to simplify your migration journey.

Best Practices for a Successful Cloud Migration with AWS Migration Hub

To ensure a successful cloud migration with AWS Migration Hub, it's important to follow best practices. Here are some best practices to consider:

- Start with a pilot project: Begin your migration journey with a small pilot project to gain hands-on experience with AWS Migration Hub. This will help you identify any challenges or issues early on and refine your migration strategy.
- Prioritize applications: Prioritize your applications based on their criticality and complexity. Start with low-risk applications and gradually migrate to more critical and complex workloads.
- Test and validate: Thoroughly test and validate your migrated workloads to ensure everything is functioning as expected. Perform performance testing, security testing, and user acceptance testing to minimize any post-migration issues.

AWS MIGRATION HUB TUTORIAL

1. *Access AWS Migration Hub*:
   i. *Sign in to AWS Management Console*: Open your Web browser and go to AWS Management Console at *https:/console.aws.amazon.com/*.
   ii. Enter your AWS credentials and log in.
   iii. *Navigate to Migration Hub*: In AWS Management Console, type *Migration Hub* in the search bar and select it from the list.

2. *Configure AWS Migration Hub*:
    i. *Set up data collection*: On the Migration Hub dashboard, select Get started to configure your account. Choose the Region where you want to create the Migration Hub home Region and click Create home region.
    ii. *Connect data collectors*: Use AWS Application Discovery Service to collect on-premises server details. Download and install the AWS Discovery Agent on your on-premises servers or use the AWS Discovery Connector for VMware environments. Agents will send data to the AWS Application Discovery Service, which populates Migration Hub with the server information.
3. *Create a migration plan*:
    i. *Discover and group servers*: After data collection, view the discovered servers in Migration Hub. Group servers based on application dependencies. This helps in migrating interconnected servers together to minimize downtime.
    ii. *Assess server readiness*: Use the Server Migration Service (SMS) or partner migration tools to assess each server's readiness for migration. Check for compatibility, performance requirements, and other critical factors.
4. *Execute the migration*:
    i. *Select migration tools*: Choose the appropriate migration tool based on your server OS and application. AWS provides tools such as AWS SMS and AWS Database Migration Service (DMS).
    ii. *Start the migration*: Initiate the migration process using the selected tools. Migration Hub will track the progress of your migrations and provide updates.
5. *Monitor and finalize*:
    i. *Monitor migration progress*: Use the Migration Hub dashboard to monitor the status of each migration task. It provides detailed information about the progress, errors, and completion status.
    ii. *Finalize the migration*: Once the migration is complete, verify that all applications and data are functioning correctly in the AWS environment. Decommission the on-premises servers if necessary.

SUMMARY

The Mobilize phase within AWS cloud migration focuses on preparing the organization for a successful large-scale change by addressing key aspects such as portfolio discovery, security, compliance, landing zone setup, and operational readiness. Following the Assess phase, the Mobilize phase refines the business case, clarifies the migration strategy, and starts migrating the initial applications to identify potential issues. AWS provides several tools for efficient mobilization of the cloud system. AWS Control Tower is used to set up a secure landing zone, AWS Application Discovery Service provides insights into infrastructure analysis, and AWS Migration Hub provides a centralized place for tracking migrations. The Mobilize phase highlights aspects such as compliance, risk management, and culture readiness, while also imparting cloud best practices to the teams. Through the effective implementation of this phase, organizations build the foundations for scalable, secure, and efficient cloud adoption.

REFERENCES

[AWS23] Amazon Web Services, "*What Is AWS Migration Hub?*", AWS documentation, 2023. Available online at: *https://docs.aws.amazon.com/migrationhub/latest/ug/what-is-migrationhub.html*.

[AWSControl23] Amazon Web Services, "*What Is AWS Control Tower?*", AWS documentation, 2023. Available online at: *https://docs.aws.amazon.com/controltower/latest/userguide/*.

[AWSADS22] Amazon Web Services, "*What Is Application Discovery Service?*", AWS Whitepaper, 2022. Available online at: *https://docs.aws.amazon.com/application-discovery/latest/userguide/*.

[McKinsey24] McKinsey & Co., "*The cloud transformation engine*", McKinsey Digital, 2024. Available online at: *https://www.mckinsey.com/capabilities/mckinsey-digital/our-insights/the-cloud-transformation-engine*.

[Gartner24] Gartner, "*Migrating to the Cloud: Why, How and What Makes Sense?*", Gartner Research, 2024. Available online at: *https://www.gartner.com/en/articles/migrating-to-the-cloud-why-how-and-what-makes-sense*.

[AWS24] Amazon Web Services, "*What is a landing zone?*", AWS documentation, 2024. Available online at: *https://docs.aws.amazon.com/prescriptive-guidance/latest/migration-aws-environment/understanding-landing-zones.html*.

KNOWLEDGE CHECK: MULTIPLE-CHOICE Q&A

Question 1

What is the primary goal of the AWS migration Mobilize phase?

A. To directly migrate applications to AWS.

B. To develop a detailed business case and prepare resources for migration.

C. To configure AWS networking infrastructure.

D. To perform cost optimization after migration.

Question 2

Which of the following activities is NOT part of the Mobilize phase?

A. Portfolio discovery and assessment.

B. Establishing a landing zone.

C. Migrating all workloads to AWS.

D. Creating an operations runbook.

Question 3

What is the purpose of AWS Control Tower in the Mobilize phase?

A. To set up a landing zone for a secure AWS environment.

B. To migrate databases to AWS RDS.

C. To manage cost optimization for AWS services.

D. To automate server provisioning for applications.

Question 4

Which AWS service helps collect data from on-premises environments for migration planning?

A. AWS CloudFormation.

B. AWS Lambda.

C. AWS Application Discovery Service.

D. AWS Glue.

Question 5

What is a key component of AWS Control Tower that helps enforce compliance?

A. AWS Glue.

B. AWS Guardrails.

C. AWS Lambda.

D. AWS Fargate.

Question 6

Which method of application discovery is best suited for VMware environments?

A. Agent-based discovery.

B. Agentless discovery.

C. Manual data entry.

D. AWS Snowball.

Question 7

What is a landing zone in AWS?

A. A secure and scalable AWS environment for migrated workloads.

B. A temporary AWS storage solution for migrating applications.

C. A network setup within an AWS VPC.

D. A data analytics platform for cloud monitoring.

Question 8

Which AWS service provides a centralized dashboard to track migration progress?

A. AWS CloudTrail.

B. AWS Migration Hub.

C. Amazon QuickSight.

D. AWS IAM.

Question 9

What is the role of the operations runbook in the Mobilize phase?

A. To automate infrastructure deployment.

B. To provide detailed instructions for managing AWS applications post-migration.

C. To analyze AWS billing and usage reports.

D. To set up machine learning models in AWS.

Question 10

Which of the following is a major focus of security in the Mobilize phase?

A. Ensuring that IAM roles are deleted before migration.

B. Checking the security and compliance of the AWS landing zone.

C. Using AWS WAF for protecting on-premises databases.

D. Deploying only AWS AI/ML services.

CHAPTER 11

AWS Migration Migrate Phase

OVERVIEW OF THE MIGRATION PHASE

In the cloud migration journey, the Migrate phase is the most important one, when the transition from on-premises or legacy systems to the AWS cloud is performed. After extensive planning and preparation during the earlier Assess and Mobilize phases, the Migrate phase comes into the picture. It involves executing the migration strategy—transferring workloads and data to the cloud without any disruption. Modernization is another aspect that needs to be considered during this phase. Please note that the Migrate and Modernize phases work simultaneously.

UNDERSTANDING THE MIGRATE PHASE

The Migrate phase can be performed using the following key activities.

Workload Migration

In simple terms, this is the process of moving servers, applications, and related components from the old environment to the cloud. It requires careful planning to ensure that applications maintain their old functionality in the cloud, with the same or even better performance. Workload migration comes in various forms, the most common of which are rehosting (lifting and shifting) applications without significant changes, or re-architecting to use cloud-native capabilities.

Data Migration

Data migration is the process of moving databases, file systems, and large datasets to cloud storage solutions while ensuring that data integrity, data security, and compliance are maintained throughout the process. This ensures that all the necessary data is in the cloud and remains functional.

It is important to check and verify that workloads and data have been migrated successfully and that everything is functioning as intended. This includes performance testing, security checks, and ensuring that the cloud environment meets the criteria that were set during the planning stage of the migration project.

Optimization and Modernization

Although migration primarily involves moving existing data and workloads to the cloud, it also provides the opportunity for management to modernize and optimize applications and infrastructure. This might include making applications more flexible to benefit from cloud-native services, optimizing resource utilization, or implemnting new security measures that were not previously possible.

AWS PRESCRIPTIVE GUIDANCE IN THE MIGRATE PHASE

Applying different aspects of AWS Prescriptive Guidance is essential for ensuring a successful and efficient migration. AWS Prescriptive Guidance encapsulates the collective wisdom and best practices developed by multiple organizations, cloud service providers, and professional services teams who have already navigated the complexities of cloud migration in the past. It is a comprehensive resource that is useful for organizations to make their migration efforts more efficient.

The three components of AWS Prescriptive Guidance can be seen in Figure 11.1.

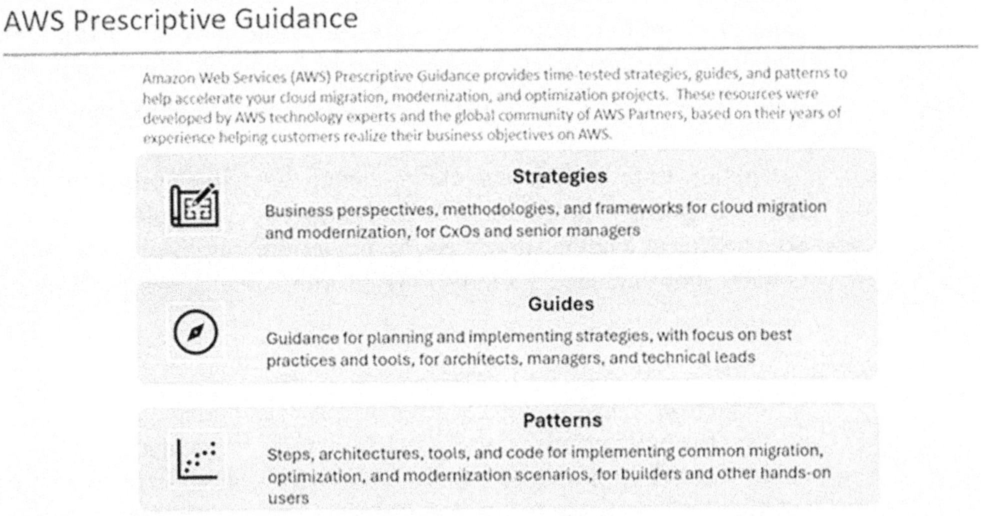

AWS Prescriptive Guidance

Amazon Web Services (AWS) Prescriptive Guidance provides time-tested strategies, guides, and patterns to help accelerate your cloud migration, modernization, and optimization projects. These resources were developed by AWS technology experts and the global community of AWS Partners, based on their years of experience helping customers realize their business objectives on AWS.

Strategies
Business perspectives, methodologies, and frameworks for cloud migration and modernization, for CxOs and senior managers

Guides
Guidance for planning and implementing strategies, with focus on best practices and tools, for architects, managers, and technical leads

Patterns
Steps, architectures, tools, and code for implementing common migration, optimization, and modernization scenarios, for builders and other hands-on users

FIGURE 11.1 Three Key Components of AWS Prescriptive Guidance.

AWS Prescriptive Guidance is organized into three key components:

- Strategies:
  - *Migration strategy development*: AWS Prescriptive Guidance includes the essentials of creating a strong migration strategy according to a company's specific requirements. This section contains business perspectives of cloud adoption alignment with the company's goals, choosing migration approaches (e.g., rehosting, refactoring, or replatforming), and governance framework establishment.
  - *Frameworks and methodologies*: This shows the use of frameworks such as the AWS Well-Architected Framework, Microsoft Azure Cloud Adoption Framework, or Google Cloud Adoption Framework. These frameworks assist organizations with choosing the most suitable solutions (i.e., architecture, security, cost management, and operational excellence) during the migration.
- Guides:
  - *Practical implementation guides*: These guides show organizations how to transform strategies into actionable plans. They provide the necessary steps to ensure a successful migration, such as establishing a secure landing zone, configuring identity and access management controls, and cloud infrastructure deployment.

- *Best practices*: The guidelines emphasize key considerations for a smooth migration, including using automation tools to cut down on manual processes, using monitoring and logging to track migration progress, and conducting regular reviews to ensure compliance with business requirements.
- *Communication and change management*: Effective communication is very important during the migration process. This guidance covers how technical leaders should communicate migration plans to stakeholders, how managers should engage their teams, and on how to manage change effectively to minimize disruption.

■ Patterns:
- *Architectural patterns*: AWS Prescriptive Guidance also provides architectural patterns with examples of how to design and implement cloud solutions for special cases. For example, an architectural pattern could include deploying microservices to various Regions, creating a multi-account cloud environment, or optimizing databases in the cloud to work together efficiently.
- *Migration patterns*: These patterns have been successful for different migration situations previously. Examples include rehosting legacy applications using tools such as AWS Server Migration Service or Azure Migrate, or refactoring an application to use cloud-native services such as serverless computing.
- *Optimization patterns*: These patterns are used for the optimization of cloud environments, such as the automation of resource scaling, the introduction of cost management, or improving the security posture through continuous monitoring and compliance checks.

Utilizing Prescriptive Guidance

There are various ways that organizations can use AWS Prescriptive Guidance, such as cloud provider documentation, partner resources, and professional services teams. Often, these systems come with a searchable database or portal, which is where the user searches for the right strategy, guide, or pattern according to their specific requirement:

■ *Large-scale migrations*: AWS Prescriptive Guidance provides information about the management of complex projects, such as migrating hundreds of servers or moving entire data centers to the cloud. It includes plans for portfolio management, project governance, and building a strong cloud foundation.

- *Tool-specific guidance*: If an organization is utilizing AWS Glue for ETL processes or Azure Data Factory for data integration, AWS Prescriptive Guidance provides specific documentation and examples on how to use those tools successfully during migration.

- *Industry-specific scenarios*: AWS Prescriptive Guidance provides industry-specific scenarios and solutions (such as financial services, healthcare, and retail). These industries often struggle with the complexity of new compliance requirements and the need to migrate to the cloud while ensuring that cloud vendors guarantee high availability, meet regulatory requirements, and offer exceptional monitoring capabilities.

- *Risk reduction*: AWS Prescriptive Guidance enables companies to greatly decrease the risks of cloud migration. It gives them the chance to learn from other people's experiences in order to avoid common mistakes and implement the best practices that have been proven to be effective in real-life cases.

More information can be found here: *https://aws.amazon.com/prescriptive-guidance/*.

DIFFERENT AWS MIGRATION PHASE TOOLS

AWS provides a comprehensive set of tools for efficient migration. These tools can be used in a wide range of scenarios for different workload types, as well as hybrid migration (coupled with on-premises servers). These tools include AWS Application Migration Service (MGN), AWS Database Migration Service, and other services that have been put together to facilitate a smooth transfer of data to the cloud, making the migration process more reliable and cost-effective.

Different AWS Migrate phase tools can be seen in Figure 11.2.

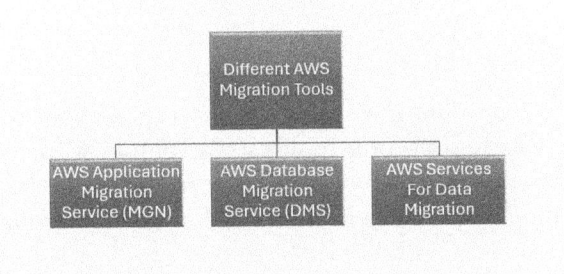

FIGURE 11.2 Different AWS Migrate Phase Tools.

AWS Application Migration Service (MGN)

MGN has replaced the Server Migration Service. It migrates entire applications (including dependencies) to AWS, aiming for modernization during the process. It was previously known as Cloud Endure.

AWS Database Migration Service (DMS)

This service helps you migrate your databases to AWS. There are two different types of database migration:

- Homogeneous database migration
- Heterogeneous database migration

AWS Services for Data Migration

AWS provides other services that can be used to migrate data to the AWS cloud. These services are:

- AWS Storage Gateway
- AWS DataSync
- AWS Snow Family

WORKLOAD MIGRATION VS. DATA MIGRATION

The cloud migration process can be broken down into workload migration and data migration. Each utilizes tools designed explicitly for that purpose, making the entire process simple and efficient. VMware Cloud on AWS and AWS MGN are used for migrating applications and workloads, while AWS Storage Gateway, AWS DMS, and AWS Snow Family are used for data migration. Collectively, these tools provide a robust framework for efficient migration and for the modernization of IT environments in the cloud, with minimal disruption.

Workload Migration

Workload migration involves moving servers, applications, and their associated workloads from on-premises environments to the cloud. This process guarantees the necessary transfer of critical business operations while avoiding any interruption in service availability and performance ratios.

VMware Cloud on AWS

VMware Cloud on AWS is a cloud service used to assist businesses in the migration of VMware systems from conventional physical servers located in on-premises data centers to the AWS cloud. This is best for organizations that use many VMware virtualization applications and want to keep a uniform system between their on-premises data centers and cloud environments.

With VMware Cloud on AWS, enterprises can move their workloads with little or no modification. This tool can also be used for activities such as expanding the data center, disaster recovery, and cloud migration. The agility of this tool to migrate workloads between on-premises and AWS environments makes it a critical utility for companies that have made significant investments in VMware technologies.

AWS MGN

AWS MGN facilitates the process of migrating applications to the AWS cloud by automating source server conversion. This solution can accommodate all kinds of applications and workloads. This service was previously known as Server Migration Service.

AWS MGN automates the lift-and-shift migration process, cutting down on manual work and ensuring that applications can be transitioned with the least amount of downtime possible. It replicates servers in AWS, converts them to the AWS-native version, and handles the primary migration tasks. This tool is essential for organizations migrating their legacy applications that are too complex or not possible to refactor or modernize immediately.

Data Migration

Data migration takes care of the movement of data from on-premises storage solutions to the cloud. This step ensures that critical data is securely and efficiently moved to the cloud, allowing the cloud to be utilized in various kinds of analytics, storage, and computing in the future.

It is a useful service that is a bridge between on-premises environments and AWS cloud storage. There are a variety of use cases, including backup and archiving, disaster recovery, and cloud-based data lakes.

AWS Transfer Family

AWS Transfer Family is a secure method of transferring files into and out of AWS storage services using protocols such as SFTP, FTPS, and FTP. This is best suited for companies that are planning to transfer a large volume of data from their existing systems to AWS storage services. It enables secure data transmission through the integration with AWS Identity and Access Management (IAM) so that only people who are authorized to access the files can do so.

AWS Database Migration Service (DMS)

AWS DMS provides flexibility and security when migrating databases to AWS. With this smart tool, you can move all your data regardless of the type of database. The software supports homogenous migrations (e.g., Oracle to Oracle) and heterogeneous migrations (e.g., Oracle to Amazon Aurora). This service ensures that continuous data replication is carried out with minimal downtime, which is why it's applicable in the migration of high-priority database systems. With AWS DMS, you won't have to be concerned with all these complexities. It automates the processes of data type conversions and schema changes based on user preferences, effectively reducing logical and migration errors in the database.

AWS DataSync

One of the main features of AWS DataSync is the built-in functionality to transmit massive amounts of data automatically between on-premises storage and AWS storage services.

DataSync saves time and effort by taking care of the process of transferring data automatically and syncing the data between different storage locations. It is ideal for the migration of various data types. It ensures data security by encrypting data and checking integrity during the migration process.

AWS Snow Family

AWS Snow Family is a series of physical devices that are specially designed to transfer a lot of data to and from on-premises and AWS, especially in situations where network connectivity is limited or unavailable.

This service is ideal for large-scale data migrations, edge computing, or environments with limited bandwidth. AWS Snow Family encompasses Snowcone, Snowball, and Snowmobile devices. These devices help organizations move volumes of petabytes of data safely and securely to AWS, allowing for rapid data integration.

VMWARE TO AWS CLOUD MIGRATION

VMware Cloud on AWS provides a robust and scalable platform for migrating existing VMware workloads to the cloud. The *Relocate* strategy, combined with VMware's Software-Defined Data Center (SDDC) and AWS's infrastructure, enables a seamless transition to the cloud while maintaining operational continuity and minimizing disruption. Whether you are looking to extend your data center, implement disaster recovery, or leverage cloud-native services, VMware Cloud on AWS offers a comprehensive solution that aligns with your cloud migration strategy.

You need to understand key functional considerations and the migration stages in this kind of process:

- Relocate strategy and its association with VMware cloud migration to AWS
- VMware SDDC
- VMware Cloud on AWS (VMC on AWS)
- Migration type: Cold migration
- Migration type: Warm migration
- Migration type: Live migration

Relocate Strategy and Its Association with VMware Cloud Migration to AWS

The Relocate strategy involves migrating applications and data from one data center or cloud provider to an equivalent cloud infrastructure of another provider or region, typically involving a hypervisor-level lift-and-shift approach. In the context of VMware migration to AWS, this strategy allows you to move your existing VMware workloads to the cloud with minimal changes to the underlying architecture.

Overview of the Relocate Strategy

Relocation refers to moving workloads from an on-premises data center or another cloud provider to AWS, retaining the same hypervisor or containerization layer. This is ideal for organizations running VMware environments that want to migrate to AWS without refactoring or re-architecting their applications. It minimizes downtime and disruptions, maintains existing operational procedures, and requires no retraining or significant changes to existing infrastructure.

Advantages of the Relocate strategy include:

- *Minimal downtime*: Users remain seamlessly connected during the migration process, with no noticeable impact on ongoing operations.
- *No need for application rewrites*: Since the underlying architecture remains unchanged, there's no need to modify the application source code.
- *Operational continuity*: Existing automation scripts, backup solutions, and monitoring tools continue to function as before.

Disadvantages of the Relocate strategy include:

- *Limited cloud-native benefits*: While migrating, you might not be able to fully use cloud-native features such as managed services, automatic scaling, or serverless platforms.
- *Operational overhead*: Maintaining the operational tasks remains the same as you control them by conducting patching and security updates, hence not exploring the power of AWS's managed services.
- *Resource and time consumption*: Ensuring the compatibility of existing applications on the new platform can be very resource-consuming and tedious.
- *Cost considerations*: You will still have to deal with the costs of hypervisor licenses as well as the daily operational overhead.

VMware SDDC

The VMware SDDC is the foundation of the VMware Cloud on AWS offering. It virtualizes the entire data center—computing, storage, networking, and management—using VMware's suite of products.

The components of VMware SDDC are as follows:

- *vSphere (ESXi Hypervisor)*: It virtualizes computing resources by converting physical CPUs, memory, and storage into virtual hardware for running multiple Virtual Machines (VMs) on a single server.
- *vSAN (Virtual Storage Area Network)*: It virtualizes storage by aggregating local disk storage from multiple ESXi hosts into a shared data store.
- *NSX (Network Virtualization)*: It virtualizes networking, allowing for the creation of entire networks in software, independent of the underlying physical infrastructure.

- *vCenter Server*: It provides centralized management for vSphere environments, allowing for easy deployment, monitoring, and management of VMs across multiple hosts.

This is how SDDC supports VMware cloud migration:

- *Unified management*: The SDDC framework provides a unified management platform, making it easier to manage hybrid cloud environments that span both on-premises data centers and AWS.
- *Scalability*: The software-defined nature allows for rapid scaling of resources, which can be seamlessly extended to the cloud with VMware Cloud on AWS.

VMware Cloud on AWS (VMC on AWS)

VMware Cloud on AWS is a jointly engineered service that integrates VMware's SDDC with AWS's Global Infrastructure, providing a consistent and scalable platform for running VMware workloads in the cloud.

Key features of VMware Cloud on AWS include:

- *Hybrid cloud capabilities*: It enables seamless integration between on-premises VMware environments and AWS, facilitating workload migration, disaster recovery, and data center extension.
- *Elastic and scalable infrastructure*: AWS provides the physical infrastructure, while VMware delivers the virtualization layer, allowing you to scale your environment as needed without worrying about the underlying hardware.
- *Access to AWS services*: It allows you to integrate with native AWS services such as S3, RDS, and Lambda, enabling you to enhance your applications with cloud-native features.
- *Management and integration*:
  - *Hybrid vCenter linked mode*: It allows you to manage both on-premises and cloud-based VMware environments from a single interface, simplifying migration and operations.
  - *AWS Global Infrastructure*: It leverages AWS's Global Infrastructure, including Regions and Availability Zones, to provide high availability and disaster recovery options.

DIFFERENT MIGRATION TYPES

As we have discussed the different terminology used in VMWare migration to AWS, we need to understand the different types of migration, as given below:

- Cold migration
- Warm migration
- Live migration

By understanding the various migration types, you can choose the method that best fits your organization's needs.

Cold Migration

Cold migration is the process of transferring VMs from one environment to another while they are powered off. This method, although requiring the most downtime, is the method that is often easier to implement.

The VMs are backed up in the source environment, transferred to the target environment, and then restored. The VMs are powered off during the migration, which means the application will be unavailable for the whole duration of the transfer and restoration process. Furthermore, VMware vSphere Replication or a third-party backup tool that is compatible with both the source and target environments can be used.

This method is ideal for applications that are not crucial or for scheduled maintenance windows, where downtime can be tolerated. The prolonged downtime and potential difficulties in data synchronization for large or complex environments are the most likely issues.

Warm Migration

Warm migration involves transferring running VMs with minimal downtime, often by replicating data to the target environment in advance. Continuous replication of VM data from the source environment to the target environment ensures that the target VM is up to date at the time of cutover. The final switch to the target environment is made during a short maintenance window, resulting in minimal downtime.

The different tools used for this migration are VMware vSphere Replication, VMware HCX, or third-party replication tools.

It is most suitable for applications that cannot afford extended downtime but can tolerate a brief outage during the final cutover. It requires careful planning and coordination to minimize disruption and may involve additional costs for replication tools.

Live Migration

Live migration, or vMotion, allows for the transfer of running VMs with no downtime, providing a seamless experience for end users. VMware vMotion is the live migration of VMs between different ESXi hosts without the deployment of active workloads. Users remain connected to the applications and view the whole process, which takes place in real time with no disruption to the service. The tools used for this type of migration are VMware vMotion and Enhanced vMotion Compatibility (EVC) for cross-cluster migrations. Applications of paramount importance that should be highly available and cannot be subject to any downtime are the best use cases for vMotion. It needs a fast and uninterrupted link between the source and the target environments and might also involve the additional cost of purchasing a license.

AWS APPLICATION MIGRATION SERVICE

AWS Application Migration Service (MGN) covers a wider range of application migrations, particularly those involving lift-and-shift strategies. It helps organizations perform lift-and-shift migration from any source infrastructure with minimum business disruption. This migration can be divided into three types:

- On-premises to AWS
- Cross-Region or Availability Zone (AWS to AWS)
- Cross-cloud

The different migration types can be seen in Figure 11.3.

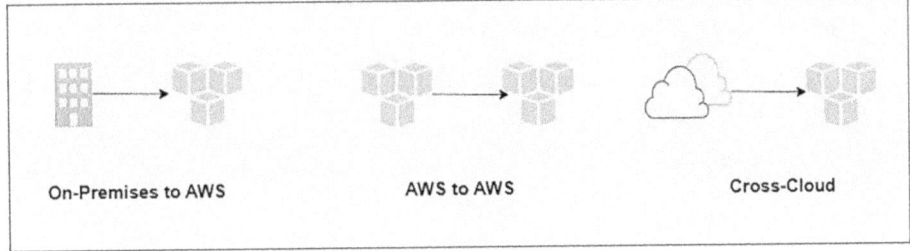

FIGURE 11.3 Different Migration Types.

The following are the fundamental attributes of MGN:

- *Lift-and-shift focus*: MGN excels in the process of transferring on-premises applications to AWS with almost no code modifications. This situation is perfect if your main objective is not modernization but a fast migration to the cloud.
- *AWS Management Console integration*: MGN easily connects to the AWS Management Console, which gives you a centralized place from which you can control the whole migration process.
- *Service integration*: MGN collaborates closely with other AWS services including EC2, S3, and VPC, simplifying the migration process and utilizing AWS functions that are already in place.
- *EC2 launch templates*: MGN makes use of EC2 launch templates to ensure that the instances of your migrated applications on AWS have the same setup. Having a consistent environment is the most important factor and makes the workplace easier to manage.
- *Network access control*: MGN provides granular control over the security of your migrated applications and network, ensuring the integrity of security and compliance within your AWS infrastructure.
- *Minimal downtime*: MGN reduces downtime during the migration. In this way, the handovers are smoother and minimize disruption to your applications.
- *Cost reduction potential*: The automation of many migration tasks and resource optimization through MGN can help reduce overall migration costs compared to manual methods.

MGN provides a comprehensive, user-friendly solution for moving complex applications to AWS. It simplifies the process, reduces downtime, and integrates seamlessly with AWS services.

Benefits of Application Migration Service

AWS MGN offers many benefits, including flexibility, reliability, and a highly automated nature:

- Flexible:

Migrate from any source: It supports numerous on-premises or cloud environments. A financial services firm could use it to replicate VMware workloads with minimal reconfiguration, ensuring compliance and reducing risk.

- *Wide range of support*: It is compatible with multiple OSs, applications, and databases. A retail company could seamlessly migrate its e-commerce application from Windows Server and SQL Server to AWS without code changes, maintaining service availability.
- *Suitable for large-scale migrations*: It handles complex migration projects with ease. An enterprise IT firm could migrate 500 VMs from a private data center to AWS, reducing project time by 40% using bulk migration capabilities.

- Reliable:
  - *Robust and predictable replication*: It provides non-disruptive, continuous data replication, ensuring data integrity. A healthcare provider could replicate patient records from legacy systems to AWS to avoid data loss during cutover.
  - *Short cutover windows*: It helps migrate critical systems without much downtime. A global airline could transfer its ticketing system onto AWS during a weekend with little effect on 24/7 services.
  - *Highly secure*: Sensitive data is kept secure using encryption and secure access. A government agency could use it to transfer citizens' information to AWS.

- Highly automated:
  - *Minimal skill requirements*: It is simple enough for non-IT teams to operate. A small start-up could use it with little assistance from outsiders to move its app stack onto AWS.
  - *Non-disruptive testing*: It offers pre-migration tests that do not affect real users. A SaaS company could use it to conduct tests before going live on AWS.
  - *Integration with COEs*: It works well with existing procedures. A multinational firm could integrate it into their COE process, helping cut costs by 30% and streamlining their cloud use strategy.

Application Migration Service Lifecycle

The MGN lifecycle simplifies the process of migrating applications to AWS using an automated approach.

The AWS MGN lifecycle can be seen in Figure 11.4.

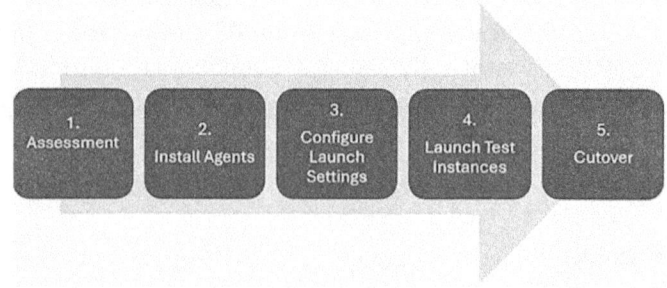

FIGURE 11.4 AWS Application Migration Service Lifecycle.

Here's the step-by-step description based on the diagram:

1. *Assessment*: This stage identifies the servers, networking configurations, and instance rightsizing. This step ensures that the existing infrastructure is analyzed and mapped to AWS capabilities.

2. *Install agents*: This process installs lightweight agents on the source servers. Once installed, these agents begin the replication process by transferring data to a staging subnet in AWS.

3. *Configure launch settings*: In this step, we need to adjust launch settings for the replicated instances. These configurations can be modified at any time without affecting the ongoing replication process.

4. *Launch test instances*: This step conducts non-disruptive tests by launching the replicated instances in AWS, which ensures that applications perform as expected before the final migration.

5. *Cutover*: Once testing is complete and the system is ready, the cutover process is initiated. During this step, the migrated instances are finalized and begin running natively in AWS.

AWS MGN is a powerful tool designed to make large-scale migrations to the cloud easier and faster. It works with all kinds of applications, so it's a great fit for different workloads. The service ensures 100% data integrity, meaning your data stays safe and accurate throughout the migration. It also allows for quick cutovers, reduces downtime, and keeps your business running smoothly. By automating key steps, AWS MGN simplifies the migration process and helps businesses move to AWS with less effort and stress.

Keys to the Successful Implementation of AWS MGN

For a successful migration, follow these guidelines:

1. Plan and organize your migration:
    i. *Identify source servers*: Begin by identifying all the servers that need to be migrated.
    ii. *Group servers into waves*: Organize the servers into migration waves. Each wave should consist of servers that are interdependent or belong to a common business application.
    iii. *Set cutover dates*: Assign specific cutover dates for each wave. This ensures proper resource allocation and seamless project continuity.
2. Install the AWS Replication Agent:
    i. *Install the agent on current wave servers*: Deploy the AWS Replication Agent only on the source servers within the current wave to avoid overloading network bandwidth.
    ii. *Monitor replication progress*: Ensure that replication is proceeding as expected. Confirm that the status of each server reaches a Healthy state and is marked as Ready for Testing.
3. Perform testing:
    i. *Launch test instances*: Initiate the launch of test instances 1 to 2 weeks prior to the scheduled cutover date. This allows sufficient time to identify and resolve any potential issues.
    ii. *Validate test results*: Test thoroughly to ensure that application functionality, data integrity, and performance meet expectations.
4. Finalize pre-cutover activities:
    i. *Verify source server health*: Ensure that all source servers have a Healthy status, have been thoroughly tested, and are marked as Ready for Cutover.

ii. *Confirm no lag*: Ensure that replication is fully synchronized, and no lag exists between source and replication servers. This reduces the cutover window and minimizes downtime.

5. Execute the cutover:

   i. *Launch target instances*: Perform the final cutover by launching target instances in AWS.

   ii. *Validate post-cutover functionality*: Verify that the target servers are functioning as expected and all applications are operational.

   iii. *Decommission source servers*: Once the target environment is stable, decommission the original source servers.

Server Migration Service (SMS) and Its Comparison with MGN

AWS used to have a tool called AWS Server Migration Service (AWS SMS), which was primarily used for bringing individual virtual servers to the AWS cloud, but it was officially discontinued on March 31, 2022. To streamline and enhance the migration process, AWS now recommends using AWS MGN, which is the primary tool for a lift-and-shift migration to AWS. This service provides a safe and secure way for enterprises to move workloads into the cloud. The following table shows the key comparisons between SMS and MGN for better understanding:

TABLE 11.1 SMS vs. MGN.

Aspect	AWS Application Migration Service (MGN)	AWS Server Migration Service (SMS)
Focus	Migrates entire applications, including dependencies, to AWS, with the goal of modernization during the process.	Focuses on migrating individual virtual servers to AWS.
Migration approach	Automatically converts source servers to run natively on AWS, with potential optimizations. Supports agentless replication for vCenter environments.	Replicates the server data to an AWS staging area before cutover. Primarily targets virtualized environments.
Downtime tolerance	Enables non-disruptive testing and cutover, minimizing downtime.	May require some downtime during the cutover phase.
Modernization	Offers built-in and custom options to optimize applications for AWS during migration.	Limited application modernization capabilities.

AWS MGN Architecture

The AWS MGN architecture is designed to facilitate seamless migration of physical, virtual, or cloud servers to AWS. The process begins with the source environment, which includes a combination of servers from various infrastructures. In this example, the source environment has two servers, with two disks attached to the top server and three disks attached to the bottom server. On the AWS side, the target environment is set up in a predefined AWS Region with configured subnets, where the migrated servers will be deployed.

The AWS MGN source and target environments can be seen in Figure 11.5.

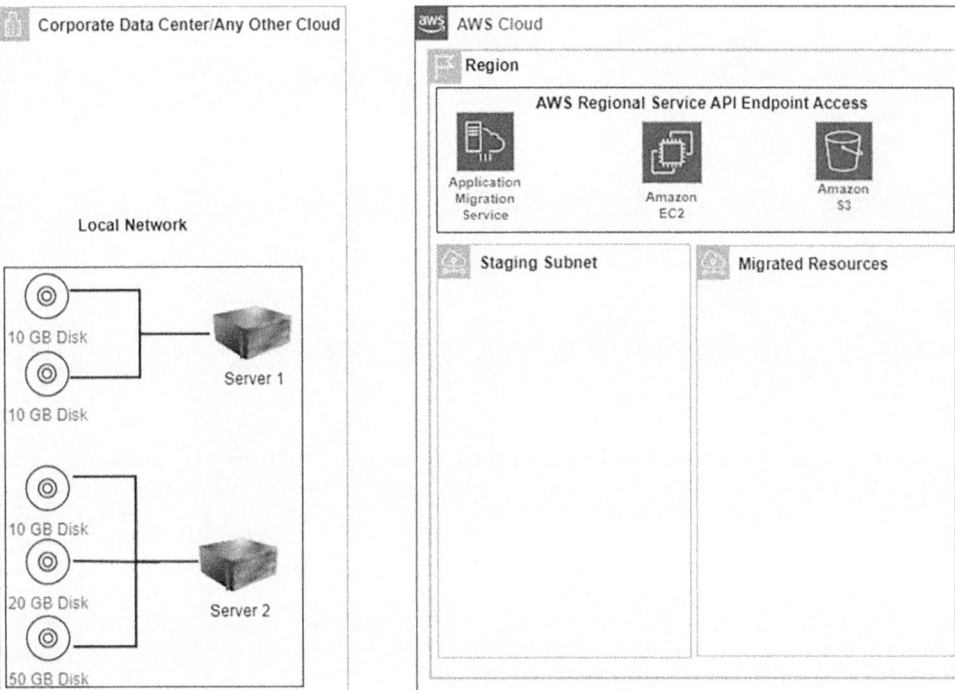

FIGURE 11.5 AWS MGN Source and Target Environments.

To initiate the migration, the AWS Replication Agent is installed on the source servers. This installation is straightforward, unattended, and does not require a server reboot. Once installed, the agent performs an encrypted handshake using TLS 1.3 with the Application Migration Service API, registering the source servers with the service. This registration automatically provisions the staging area subnet within AWS, which serves as a low-cost environment to keep the data synchronized.

The AWS MGN architecture with the AWS Replication Agent can be seen in Figure 11.6.

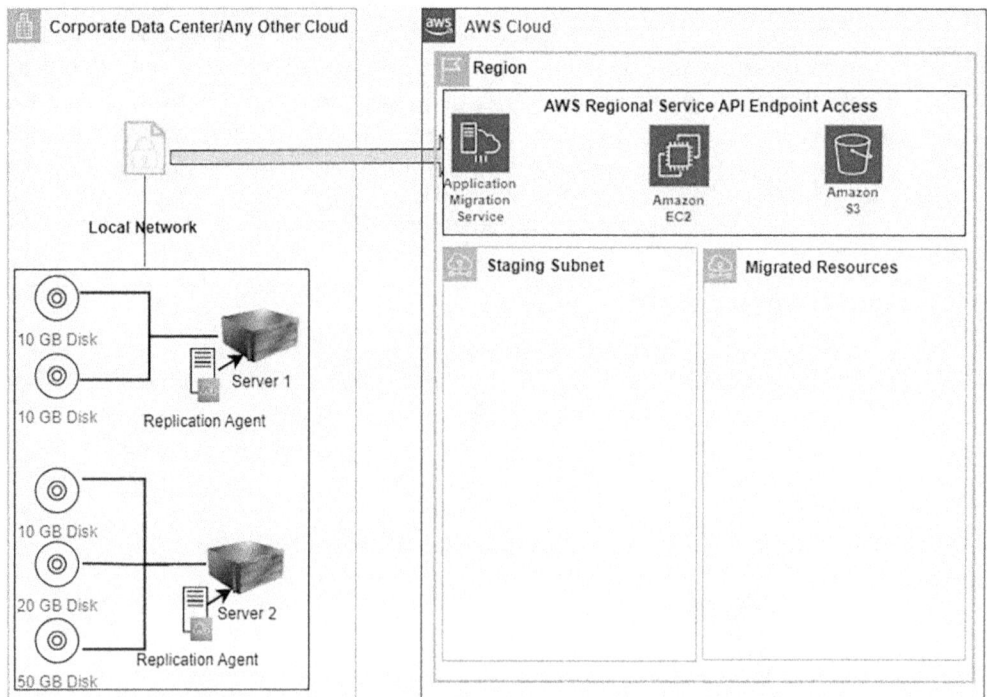

FIGURE 11.6 AWS Application Migration Service with AWS Replication Agent.

The staging area subnet uses low-cost compute and storage to keep the data from the source environment in sync on AWS. The staging area subnet consists of the following resources:

- *Replication servers*: These are lightweight Amazon Elastic Compute Cloud (EC2) instances.
- *Staging volumes*: These are low-cost Amazon Elastic Block Store (EBS) volumes.
- *Amazon EBS snapshots*: These are incremental EBS snapshots.

The AWS MGN architecture with added replication servers can be seen in Figure 11.7.

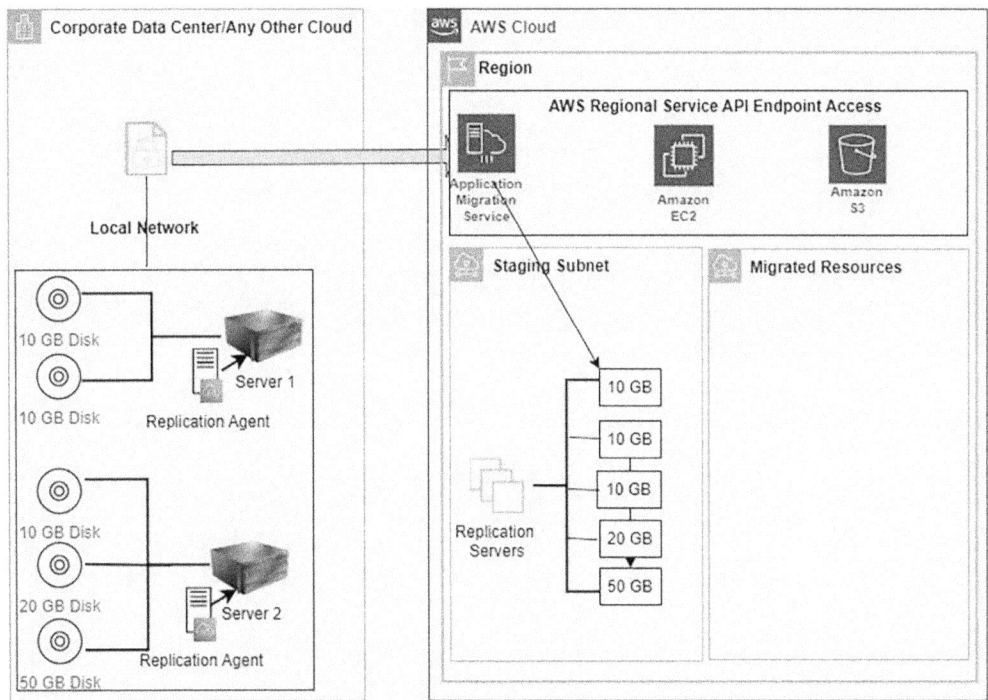

FIGURE 11.7 AWS Application Migration Service with Added Replication Servers.

For every source disk, the service creates an equivalent Amazon EBS volume in the staging area, ensuring precise data synchronization. In this example, the five replicating source disks result in five equivalent EBS volumes attached to the staging area replication servers.

The AWS MGN architecture with added replication servers and data encryption can be seen in Figure 11.8.

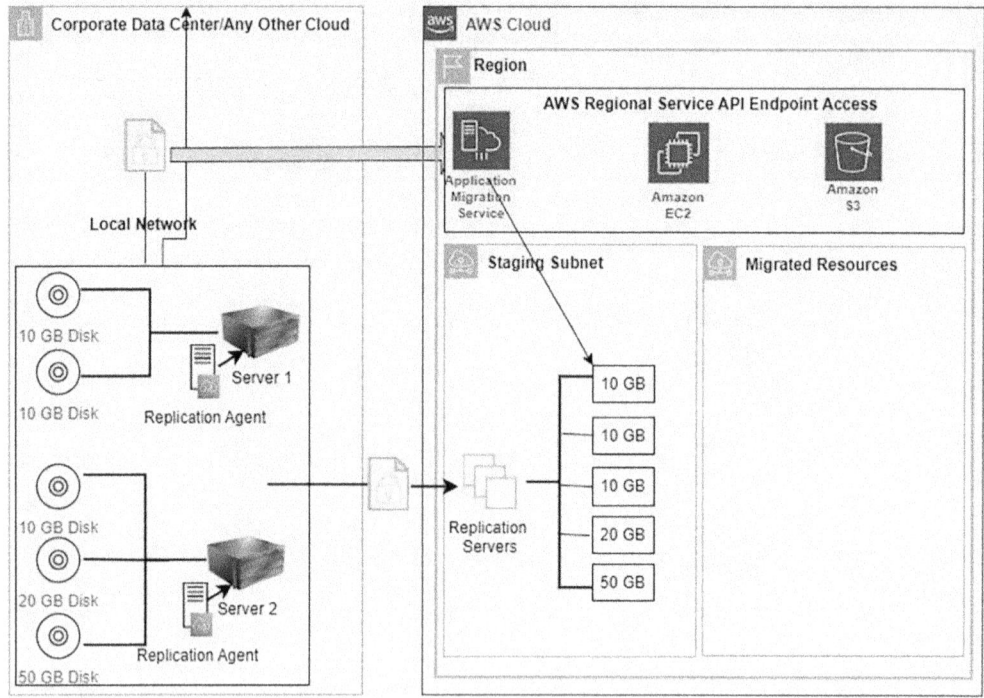

FIGURE 11.8 AWS Application Migration Service with Added Replication Servers and Data Encryption.

The replication process begins with an initial sync, during which all data from the source server is transferred to the staging volumes. Following this, continuous replication tracks and replicates changes asynchronously. The data is securely transmitted using AES 256-bit encryption in transit and can be encrypted at rest in AWS.

The service automatically manages the staging area subnet resources, scaling resources up or down as needed based on concurrently replicating source servers and disks. This means no maintenance operations are required from the user to manage the staging area subnet. AWS MGN servers are ephemeral resources and are automatically rotated from time to time by the service.

Important information to note includes:

- Replication servers use t3.small Linux instances by default with T3 unlimited pricing enabled.
- A general rule of thumb is that one replication server can handle up to 15 concurrently replicating disks.

- Data is compressed and encrypted in transit using an AES 256-bit encryption key by default. It can also be encrypted at rest in your AWS Region using Amazon EBS encryption.

Replication starts with an initial sync. During the initial sync, the agent replicates all of the content on the source disks to EBS volumes in the staging area subnet. In parallel, the agent tracks and continuously replicates data rights as they occur and asynchronously replicates the data to the relevant resource in the staging area subnet. Continuous replication continues indefinitely after the initial sync is complete.

Once the replication is underway, launch settings are configured. These settings define how and where the migrated instances will be launched in AWS, including the choice of subnet, security groups, instance type, volume type, and associated tags. After the initial synchronization is complete, the source servers are marked as *Ready for Testing*, allowing users to test or perform a cutover by launching instances. The launch process involves spinning up a temporary conversion server that adapts the migrated instance to run natively on AWS by modifying drivers, network configurations, and operating system licenses.

The AWS MGN architecture with a conversion server can be seen in Figure 11.9.

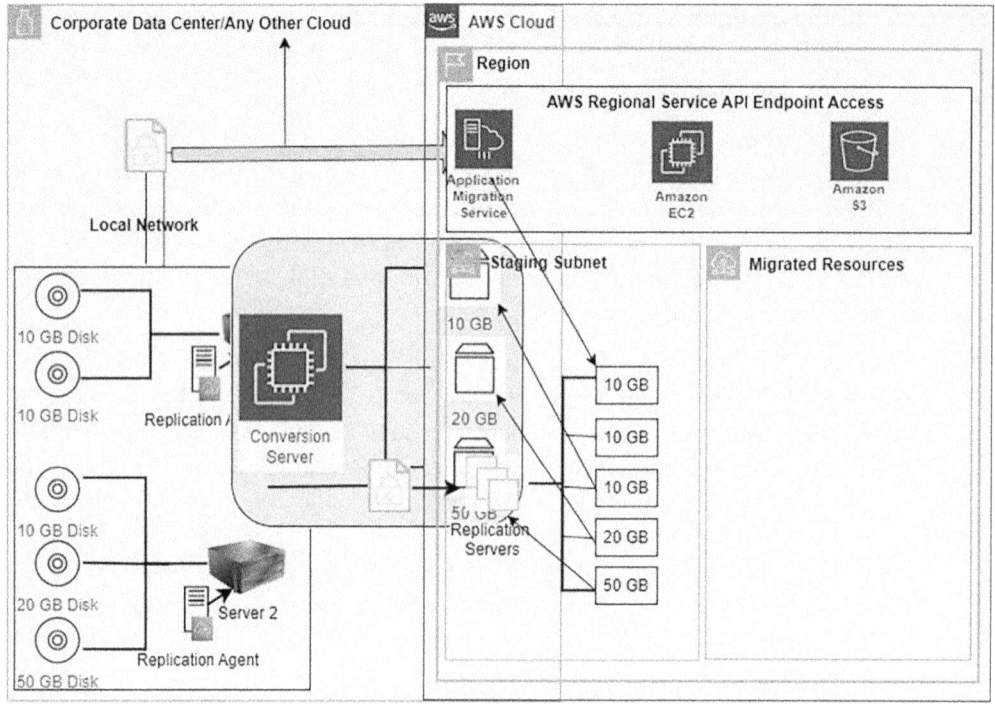

FIGURE 11.9 AWS Application Migration Service Architecture with Conversion Server.

Unlike the replication servers, which are active as long as replication is active, the conversion server is spun up only for the specific purpose of converting servers during the launch process and is then immediately terminated. After the conversion is complete, the new instance is spun up on AWS and ready for use. Note that the volumes attached to the launched instance represent the source servers' state at the time of the launch.

The AWS MGN architecture with migrated resources can be seen in Figure 11.10.

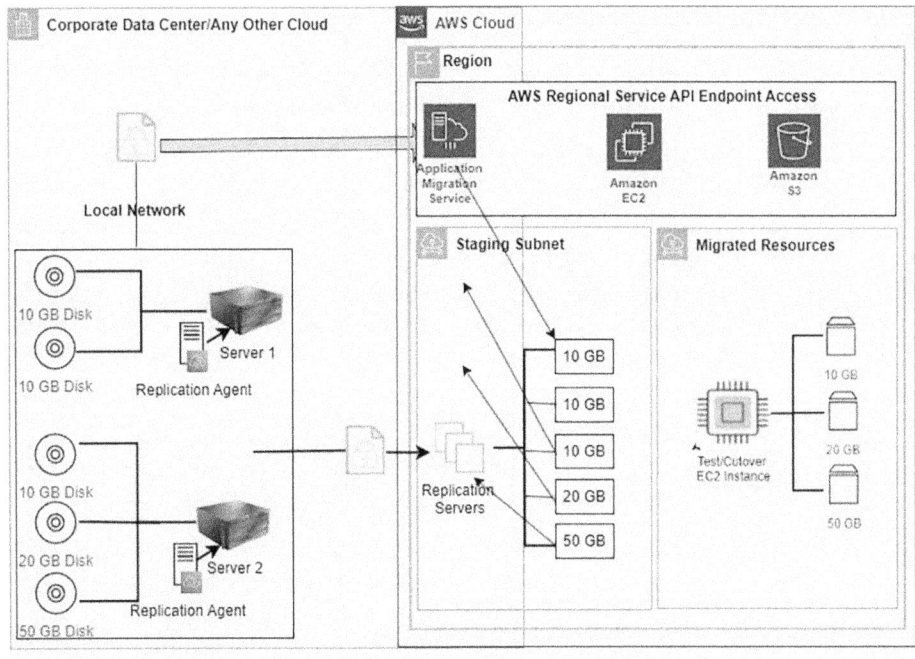

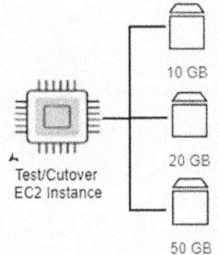

FIGURE 11.10 AWS Application Migration Service Architecture with Migrated Resources.

Once the instance is launched, it reflects the state of the source server at the time of launch. Continuous replication from the source server to the staging area continues, but these updates do not affect the launched instance. Each new test or cutover instance reflects the most recent replicated data, allowing users to test deployments without interrupting the ongoing replication or source server operations.

Setting Up Network Connectivity to Run AWS MGN Properly

To run AWS MGN, the network connectivity architecture needs to be set up properly to ensure smooth replication and migration:

- The first critical connectivity requirement is between the source servers and the AWS MGN API endpoints. This connectivity must allow communication on port 443 between the AWS replication agent installed on the source servers and the AWS MGN endpoint. This connection is essential for authentication, configuration, and monitoring. It must be maintained throughout the replication process, including during the installation of the AWS replication agent. Since the communication is over HTTPS, it can be configured to go through a Web proxy using standard settings on the source server. Additionally, you need to allow connectivity between the source servers and Amazon S3, enabling the AWS replication agent to retrieve necessary software components from an S3 bucket.

- The second aspect of connectivity involves the source servers and the staging area subnet. The AWS replication agent sends data from the source servers directly to the replication servers in the staging area subnet over port 1500. Therefore, it is crucial to allow connectivity on port 1500 for continuous data replication between the source servers and the replication servers.

- The third requirement is for connectivity out of the staging area. The AWS MGN replication and conversion servers, which are launched within the staging area subnet, must maintain continuous communication with the AWS MGN API endpoints on port 443 for ongoing authentication, configuration, and monitoring. This connection is necessary as long as the replication process is active. Additionally, the staging area servers need to have connectivity to Amazon S3 to download any software and configuration files needed during the replication or conversion process.

- Finally, one of the roles of the replication server is to issue API calls to take snapshots of the staging EBS volumes during the replication process. To accomplish this, connectivity to an EC2 API endpoint on port 443 must also be established. This enables the replication server to trigger the snapshot process for the volumes in the staging area. This connectivity ensures that the migration process is efficient and smooth, maintaining the integrity and synchronization of the data throughout the entire operation.

The AWS MGN architecture with a cutover instance can be seen in Figure 11.11.

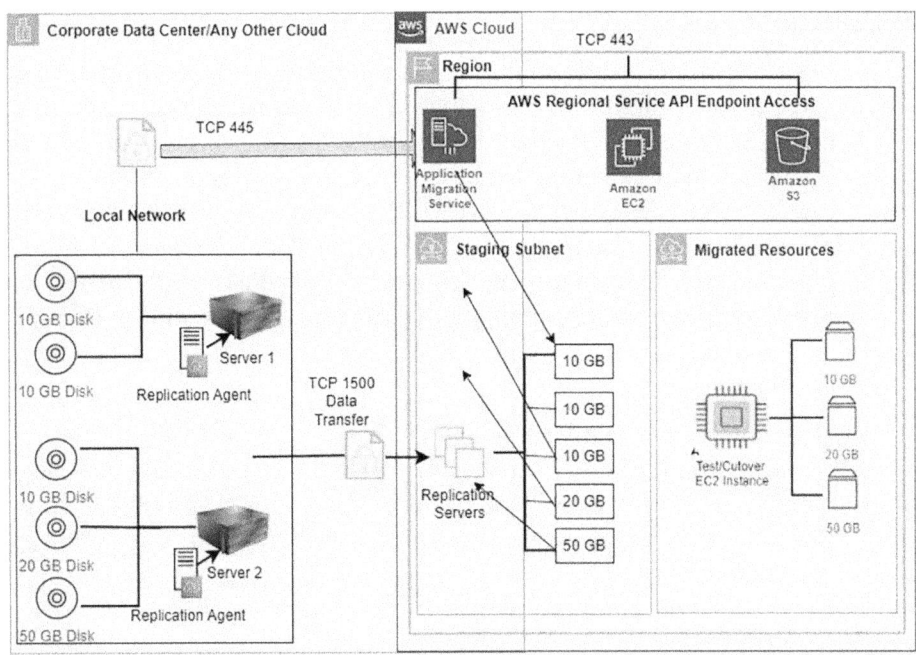

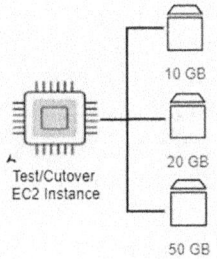

FIGURE 11.11 AWS Application Migration Service Architecture with Cutover Instance.

KPIS FOR SUCCESSFUL IMPLEMENTATION

There are five key activities that are crucial for the successful implementation of AWS migration. By carefully following the detailed steps for each phase, you can achieve a seamless and efficient migration with minimal risk and optimal performance.

Implementation

These activities include identifying the source servers that need to be migrated and grouping them into waves based on workload priorities, dependencies, or business needs. Once the identification and grouping are completed, it is essential to set a cutover date for each wave, which determines when the migration process for that wave will be finalized. This structured approach ensures better resource allocation by systematically organizing the migration process and promotes project continuity by dividing the workload into manageable phases, thereby avoiding confusion and last-minute rush.

Initial Replication

During the initial replication phase, it is important to install the migration agent only on the servers involved in the current wave. This step helps avoid network overloading by limiting replication activities to the planned wave and ensures optimal use of network bandwidth without impacting existing applications.

Ready for Testing

To ensure a successful AWS migration, it is essential to confirm that data replication has reached a *Healthy* status, indicating that the replicated data is synchronized and consistent. Once this is achieved, the wave should be marked as *Ready for Testing* before proceeding further. This step is crucial as it guarantees that instances can only be launched after the initial replication is complete, thereby ensuring data consistency. Additionally, it provides a solid foundation for testing without the risk of data corruption or missing configurations, which are critical for maintaining the integrity and reliability of the migration process.

Testing

For a smooth migration process, it is essential to launch test instances of the migrated workloads 1–2 weeks before the planned cutover date. During this period, rigorous testing should be performed to validate application functionality, data integrity, and performance within the new environment. This approach allows ample time to identify and address any potential issues, such as misconfigurations, connectivity problems, or performance bottlenecks, before the final cutover. By proactively addressing these challenges, the risk of unforeseen failures during the critical migration phase is significantly reduced, ensuring a seamless transition to the new environment.

Cutover

To complete the AWS migration successfully, it is important to confirm that data replication has once again reached a *Healthy* status and is marked *Ready for Cutover*. Once this is verified, the cutover process can be executed to transition production workloads to the migrated environment. This step is critical as it helps to shorten the cutover window, minimizing downtime for end-users or customers. Additionally, it ensures a seamless transition with minimal disruption to business operations, maintaining continuity and reducing potential impacts on productivity.

The KPIs for successful implementation can be seen in Figure 11.12.

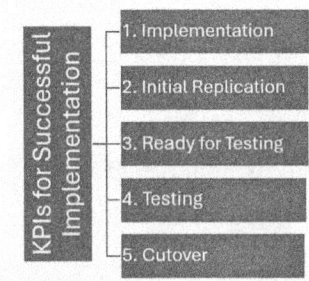

FIGURE 11.12 KPIs for successful implementation.

LAB: AWS APPLICATION MIGRATION SERVICE TUTORIAL

Case Study

We are migrating an on-premises-based WordPress server into a AWS cloud environment located in AWS US East North Virginia.

The on-premises to AWS migration can be seen in Figure 11.13.

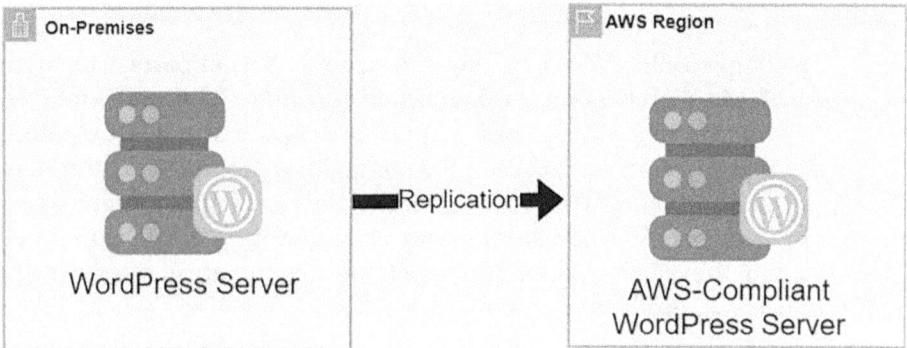

FIGURE 11.13 On-Premises Environment to AWS Region Migration.

We need to follow the steps outlined below to complete this exercise.

Prerequisites

We need to complete two important network settings and ensure the following before starting the migration process:

- Set up the source server:
  1. *Access to Amazon S3*: For downloading agent components.
  2. *Access to Application Migration Service API endpoint*: For control messages and status updates.
  3. *Firewall configuration*: Open outbound TCP port 443 for both S3 and API endpoint communication.
  4. *Staging subnet access*: Allow outbound TCP port 1500 to the staging subnet's network IP CIDR for data transmission.

All data transmission occurs over a secure TLS 1.3 AES-256 encrypted tunnel.

- Configure the staging area subnet:
  1. *TCP port 1500 inbound*: Allow to complete the connection from the agent to the replication server.
  2. *Access to Amazon S3*: For downloading required software components.
  3. *Access to Application Migration Service API endpoint*: For control communication.
  4. *Access to Amazon EC2 API endpoint*: For operational purposes.

Step 1: Creating an IAM User

An IAM user is created to facilitate the migration process by generating the necessary AWS credentials. These credentials are used to install the AWS Replication Agent on the source server. Once installed, the Replication Agent establishes a connection between the source server and AWS Application Migration Service, allowing the server to be added to the service for continuous data replication:

1. *Access IAM*: Search for IAM in the AWS services search bar and select it.
2. *Add user*: From the IAM console, go to Users and click Add user.
3. *Set username*: Enter a name (e.g., demo-user) and proceed by clicking Next.
4. *Set permissions*: On the Permissions screen, choose Attach policies directly and filter for AWSApplicationMigrationAgentPolicy. Select it and click Next.
5. *Review and create*: Review the settings, add tags if desired, and click Create user.
6. *Retrieve credentials*: Download the CSV file or copy the access and secret keys directly.
7. *Generate access keys*: In the user configuration panel, go to the Security credentials tab, select Create access key, and choose the use case Application running outside AWS.
8. *Tag keys (optional)*: Tag the keys (e.g., demo-keys) for easier management and click Create access key.
9. *Save keys*: Download the keys or securely save them, as the secret key will not be shown again.

Step 2: Accessing the Application Migration Service Console

1. Go to the AWS Management Console, select Services, and choose Application Migration Service to open the dashboard.

Step 3: First Time Setup (Replication Template/Tags)

1. Clicking the Get Started button for the first time will automatically direct you to the Setup page and you will be prompted to create a Replication Settings template.

2. The Replication Settings determine how data will be replicated from source servers to AWS. To access or update it, go to Settings in the left navigation pane. Review and adjust the following options:

   Subnet: Choose your staging area subnet or use the default.

   Replication Server Instance Type: The default is t3.small, but you can modify it based on your needs.

   EBS Volume Type: Modify for cost or performance if disks are over 500 GB.

   EBS Encryption: This is enabled by default for encrypted data at rest.

   Security Group: Use the default or specify your own for traffic control.

   Data Routing: Choose public or private IP for replication communication or enable Site-to-Site VPN/Direct Connect for private IP.

   Throttling: Limit network bandwidth if needed.

   Custom Tags: Apply tags for resource identification, such as billing.

   After reviewing, click Create template to save the configuration. This completes the setup.

Step 4: Configuring the Launch Template

Before installing the AWS Replication Agent, you can set up the launch template, which preconfigures settings for source servers. The template applies to newly added servers, not those already in the Application Migration Service console. After adding a source server, you can modify its launch settings at any time. The launch template includes three sections: general launch settings, default EC2 launch template, and MAP program tagging:

1. Access the launch template:

   Open the Application Migration Service console, navigate to the Settings option in the navigation pane, and select the Launch Template tab.

2. Review and edit launch template settings:

   The launch template has three sections:
   - *General Launch Settings*: Configure default launch options.
   - *Default EC2 Launch Template*: Define EC2 instance settings for target servers.

- *MAP Program Tagging*: Set tags for resources if participating in the Migration Acceleration Program (MAP).

Click Edit to begin customization.

3. General Launch Settings configuration:
   - *Instance Type Right-Sizing*: Enable this option to let AWS MGN select the best-matching instance type based on source server hardware (optional).
   - *Start Instance upon Launch*: Choose whether to start test or cutover instances automatically after launch or leave them in a stopped state.
   - *Copy Private IP*: Enable this to replicate the source server's private IP on the target instance (optional).
   - *Transfer Server Tags*: Allow the transfer of custom tags from source servers to the target instances and resources (optional).
   - *Operating System Licensing*: Select BYOL for Linux servers or if you want to bring your own license (e.g., RHEL, SUSE, Debian). Choose AWS-Provided License for other scenarios.

4. Default EC2 Launch Template settings:
   - *Target Subnet*: Select the target subnet for launching test and cutover instances.
   - *Security Groups*: Assign at least one security group to allow traffic for the test and cutover machines.
   - *Default Instance Type*: Choose an EC2 instance type for the target servers. This will be overridden if Instance Type Right-Sizing is enabled.
   - *EBS Volume Type*: Select the desired volume type (e.g., gp3, io1, or io2). The default is gp3.

5. MAP Program Tagging (optional):
   - If participating in MAP, configure tags to help track migrated resources. Enter the tag value for map-migrated, which will automatically be applied to eligible resources.

6. Save the template:
   - Once all desired settings are configured, click Save Template to finalize the changes. This completes the launch template configuration.

Step 5: Creating the WordPress Content and Installing the AWS Replication Agent

With the replication settings and launch template ready, proceed to install the agent. For this workshop, a preconfigured training machine has been set up. From the EC2 dashboard, select Launch Instance and search for Application Migration Service Workshop Training. Verify that the AMI name and owner match the provided details, even if the AMI ID differs. Note that the WordPress server is configured for unsecured HTTP access over TCP port 80, solely for this exercise. A video demonstration will guide you through adding content to the WordPress site and installing the AWS Replication Agent:

1. Launch the source server instance:
   - Open the AWS Management Console and search for EC2.
   - Navigate to AMI Catalog in the EC2 dashboard.
   - Search for AWS MGN Workshop under the Community AMIs tab.
   - Verify that the AMI owner's field ends with 3848 and select it.
   - Click Launch Instance with AMI and provide a name for the instance.

2. Configure instance settings:
   - Use the default instance type (t2.micro is suitable for this demo).
   - Choose a key pair or create a new one for SSH access.
   - In Network settings, allow HTTP traffic and, optionally, HTTPS traffic.
   - Select the desired VPC and subnet, and enable Auto-assign public IP.
   - Configure a security group to allow inbound SSH and HTTP traffic.
   - Leave other options at their defaults and click Launch Instance.

3. Access the instance:
   - Once the instance is launched, wait for the status check to display 2/2 checks passed.
   - Locate the public IPv4 address of the instance from the details panel.
   - Open the IP address in your browser to verify the setup (avoid using HTTPS as no certificate is configured).

4. Test the WordPress setup:
   - Interact with the WordPress site by adding a comment, name, and email address.
   - Confirm that your comment is posted and return to the AWS Management Console.

5. Connect via SSH:
   - From the EC2 Instances panel, choose Connect and select the SSH Client tab.
   - Follow the instructions to connect to the instance using SSH.
   - Keep the SSH session open for subsequent steps.
6. Install AWS Replication Agent:
   - In the AWS Management Console, search for Application Migration Service and select Get started.
   - On the Add server page, configure the source server details:
     - Select the operating system.
     - Choose the disks to replicate.
     - Provide IAM access credentials (set up or retrieve credentials as needed).
   - Copy the provided installation command and execute it in the SSH terminal to install the Replication Agent.
7. Complete the configuration:
   - After installation, execute the provided configuration command in the terminal.
   - Wait for the terminal to display Finished after syncing with the Application Migration Service console.
   - Return to the Application Migration Service console to finalize the setup.
8. Begin replication:
   - Monitor the replication initialization, which may take 10 minutes to several hours, depending on the workload.

Step 6: Configuring the Launch Settings

You've set up a launch template with global migration settings; however, individual servers may require unique configurations. Now that replication is underway, configure the launch settings for the source server. These settings dictate how an instance of the source server will be launched. Adjustments can be made after launching a test or cutover instance, but changes require relaunching the instance to take effect. To configure, go to the Source Servers page, select the source server, and access the Server Details page. Follow the video demonstration to configure launch settings for a single server:

1. Access the launch settings:
   - Navigate to the Source Servers page.
   - Select the server by its hostname and choose Launch Settings.
2. Modify the general launch settings:
   - *Turn off Instance Type Right-Sizing*: AWS will not auto select an instance type; you will define it in the EC2 launch template.
   - *Start Instance*: Decide whether the instance should start automatically or remain stopped (set to Stop for this demo).
   - *Private IP Option*: Set to No to assign a new private IP to the migrated instance.
   - *Tags*: Enable transferring tags if the source server exists in AWS.
   - *OS Licensing*: Choose BYOL for Linux or AWS license-included for Windows (depending on your setup).
   - Save the changes.
3. Modify the EC2 launch template:
   - In the EC2 Launch Template section, choose Modify to edit parameters.
   - Define the instance type (set to m5.large for this demo).
   - Add a custom resource tag.
   - Enable a public IP address on launch.
   - Avoid changing parameters such as key pair, certain network, and storage options (refer to the documentation).
4. Save the template changes:
   - Save the changes as a new template version by selecting Create template version.
   - Set the latest template version as default:
     - Go to the Launch Templates page, select the template name, and choose Actions > Set Default Version.
5. Verify the changes:
   - Return to the Launch Settings page. Confirm that the updated instance type and settings are reflected in the EC2 launch template.

6. Next steps:
   - The configured settings will apply when launching test or cutover instances.

   This completes the launch settings configuration.

Step 7: Launching a Test Instance

Ensure your instance status is Ready for testing under the Lifecycle section on the Migration dashboard. In the Source Servers window, select your server, choose Test and Cutover, and click Launch test instances:

1. Prepare for testing:
   - Perform the test launch at least 1 week before migration to identify and resolve issues.
   - On the Source Servers page, ensure that the following settings are shown:
     - *Migration lifecycle status*: Ready for testing.
     - *Data replication status*: Healthy, with no replication lag.
     - *Next step status*: Launch test instance.
2. Launch the test instance:
   - Select the source server (or multiple servers for batch testing).
   - From the Test and Cutover dropdown, choose Launch test instances.
   - Confirm the launch prompt and select Launch.
   - Monitor the progress via the View job details banner.
3. Verify the test instance:
   - Check the Job log for sub-tasks such as snapshot creation and conversion.
   - Navigate to the Source Servers page. The statuses should update:
     - *Alerts status*: Launched.
     - *Migration lifecycle status*: Test in progress.
     - *Next step status*: Complete testing and mark as Ready for cutover.
   - Review the test EC2 instance in the console:
     - Confirm the instance type (e.g., m5.large) and custom tags.
     - Copy the public IP to verify WordPress functionality via a Web browser.

- Log in via SSH using the same credentials as the source server.
4. Finalize testing:
    - In the Application Migration Service console, select the server.
    - From the Test and Cutover dropdown, choose Mark as Ready for cutover.
    - Decide whether to terminate the test instance:
        - For this demonstration, terminate the instance.
        - Select Continue.
5. Completion:
    - A banner confirms the instance termination and readiness for cutover.
    - The test is now complete.Top of FormBottom of Form

Step 8: Launching a Cutover Instance

Once the source server is ready for cutover, you will follow a similar procedure to testing. You will launch a cutover instance and validate the state of the launched instance. If the launch fails, you can revert to Ready for Cutover, and if successful, finalize the cutover. Cutover means that the launched instance is now live and should have replaced your source server as the active production instance:

1. Verify the server status:
    - Check that the Migration lifecycle status is Ready for cutover.
    - Ensure that Data replication status is Healthy with no lag.
    - Confirm that the next step is Launch cutover instance.
2. Launch the cutover instance:
    - Select your server(s) from the Source Servers page.
    - Under Test and Cutover, choose Launch cutover instances.
    - Confirm and start the launch.
3. Monitor the job status:
    - View the job details to track progress.
4. Verify the instance:
    - Check the EC2 instance in the Migration dashboard.
    - Verify functionality (e.g., WordPress) using the public IP.

5. Finalize the cutover:
   - In Application Migration Service, select the server and choose Finalize cutover.
   - Confirm that data replication stops and replication servers terminate.
6. Complete the migration:
   - Mark the source server as archived.

   The migration is now complete!

Step 9: Applications and Waves

AWS MGN introduces the concept of an application, which enables you to group and manage servers as a single application. This helps handle dependencies such as network configurations and security policies effectively. Users can perform bulk actions, migrate servers as one unit, monitor their aggregated status, and configure the application environment seamlessly.

A wave in MGN enables users to group applications and perform bulk operations on applications and servers. Waves help customers plan, implement, and monitor migrations by organizing applications to be migrated together within a specified time frame. Grouping is based on customer migration needs and not on application dependencies. Users can add applications, associate servers, and migrate them in a single wave. You can find more details about the servers of an application by selecting the wave from the wave's dashboard. The wave details page will have three tabs: Applications, Source servers, and Tags.

To create an application and add servers:

1. Navigate to Applications from the navigation pane.
2. On the Applications page, click Add Application.
3. Provide the application name and an optional description.
4. From the Servers dropdown, select the source servers to add (only unassociated servers are listed).
5. Optionally, add tags to the application.
6. Click Add Application.
7. Review the application's details, including migration status, alerts, and the number of associated servers.

8. Use the Actions dropdown to:
   - Launch test or cutover instances.
   - Revert the status (e.g., Ready for Testing, Ready for Cutover).
   - Finalize cutover or add the application to a wave.

To create a wave and associate applications:

1. Navigate to Waves in the navigation pane.
2. Click Add Wave.
3. Provide a wave name and an optional description.
4. From the Applications dropdown, select applications to associate (only unassociated applications are listed).
5. Optionally, add tags to the wave.
6. Click **Add Wave.**

To manage and monitor the wave:

1. In the Waves section, review details such as migration status, alerts, and the number of associated applications.
2. Select the wave name, then use the Actions dropdown to:
   - Launch test instances for application servers.
   - Finalize or monitor cutover processes.

To view the wave details:

1. On the Wave details page, view:
   - *Applications tab*:
     - Color-coded pie charts show the health status of applications and the cutover status of servers.
   - *Source Servers tab*:
     - Charts on server health, replication status, and migration lifecycle.
2. Scroll to the bottom of each tab to see detailed lists of applications and source servers.

Step 10: Post-Migration Modernization

The post-migration modernization feature enables disaster recovery configuration, OS upgrades, subscription conversions, and custom actions using AWS Systems Manager documents. It uses an account-wide post-launch template to manage post-launch settings for newly added servers. These settings, created automatically, control actions performed after a server is launched in AWS. Users can modify the template or server-specific settings anytime and run predefined or custom actions via AWS Systems Manager. The post-launch template and the post-launch settings of any source server can be modified at any time.

Access and Activate Post-Launch Actions

1. Go to Settings in the navigation pane and select the Post-launch Template tab.
2. Click Edit to configure post-launch actions.
3. Toggle to activate the feature, which installs the Systems Manager Agent:
   - Ensure proper networking and permissions for communication with Systems Manager endpoints (e.g., security groups permitting port 443).
4. Choose a deployment option:
   - Run actions on Test and Cutover instances (recommended), Cutovers only, or Test instances only.

Configure Custom Actions

1. Click Add custom action at the bottom of the post-launch template.
2. Provide a name for the custom action.
3. Select a Systems Manager Document (SSM Document) to run (e.g., AWS-RunPatchBaseline for patching).
4. Choose a document version: Latest, Default, or a specific version.
5. Specify:
   - Order Number (1,001–10,000 for execution sequence).
   - Target Operating System (Windows, Linux, or both).
6. Optionally, select Activate this custom action and whether the action must complete successfully before finalizing the migration.
7. Configure action-specific parameters based on the selected SSM document and click Add Action.

Select Predefined Modernization Actions

1. Choose predefined actions to include:
   - *Disaster Recovery*: Installs AWS Elastic Disaster Recovery Agent and configures replication to a target region.
   - *Operating System Migration*: Converts CentOS 8 to Rocky Linux.
   - *License Conversion*: Switches SUSE Linux subscriptions to AWS-provided subscriptions.
2. For Disaster Recovery, select the target AWS Region (e.g., us-east-1) where instances will be replicated.
3. Save the template.

Monitor Post-Launch Actions

1. Launch a test or cutover instance for a server with post-launch settings.
2. Monitor the results on the Source Servers Details page:
   - For detailed logs, click the action name to view it in the AWS Systems Manager console.

Additional Notes

- Post-launch settings only apply to new servers added after configuring the template.
- For existing replicated servers, modify their post-launch actions via the Post-launch Settings tab on their details page.

This streamlined process ensures effective post-migration modernization and management of your servers.

Step 11: Cleaning Up After Final Cutover

Once you complete migration or cut over the source server, you need to remove all unnecessary resources so that your account does not continue to accumulate charges from running the server:

- Select the source server and then choose the Actions drop-down menu. Select Mark as Archived. Confirm by choosing Archive.

DATABASE MIGRATION

Overview of Amazon Database Migration (DMS)

AWS Database Migration Service (DMS) is a highly efficient cloud-based service that allows database migrations to be done to AWS in seamless manner. Designed to support both homogeneous (same database engine) and heterogeneous (different database engines) migrations, DMS is the tool for the organizations that want minimal downtime and disruption during the migration process. This service is particularly beneficial for companies looking to move their on-premises databases to the cloud or shift between different database engines to take advantage of cost savings, scalability, and performance enhancements offered by AWS.

AWS DMS helps you migrate relational databases, data warehouses, NoSQL databases, and other types of data stores into the AWS cloud or between combinations of cloud and on-premises setups.

Some of the supported environments from DMS are:

- *RDBMS*: Oracle, PostgreSQL, MySQL, SQL Server, Sybase, and Db2
- *Data warehouse services*: Amazon Redshift
- *NoSQL database services*: Amazon DynamoDB and MongoDB.

AWS DMS supports object storage services such as Amazon Simple Storage Service (Amazon S3) and several AWS stream services, such as Amazon Kinesis and Amazon Managed Streaming for Apache Kafka (Amazon MSK).

The source and target environments can be seen in Figure 11.14.

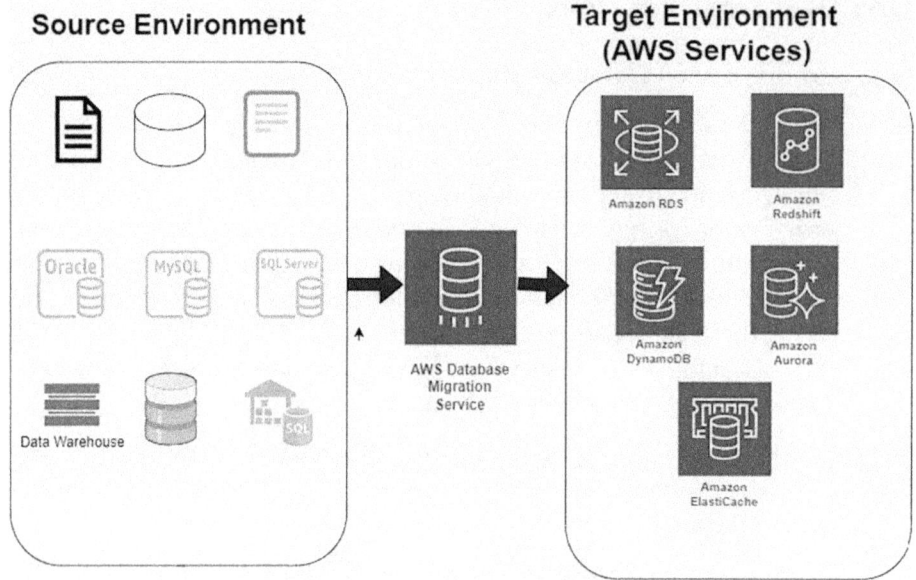

FIGURE 11.14 Source and Target Environments.

DMS is integral to the broader strategy of cloud migration, aligning with the three-phase approach commonly used in migrations: assess, mobilize, and migrate and modernize. The structured methodology ensures that migrations are carefully planned, resources effectively used, and the migration is carried out, followed by modernization efforts to fine-tune the new environment.

DETERMINING THE RIGHT TOOL OR APPROACH FOR DATABASE MIGRATION

Choosing the right migration option depends on the circumstances. When the source and target data stores are using the same database management system (e.g., Oracle to Oracle or MySQL to MySQL), you can generally migrate data by means of the features and tools of the data store. For instance, in the case of the MySQL server, you can use the MySQL tool *mysqldump* for importing/exporting data and binary log (binlog) replication for data synchronizing. This migration approach is called homogenous migration. Using the original tools for the homogenous migration is frequently the most cost-effective and the best performing, especially for open-source databases such as MySQL and PostgreSQL, since they eliminate the need for additional software.

Migration between different database system (e.g., Oracle to MySQL) is a much more difficult process because of differences in data format and the uniqueness of every database engine. This challenge increases when migrating between RDBMS and NoSQL systems due to their fundamentally different storage methods. . This kind of migration method is known as heterogeneous migration. AWS DMS is highly recommended for heterogeneous migrations as it supports these complex scenarios

In addition to homogeneous or heterogeneous migration, when migrating data across data stores, there are various methods and tools. Determining which tool to use depends on whether you want to migrate data physically or logically and migrate online or offline. AWS DMS is one of the logical data migration methods, and you can use it for both online and offline migrations:

- *Physical data migration*: Physical data migration involves migrating data files from the source data store to target the data store directly (often without format conversion). These methods are typically used for homogeneous migration.
- *Logical data migration*: Logical data migration methods migrate data logically retrieved from a data store, for example, with a SELECT statement, and write it to a target data store. These methods are used for both homogeneous and heterogeneous migration.
- *Online data migration*: Online data migration methods incur zero or minimal downtime and can use either physical or logical migration methods.
- *Offline data migration*: Offline data migration methods will incur downtime on the source database as part of the migration process. It can use either physical or logical migration methods.

Three-Phase Approach to Database Migration

Typically, a migration process follows three key phases: assess, mobilize, and migrate and modernize. It is applicable to databases, applications, or entire data centers and helps in minimize risk and maximizing benefits.

Assess Phase

Understanding the existing database environment, dependencies, and the complexity of the migration is the main purpose of this phase. It is the most important phase for creating a detailed migration plan that ensures a seamless transition and reduces downtime. AWS DMS *Fleet Advisor* is the tool that is used in this phase. This thoroughly reviews the source database environment and presents a database inventory, usage patterns, and dependencies. This is the data we need for planning the migration and estimating the required resources.

The core functions of AWS DMS Fleet Advisor are inventory and dependency analysis, migration feasibility study generation, and time and cost estimation.

Mobilize Phase

During this phase, the focus is on setting up the target environment on AWS and ensuring that all the necessary tools and configurations are ready for a smooth migration. AWS Schema Conversion Tool (SCT) is one of the most important components of this phase, primarily for heterogeneous migrations in which the database engine is different (i.e., from Oracle to Amazon Aurora). SCT assists in transforming the source database schema into a format that is compatible with the target database engine. This tool automates much of the conversion process, reducing manual effort and potential errors. The key activities of AWS SCT are schema conversion, target environment setup, and testing and validation.

Migrate and Modernize Phase

This final phase is where the actual data migration occurs. During this phase, databases are moved from the source to the target environment, and modernization objectives are achieved to configure the new environment for the best performance, cost, and scalability.

AWS DMS is the primary service for the actual migration process. DMS can do both full load migrations (migrating the whole database) and continuous data replication, thus minimal downtime is ensured.

The key activities of DMS during this phase are given below:

- *Full load migration*: This is when the whole database is moved, including schema, data, and objects, from the source to the target. It is a challenging process and needs to be managed very carefully for successful completion.

- *Continuous data replication*: DMS can efficiently replicate any change that happens during the ongoing process from the source database to the target database. It ensures that the target database has the latest information from the source database continuously throughout the migration.

- *Modernization*: The workflow from the legacy system to the target is cumbersome. Post-migration, the target database environment can be optimized by means of AWS-native features such as auto-scaling, managed backups, and performance monitoring tools.

As you can see, AWS owns a plethora of tools and services that are used together with DMS and support various aspects of database migration. These tools make it possible to streamline the migration process and ensure that migrations are successful:

- *DMS Fleet Advisor*: As discussed earlier, this is primarily used in the assessment stage. It assists companies in gaining knowledge about their database landscape and making them ready for the migration by providing detailed insights into the source environment.
- *AWS SCT*: This is a crucial element for heterogeneous migrations, when the database engine is different in the source and target environment. It does almost everything in the schema conversion process, translating the source engine's database schemas, stored procedures, and other database objects to the target engine.
- *AWS DMS*: This is the most important tool for executing the database migration. It deals with data migration and replication with little downtime, which is why it can be considered as fundamental for any database migration.

Native Database Migration Tools

At times, native database migration tools that are offered by database vendors may be used, especially when the migrations are homogeneous. These tools are usually well known and can be a great help for DBAs since they can reduce the migration process for some databases. Some examples of such tools are Oracle Data Pump, SQL Server Migration Assistant, and MySQL's mysqldump.

Different Types of Database Migration

There are two different types of database migration:

- Homogeneous migration
- Heterogeneous migration

The choice between homogeneous and heterogeneous migrations depends on the business's objectives and the source and target database environment.

Homogeneous Migration

In homogeneous database migration, both the source and target database have the same database engine (e.g., Oracle to Oracle or SQL Server to SQL Server). These migrations are quite simple because the database structures and syntax remain consistent.

Homogeneous database migrations can be seen in Figure 11.15.

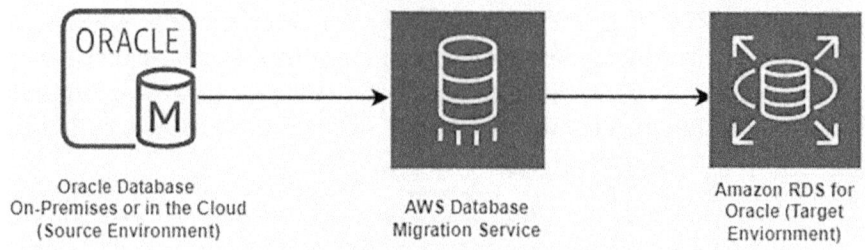

FIGURE 11.15 Homogeneous Database Migrations.

Tools used in these migrations include:

- *Native migration tools*: Tools such as Oracle Data Pump, SQL Server Management Studio (SSMS), and MySQL mysqldump are commonly used.
- *AWS DMS*: Even though native tools are usually the best option for homogeneous migrations, DMS can still be used, especially when minimal downtime is a priority.

The benefits of these migrations are:

- *Simplicity*: The migration process is straightforward as database engines are not changing.
- *Familiarity*: DBAs and developers are mostly aware about the environment and processes involved.

Heterogeneous Migrations

Heterogeneous migrations are those in which different types of database are used in the source to target environment (e.g., from Oracle to Amazon Aurora or from SQL Server to MySQL). Such migrations are further complicated by the difference in database syntax, schema, and features.

Heterogeneous database migrations can be seen in Figure 11.16.

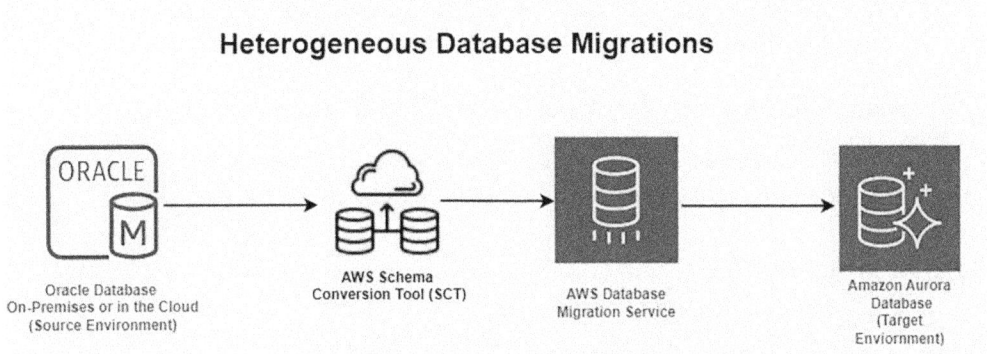

FIGURE 11.16 Heterogeneous Database Migrations.

Tools used in these migrations include:

- *AWS Schema Conversion Tool (SCT)*: This is used for converting schemas and code from the source engine to the target engine.
- *AWS DMS*: This handles data migration, which includes any necessary transformations to ensure that the source and target engines are compatible.

These migrations have some challenges:

- *Complexity*: The discrepancy of the database engines can be an issue in schema conversion, data transformation, and application compatibility.
- *Testing requirements*: Thorough testing is needed to ensure that the migrated database functions correctly in the new environment.

Key Concepts in Database Migration

For a successful migration, you need to understand the concepts of transaction logs and Change Data Capture (CDC).

Transaction Logs

Transaction logs are records of all the changes that have been made to a database, ensuring a sequential order of transactions. They are crucial to ensure data integrity and enable recovery in the event of a failure or breakdown.

Transaction logs are used to ensure that the whole migration process is captured, and the target database is updated with all the changes made.

Change Data Capture (CDC)

CDC identifies and tracks all changes that were made to a database, including the insert, update, and delete operations. It replicates these changes onto another database to ensure that the two databases remain in sync.

CDC is beneficial to applications where continuous data replication is needed, and it can create and migrate a live database with zero downtime.

Key Features of AWS DMS

The key features of AWS DMS are:

- *Supported environments*: It supports a wide range of database engines for migration, including popular options such as Oracle, SQL Server, PostgreSQL, MySQL, MongoDB, and MariaDB.

TABLE 11.2 Source and Target AWS Support Database Environment.

Source Database Engines	Target Database Engines
Oracle Database and Data Warehouse	Amazon Aurora MySQL
Microsoft Azure SQL Database and Server	Amazon Aurora PostgreSQL
Teradata	MariaDB
IBM Netezza	MySQL
Greenplum	PostgreSQL
HPE Vertica	Amazon Redshift
MySQL	Aurora MySQL
PostgreSQL	Aurora PostgreSQL
IBM DB2 LUW	Microsoft SQL Server
Apache Cassandra	Amazon DynamoDB
SAP ASE	Amazon Aurora MySQL
Amazon Redshift	Amazon Redshift
Azure Synapse Analytics	Amazon Redshift
Snowflake	Amazon Redshift

- *Minimal downtime*: It is designed to minimize disruption to your applications during the migration process. This is implemented by keeping the source database operational throughout the migration.

- *Data replication*: It can establish a continuous data replication process, ensuring that your target data environment is always in sync with source data. This is most common in daily data change scenarios. ·

- *Cost-effective*: You only pay for the compute resources and additional data storage in the migrating process, making it a very cost-effective approach, even for large database migrations.

- *Multiple migration options*: It enables you to migrate similar (homogeneous) or different (heterogeneous) database platforms smoothly and efficiently.

Different Challenges During Database Migration

While transferring a database from a source to target environment, you might face some of the challenges that are given below:

- *Migration time*: Transferring all the data from the source database to the target database can be time-consuming. This can also sometimes cause applications downtime if the database is unavailable.

- *Schema conflicts*: Differences between the source database's schema and the target database's schema can slow down the migration process. For instance, data types or column names might not be compatible.

- *Application downtime*: The database could be unavailable during the migration, which would make the applications unable to run. This downtime could lead to reduced business efficiency.

- *Data consolidation and refactoring*: This could be a potential issue if you need to aggregate data from different sources to the target database. This includes cleaning and transforming the data in order to make sure that it is consistent. Additionally, refactoring might also be necessary for the data structure to be altered to fit the target database schema.

These challenges can be eliminated by means of proper planning and execution. Here are a few strategies to look into:

- *Minimize downtime*: Use methods such as database replication to keep the source database running while the data is being migrated to the target.

- *Schema conversion*: Employ tools that take care of converting the schema of the source database to a format that is in line with the target database.

- *Phased migration*: Perform data migration in a stepwise manner so that applications are not disrupted.
- *Testing*: Thoroughly test the migrated database server to verify that it operates properly.

Database Migration Patterns

A database migration pattern refers to moving data and underlying schema (structure) from one database system to another in a structured approach. This process can consist of migrating from an on-premises database to a cloud-based solution, transferring between different clouds, or even consolidating many databases into a single system. There are two kinds of database migration patterns:

- Lift and shift
- Replatforming

Lift and Shift

Lift-and-shift database migration is the process of moving a database from one environment to another with minimal changes to the database itself. Lift-and shift migration can be used to move a database from an on-premises server to the cloud. In this scenario, the database would be "lifted" from the on-premises server and "shifted" to a database instance in the cloud, such as AWS. This would allow the organization to take advantage of the scalability and elasticity of the cloud without having to redesign the database.

Lift-and-shift database migrations can be seen in Figure 11.17.

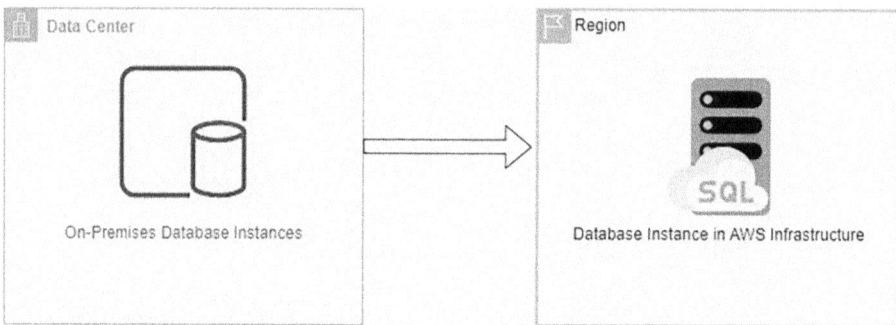

FIGURE 11.17 Lift-and-Shift Database Migrations.

Replatforming

Replatforming is the process of moving a database from one platform to another, making significant alterations in the database schema and functionality to optimize it for the target platform. This approach contrasts with a lift-and-shift migration, which involves minimal changes to the database.

AWS DMS Architecture Types

As mentioned previously, databases can be categorized as homogeneous and heterogeneous with respect to AWS migration. Both forms of architecture are similar, but heterogeneous migrations require the Schema Conversion Tool (SCT) to convert the source database schema into a format that is compatible with the target database. Let's explore the architecture of both types of AWS DMS.

AWS DMS Homogeneous Architecture

Migrating data from an AWS database first involves connecting to the data source, extracting the data, and preparing it for migration to the target database. Data is imported from one database to another. As the data is transferred, the server cache quickly captures updates to the database, enhancing system performance. Once the full load is complete, AWS DMS applies the cached changed data to the target database server, ensuring synchronization between the source and target databases.

The AWS DMS homogeneous architecture can be seen in Figure 11.18.

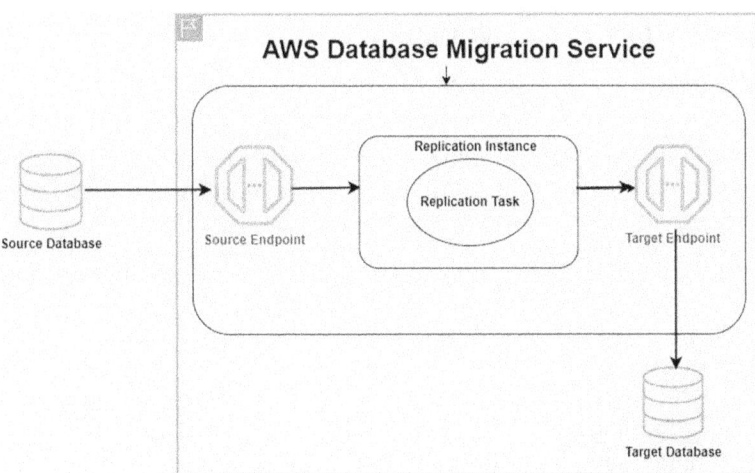

FIGURE 11.18 AWS DMS Homogeneous Architecture.

AWS DMS consists of three key components:

- Replication instance
- Source and target endpoints
- Replication tasks

Replication Instance

A replication instance is a managed Amazon EC2 instance that runs one or more replication tasks. There are different types of replication instances, each suited for specific migration scenarios:

- *T2/T3*: Designed for configuring, designing, and testing database migration strategies, as well as supporting ongoing migration processes.
- *C4*: Optimized for compute-intensive workloads, making them ideal for heterogeneous migrations requiring high performance.
- *R4/R5*: Memory-optimized instances used for high-throughput transactions and continuous migrations.

Source and Target Endpoints

Endpoints in AWS DMS are used to connect source and target databases for data transfer. The specifics of each endpoint depend on the database type but generally include the database engine, credentials, encryption methods, port number, hostname, and endpoint type.

Replication Tasks and CDC

Replication tasks define how data is moved from the source to the target endpoint, specifying which tables and schemas are migrated and when. Before a migration can begin, replication tasks must be created, requiring all necessary credentials and the appropriate replication instance. AWS provides different types of data migration options:

- *Full Load*: This migrates all the data currently in your database; it does not copy data updates. This is a great choice if you simply want to migrate once and do not need to record continuing changes.
- *Full Load + CDC*: This will migrate all your data first and replicate any later changes at the source. While the operation is being performed, your database will be monitored. This is beneficial when you have large databases and don't want to pause tasks.

- *CDC Only*: This will only duplicate database updates, not the initial complete load of data. This approach is appropriate if you are transferring your database through another technique but still want to keep up with changes occurring at the source.

The replication job in the CDC process streams updates from the source to the target, employing in-memory buffers to store data while it is being transferred.

The replication process will leak any unfinished modifications to the disk's change cache if the in-memory buffers run out of space.

Lab: Getting Started with Homogeneous AWS Database Migration Service

In this tutorial, we will walk you through the various steps involved in performing a homogeneous database migration using AWS DMS. To perform a homogeneous database migration to AWS DMS, you need to complete the following steps:

1. Create an AWS DMS replication instance.
2. Create AWS DMS source and target endpoints.
3. Create and run an AWS DMS migration task.

Step 1: Create an AWS DMS Replication Instance

1. Navigate to AWS DMS.
2. Go to the AWS Management Console.
3. In the search bar, type Database Migration Service and select it from the search results.
4. From the AWS DMS dashboard, click on Replication Instances from the navigation pane.
5. Create the replication instance:
   - Click Create replication instance to begin the process.
6. Enter the instance details:
   - *Name*: Provide a name for your replication instance (e.g., demo-DMS-instance).
   - *Description*: Optionally, add a description.

- *Instance Class*: Use the preselected dms.t3.medium.
- *Engine Version*: Keep the default value.

7. Choose Multi-AZ Deployment:
   - For Multi-AZ, select Dev or test workload (Single-AZ).
8. Configure Storage:
   - *Allocated Storage*: Accept the default of 50 GiB.
   - *Note*: Storage in AWS DMS is used mainly for log files and cached transactions. The amount used for caching is minimal.
9. Set the VPC settings:
   - Select the Amazon VPC in your account where the replication instance will reside.
10. Set the replication subnet group:
    - Leave the default Replication subnet group selected.
11. Make the instance publicly accessible:
    - Check the Public accessible checkbox.
12. Expand Advanced settings to adjust network and encryption settings as needed:
    - *Availability Zone*: Choose the desired Availability Zone.
    - *VPC Security Groups*: Ensure that the default security group is selected.
    - *AWS KMS Key*: Leave the default selection.
13. Review the Maintenance settings:
    - On the Maintenance tab, leave the default settings for a 30-minute maintenance window selected randomly within an 8-hour block for the AWS Region.
14. Create the replication instance:
    - Click Create replication instance to initiate the creation process.
15. Monitor the instance creation:
    - The creation process may take a few minutes. Once complete, the status of the replication instance will change to Available.

Step 2: Create AWS DMS Source and Target Endpoints

1. Create a source endpoint:
   - *Access Endpoints*: From the AWS DMS navigation pane, select Endpoints, then click Create endpoint.
   - *Set Endpoint Type*: Choose Source endpoint.
2. Configure the endpoint:
   - Enter an Endpoint identifier.
3. In the Source engine dropdown, select MySQL.
4. Under Access to endpoint database, select Provide access information manually.
5. Enter the Server name (source database name).
6. Set Port to 3306.
7. Provide a username and password.
8. Leave SSL mode at its default value, none.
9. Test the connection (optional):
   - Expand the Test endpoint connection (optional) section.
   - Select the VPC where your replication instance is located.
   - For Replication instance, leave the default value.
   - Choose Run test.
   - If the replication instance is not yet active, you may receive a Replication instance not active message. Wait for the instance to be ready or skip the test and perform it later.
10. Complete the setup by clicking Create Endpoint.
11. Create a target endpoint:
    - *Access Endpoints*: On the Endpoints page, click Create endpoint.
    - *Set Endpoint Type*: Choose Target endpoint.
12. Connect to the RDS DB instance:
    - Check the Select RDS DB instance box.
    - The wizard will automatically populate the endpoint details for the RDS instance.

13. Create and enter a password for the administrative user account.
14. Complete the setup by scrolling to the bottom of the page and clicking Create endpoint.
15. Verify endpoint connections by testing the connection:
    - On the Endpoints page, select an endpoint, then go to the Actions dropdown and choose Test connection.
    - Ensure the replication instance is set to your instance (e.g., demo-DMS-instance).
    - Click Run test.
    - If the test fails, review the error message, edit the endpoint configuration if necessary, and test the connection again.
    - When the test completes with a successful status, the endpoint connection is established and ready for use.

Step 3: Create and Run an AWS DMS Migration Task

1. Access the database migration tasks:
   - Navigate to the Database migration tasks section from the AWS DMS navigation pane.
   - Click Create task to open the task configuration page.
2. Configure the task:
   - *Task Identifier*: Enter a name for your task (e.g., mytask).
   - *Replication Instance*: Choose your previously created replication instance.
   - *Source Database Endpoint*: Select the source endpoint (e.g., mysql8-source).
   - *Target Database Endpoint*: Select the target endpoint (e.g., pgsql13).
   - *Migration Type*: From the dropdown, choose Migrate existing data and replicate ongoing changes.
3. Set the task settings:
   - *Target Table Preparation Mode*: Set to Do nothing.
   - *Stop Task After Full Load Completes*: Select Don't stop.
   - *Include LOB Columns in Replication*: Select Limited LOB mode.
   - *Maximum LOB Size (KB)*: Ensure it is set to 32.

4. Enable CloudWatch Logs:
   - Scroll down to the Task logs section and enable Turn on CloudWatch logs.
5. Define table mappings:
   - Expand the Selection rules in the Table mappings section.
   - Click Add new selection rule and configure the settings:
     - *Schema*: Choose Enter a schema.
     - *Schema Name*: Enter the schema name from your source database.
6. Set the task startup configuration:
   - Scroll to Migration task startup configuration and select Manually later.
   - Click Create task.
7. Monitor the task creation:
   - Wait a few minutes for the task creation to complete.
   - Once the Status column displays Ready, you can start the task.
8. Start the task.
9. If you did not choose the Automatically on create option:
   - Select the checkbox next to your task.
   - From the Action menu, select Restart/Resume.
   - The status will change to Starting and, upon successful startup, will display Running.
10. Monitor task progress:
    - *Overview Details*: Click on the task identifier to monitor the overall progress in the Overview details tab.
    - *Table Statistics*: Check the progress of individual tables in the Table statistics tab.

HETEROGENEOUS AWS DATABASE MIGRATION SERVICE

The migration of databases across various platforms is a complex procedure, particularly when heterogeneous databases are involved (different source and target databases, such as Oracle to Postgres). AWS DMS simplifies the process by offering appliances and services that enable seamless migration of databases to AWS.

Heterogeneous Database Migration

This type of migration involves moving data from one type of database management system to another, such as from an on-premises Oracle database to an Amazon Aurora PostgreSQL database. This is more complicated than homogeneous migration because of the differences in database structure, data types, and the use of different SQL dialects.

The heterogeneous AWS DMS architecture can be seen in Figure 11.19.

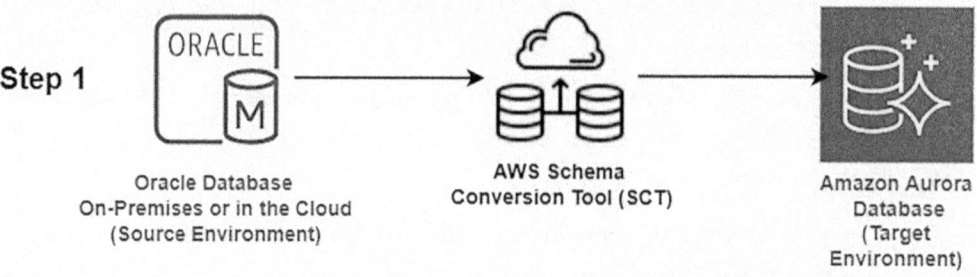

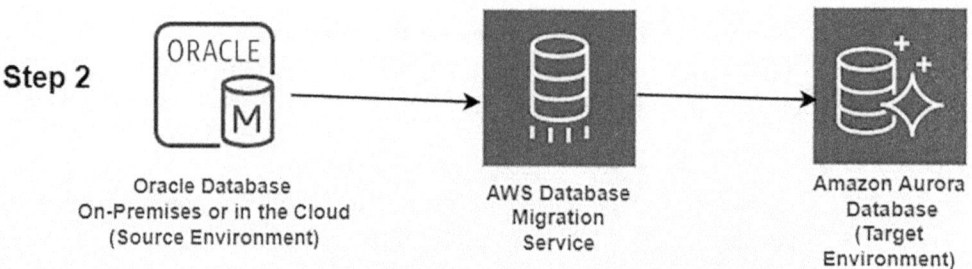

FIGURE 11.19 Heterogeneous AWS DMS Architecture.

Key challenges in heterogeneous migrations include:

- *Schema and data type differences*: Source and target databases often have different schemas, data types, and SQL syntax.
- *Data transformation*: Some transformations are required to align the data model of the source with that of the target.

- *Complex query handling*: Stored procedures, triggers, and other database-specific constructs need to be manually or semi-automatically translated.

In the case of heterogenous database migration, AWS provides a range of tools, as given below:

- *AWS DMS*: This facilitates data movement with minimal downtime.
- *AWS SCT*: AWS SCT identifies and converts the database of a source platform to the target platform, including the database's tables, indexes, views, and stored procedures as well as the application code. In the event that the schema of your source database can't be automatically converted, AWS SCT provides guidance on how to create the same schema in your target database engine.
- *AWS Glue (optional)*: This is used for advanced data transformation and ETL workflows.
- *CloudWatch and CloudTrail*: These are used for auditing and monitoring migration progress.

Heterogeneous database migration involves the following steps:

1. *Assessment and planning*: Evaluate the source and target databases' compatibility and the strategy to be followed, considering factors such as compatibility, required downtime, and the data volume.
2. *Schema conversion*: Utilize AWS SCT for the transformation of the source schema and the database code (i.e., stored procedures, functions, and triggers) to the target database, and achieve the highest possible compatibility between the source and target databases.
3. *Data migration*: By employing AWS DMS, the data from the source will be transferred to the target database. DMS will handle all the data Extraction, Transformation, and Loading (ETL) processes.
4. *Testing and validation*: When the migration process is complete, test all the parts of the newly migrated database to see whether there are any issues such as data integrity, speed, and functionalities that need attention.
5. *Cutover*: Test and verify that the migration process was successful and then proceed to change to the new database as the production system.

AWS Schema Conversion Tool

AWS SCT is used to simplify the task of migrating database schemas from a source to target environment in heterogeneous migrations. It automates the conversion of schema objects (tables, indexes, views, and stored procedures) of the source database to the target database.

SCT provides support to different database engines such as Oracle, Microsoft SQL Server, PostgreSQL, and MySQL, as well as Amazon services such as Amazon Aurora and Amazon Redshift.

This desktop application streamlines schema conversion, reducing manual effort and ensuring compatibility between different database systems.

AWS SCT working mechanism can be seen in Figure 11.20.

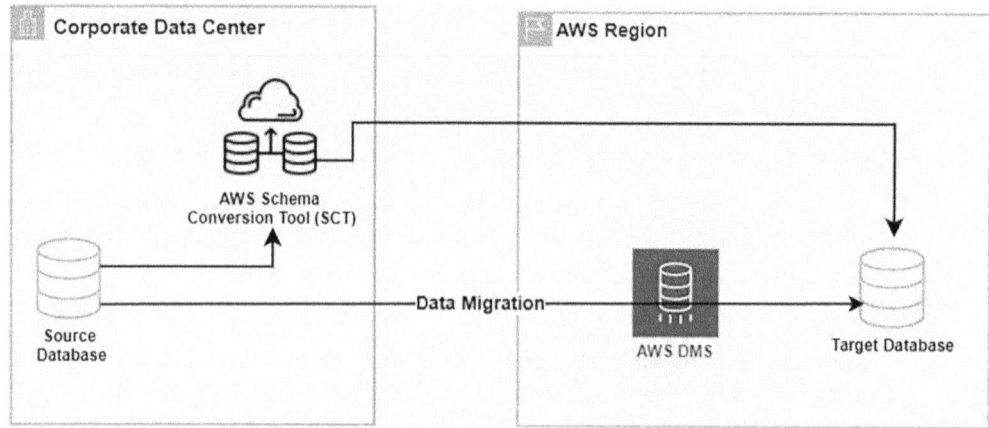

FIGURE 11.20 AWS SCT Workflow.

What Is a Database Schema?

Each database has a different way of storing data. The structure and its corresponding relationship with the data is called a schema. This represents any kind of structure that we define around that data, including tables, views, fields, relationships, packages, procedures, indexes, functions, types, materials, sequences, materialized views, queues, triggers, synonyms, database links, directories, and other elements.

In this section, we will look at the step-by-step process for migrating an on-premises Oracle database (the source endpoint) to Amazon Aurora with MySQL compatibility (the target endpoint) using AWS DMS.

LAB: HETEROGENEOUS AWS DATABASE MIGRATION SERVICE

This lab demonstrates heterogeneous database migration from an on-premises Oracle database to Amazon Aurora MySQL.

Prerequisites

You need to create and secure an AWS account:

1. Create an AWS account:
   - Visit *https://portal.aws.amazon.com/billing/signup*.
   - Complete the registration, including phone verification and setting up an account root user.
   - AWS will send a confirmation email upon completion.
2. Secure the root user:
   - Sign in as the root user and enable Multi-Factor Authentication (MFA) for added security.
   - Use the root user only for tasks that require full account access.
3. Set up administrative access:
   - Enable IAM Identity Center and create a new administrative user to manage the account instead of the root user.
4. Assign permissions:
   - Create a permission set using the principle of least privilege and assign permissions to groups or users.
5. Sign in as the admin user:
   - Use the sign-in link sent to your email to access the account as the admin user.

After completing the prerequisites, follow these steps to successfully complete the tutorial:

1. Configure the Oracle source database.
2. Configure the Aurora target database.
3. Create a replication instance.
4. Set up the Oracle source endpoint.
5. Set up the Aurora MySQL target endpoint.

6. Create a migration task.
7. Monitor the migration task.

Step 1: Configure the Oracle Source Database

To configure your Oracle source database, do the following:

1. Enable database-level supplemental logging:
   - Run the following command to enable supplemental logging at the database level, which AWS DMS requires:
     ```
     ALTER DATABASE ADD SUPPLEMENTAL LOG DATA
     ```
2. Enable identification key supplemental logging:
   - Use the following command to enable identification key supplemental logging at the database level. AWS DMS requires supplemental key logging at the database level unless you allow AWS DMS to automatically add supplemental logging as needed or enable key-level supplemental logging at the table level:
     ```
     ALTER DATABASE ADD SUPPLEMENTAL LOG DATA (PRIMARY KEY) COLUMNS
     ```
3. Enable key level supplemental logging at the table level (optional):
   - Your source database incurs a small bit of overhead when key-level supplemental logging is enabled. If you are migrating only a subset of your tables, you might want to enable key-level supplemental logging at the table level. To enable key-level supplemental logging at the table level, use the following command:
     ```
     ALTER TABLE TABLE_NAME ADD SUPPLEMENTAL LOG DATA (PRIMARY KEY) COLUMNS
     ```
4. Create or configure a database account to be used by AWS DMS:
   - We recommend that you use a user with the minimal privileges required by AWS DMS for your AWS DMS connection. AWS DMS requires the following privileges:
     - `CREATE SESSION`
     - `SELECT ANY TRANSACTION`
     - `SELECT` on `V_$ARCHIVED_LOG`
     - `SELECT` on `V_$LOG`

- SELECT on V_$LOGFILE
- SELECT on V_$DATABASE
- SELECT on V_$THREAD
- SELECT on V_$PARAMETER
- SELECT on V_$NLS_PARAMETERS
- SELECT on V_$TIMEZONE_NAMES
- SELECT on V_$TRANSACTION
- SELECT on ALL_INDEXES
- SELECT on ALL_OBJECTS
- SELECT on ALL_TABLES
- SELECT on ALL_USERS
- SELECT on ALL_CATALOG
- SELECT on ALL_CONSTRAINTS
- SELECT on ALL_CONS_COLUMNS
- SELECT on ALL_TAB_COLS
- SELECT on ALL_IND_COLUMNS
- SELECT on ALL_LOG_GROUPS
- SELECT on SYS.DBA_REGISTRY
- SELECT on SYS.OBJ$
- SELECT on DBA_TABLESPACES
- SELECT on ALL_TAB_PARTITIONS
- SELECT on ALL_ENCRYPTED_COLUMNS
- SELECT on all tables migrated

- If you want to capture and apply changes (CDC), you also need the following privileges:
  - EXECUTE on DBMS_LOGMNR
  - SELECT on V_$LOGMNR_LOGS
  - SELECT on V_$LOGMNR_CONTENTS
  - LOGMINING (for Oracle 12c and higher)
  - ALTER for any table being replicated (if you want to add supplemental logging)

- For Oracle versions before 11.2.0.3 or if views are exposed, you need the following privileges:
  - `SELECT` on `DBA_OBJECTS` (versions before 11.2.0.3)
  - `SELECT` on `ALL_VIEWS` (required if views are exposed)

Step 2: Configure the Aurora Target Database

As with your source database, it's a good idea to restrict access of the user you're connecting with. You can also create a temporary user that you can remove after the migration:

```
CREATE USER 'dms_user'@'%' IDENTIFIED BY 'dms_user';

GRANT ALTER, CREATE, DROP, INDEX, INSERT, UPDATE, DELETE,

SELECT ON <target database(s)>.* TO 'dms_user'@'%';
```

AWS DMS uses some control tables on the target in the database `awsdms_control`. The following command ensures that your `dms_user` has the necessary access to the `awsdms_control` database:

```
GRANT ALL PRIVILEGES ON awsdms_control.* TO 'dms_user'@'%';

FLUSH PRIVILEGES;
```

Step 3: Create an AWS DMS Replication Instance

1. Access the AWS DMS console:
   - Sign in to *https://console.aws.amazon.com/dms/v2/*.
   - Navigate to Replication instances. Ensure you have the required IAM permissions.
2. Create the replication instance:
   - Click Create replication instance on the page.
3. Configure the instance:
   - *Name*: Use a descriptive name to differentiate instances.
   - *Description*: Add a meaningful description for clarity.
   - *Instance Class*: Select based on database size and workload. Monitor CPU/memory usage to scale as needed.
   - *VPC*: Choose the VPC where your source/target database resides. Adjust firewall rules if necessary.

- *Multi-AZ*: Use for high availability if syncing source and target databases for extended periods.
- *Publicly Accessible*: Enable if databases are outside the VPC.

4. Set Advanced Options:
   - *Allocated Storage*: The default is usually sufficient but monitor for large tables or high transaction loads. Scale as needed.
   - *Replication Subnet Group*: Ensure at least two subnets for Multi-AZ setups.
   - *Availability Zone*: Prefer the same zone as the target database.
   - *VPC Security Group*: Configure to control network access.
   - *KMS Key*: Use the default encryption key or specify an existing one.

5. Finalize and launch:
   - After configuring all settings, click Next and follow the prompts to complete the setup.

Step 4: Create the Oracle Source Database Endpoint

1. Access the Endpoints section:
   - In the AWS DMS console, select Endpoints from the navigation pane and click Create endpoint.
2. Create source and target endpoints:
   - *Endpoint Type*: Choose Source or Target.
   - *Endpoint Identifier*: Enter a unique identifier for the endpoint within the AWS Region.
   - *Source Engine*: Select Oracle.
   - *Server Name*: Provide the database's IP address.
   - *Port*: Specify the port (the default for Oracle is 1521).
   - *SSL Mode*: Configure SSL for encrypted connections, if needed.
   - *Username and Password*: Enter the credentials for database access.
3. Advanced options (optional):
   - Extra connection attributes:
     - *addSupplementalLogging=Y*: Enable supplemental logging.
     - *useLogminerReader=N*: Disable LogMiner if using Oracle 12c with LOBs.

- *numberDataTypeScale*: Specify precision for Oracle NUMBER type.
- *archivedLogDestId*: Set the destination for archived redo logs.
- *KMS Key*: Choose an encryption key (default or custom).

4. Test the endpoint:
   - Before saving, test the endpoint by selecting a VPC and replication instance. AWS DMS refreshes the schema list for validation.
   - Save the endpoint once testing is successful.

Step 5: Create the Aurora MySQL Target Endpoint

1. In the AWS DMS console, navigate to Endpoints and select Create endpoint.
2. Configure the target endpoint:
   - *Endpoint Type*: Choose Target endpoint.
   - *Endpoint Identifier*: Provide a unique name for the Aurora MySQL endpoint.
   - *Target Engine*: Select Amazon Aurora MySQL.
   - *Access to Endpoint Database*: Choose Provide access information manually.
   - *Server Name*: Enter the writer endpoint (primary instance) of the Aurora MySQL database.
   - *Port*: Specify the assigned port.
   - *SSL Mode*: Enable SSL for encrypted connections if required.
   - *Username and Password*: Provide credentials for database access.
3. Advanced settings:
   - Use the wizard or editor in Endpoint settings for additional configurations:
     - *KMS Key*: Select an encryption key (default or custom) to secure replication storage and connection data.
     - *Tags*: Add tags to organize resources, manage IAM roles, and track costs.

4. Test the endpoint (optional):
   - Test the endpoint connection by selecting a VPC and replication instance before saving.
5. Save the endpoint once testing is successful.

Step 6: Create a Migration Task

1. Access the Tasks section:
   - In the AWS DMS console, go to Tasks and select Create Task.
2. Specify task options:
   - *Task Name*: Provide a descriptive name.
   - *Description*: Add a brief task description.
   - *Source and Target Endpoints*: Select the appropriate endpoints.
   - *Replication Instance*: Choose an instance accessible to both endpoints.
   - *Migration Type*: Choose one of the following:
     - *Migrate existing data*: For initial data load only.
     - *Migrate data and replicate changes*: For minimal downtime migrations with ongoing change replication.
     - *Replicate changes only*: For syncing data after a separate bulk load.
   - *Start Task on Create*: Enable this to start the task immediately or delay as needed.
3. Configure advanced settings:
   - *Target Table Preparation Mode*: Choose how to handle target tables:
     - *Do nothing*: Retain existing structure and data.
     - *Drop tables*: Recreate tables before migration.
     - *Truncate*: Clear table data but retain structure.
   - *LOB Columns*: Set LOB handling:
     - *Don't include LOBs*: Exclude LOB data.
     - *Full LOB mode*: Migrate all LOBs, piece by piece.
     - *Limited LOB mode*: Set a maximum LOB size for faster performance.
     - *Max LOB Size*: Specify a maximum size for LOBs in limited mode.
     - *LOB Chunk Size*: Set a chunk size for LOBs in full mode.

- *Custom CDC Start Time*: Define where to start capturing changes (for change replication).

4. Set additional parameters:
   - *Logging*: Enable logging for better debugging.
   - *Control Tables*: Specify a schema for control tables if needed.
   - *Parallel Table Loads*: Adjust the number of tables to load in parallel (the default is 8).
5. *Table mappings in AWS DMS*: Table mappings define which tables are migrated from source to target and allow transformations, such as converting table names to lowercase.

   Specify any table mapping settings:
   - By default, AWS DMS generates table mappings for all non-system schemas. To customize these mappings, select the Custom option in the console or modify the JSON configuration. For example:
     - Includes the DMS_SAMPLE schema.
     - Excludes tables: NFL_DATA, MLB_DATA, NAME_DATE, and STADIUM_DATA.
   - Convert schema, table, and column names to lowercase.

Step 7: Monitor the Migration Task

The console provides three key sections for monitoring migration tasks:

- *Task Monitoring*: Displays full load throughput and change capture/apply latencies.
- *Table Statistics*: Shows details such as rows processed, transaction types, and DDL operations.
- *Logs*: Allows viewing the task log (if logging is enabled) for errors, warnings, or data truncation. Logging levels can be adjusted using the AWS CLI.

AWS DMS SERVERLESS

AWS DMS Serverless is a feature designed to simplify and enhance the migration process by automating the management of replication instances.

When it comes to traditional migration scenarios, you usually need a replication instance to manage data between source and target databases. This instance comes with the already specified CPU, memory, and disk capacity. Nevertheless, handling this manually may not be the most productive way since it might lead to either a lower or higher level of resource usage than you have. Moreover, the migration team will still need to handle the updates, scaling, and patching.

AWS DMS Serverless automates the provisioning, scaling, and management of replication instances, ensuring high availability and optimizing cost. This means you only pay for the resources you consume, whether you use minimal or maximal capacity.

While using Serverless, AWS acts as a replication instance manager. Users simply specify the job, source, and target endpoints, and AWS automatically adjusts the resources as the workload changes. Users set up the minimum and maximum capacity levels, and the AWS server dynamically adapts capacities as the amount of data changes.

DMS AWS Serverless eliminates all manual activities, including capacity estimation, provisioning, cost optimization, and version management for the replication engine. AWS takes care of all these tasks, allowing users to focus more on the migration process itself rather than the underlying infrastructure management.

The AWS DMS Serverless architecture can be seen in Figure 11.21.

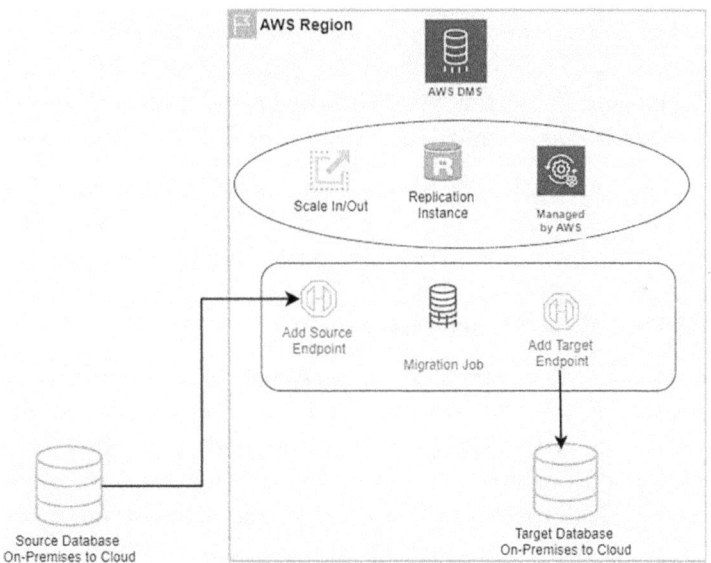

FIGURE 11.21 AWS Database Migration Service Serverless Architecture.

AWS DMS FLEET ADVISOR

AWS DMS Fleet Advisor is a service that simplifies the process of migrating on-premises databases and analytics workloads to the AWS cloud. It is designed to help organizations assess, plan, and execute their migration strategies by providing tools and insights into their existing IT environment.

Key features and benefits include:

- *Automated discovery*: Fleet Advisor automates the discovery of on-premises databases and analytics workloads. It scans your environment to identify databases, including their configurations, usage patterns, and dependencies, providing a comprehensive inventory.

- *Migration recommendations*: Based on the inventory discovered. Fleet Advisor offers migration recommendations. It helps determine the best AWS services to use for your specific workloads, such as Amazon RDS, Amazon Aurora, or Amazon Redshift. These recommendations consider factors such as compatibility, performance, and cost.

- *Data-driven insights*: Fleet Advisor provides detailed insights into your existing infrastructure, including hardware and software configurations, database versions, and utilization metrics. This information is crucial for planning the migration, ensuring that workloads are moved to the cloud efficiently and with minimal disruption.

- *Streamlined migration planning*: Fleet Advisor helps in creating a migration plan by grouping databases and workloads based on their dependencies and characteristics. This ensures a more organized and systematic migration process, reducing the complexity of large-scale migrations.

- *Integration with AWS migration tools*: Fleet Advisor integrates with other AWS migration tools, such as AWS DMS and AWS SCT, to facilitate a smooth migration process from assessment to execution.

AWS DMS Fleet Advisor Architecture

The AWS DMS Fleet Advisor architecture and workflow show a comprehensive approach to assessing and planning the migration of on-premises databases to AWS. This process is designed to be efficient and streamlined, leveraging automated tools to minimize manual effort and reduce the complexity typically associated with large-scale database migrations:

- *The on-premises data center*: The journey begins with the existing database servers in the on-premises data center, which house the data that needs to be migrated. These servers are connected to an LDAP server, which plays a crucial role in managing user authentication and authorization. To access and collect data from these database servers, user credentials are required. Organizations can either create new user accounts with the necessary permissions or use existing credentials to facilitate this access. Additionally, server details can be imported through a CSV file, which aids in the discovery process by providing a structured way to input essential information about the servers.

- *Data collection with the AWS DMS data collector*: At the heart of the data collection process is the AWS DMS data collector, which runs on a Windows server within the on-premises environment. This data collector is responsible for gathering detailed metadata and performance metrics from the database servers and the underlying operating systems. The discovery process is divided into two phases. The first phase focuses on discovering operating system details, while the second phase delves into the specifics of the databases themselves. Once this data is collected, it is securely transmitted to an S3 bucket in the AWS cloud, where it serves as the foundation for further analysis.

- *Processing in the AWS cloud with Fleet Advisor*: In the AWS cloud, the data stored in the S3 bucket is processed by AWS DMS Fleet Advisor. This tool plays a pivotal role in analyzing the collected data, performing discovery, and creating an inventory of the existing on-premises infrastructure. Fleet Advisor then generates detailed recommendations for migrating these workloads to AWS. These recommendations are tailored to the specific characteristics of the databases and are designed to optimize the migration process, ensuring that the selected AWS services (such as Amazon RDS) are well-suited to the organization's needs.

- *Guiding migration to Amazon RDS*: Finally, the recommendations provided by AWS DMS Fleet Advisor can guide the organization in transitioning their databases to Amazon RDS, a fully managed database service in AWS. This service offers scalability, reliability, and cost-effectiveness, making it an ideal target for databases migrating from on-premises environments. Through this entire process, AWS DMS Fleet Advisor simplifies the migration journey, providing automated discovery, detailed insights, and actionable recommendations, all of which contribute to a smooth and successful migration to the AWS cloud.

The AWS DMS Fleet Advisor architecture can be seen in Figure 11.22.

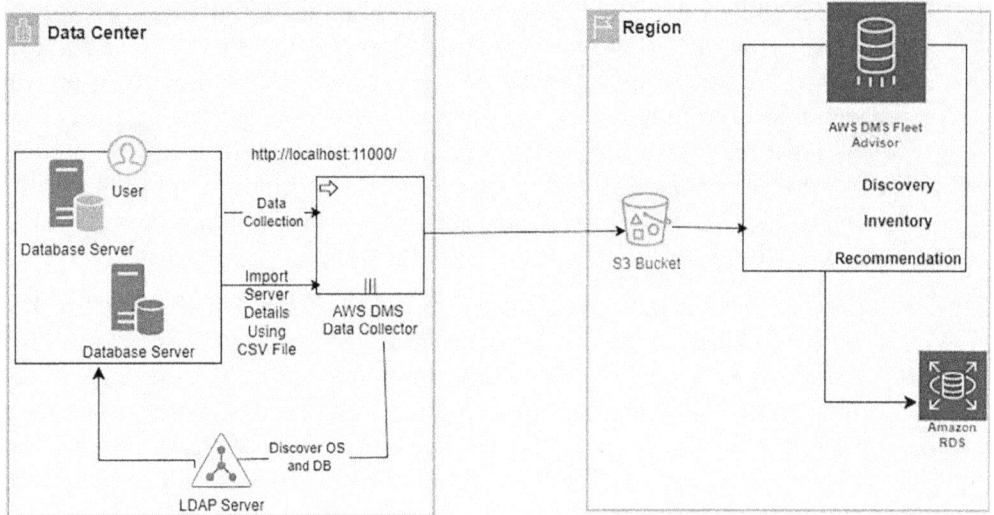

FIGURE 11.22 AWS DMS Fleet Advisor Architecture.

DATA MIGRATION TO AWS

One of the biggest challenges in deploying application infrastructure in the cloud is transferring data to and from the cloud. AWS offers a range of solutions for data migration, each with varying speeds, security, costs, and performance. This section explores the different AWS services that facilitate smooth data transfer to and from the AWS cloud.

We have already touched upon the complexities of application migration, a critical step that demands thorough planning; however, application migration is only part of the picture. Data migration is an equally important aspect that requires its own set of strategies, tools, and careful considerations.

Data migration is vital for ensuring the successful transition of your organization's digital assets to the cloud. It's important to remember the broader context of our migration journey, which has spanned from assessment to mobilization and now moves toward migration and modernization. Throughout this process, we have discussed various tools and techniques available to aid in each phase. Having covered AWS DMS, we will now delve into additional tools specifically designed to handle data migration.

Data migration is a critical component of your cloud migration strategy. By thoroughly understanding your data portfolio and selecting the right AWS services, you can ensure a successful and seamless transition of your organization's data to the cloud. Each tool we have discussed plays a crucial role in this process, and by leveraging them effectively, you can overcome the challenges of data migration and fully realize the benefits of the cloud.

In data migration, we transfer all the data from the source environment to the target environment (AWS storage).

Data Migration Process Overview

The data migration process is a structured approach to transferring data from one environment to another. The five phases (Discovery, Planning, PoC & Optimization, Implementation, and Verification) work together to minimize risks, ensure data quality, and achieve successful migration with minimal disruption.

Understanding Online and Offline Data Migration

Data migration can be done either online or offline, based on the use case, resources, and constraints.

Online Data Migration

Online data migration refers to the use of live network connections to transfer data between the on-premises system and the cloud. This method generally uses WAN (Wide Area Network) connections; for instance, it can use the Internet in conjunction with dedicated high-bandwidth connections (such as AWS Direct Connect).

Key characteristics include:

- *Bandwidth consideration*: One of the main factors that need to be included in online migration is bandwidth. Data that will be transferred needs a high bandwidth connection to minimize downtime.
- *Network requirements*: High-bandwidth solutions such as WAN or AWS Direct Connect guarantee faster and smoother data migration. Firewall configurations may need to be adjusted to allow data transfer.
- *Immediate availability*: Once the data is transferred, it becomes immediately available in AWS or the target cloud environment. This method is more suitable for smaller datasets or where minimal disruption is critical.

Offline Data Migration

Offline migration is the process of moving data from one place to another, using only physical hardware devices. It is primarily used when the network bandwidth is inadequate or there is a large amount of data.

Key characteristics include:

- *Bandwidth limitations*: Offline migration is ideal when the bandwidth is low and the data cannot be transferred quickly. It is also useful for air-gapped systems (isolated from the Internet).
- *Security policies*: Stringent security policies can limit data transfers over WAN or Internet connections, making offline transfer a secure alternative.
- *Resource and device management*: This method requires data center capacity to store devices during the migration process. Device management is critical, as physical devices must be handled securely to avoid data loss or corruption.

TABLE 11.3 Online vs. Offline Data Migration.

Aspect	Online Migration	Offline Migration
Bandwidth	Requires high-bandwidth WAN or Direct Connect	Suitable for low or constrained bandwidth
Network dependencies	Require firewall configurations and WAN access	Air-gapped or offline; avoids network use
Data availability	Data is available immediately after transfer	Data availability depends on device handling
Security policies	May require network-based security configurations	Avoids security restrictions over the network
Hardware requirements	No physical devices needed	Requires physical storage devices and capacity
Management overhead	Minimal management and automated transfer	Requires manual device and logistics management

Based on the above comparison, we can say that online migration is more suitable for smaller datasets, environments with robust network connectivity, or scenarios demanding real-time data availability. Offline migration is ideal for massive datasets, constrained network resources, or stricter security requirements.

Understanding these differences helps organizations choose the right approach for efficient and secure data migration.

Understanding Your Data Portfolio (Source Environment)

Before diving into the specifics of data migration tools, it's essential to understand your current data portfolio. Your data might be scattered across different environments, particularly in on-premises setups. For instance, you may be dealing with various file systems such as Network File System (NFS), Server Message Block (SMB) servers, or even a Hadoop file system. The specifics can vary greatly depending on your existing infrastructure.

In addition to these file systems, your organization may rely on object storage solutions. These can range from open-source options to more proprietary systems offered by vendors such as Hitachi, IBM, or Huawei. Each of these solutions presents unique challenges when planning a migration to the cloud.

Moreover, block storage is another common storage solution that might be part of your environment. This could involve Storage Area Networks (SANs) or local storage associated with backup servers. Although these systems might not always be extensive in size, they are crucial and must be considered during the migration process.

It's also possible that your organization has tape devices in place, perhaps due to compliance requirements or legacy systems. These tape drives could be vendor-specific or interfaced through a Virtual Tape Library (VTL). They add another layer of complexity to the migration process.

Furthermore, your data might also reside in multiple cloud environments, such as Azure or Google Cloud. This could be the result of mergers, acquisitions, or expanding operations into new regions. In such scenarios, it's important to consider how this data will be integrated into your AWS environment.

These scenarios represent some of the most common data storage configurations you might encounter in both on-premises and cloud environments. For the purposes of this discussion, our focus will be on standard data storage, excluding databases since we have already covered that topic.

TARGETING AWS STORAGE SERVICES

Once you've gained a clear understanding of where your data currently resides, the next step is determining where you will be moving it within AWS. AWS provides a variety of storage services designed to accommodate different types of data. Among the most common options are Amazon S3, Amazon EFS, Amazon FSx, and Amazon EBS.

Amazon S3 is a highly scalable object storage service that is often used for backup and archiving, big data analytics, and even as a data lake for your organization's data. Amazon EFS is built for scalable and elastic file storage, particularly in applications that call for shared access to a file system.

Amazon FSx offers fully managed storage built on popular file systems such as Windows File Server or Lustre, making it ideal for specialized workloads. Lastly, Amazon EBS provides block storage that is optimized for use with Amazon EC2, offering persistent storage for your instances.

Depending on your specific use cases, your data might end up in one or more of these services. Each of these storage solutions comes with its own set of features and capabilities, making them suitable for different types of data and workloads.

Large vs. Medium vs. Small Data Based on Terabyte Size

The size of a given dataset can be basically divided into three different levels based on its total volume. In the above range, a dataset that is up to 20 TB is considered to be a small dataset, as is usually the case with standard methods of the Internet. A medium dataset can comprise from 20 TB to 100 TB, and the user needs to plan more carefully and use advanced methods for the efficient transfer of this data. Datasets that are classified as large are 100 TB or more and, at times, they necessitate using special tools and tactics to make them operable on a given scale and to decrease the transfer time.

For instance, it is possible to move 10 TB of data from a local PC with a 10 Gbps connection to an AWS data center in one day; however, this can only be achieved with network stability, available bandwidth, and infrastructure capabilities. In practical situations, these variables may slightly impact transfer speeds, requiring businesses to plan accordingly to meet their migration timelines effectively.

Different data volume tiers can be seen in Figure 11.23.

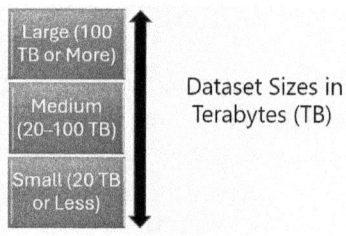

FIGURE 11.23 Data Volume Tiers.

Large-Scale and Small-Scale Data Migrations to AWS

Data migrations, whether large or small, require careful planning, coordination, and the use of appropriate AWS tools and services to ensure a smooth and efficient transfer.

Large-scale data migrations involve moving large datasets, often exceeding hundreds of terabytes. Successfully migrating such data requires specialized AWS services such as AWS DataSync or AWS Snow Family devices (such as Snowcone, Snowball Edge, or Snowmobile). These migrations typically involve close coordination between your company's IT team and AWS to manage timelines, resources, and infrastructure. Large-scale migration necessitates efficiency in planning while guaranteeing data integrity, downtime reduction, and speed optimization. This section will give a detailed breakdown of how to manage large-scale migrations by properly utilizing AWS services and best practices.

Conversely, small-scale data migrations involve moving 20 TB (or less) of data to AWS. Even with the limited size, AWS delivers powerful tools for both online and offline migrations. DataSync moves data between on-premises and AWS cloud storage automatically, speeding up the process. If the user prefers an offline transfer, AWS Snow Family products such as Snowcone or Snowball Edge can be utilized to ensure the safe transfer of data to AWS.

Furthermore, AWS also brings about a plethora of scripting and CLI tools to automate small-scale data transfers:

- The AWS Command Line Interface (AWS CLI) can sync files directly to an Amazon S3 bucket using the `aws s3 sync` command (*https://awscli.amazonaws.com/v2/documentation/api/latest/reference/s3/sync.html*).

- If the target destination is Amazon S3 Glacier, the `aws glacier` CLI command can be used for efficient archiving (*https://docs.aws.amazon.com/cli/latest/userguide/cli-services-glacier.html*).

Third-party tools, either open-source or commercial, can also be used to copy data directly into the desired AWS storage service. Through the use of AWS tools, scripts, and best practices, data migrations can be finished quickly and efficiently with minimal disruption to operations.

Large-Scale Data Migration Challenges in AWS

Migrating large datasets of 100 TB or more to AWS demands thorough planning and coordination. The migration timeline can vary significantly, ranging from days to weeks or even months, depending on the data size and available resources.

Insights provided by professionals who have been actively involved with customers on large-scale data migrations highlight several key challenges commonly faced during the process, it is essential that your data migration plan proactively addresses these challenges. These common large-scale data migration challenges are as follows:

- Migration plan and scripts
- Data security and validation
- Error management and recovery
- Network stability and bandwidth
- Performance optimization
- Time estimation and planning
- Compliance and governance

Large-scale data migration challenges can be seen in Figure 11.24.

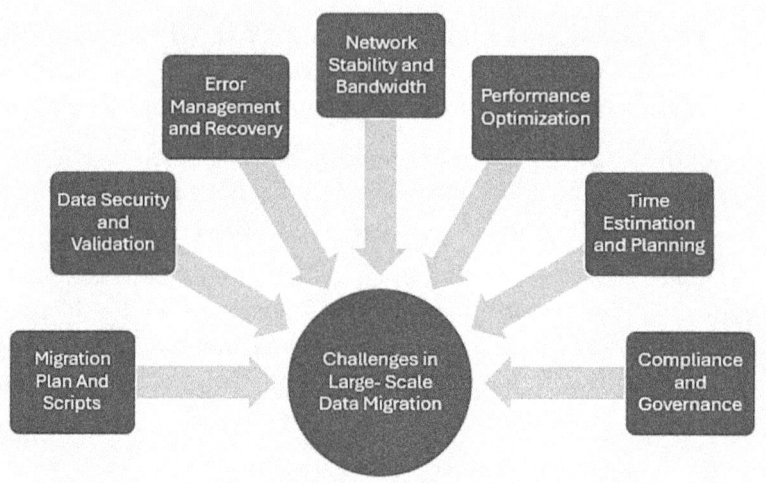

FIGURE 11.24 Large-Scale Data Migration Challenges.

Migration Plan and Scripts

The large-scale data migration plan must clearly mention the details of the migration process. For example, the company must prepare, test, and deploy those migration scripts on the source storage and make sure to keep them operational throughout the migration period. The writing of these scripts identifies key environment components, such as what data is to be migrated, which file transfer protocols are to be used, and the access credentials for the data at both the source and target locations. The plan should also define exactly who will oversee and carry out this phase of the migration, either an individual or a group of IT professionals.

Data Security and Validation

Migrating data to AWS in a secure and encrypted manner, including encrypted data transfers, is a top priority. A comprehensive data migration plan should contain the data encryption strategy during the transfer process. Secure protocols such as HTTPS (TLS) or a Virtual Private Network (VPN) can be used online to protect data. On the other hand, for offline transfers, AWS Snow Family devices offer built-in encryption capabilities with AWS performing the encryption on the customer's behalf.

After the data migration has been completed successfully, the next critical step is data verification. The migration plan should have a step-by-step approach to verify data integrity at the destination. Missing or incomplete data, which might need the migration process to be carried out again, could be the result of skipping this step, and that will be costly and time-consuming so it is better to do it right the first time.

Error Management and Recovery

An infrastructure issue that might be encountered is that the source and target locations go offline, or the network connections drop. When writing scripts for the automation of the migration process, the input of mechanisms to handle and recover from infrastructure errors is necessary. For example, your script should be able to recognize failures such as errors during data verification, and then proceed with problem-solving. Moreover, the plan should state the script recovery methods when there is a breakdown and include details of the person to be informed in the case of issues in order to ensure their immediate resolution.

Network Stability and Bandwidth

If an online transfer is the main part of your data migration plan, you should also include details of the network's availability and bandwidth. The time scales for migrating large datasets are quite uncertain, from days to weeks or even months, so the plan needs to be flexible enough for the periods when bandwidths are not available during the whole migration. Doing a complete evaluation of bandwidth in the project planning stage will enable you to identify the most efficient ways to manage network resources. One method is to optimize your migration scripts to use the bandwidth you have more efficiently and effectively over the entire transfer period.

Performance Optimization

A large-scale data migration at the scale of petabytes is a very complex action and its success requires clear observability. If you are writing your own tools for the migration, it is important to add a tracking feature to follow the progress of the migration. This will allow you to monitor the migration in the real world and take the necessary actions if there are any problems. By adding this to your plan, you can certify that the data is moving smoothly and performing optimally.

Time Estimation and Planning

Planning and time estimation for large-scale migration are the core part of the migration process. To accurately determine the duration of the operation, you must consider factors such as the speed of the network, the availability of resources, and the possibility of failure during the migration. These are crucial factors that could greatly influence the overall duration of the process, so they must be included in the planning phase. The time estimation should account for network performance fluctuations and unexpected delays in fetching resources. Defined solutions are the key to addressing delay issues, and ensuring reliable and well-planned engagement measures. With the help of a well-thought-out plan, the migration can take place on schedule, reducing the risks of the project taking too long and causing business disruptions.

Compliance and Governance

As organizations move significant amounts of data to the cloud, the migration process must comply with all legal requirements, ensure personal data protection, and align with industry standards. This includes confirming that the company complies with frameworks such as GDPR, HIPAA, and other regional regulations.

During migration, proper governance must be implemented to enforce access controls, data privacy, and security practices, ensuring that sensitive data is protected throughout the process. A strong compliance and governance strategy should include detailed auditing, logging, and documentation to maintain transparency and accountability. This will mitigate legal risks and ensure that the migration is carried out within the existing policies and external regulations.

DATA MIGRATION FRAMEWORK AND AWS DATA STORAGE MAPPING

So far, we have covered various aspects of data migration. Now, let's explore the relationship between data storage, AWS migration services, and AWS storage services. In essence, data from the source environment is migrated to different AWS storage solutions (target environment) using a range of AWS migration services.

AWS data storage mapping with traditional storage systems can be seen in Figure 11.25.

376 • AWS Cloud Migration: A Modern Approach

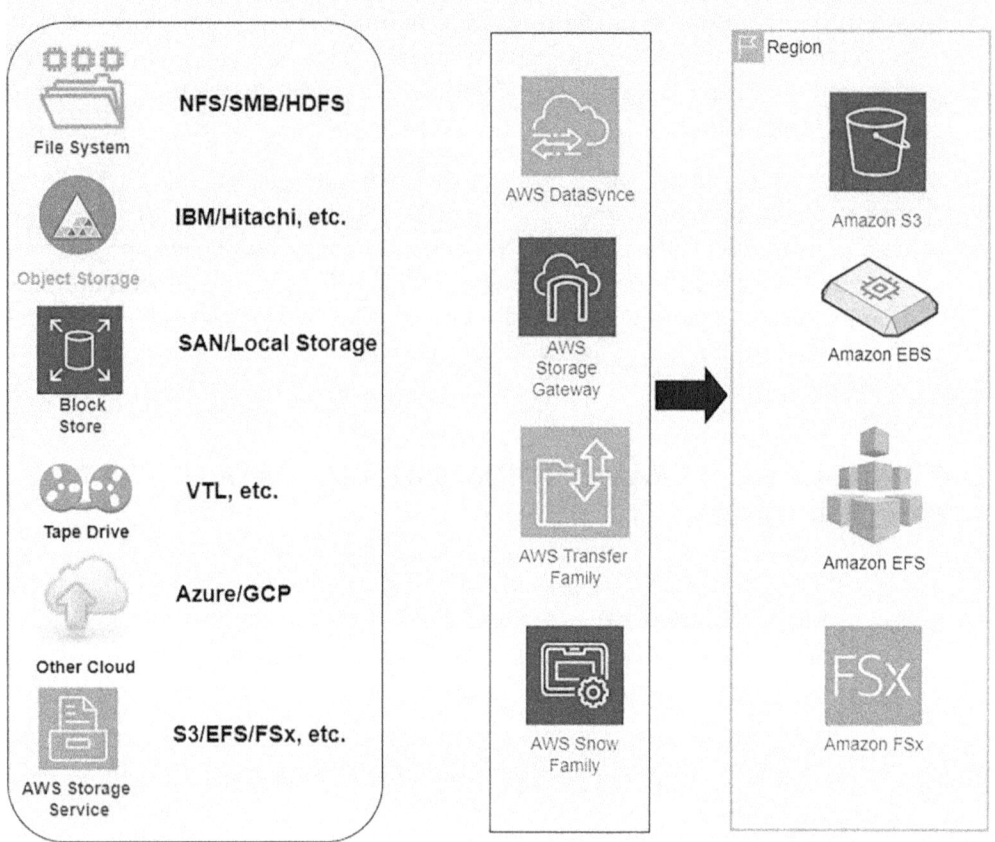

FIGURE 11.25 AWS Data Storage Mapping with Traditional Storage Systems.

This figure illustrates a data migration framework that maps different types of data storage systems to relevant AWS migration services and AWS storage services. Here is a detailed breakdown of this.

File Systems (Source Storage Systems)

This column lists different data storage types that businesses may currently use as their source data systems:

- *File systems*: These include traditional systems such as NFS, SMB, and HDFS (Hadoop Distributed File System).
- *Object storage*: This includes systems such as Hitachi, IBM, or Huawei for unstructured data storage.
- *Block storage*: This refers to SAN and local storage systems used for structured data.
- *Tape drives*: This refers to older technologies such as vendor-specific or Virtual Tape Library (VTL) systems.
- *Other cloud*: This covers other cloud platforms such as Azure or Google Cloud.
- *AWS storage services*: This directly references AWS-native storage solutions such as S3, EFS, and FSx.

AWS Migration Services (Migration Tools)

This column identifies the AWS services that facilitate the migration of data from the source systems to the AWS cloud:

- *AWS DataSync*: This is a managed data transfer service that automates data migration, replication, and synchronization between on-premises systems and AWS.
- *AWS Storage Gateway*: This is a hybrid cloud storage service that connects on-premises environments to AWS storage.
- *AWS Transfer Family*: This offers fully managed SFTP, FTP, and FTPS protocols to transfer data securely to AWS.
- *AWS Snow Family*: These are physical devices that are used for offline data transfer, and are ideal for large-scale migrations or scenarios where high bandwidth is not available.

AWS Storage Services (Target Storage Systems)

The third column shows the AWS storage services where the data is migrated and stored:

- *Amazon S3*: This is an object storage service designed for scalability, data availability, and security.
- *Amazon EFS*: This is a managed file storage service for EC2 instances that is scalable and offers file storage with shared access.
- *Amazon FSx*: This is a managed file storage service for Windows and Lustre-based workloads.
- *Amazon EBS*: Elastic Block Store is a high-performance block storage service for EC2 instances.

These data migration services can be used in various combinations, depending on your source and destination requirements. For example, you might use AWS DataSync to pull data from an on-premises NFS file system and then use AWS Storage Gateway to bridge that data into Amazon S3. Alternatively, AWS Transfer Family might be employed to transfer files from a legacy FTP server directly into Amazon S3, while AWS Snow Family could be used for a massive data migration project where network limitations would otherwise slow down the process.

Each tool has its strengths, and by understanding the specific needs of your data migration project, you can select the appropriate combination of services to ensure a smooth and efficient transition to AWS.

Key AWS Data Migration Services

To effectively transfer your data into these AWS storage services, you'll need robust data migration tools. AWS offers several services designed to facilitate the secure and efficient transfer of data into the cloud. The four primary tools or services we will focus on are:

- AWS DataSync
- AWS Storage Gateway
- AWS Transfer Family
- AWS Snow Family

AWS DataSync is a service that simplifies and automates the process of moving large amounts of data between on-premises storage and AWS. It's particularly useful for scenarios where you need to move data continuously or periodically. DataSync supports file systems such as NFS and SMB, making it a versatile option for many migration scenarios. AWS DataSync supports online data migration. You can use the Internet and Direct Connect to perform migration using AWS DataSync.

AWS Storage Gateway bridges the gap between on-premises environments and AWS by providing hybrid cloud storage. It allows you to seamlessly integrate your existing on-premises infrastructure with AWS, supporting various use cases, from backup and archiving to disaster recovery.

AWS Transfer Family enables you to transfer files directly into and out of Amazon S3 or Amazon EFS using the Secure File Transfer Protocol (SFTP), File Transfer Protocol over SSL (FTPS), and File Transfer Protocol (FTP). This service is particularly useful for organizations that rely on traditional file transfer methods but need to modernize their infrastructure.

AWS Snow Family is a set of physical devices that help you transfer large amounts of data to AWS, especially in scenarios where network bandwidth is limited. Snow Family devices are ruggedized and designed for environments where traditional online data transfer might not be feasible. Overall, AWS Snow Family is suitable for offline data migration and recommended when there is limited or unstable network bandwidth.

AWS DataSync

AWS DataSync is a fully managed, online data transfer service that simplifies, automates, and accelerates the movement of large volumes of data to and from AWS cloud storage services.

The AWS DataSync process of transferring data from on-premises to AWS service is shown in the following figure. AWS DataSync can also move data to and from other public cloud storage systems.

The AWS DataSync architecture can be seen in Figure 11.26.

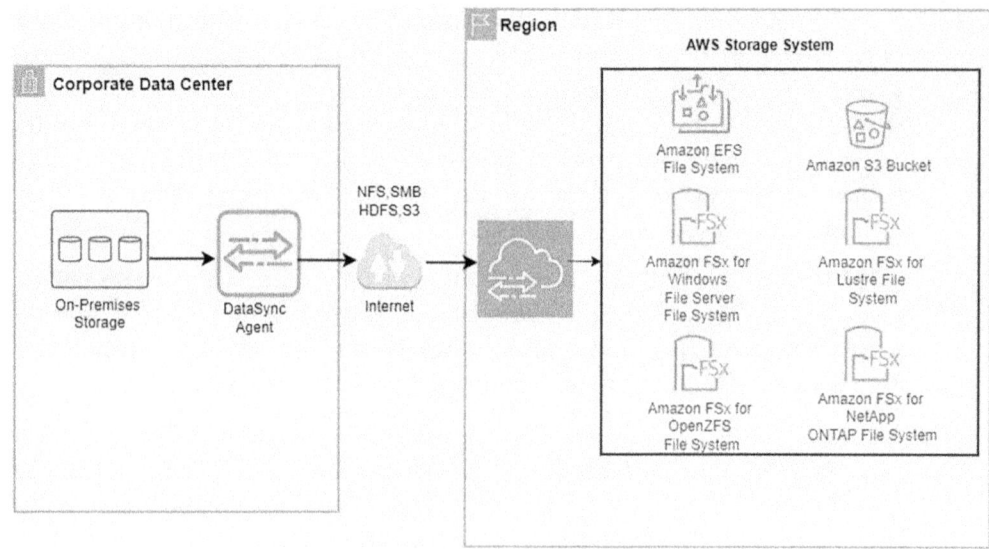

FIGURE 11.26 AWS DataSync Architecture.

The AWS DataSync architecture provides a secure, efficient, and scalable solution for migrating data from on-premises environments to AWS cloud storage services. The process begins with the source environment, where data resides in a shared file system using the NFS protocol. AWS DataSync also supports data transfers from other storage systems, including SMB file servers, HDFS, and on-premises object storage systems. A DataSync agent is deployed as a VM in the on-premises environment to act as a bridge between the source storage and the AWS cloud. The agent is configured with NFS permissions (or relevant protocol access) to securely read the data for migration.

The data transfer process is handled securely using your existing Internet connection, and the data is encrypted during transit with Transport Layer Security (TLS) version 1.2. For enhanced security and performance, AWS DataSync supports private connectivity options such as AWS Direct Connect. Once the DataSync agent establishes a connection, the AWS DataSync service coordinates and manages the migration process. It validates, optimizes, and transfers the data while ensuring high performance, integrity, and reliability.

In this example, the target storage destination is Amazon S3, where data is securely copied into the designated S3 bucket. Other AWS storage service destinations include the following:

- Amazon Elastic File System (Amazon EFS)
- Amazon FSx for Windows File Server
- Amazon FSx for Lustre
- Amazon FSx for OpenZFS
- Amazon FSx for NetApp ONTAP

Once the file transfer process is complete, the migrated data is immediately accessible in the target AWS storage service. For example, in the case of Amazon S3, the data can be utilized for long-term archiving, analytics pipelines, or integration with AWS services such as Amazon Athena and Amazon Redshift. The architecture ensures that data is securely migrated, encrypted, and transferred with high performance while maintaining flexibility across different storage options in the AWS cloud.

The benefits of AWS DataSync include:

- *Simplify and automate data movement*: AWS DataSync simplifies the process of transferring data over a network between on-premises storage systems and AWS cloud services. It automates the management of complex data transfer tasks, eliminating the need for manual intervention. This includes orchestrating the data transfer process and managing the infrastructure needed to ensure high performance and secure data movement. By automating these aspects, DataSync significantly reduces operational overhead, enabling seamless and reliable data migration.

- *Secure data transfer*: AWS DataSync ensures end-to-end security throughout the data transfer process. It encrypts data in transit and performs integrity validation to guarantee that your data arrives intact and ready for use. DataSync integrates seamlessly with AWS IAM roles to securely access AWS storage services, ensuring robust authentication and authorization. Additionally, it supports VPC endpoints, which allow you to transfer data securely without traversing the public Internet. This added layer of security ensures that your sensitive data remains protected during online transfers.

- *Faster data movement*: AWS DataSync enables rapid data transfer into AWS using a purpose-built network protocol and a parallel, multi-threaded architecture. This optimized approach accelerates the movement of large datasets, making it ideal for scenarios such as cloud migrations, recurring data processing workflows for analytics and Machine Learning (ML), and data protection processes such as backups. The speed and efficiency of DataSync help minimize transfer time, ensuring quicker access to data for critical workloads.

- *Reduced operational costs*: AWS DataSync offers a cost-effective solution for data movement with its flat, per-gigabyte pricing model. This eliminates the need for costly commercial transfer tools and reduces expenses associated with developing, deploying, and maintaining custom scripts. By automating data transfers and reducing manual work, DataSync helps lower operational costs, providing a streamlined and economical approach to data migration.

When to Use AWS DataSync

AWS DataSync is a versatile service that supports a variety of use cases for efficient and secure data transfer. Below are some of the key scenarios where AWS DataSync is highly beneficial:

- *Online data migration*: AWS DataSync is ideal for moving active datasets quickly over the network into AWS storage services such as Amazon S3, Amazon EFS, and all supported Amazon FSx file systems. It ensures that data migration is secure and reliable with features such as automatic encryption and data integrity validation, guaranteeing that your data arrives securely, intact, and ready for use.

- *Archiving cold data*: DataSync helps efficiently transfer cold or infrequently accessed data from on-premises storage systems to cost-effective, long-term storage options such as Amazon S3 Glacier Flexible Retrieval or S3 Glacier Deep Archive. This capability allows you to free up on-premises storage capacity, reduce costs, and decommission outdated or legacy storage systems.

- *Data protection*: AWS DataSync enables you to protect critical data by transferring it into any Amazon S3 storage class, including the most cost-effective options for backup and disaster recovery. Additionally, you can replicate data to Amazon EFS or supported Amazon FSx file systems, ensuring you have a reliable standby file system for redundancy and recovery purposes.

- *Timely data movement for in-cloud processing*: DataSync accelerates data movement into and out of AWS to support timely in-cloud processing. This is especially useful for speeding up hybrid cloud workflows across various industries. For instance, it supports ML workloads in the life sciences industry, video production workflows in media and entertainment, big data analytics in financial services, and seismic data research in the oil and gas industry. By enabling fast and secure data transfers, AWS DataSync ensures that businesses can process critical workloads efficiently and meet tight deadlines.

AWS Storage Gateway

AWS Storage Gateway is a hybrid cloud storage service that enables seamless integration between on-premises applications and AWS storage services. It provides a cost-effective, secure, and scalable solution for extending your on-premises storage infrastructure to the AWS Cloud. AWS Storage Gateway allows businesses to utilize the benefits of AWS storage for backup, archiving, disaster recovery, cloud bursting, and data migration while maintaining low-latency access to data for on-premises applications.

The service acts as a bridge that connects your on-premises environment to AWS, using standard storage protocols such as NFS, SMB, and iSCSI. It provides three main types of gateways, each designed to address specific storage use cases:

- File Gateway for file-based storage
- Volume Gateway for block-based storage with cached and stored options
- Tape Gateway for VTLs

Each type addresses unique use cases such as backups, archiving, disaster recovery, and hybrid cloud storage, helping organizations optimize their storage infrastructure while leveraging the scalability and cost benefits of AWS. We will explore Amazon S3 File Gateway in greater detail to gain a deeper understanding of AWS Storage Gateway.

What Is Amazon S3 File Gateway?

Amazon S3 File Gateway is a hybrid cloud storage solution offered as part of AWS Storage Gateway. It provides a file-based interface to Amazon S3, combining a cloud service with a virtual software appliance. This solution enables you to store and retrieve data as objects in Amazon S3 using standard file protocols such as NFS and SMB.

Amazon S3 File Gateway facilitates efficient data transfer between your on-premises applications and AWS, optimizing the process by buffering data to handle network congestion, streaming data in parallel for improved performance, and managing bandwidth consumption to ensure seamless data movement. This makes it ideal for use cases such as file-based backups, cloud data archiving, and hybrid cloud file storage.

Amazon S3 File Gateway Architecture

The Amazon S3 File Gateway architecture can be seen in Figure 11.27.

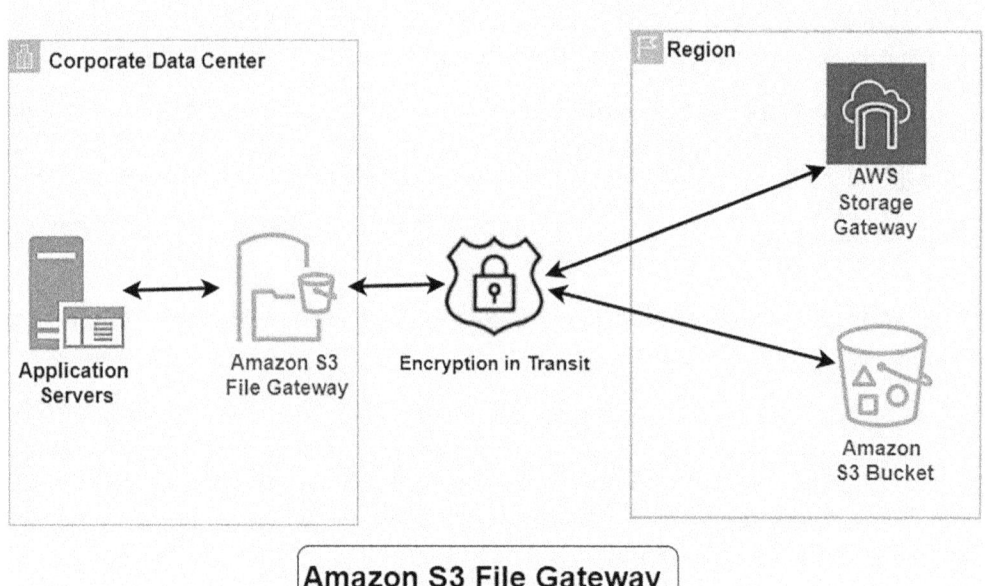

FIGURE 11.27 Amazon S3 File Gateway Architecture.

On-premises application servers connect to the Amazon S3 File Gateway appliance using either the NFS or SMB protocol. S3 File Gateway acts as a local file storage cache, providing a seamless interface for applications to access and store data. The gateway performs two critical functions: it offers low-latency access to recently accessed or stored data, ensuring optimal performance for applications, and seamlessly transfers data from the on-premises environment to Amazon S3, enabling secure and efficient cloud storage. S3 File Gateway can run as a virtual appliance hosted on a VM in your data center or as a physical appliance, such as a 1U rack-mounted server.

All network communication between the S3 File Gateway appliance and AWS is securely encrypted using the SSL protocol, also referred to as HTTPS, ensuring data confidentiality and integrity. Once data is transferred, it is stored as objects in the designated Amazon S3 bucket, providing durable, scalable, and cost-effective cloud storage for your files.

You can manage and monitor the Amazon S3 File Gateway appliance through the AWS Storage Gateway Service. The service allows you to view detailed configuration information for S3 File Gateway and monitor the health, performance, and overall status of the appliance through the AWS Storage Gateway service console.

What Are the Benefits of Amazon S3 File Gateway?

Amazon S3 File Gateway offers several key benefits, as given below:

- *Extends AWS services to your data center*: For critical workloads that rely on on-premises data access, Amazon S3 File Gateway enables seamless integration with AWS services. This allows you to gain valuable insights from your data through analytics, media processing, or other AWS capabilities, starting with migrating your data to Amazon S3.

- *No changes to existing applications*: The S3 File Gateway appliance runs within your existing data center infrastructure, providing file-sharing access via NFS or SMB protocols. This eliminates the need to refactor or modify your on-premises applications to access data hosted on the gateway.

- *Reduces infrastructure costs and complexity*: Managing and scaling on-premises storage can be expensive and complex, requiring hardware upgrades, data center expansion, and ongoing software licensing costs. Amazon S3 File Gateway simplifies infrastructure management and reduces costs while offering scalable storage capacity.

When Should You Use Amazon S3 File Gateway?

Amazon S3 File Gateway is ideal for addressing various application storage needs. Here are common scenarios where it is most beneficial:

- *Low-latency access to AWS stored data*: Some on-premises applications cannot directly access data stored in AWS due to network latency or protocol incompatibility with Amazon S3. Amazon S3 File Gateway provides low-latency, on-premises access to data stored in Amazon S3, ensuring seamless performance.

- *Tiering on-premises file storage to Amazon S3*: When managing large datasets or files, you may want to retain access to data while reducing costs. Once stored in Amazon S3, you can tier this data to cost-effective options such as S3 Glacier storage classes, aligning with your Service-Level Agreements (SLAs) and optimizing storage costs.

- *Preserving file metadata*: Files stored as objects in Amazon S3 typically lose metadata such as Access Control Lists (ACLs), extended attributes, and file-sharing permissions. S3 File Gateway overcomes this limitation by storing both files and their metadata as objects. This ensures that all the metadata is restored when files are retrieved to the local S3 File Gateway appliance.

- *Populating data lakes*: Amazon S3 File Gateway enables easy access to data both on-premises and in Amazon S3. Files written to the gateway are converted into objects in Amazon S3 while maintaining their original format. This makes it simple to use AWS analytics tools suc as Amazon EMR or Amazon Athena to process and analyze the data.

AWS Snow Family

AWS Snow Family is a set of physical devices designed to help customers move large amounts of data into and out of AWS. These devices are particularly useful in situations where transferring data over the Internet is impractical due to its size, cost, or network limitations. Snow Family also provides edge computing capabilities to process data locally before transferring it to AWS.

AWS Snow Family consists of the following services:

- AWS Snowcone
- AWS Snowball Edge
- AWS Snowmobile

We will explore AWS Snowball Edge in greater detail to gain a deeper understanding of AWS Storage Gateway.

What Is AWS Snowball Edge?

AWS Snowball Edge is a specialized Snowball device equipped with both storage and compute capabilities. It enables local data processing, edge-computing workloads, and efficient data transfer between your on-premises environment and the AWS cloud.

To manage significant data migrations, you can use multiple Snowball Edge devices simultaneously. If your needs exceed the default service limit (currently set to one device), you can contact your AWS account team to request an increase.

AWS Snowball Edge Workflow

AWS Snowball Edge simplifies large-scale data transfers between on-premises infrastructure and AWS by leveraging secure physical devices. It helps reduce data migration time, improves security during transit, and integrates seamlessly with Amazon S3 for cloud storage.

The AWS Snowball Edge workflow can be seen in Figure 11.28.

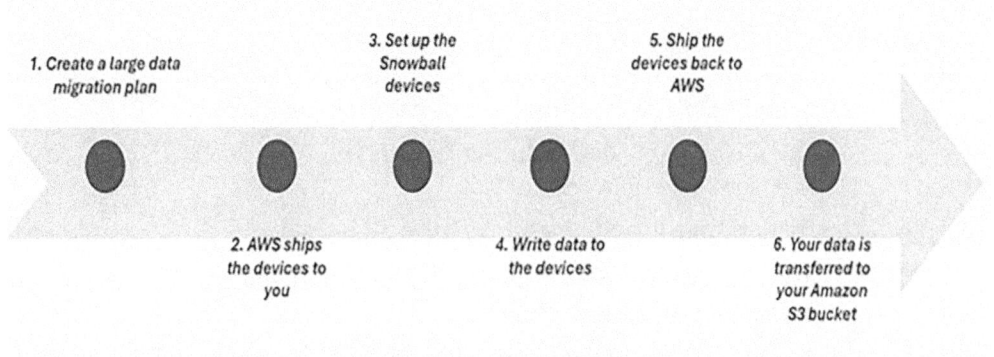

FIGURE 11.28 AWS Snowball Edge Workflow.

Here is a step-by-step breakdown of the AWS Snowball Edge data transfer process between on-premises and AWS:

1. Create a large data migration plan:
   - Start by identifying the data that needs to be migrated to AWS.
   - Use the AWS Management Console or AWS CLI to create a migration job and order Snowball Edge devices.

- AWS helps you design a plan for moving large amounts of data efficiently and securely.
2. AWS ships the devices to you:
   - AWS prepares and ships the Snowball Edge devices to your on-premises location.
   - These devices are rugged, secure, and tamper-resistant, designed to handle large-scale data transfers.
3. Set up the Snowball devices:
   - Once the devices arrive, set up Snowball Edge on your premises.
   - Connect the devices to your network, power it on, and use the AWS OpsHub software or other tools to initialize and configure the Snowball device.
4. Write data to the devices:
   - Start transferring data to the Snowball Edge devices from your on-premises servers or storage.
   - The devices use high-speed connections for rapid data transfer while ensuring data encryption for security.
5. Ship the devices back to AWS:
   - Once the data transfer is complete, power down the devices and ship them back to AWS using the pre-paid shipping labels.
   - The devices are secure during transit, and AWS tracks their progress to ensure safe delivery.
6. Your data is transferred to your Amazon S3 bucket:
   - AWS receives the Snowball Edge devices and uploads the data to your designated Amazon S3 bucket.
   - After the upload, AWS wipes the devices clean to maintain data privacy and security.

What Are the Benefits of AWS Snowball Edge?

AWS Snowball Edge offers several key benefits for data migration and processing:

- *Offline data transfers to AWS*: When dealing with large amounts of data in locations with limited or no Internet connectivity, AWS Snowball Edge provides an ideal solution. Devices are shipped directly to your location and come equipped with network adapters capable of supporting transfer speeds of up to 40 Gbps, ensuring fast and efficient data movement.

- *Process data before migration*: If you need to process or analyze data locally before transferring it to AWS, Snowball Edge allows you to select devices with compute capabilities tailored to your requirements. This ensures data is prepared, validated, and processed to your specifications before the devices are returned to AWS, enabling early-stage data integrity checks.
- *End-to-end data security*: AWS Snowball Edge devices are designed for secure, rugged, and reliable data transfers. Each device is:
  - Tamper-resistant and enclosed in a durable case.
  - Protected by 256-bit encryption, ensuring your data remains secure throughout the migration.
  - Verified for data integrity using checksums when importing to Amazon S3.
  - Securely wiped after successful transfer, ensuring your data cannot be accessed before the device is reused.

These features make AWS Snowball Edge a reliable and secure choice for data migration, local processing, and operations in environments with connectivity challenges.

When Should You Use AWS Snowball Edge?

AWS Snowball Edge is an excellent solution for offline data migrations. Here are some common scenarios where AWS Snowball Edge is the right choice:

- *Large-scale data migrations with limited online transfer options*: If an online data migration to AWS is not feasible due to reasons such as limited Internet bandwidth or tight migration schedules, AWS Snowball Edge provides an efficient alternative for transferring large datasets offline.
- *Decommissioning on-premises storage devices*: When you need to decommission on-premises storage devices—whether due to hardware refreshes, data center closures, or cost-cutting initiatives—AWS Snowball Edge devices help you offload your data securely to the cloud as part of your migration strategy.
- *Data lake creation or migration*: If you are creating a new data lake or migrating an existing one to the cloud, Snowball Edge is ideal for

transferring large volumes of data. Once stored in Amazon S3, your data can be easily processed using AWS analytics services such as Amazon Athena and AWS Glue for transformation.

- *Process data before migration*: In scenarios where data processing is required before migration, you can use Snowball Edge Storage Optimized devices. With 80 TB of usable storage, 24 vCPUs, and 80 GB of memory, these devices allow you to perform local processing before securely migrating the data to AWS.

These cases make AWS Snowball Edge the perfect choice for secure, efficient, and scalable data migrations and edge computing tasks.

SUMMARY

The Migrate phase is an important stage of the AWS cloud migration process since it is the step where the workloads and data are migrated from on-premises systems to the AWS cloud. This involves workload migration, data migration, and optimization, ensuring minimal business disruption. AWS offers a variety of tools that work to simplify the process, including AWS Application Migration Service (MGN) for lift-and-shift migrations, AWS Database Migration Service (DMS) for seamless database transitions, and AWS other data migration solutions such as AWS DataSync, AWS Snow Family, and AWS Storage Gateway. Moreover, organizations can use AWS Prescriptive Guidance, which contains best practices, architectural patterns, and migration strategies to ensure efficiency and security. By adding optimization and modernization into the migration phase, companies are able to enrich their performance, scalability, and cost efficiency, and take advantage of AWS cloud-native services.

REFERENCES

[AWSMGN22] AWS, "*AWS Application Migration Service*". Available online at: *https://aws.amazon.com/application-migration-service/*, 2022.

[AWSMSK23] AWS, "*Amazon Managed Streaming for Apache Kafka*". Available online at: *https://aws.amazon.com/msk/*, 2023.

[AWSMigrate23] AWS, "*AWS Migration and Modernization Competency Partners*". Available online at: *https://aws.amazon.com/migration/*, 2023.

[AWSDataSync22] AWS, *"AWS DataSync"*. Available online at: *https://aws.amazon.com/datasync/*, 2022.

[AWSStorage23] AWS, *"AWS Storage Gateway"*. Available online at: *https://aws.amazon.com/storagegateway/*, 2023.

[AWSGlue22] AWS, *"AWS Glue"*. Available online at: *https://aws.amazon.com/glue/*, 2022.

[AWSWellArch23] AWS, *"AWS Well-Architected"*. Available online at: *https://aws.amazon.com/architecture/well-architected/*, 2023.

[AzureCAF23] Microsoft, *"Microsoft Cloud Adoption Framework for Azure"*. Available online at: *https://learn.microsoft.com/en-us/azure/cloud-adoption-framework/*, 2023.

[GCPMigrate23] Google Cloud, *"Google Cloud Migration Center documentation"*. Available online at: *https://cloud.google.com/migrate/*, 2023.

[AWSRefactor23] AWS, *"Application Refactoring Strategies for AWS"*. Available online at: *https://docs.aws.amazon.com/prescriptive-guidance/latest/large-migration-guide/migration-strategies.html#refactor*, 2023.

[AWSOptimization22] AWS, *"AWS Cost Optimization Strategies"*. Available online at: *https://aws.amazon.com/aws-cost-management/cost-optimization/*, 2022. .

[SmartDraw09] SmartDraw.com, *"A Unified Collaboration App"*. Available online at: *https://www.smartdraw.com/*, 2009.

[Neider93] Neider, Jackie, et al., *"OpenGL Programming Guide"*, Addison-Wesley Publishing Co., 1993.

[AWSDBM23] AWS, *"AWS Database Migration Service"*. Available online at: *https://aws.amazon.com/dms/*, 2023.

[AWSCDC22] AWS, *"Creating tasks for ongoing replication using AWS DMS"*. Available online at: *https://docs.aws.amazon.com/dms/latest/userguide/CHAP_Task.CDC.html*, 2022.

[AWSS3Migrate23] AWS, *"Cloud Data Migration on AWS"*. Available online at: *https://aws.amazon.com/cloud-data-migration/*, 2023.

KNOWLEDGE CHECK: MULTIPLE-CHOICE Q&A

Question 1

What does the term "hybrid cloud" refer to?

A. Public cloud.

B. Private cloud.

C. Combination of public and private cloud.

D. None.

Question 2

Which of the following is a key advantage of cloud migration?

A. Increased latency.

B. Reduced scalability.

C. Cost optimization.

D. Higher capital expenditure.

Question 3

In cloud migration, which phase involves assessing the existing IT landscape?

A. Mobilize.

B. Migrate.

C. Assess.

D. Modernize.

Question 4

Which of the following is NOT a cloud migration strategy?

A. Rehost.

B. Replatform.

C. Refactor.

D. Redistribute.

Question 5

Which AWS service is primarily used for migrating databases to the cloud?

A. AWS Lambda.

B. Amazon RDS.

C. AWS Database Migration Service (DMS).

D. Amazon S3.

Question 6

What is the primary advantage of using microservices in cloud-native design?

A. Monolithic application structure.

B. Easier scalability and maintainability.

C. Centralized architecture.

D. Increased dependency between components.

Question 7

Which cloud service model provides infrastructure components such as virtual machines and networking?

A. SaaS.

B. PaaS.

C. IaaS.

D. FaaS.

Question 8

Which AWS service provides automatic scaling for applications?

A. Amazon S3.

B. AWS Auto Scaling.

C. AWS IAM.

D. AWS Snowball.

Question 9

What is the purpose of Google's BigQuery in cloud computing?

A. Cloud storage solution.

B. Serverless data warehouse.

C. Virtual machine management.

D. Edge computing service.

Question 10

What is a key characteristic of a serverless computing model?

A. Requires dedicated infrastructure management.

B. Auto-scales based on demand.

C. Always-on virtual machines.

D. No support for event-driven architecture.

Question 11

Which component is essential for Change Data Capture (CDC) in database migration?

A. Static data storage.

B. Transaction logs.

C. Data lakes.

D. Load balancer.

Question 12

Which tool is commonly used in the assessment phase of cloud migration?

A. AWS Snowcone.

B. Azure Migrate.

C. Google Firebase.

D. Kubernetes.

Question 13

Which cloud security feature ensures access control and identity management?

A. AWS IAM.
B. Amazon S3.
C. AWS Auto Scaling.
D. AWS Lambda.

CHAPTER 12

AWS Migration Modernization Phase

OVERVIEW OF THE MODERNIZE PHASE

Modernization is the process in which we take our current environment and transform it into something that is more adaptable, elastic, and reliable. Typically, this current or source environment is legacy and monolithic in nature.

While there isn't an official separate "Modernize" phase, combining the "Migrate" and "Modernize" stages of AWS application migration is a crucial step in maximizing the benefits of the cloud. If migration and modernization are the two crucial steps of the AWS application migration process, the latter is a decisive moment in harvesting the power of the cloud. This phase is realized if all the source components are successfully migrated into the AWS environment. Therefore, the migration and modernization steps have a parallel working relationship.

This chapter delves into the various facets of modernizing applications during AWS migration. You will take a detailed look at the ideas of the functions—rehosting, refactoring, rearchitecting, and replacing legacy applications with SaaS solutions. In addition to computing, data, and application services, AWS also offers other services related to migration that will be explained in this chapter. The chapter will also explore the common problems that most organizations face during modernization and the most effective ways to tackle these to provide a complete understanding of how organizations can navigate the modernization phase within an AWS migration context.

KEY OBJECTIVES OF MODERNIZATION

In today's modern digital world, companies are constantly looking for ways to be more agile, scalable, and cost-effective. This often implies moving away from existing, on-premises legacy applications to modern, cloud-based solutions.

One of the main reasons for the introduction of modernization in cloud migration is its ability to fully utilize cloud capabilities. Cloud environments are formed by scalability, flexibility, and sophisticated features that old systems cannot exploit. By modernizing their IT environment, companies can bring in automated scaling, load balancing, and several other performance-enhancing tools supported by cloud service providers such as AWS.

Moreover, the factor of technology modernization is the main driver of the innovation process for businesses. The power of cutting-edge, cloud-centered infrastructure makes it possible for companies to experiment with technology such as the Internet of Things (IoT), blockchain, and augmented reality in a much more comfortable way.

These technologies utilize very large volumes of data and require computation power and storage that are only offered by highly elastic cloud environments; however, by upgrading, businesses can shorten their innovation cycles and thus bring new products and services to the market faster than before.

The key objectives of the modernization phase can be seen in Figure 12.1.

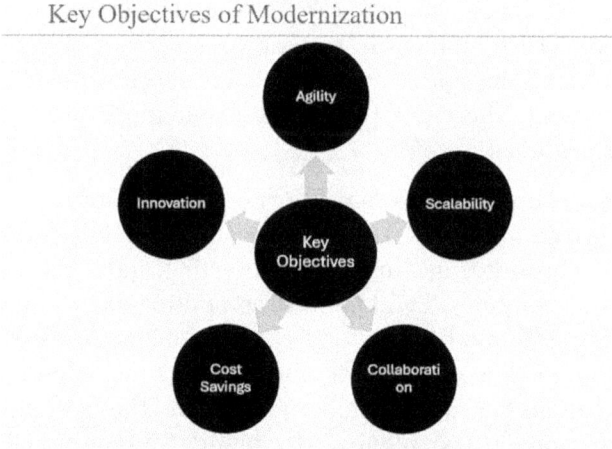

FIGURE 12.1 Key Objectives of the Modernization Phase.

Agility

One of the critical success factors for a modern fast-evolving business that emerges at the very beginning is the necessity to promptly address changes in the market. Developers utilize the next generation of cloud technologies to streamline the work process and make it possible to use modern development methodologies such as DevOps and CI/CD pipelines in the projects. By doing so, companies can rapidly develop and implement applications, and hence, they can react promptly to new opportunities or challenges that result from those actions. In addition, companies can gain an advantage over their rivals by being more agile and adaptable in their business actions.

Scalability

Scalability is another main factor when talking about the modernization process. Sometimes, traditional IT infrastructure becomes a burden with fluctuating workloads, either they are underused by the different resources they consist of or are completely overloaded by the systems they support. Cloud computing environments address this problem by providing dynamic scaling. Applications can scale in or scale out in the most optimal way, hence only the necessary resources will be used, reducing resource wastage. Businesses can then deal with peak loads during high demand and conserve resources during idle times, improving overall efficiency.

Cost Saving

Modernization significantly improves cost efficiency. Maintaining legacy systems is expensive, as these systems have higher running and maintenance costs; however, cloud migration offers you a pay-as-you-go pricing model. Through the process of modernization and cloud migration, organizations can reduce their IT costs by a significant amount while reaping the benefits of more durable variants and better performance. Additionally, to further increase the share of the public clouds, cloud providers constantly work on their infrastructure, and this allows clients to experience cutting-edge technology at a far lower cost than that for an equivalent on-premises system.

Innovation

Innovation is key for any business aiming to stay competitive. Modernizing the business allows for a culture of experimentation and fast prototyping to be implemented as it is easily accessible to advanced technological tools. Cloud platforms provide a lot of services and APIs that developers can introduce in their applications, enabling them to create complicated functions with little effort. This speeds up the innovation process, enabling firms to test new ideas in a fast and cost-efficient manner. Moreover, modern systems are mostly embedded with the automation of monitoring and management tools, thus enabling staff to focus on more strategic initiatives rather than the usual maintenance tasks.

Collaboration

As well as supporting innovation, the modernization phase goes further to facilitate teamwork. Often, software developers adopt cloud-based solutions that include collaboration tools to enable team members to work together from any location more efficiently. This has special significance in current times now that people are compelled to work from remote locations. Teams can co-author documents, communicate in real time, and collaborate on projects together; as a result, they become more productive and projects are completed at a faster pace.

WHY IS AWS THE BEST CHOICE FOR APPLICATION MODERNIZATION?

AWS predominates over other cloud providers, as it provides a full range of tools and services used in cloud application modernization.

The main benefits of AWS in the modernization phase can be seen in Figure 12.2.

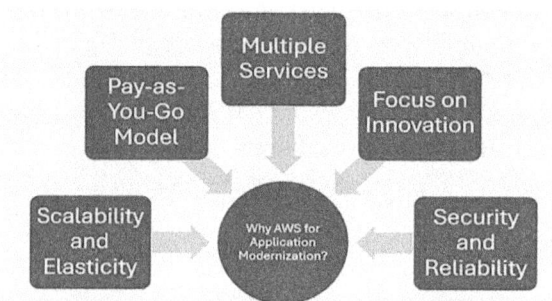

FIGURE 12.2 Main Benefits of Using AWS in the Modernization Phase.

There are several reasons why AWS is the best choice for application modernization, which are listed below:

- *Scalability and elasticity*: In the case of legacy applications, the use of old applications makes it difficult to handle workloads that are loading or unloading. AWS offers elastic and scalable resources that are adaptable to your needs. Thus, over-provisioning infrastructure is no longer an issue, and the cost is reduced as well.

- *Pay-as-you-go model*: AWS uses a pay-as-you-go pricing model. Unlike the fixed expenses for on-premises resources, in the AWS pay-as-you-go model, we only need to pay for active resources. This is translated into substantial cost savings by using resources only when they are needed.

- *Wide range of services*: AWS comprises various services such as compute power, storage, databases, analytics, and machine learning to an extent no one has seen before. This allows you to find the specific orchestration for your application needs, providing a ground for innovation.

- *Security and reliability*: The primary concern of the AWS team is security, which is why it offers identity management and encryption at rest as well as in transit. Additionally, AWS's geo-redundant network enhances availability and mitigates failures, which is undoubtedly beneficial for your business.

- *Focus on innovation*: With AWS as the backbone of infrastructure, your team can focus on development and innovation only. This ensures a very flexible approach, and the development of new features will also be expedited.

All modernization projects are different in nature; AWS helps thousands of organizations successfully achieve their business goals.

MODERNIZATION STAGES

There are two distinct modernization stages. Many AWS customers have found it beneficial to break the larger digital transformation effort into these two stages:

- IT modernization
- Application modernization

IT Modernization

IT modernization involves optimally transforming legacy systems, processes, workloads, and infrastructure to function in the cloud. This initial stage will be the primary focus area. The cloud provides the ideal environment for IT modernization. Cloud vendors build elastic compute, networking, and storage infrastructures with a global footprint, enabling your IT team to spend less time on infrastructure needs and more time pursuing other work.

Application Modernization

Application modernization is an ongoing process that aims to achieve operational excellence in the organization. It is the process of updating and improving the existing applications so that they comply with current business needs and technological advancements. A successful modernization project accomplishes key business results, including enhanced business agility, improved organizational agility, and effective engineering.

The AWS approach to application modernization is a repeated process and is divided into three main phases: Assess, Modernize, and Manage.

The different phases of application modernization can be seen in Figure 12.3 and the following list:

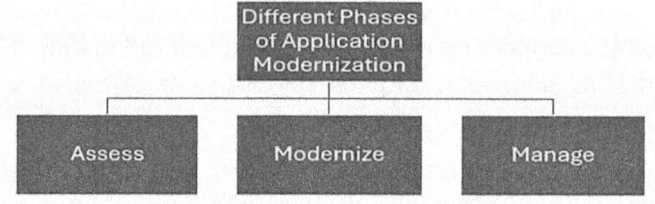

FIGURE 12.3 Different Phases of Application Modernization.

- *Assess*: Examining the current state of the application and identifying areas that need to be improved
- *Modernize*: Implementing the changes necessary to bring the system up to date and make it more useful to users
- *Manage*: Consistently managing and improving applications to ensure they perform well and are capable of dealing with new issues

This approach ensures that organizations can continuously evolve their applications to meet the demands of a dynamic business environment.

In the modernization phase, the company can build a more efficient and reliable AWS environment that is less prone to errors and disruptions by applying four key steps of operational excellence that can be implemented in an AWS environment after a successful migration.

The key operational excellence principles can be seen in Figure 12.4.

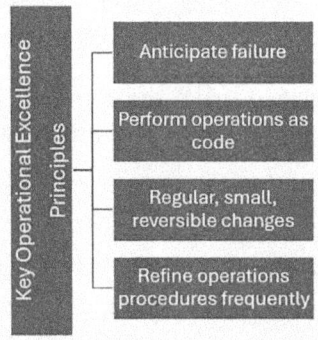

FIGURE 12.4 Key Operational Excellence Principles.

These are the principles:

- *Anticipate failure*: Proactively identify threats and then take preventive measures before they can disrupt your operations. In an AWS environment, this can be done by the use of AWS services such as CloudWatch to monitor your applications for any errors that might occur and by implementing automated scaling to handle unexpected spikes in traffic.

- *Perform operations as code*: This means treating infrastructure and application deployment as code. This approach gives options for automation and version control and guarantees consistency and reliability in your application implementation. AWS CloudFormation and AWS CodePipeline are the main tools for the accomplishment of this with AWS.

- *Make regular, small, reversible changes*: This principle emphasizes the importance of making incremental changes to your applications and infrastructure. This can help to minimize the risk of introducing errors and make it easier to roll back changes if necessary. AWS version control features such as AWS CodeCommit can simplify this process.

- *Refine operations procedures frequently*: This involves continuously monitoring and improving your operations processes. In an AWS environment, this might involve using Amazon CloudWatch metrics to identify bottlenecks and areas for improvement.

DIFFERENT MODERNIZATION STRATEGIES

In this section, we will discuss the most important areas of the Modernize phase in the AWS cloud migration process. These essential components are intended to assist you with refactoring and replatforming your applications—as well as in making use of the AWS Managed Services that are already in place—so that you can make the most of the cloud environment. We will consider three main strategies that are related to the modernization phase, as below:

- Refactoring
- Replatforming
- AWS Managed Services

Different modernization strategies can be seen in Figure 12.5.

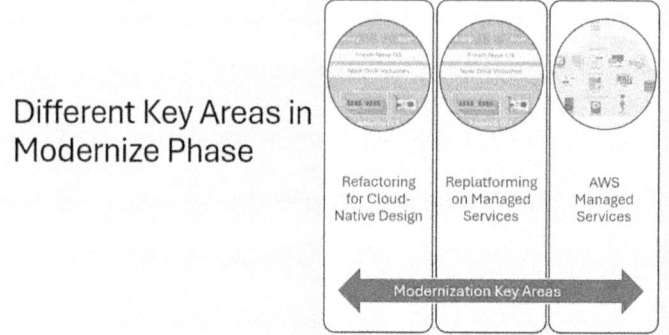

FIGURE 12.5 Different Modernization Strategies.

We already discussed the 7 Rs of migration strategies in a previous chapter. Out of these strategies, refactoring and replatforming are associated with the cloud migration modernization process. Let's delve deeper into the key strategies.

Refactoring for Cloud-Native Design

Refactoring represents a more involved modernization strategy that aims to optimize applications by aligning them with cloud-native designs. Refactoring for cloud-native design is the process of significantly changing the application's code and architecture to enable the application to take full advantage of the cloud features. This approach is important for cloud modernization because it ensures applications are optimized for scalability, resilience, and cost-efficiency. Refactoring often involves decomposing monolithic applications into microservices and utilizing serverless architectures such as AWS Lambda. By doing so, applications become more agile and resilient, capable of handling varying workloads efficiently. Below are the key strategies involved in refactoring for a cloud-native design:

- *Microservices architecture*:
    - *Decoupling Monoliths*: Moving to a microservices architecture from a monolithic approach implies the breaking down of a big complex application into multiple smaller quite independent tiered services. Every microservice is dedicated to a particular business process and it can be developed, launched, and scaled separately.
    - *Agility and resilience*: Microservices implementation can help organizations be more flexible, as teams can work on different services that are isolated and need not deal with the entire application. Additionally, this architecture is more resilient because the failure of one service does not lead to the whole system crashing.
    - *Maintainability*: Because microservices are standalone components, it is simpler to undertake maintenance, which makes it easy to update and identify problems without affecting other parts of the system.
- *Serverless functions*:
    - *Stateless design*: In serverless computing, services are designed to be stateless, which means that they do not save information or know about the user's session between executions. External databases or storage services are used for persistence. This stateless nature simplifies scaling and reduces the risk of single points of failure.
    - *Event-driven*: These functions are typically event-driven, and they are only triggered by events such as HTTP requests, database alterations, or message queue entries. By introducing this event-driven model, higher resource efficiency is obtained since scalability occurs only

when compute power is strictly needed. Therefore, expenditure will be significantly minimized.
- *Cost-effectiveness*: Since serverless functions are billed based on usage (e.g., execution time and number of requests), organizations can achieve significant cost savings compared to traditional always-on server models.

- *Containerization*:
  - *Consistency across environments*: Containerization involves the grouping of application code with its related dependencies into one standardized unit (a container), making sure that the application runs the same way everywhere, including the developer's laptop, testing environment, and production server.
  - *Simplified deployment and management*: Containers, such as those controlled by Docker, are utilized extensively to provide a proper environment for application deployment and administration. An abstraction layer is provided that isolates the application from the infrastructure, making the task simpler when switching from one cloud to another.
  - *Scalability and resource efficiency*: Containers are lightweight and can be easily scaled horizontally by adding more instances. This leads to optimal resource utilization because multiple containers can run on just one host, sharing the same kernel of the operating system, while being completely isolated from each other.

By embracing these cloud-native design principles (microservices architecture, serverless functions, and containerization), organizations can refactor their applications to be more agile, resilient, and cost-effective, positioning themselves for success in a modern cloud environment.

Replatforming on Managed Services

Replatforming on managed services is the process of converting already existing applications to cloud-native managed services provided by AWS. This way, the managed services for core functionalities such as databases, caching, and messaging are used rather than rewriting the application code from scratch. The most significant advantage of replatforming is the reduction in development and maintenance overhead, enabling organizations to concentrate more on business logic and not much on infrastructure management. The main managed services and their benefits are listed below:

- *Databases*:
    - *Migrating to managed databases*: Instead of maintaining on-premises databases, organizations can migrate to AWS-managed database services such as Amazon RDS (Relational Database Service) or Amazon Aurora. These services offer automatic scaling, high availability, and automated patching, which significantly reduces the operational burden on IT teams.
    - *Scalability and availability*: Amazon RDS and Aurora are designed to automatically scale based on demand, ensuring that the application can handle varying workloads without manual intervention. Additionally, these services provide built-in redundancy and failover mechanisms, enhancing the overall availability of the application.
    - *Automated maintenance*: Managed database services on AWS take care of routine maintenance tasks such as software patching, backups, and monitoring. This automation allows teams to focus on optimizing the application rather than managing the underlying infrastructure.
- *Caching*:
    - *Utilizing Amazon ElastiCache*: Organizations can enhance application performance and minimize database load by utilizing Amazon ElastiCache caching. This managed service, which offers storage engines such as *Memcached* and *Redis*, facilitates quick retrieval of frequently accessed data by allowing the storing of data in cache.
    - *Performance boost*: With the help of caching data that is frequently used and closer to the application, Amazon ElastiCache reduces the time of data retrieval, resulting in a better and quicker experience for the end users.
    - *Reduced database load*: Incorporating a caching layer with ElastiCache shifts the storage of read requests away from the database; therefore, the database is less overloaded and hence more capable of handling transactional requests efficiently.
- *Messaging*:
    - *Serverless messaging deployment*: AWS provides serverless messaging services such as Amazon SQS (Simple Queue Service) and Amazon SNS (Simple Notification Service) that enable asynchronous communication between application components. These services enable

decoupled communication, allowing different parts of the application to operate independently and asynchronously:

- *Amazon SQS*: The use of SQS brings about efficient, scalable, and fully managed message queuing capabilities that not only serve but also keep and receive messages between software components. Microservices decoupling is enabled by SQS, which, in turn, ensures that the application remains resilient even in the case of a temporary unavailability of one of the components hence no message is lost.
- *Amazon SNS*: SNS is a managed messaging service for sending notifications and messages to distributed systems and services. SNS, being a multi-protocol communication platform, has email, SMS, and HTTP in its lineup, thus it is a relevant solution to distribute messages among the various platforms.
- *Decoupling components*: By using SQS and SNS, organizations can create a loosely coupled architecture where components communicate without direct dependencies, enhancing the flexibility and scalability of the application.

Replatforming on managed services allows organizations to leverage AWS's powerful and reliable infrastructure, reducing the complexity and cost of managing application components. By migrating databases, caching, and messaging to AWS managed services, organizations can achieve greater scalability, performance, and resilience in their cloud modernization journey.

AWS Managed Services in Cloud Modernization

AWS Managed Services play a crucial role in the cloud modernization process, giving companies the tools and resources essential for performance improvement, cost reduction, and security assurance. The following subsections explore the main features of AWS Managed Services used in the cloud modernization context.

Scalability and Elasticity

Auto Scaling is one of the key services for scalability and elasticity, and we can consider the following aspects:

- *Dynamic resource allocation*: Leveraging AWS Auto Scaling can give your application the autonomous ability to modify the number of running Amazon EC2 instances based on real-time demand. By defining such metrics as CPU utilization or request count, Auto Scaling can instantly rush the application to handle the surge and snap it back to normal during periods of low demand. This automated tweaking can not only contribute to better resource utilization but can also bring about cost reduction.

- *Optimized performance*: Auto Scaling ensures that the application is always ready and delivered even in times of high traffic spikes. By automatically adding or removing instances, it helps maintain a consistent performance level.

Elastic Load Balancing (ELB) is another key service with the following benefits:

- *Traffic distribution*: AWS ELB automatically distributes incoming application traffic across multiple EC2 instances, ensuring no single instance becomes overwhelmed. This improves the availability and fault tolerance of your application by directing traffic to healthy instances and rerouting it if an instance fails.

- *Handling high traffic*: ELB can handle varying traffic levels, making it ideal for applications that experience fluctuating workloads. It supports different types of load balancers, including Application Load Balancers for HTTP/HTTPS traffic and Network Load Balancers for ultra-low latency requirements.

Cost Optimization

Rightsizing EC2 instances helps in the following ways:

- *Resource matching*: Analyzing your application's resource needs is essential for cost optimization. AWS offers a variety of EC2 instance types tailored for different workloads. By choosing the most appropriate instance type based on CPU, memory, and storage requirements, you can avoid over-provisioning and reduce costs.

- *Cost efficiency*: Regularly reviewing and correcting your instances ensures that you are not paying for unnecessary resources. This practice helps align your infrastructure costs with actual usage.

Reserved Instances and Spot Instances can be used as follows:

- *Reserved Instances*: For predictable workloads, AWS offers Reserved Instances, which provide significant discounts compared to on-demand pricing. Companies can achieve remarkable cost savings by committing to a period of one or three years.

- *Spot Instances*: Spot Instances offer a selection of prices that are relatively cheap for workloads that can bear disruption. Spot Instances make use of unused EC2 capacity and are the right choice for stateless applications, batch jobs, or distributed processing.

AWS Cost Management Tools

AWS provides cost management tools such as Cost Explorer and Trusted Advisor that recommend ways to reduce costs. They can inform you of your usage patterns, advise you to resize your instances, suggest that you use Reserved Instances, and show you the resources that are underutilized and can be eliminated.

Monitoring and Logging

Amazon CloudWatch can be used for monitoring purposes:

- *Comprehensive monitoring*: Amazon CloudWatch is a monitoring service that collects and visualizes key metrics such as CPU usage, memory usage, and application error rates. It gives you a quick overview of your AWS resources, allowing for timely reviews of problems and quick actions on issues.

- *Dashboards*: You can use CloudWatch to build an array of customized dashboards that render real-time metrics, thus making it easier to look after the health or performance level of your application.

- *CloudWatch alarms*: Set up CloudWatch alarms to receive notifications about potential issues before they impact users. Alarms can be configured based on specific metric thresholds or log patterns, enabling early detection and resolution of problems.

- *Automated actions*: Alarms can also trigger automated actions, such as scaling instances or restarting services, to resolve issues without human intervention.

- *Advanced log analysis*: CloudWatch Logs Insights enables you to search, filter, and analyze log data from your applications. This powerful tool helps identify trends, troubleshoot issues, and gain deeper insights into your application's behavior.

Centralized Logging

For a more robust logging solution, integrate your application logs with the Amazon Elasticsearch service. This service allows for centralized log management and analysis across your entire AWS infrastructure, making it easier to detect and resolve issues.

Security Best Practices

AWS Managed Services can be used to follow best practices as follows:

- *Principle of least privilege*: Implementing the principle of least privilege ensures that users and applications have only the permissions they need to perform their tasks. AWS IAM (Identity and Access Management) allows you to create fine-grained access controls to enforce this principle, reducing the risk of unauthorized access to sensitive resources.

- *Data protection*: Ensuring that data is encrypted both at rest and in transit is the key to the protection of sensitive information. The simplification of the process of deploying encryption across the AWS setup has become more straightforward thanks to AWS Key Management Service (KMS), which can secure the encryption keys.

AWS Security Services

AWS provides the following services for security purposes:

- *Traffic control*: Security groups act as virtual firewalls, controlling inbound and outbound traffic to your resources. Rules that specify allowed protocols, ports, and IP addresses are used for protecting applications from unauthorized access.

- *Web Application Firewall*: When it comes to a Web application firewall, Amazon WAF (Web Application Firewall) is a good option since it can prevent the most common Web attacks, such as cross-site scripting and SQL injection. It is designed to enable you to establish rules that can filter and control HTTP requests, thus leading to the protection of your Web applications from getting compromised.

By leveraging these AWS Managed Services, companies can achieve cost-effective, scalable, and secure cloud environments, speeding up their cloud modernization journey and reducing operational costs.

Besides the above-mentioned modernization strategies, companies can also think about options such as rehosting and replacing legacy applications. Following established guidelines is essential to enhance the effectiveness of the process and ensure that optimization tasks are properly allocated.

REHOSTING

This is also called lift and shift, which is one of the simplest approaches to migrating applications to AWS. This strategy deals with the moving of applications from the on-premises environment to the cloud with the least or even no modifications. Rehosting helps organizations that want to migrate workloads quickly without overheads from application redesign. The main positive side of this approach is its simplicity and speed; therefore, it comes as an attractive option to companies that need to reduce their data center's footprint. Nevertheless, it is essential to understand that although rehosting offers immediate benefits, it may not make the best use of the cloud's full capabilities.

REPLACEMENT OF LEGACY APPLICATIONS

Another worthy option for AWS migration modernization is the transition from a legacy application to a Software as a Service (SaaS) solution. The procedure involves replacing already used software with SaaS alternatives that will perform the same functions and offer a good level of flexibility and simplicity. SaaS solutions remove the redundant need for extensive infrastructure management, which, in turn, helps organizations focus on their main business processes.

An illustration of such a setup is the replacement of the on-premises email system for a SaaS solution such as Office 365. This can result in faster procedures, improvements in the relationship between all departments, and cost savings for the IT department.

CHALLENGES AND SOLUTIONS IN MODERNIZATION

Modernizing applications during an AWS migration comes with several challenges, each requiring a strategic approach to ensure a successful transition.

Some challenges of modernization and their solutions can be seen in Figure 12.6.

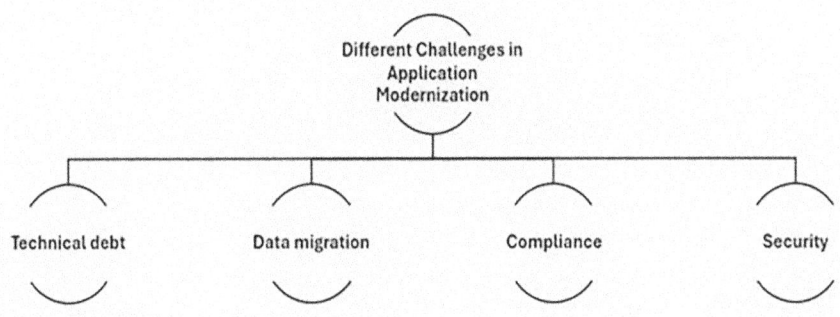

FIGURE 12.6 Challenges and Solutions in Modernization.

Technical Debt

Challenges

The technical debt that comes from legacy systems is a big challenge. Technical debt occurs when existing code or architecture is not optimal or is already outdated and it can harm progress not just today but also in the long term. Solving this problem can only be done with complete refactoring and update strategies. The way to do it is to revisit the existing code base, find the inefficient components, and optimize them in a way that is the most logical and efficient. The refactoring stage can be simplified by using digestible blocks of actions or even prioritization of key tasks that organizations can solve, thereby diminishing complex issues and overall efficiency improvement.

Solution

To minimize technical debt, organizations should consider adopting a microservices architecture strategy as a possible solution to the problem. The migration from a monolithic to a microservices architecture is a very tricky process that involves breaking up large, complex applications into numerous smaller, independently launchable applications that can generate specific functionalities due to the modularity of the systems. This process also contributes to augmenting scalability and being more adaptable to changing events. It is also simpler and faster to release updates, and less effort is needed for maintenance. A microservices architecture also makes it possible to confine technical debt in various individual services to services, thus not affecting the whole application.

Data Migration

Challenges

One of the most significant issues in improving modernity is data migration. The key to a successful transition is to guarantee that the data is intact and there are no interruptions. The difficulties associated with data migration include moving huge amounts of data between distinct storage options, which are full of risks if they are not properly managed. Efficient methods to avoid these problems include phased migration and synchronization devices. With phased migration, the transferring of the data involves small steps, hence fewer chances of disruption of business processes. Moreover, synchronization tools guarantee that the data is up to date and consistent in old and new systems during the entire migration process, thus data integrity is protected.

Solution

It is also necessary to focus migration strategies on making the best use of AWS data migration services, which include AWS Database Migration Service (DMS) and AWS Snowball. AWS DMS allows you to achieve both the simplification and acceleration of your database migration with minimal downtime, ensuring that data is transferred securely and efficiently. AWS Snowball backs the migration of large datasets while taking care of the bandwidth constraints and the data transfer periods. By using these AWS tools, transfer time is reduced, and the procedure of data transfer is more stable, thereby making the transfer more reliable and faster.

Security

Challenges

Security considerations are important while upgrading applications on AWS. The cloud environment brings specific security issues such as managing access controls, protecting data at rest and in transit, and mitigating sophisticated cyber threats. Based on the use of AWS security services such as AWS IAM and AWS Shield, these risks can be considerably lowered. IAM gives you the fine-tuned ability to control the permissions of a user so that only authorized users can access confidential information. AWS Shield safeguards the system by providing insurance against Distributed Denial of Service (DDoS) attacks from outside. Through the implementation of these services, the customer's security is protected, and modernization is promoted.

Solution

Security measures should also encompass automated security assessments and continuous monitoring. Automated security assessments, such as AWS Inspector and AWS Security Hub, are tools that identify vulnerabilities and offer actionable insights. Continuous monitoring through Amazon CloudWatch and Amazon GuardDuty for real-time threat detection, reaction, and maintenance of a secure IT environment throughout modernization is enabled.

Compliance

Challenges

Compliance with regulations is another critical aspect of modernization. Different industries are required to follow different regulatory requirements; therefore, breaching them would be a serious legal and financial problem. Compliance is a matter of understanding the laws that are characteristic of the industry and involving them in the modernization plan. An example is the healthcare sector, where HIPAA regulation is vital for the protection of data. Financial institutions must be compliant with clear regulations from the likes of FINRA or the SEC. The utilization of AWS compliance programs and services such as AWS Artifact and AWS Config is advantageous to organizations that strive to ease their compliance with regulatory requirements.

Solution

Implementing a comprehensive governance framework is critical for compliance purposes. The framework should outline the rules, processes, and mechanisms that handle compliance effectively. Periodic audits and reviews confirm that the organization is consistently sticking to regulatory requirements. AWS offers built-in compliance features and some third-party audit reports that simplify the validation process.

TABLE 12.1 Modernization Challenges and Solutions.

Category	Challenges	Solution
Technical debt	Legacy systems with outdated code and architecture can hinder progress and increase complexity.	Transition to a microservices architecture to isolate and resolve technical debt within smaller, independent services.
Data migration	Ensuring data integrity and minimizing disruptions during large-scale data transfers is challenging.	Use AWS DMS and AWS Snowball for secure, efficient, and reliable data migration.
Security	Managing access controls, data protection, and cyber threat mitigation in a cloud environment is complex.	Employ AWS services such as IAM, AWS Shield, and continuous monitoring tools for comprehensive security and threat detection.
Compliance	Meeting industry-specific regulations is critical, and non-compliance has severe consequences.	Establish a governance framework and use AWS compliance services (AWS Artifact, AWS Config) to streamline regulatory adherence.

SUMMARY

Modernizing applications during AWS migration provides a lot of benefits, and organizations have the chance to improve their IT infrastructure. This chapter has explored a range of strategies, including the rehosting, refactoring, and replatforming of legacy systems with SaaS solutions. By applying these techniques, organizations can leverage cloud-native capabilities that lead to improved performance, scalability, and cost savings. Moreover, AWS services are essential because they are used for workload optimization, data management, application integration, and monitoring of the operation, and thus the modernization process is streamlined. Nevertheless, the process is quite a challenging and complex one. It is necessary to tackle technical debt, cloud migration challenges, security issues, and compliance requirements to achieve an effective transition. A successful way of dealing with these problems is through the use of phased migration, synchronization tools, and the use of robust security measures such as IAM and AWS Shield to mitigate risks effectively.

Furthermore, AWS's array of compliance services ensures compliance with the relevant industry regulations. As organizations deal with these issues, it is vital to highlight the need for continuous improvement and adaptation, thus leading to a climate of innovation and agility in the fast-changing digital landscape.

REFERENCES

[AWS01] Amazon Web Services, *"Phases of a large migration"*, AWS whitepaper. Available online at: *https://docs.aws.amazon.com/prescriptive-guidance/latest/large-migration-guide/phases.html*.

[AWS02] Amazon Web Services, *"Strategy for modernizing applications in the AWS Cloud"*, AWS whitepaper. Available online at: *https://docs.aws.amazon.com/prescriptive-guidance/latest/strategy-modernizing-applications/welcome.html*.

[AWS03] Amazon Web Services, *"AWS Migration Hub: Planning and Tracking Migrations to AWS"*. Available online at: *https://aws.amazon.com/migration-hub/*.

[Lewis15] Lewis, James, and Martin Fowler, *"Microservices: a definition of this new architectural term"*, ThoughtWorks, 2015. Available online at: *https://martinfowler.com/articles/microservices.html*.

[Boyd19] Boyd, Greg, *"Cloud-Native Application Design"*, O'Reilly Media, 2019.

[Hendrickson21] Hendrickson, Mark, *"Serverless Computing: Architecture and Best Practices"*, Pearson Education, 2021.

[Patel20] Patel, Rohan, *"Refactoring Legacy Applications for the Cloud"*, Packt Publishing, 2020

[Smith18] Smith, George, *"Scalable Cloud Applications: Designing for Performance and Cost Efficiency"*, Wiley, 2018.

[Spillner19] Spillner, Josef, *"Serverless Computing and Functions as a Service,"* Springer, 2019.

[Vohra20] Vohra, Parth, *"Application Modernization Strategies: From Monolith to Microservices"*, Manning Publications, 2020.

KNOWLEDGE CHECK: MULTIPLE-CHOICE Q&A

Question 1

What is the main goal of the Modernize phase in AWS migration?

A. To maintain legacy systems.

B. To transform the current environment into one that is more adaptable, elastic, and reliable.

C. To migrate on-premises systems without modification.

D. To replace cloud applications with on-premises solutions.

Question 2

Which of the following is NOT a key objective of the Modernize phase?

A. Scalability.

B. Cost saving.

C. Innovation.

D. Retaining all legacy systems.

Question 3

What does refactoring for cloud-native design primarily involve?

A. Rehosting applications without changes.

B. Decomposing monolithic applications into microservices.

C. Retaining legacy infrastructure for cost savings.

D. Using manual scaling for applications.

Question 4

Which AWS service is used for monitoring applications and resources?

A. Amazon ElastiCache.

B. Amazon CloudWatch.

C. AWS IAM.

D. AWS Shield.

Question 5

What is the purpose of using AWS Database Migration Service (DMS) in the Modernize phase?

A. To replace on-premises applications with SaaS solutions.

B. To migrate large datasets quickly without bandwidth constraints.

C. To ensure secure and efficient database migration with minimal downtime.

D. To automate compliance with regulatory standards.

Question 6

Which of the following is an AWS managed service used to enhance application performance by reducing database load?

A. Amazon SNS.

B. Amazon SQS.

C. Amazon ElastiCache.

D. AWS Artifact.

Question 7

What is a key feature of AWS Elastic Load Balancing (ELB)?

A. Automatically encrypting all data in transit.

B. Distributing incoming traffic across multiple EC2 instances.

C. Replacing legacy applications with SaaS solutions.

D. Performing automated refactoring for cloud-native design.

CHAPTER 13

GENERATIVE AI IN AWS CLOUD MIGRATION

WHAT IS ARTIFICIAL INTELLIGENCE?

Artificial Intelligence (AI) has no clear definition. Many people talk about it but there is still no agreement on how to define or measure this intelligence. Some of the definitions can be given as below:

- Science that empowers computers to mimic human intelligence such as decision-making, text processing, and visual perception. The ability of a machine to replicate natural intelligence.
- The theory and development of computer systems that can perform tasks that usually require human intelligence, such as visual perception, speech recognition, decision-making, and translation between languages.
- The ability of a man-made system to replicate human thoughts. Some examples are given below:
    - Predicting whether an airplane will arrive early, on-time, or late
    - Determining the likely repair costs for an accident involving a vehicle
    - Stock prices, weather conditions, electricity consumption in a household, and total sales in a store

An AI symbolic picture can be seen in Figure 13.1.

FIGURE 13.1 AI Symbolic Picture (AI-generated image).

COMMON AI WORKLOADS

AI workloads are used to enable machines to perform tasks that typically require human-level intelligence. These workloads are designed to help machines interpret and understand complex data, learn from past experiences, make predictions, and perform tasks autonomously.

By achieving these objectives, AI workloads can improve the efficiency, accuracy, and speed of various processes across different industries.

Common AI workloads can be seen in Figure 13.2.

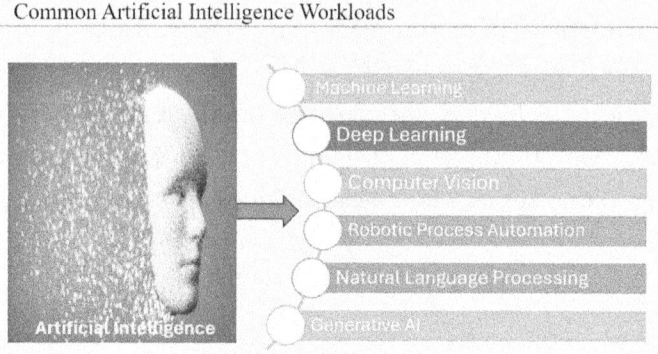

FIGURE 13.2 Common AI Workloads.

Many common AI workloads are used in various applications, including the following.

Machine Learning

This is often the foundation for an AI system and is the way we "teach" a computer model to make predictions and draw conclusions from data.

Machine Learning (ML) has emerged as one of the most revolutionary technological developments. The use of ML is enabling businesses to accelerate digital transformation and enter the age of automation in the fiercely competitive corporate world. Some people would even argue that in some industries, AI/ML is necessary to remain relevant, such as digital payments, fraud detection in banking, or product recommendations.

An ML symbolic picture can be seen in Figure 13.3.

FIGURE 13.3 ML Symbolic Picture (AI-generated image).

Examples include:

- Determining whether a customer is likely to switch to a competitor
- Detecting credit card fraud
- Scheduling the time to perform preventive maintenance on a production robot

Deep Learning

Deep Learning (DL) is part of ML, and it is used for complex algorithms to train models.

DL uses artificial neural networks with many layers, which is why it's called "deep." These layers can be compared to the neurons found in the human brain, which interact to create DL algorithms capable of recognizing complex patterns in data.

DL, with its artificial neural networks with many layers, can be seen in Figure 13.4.

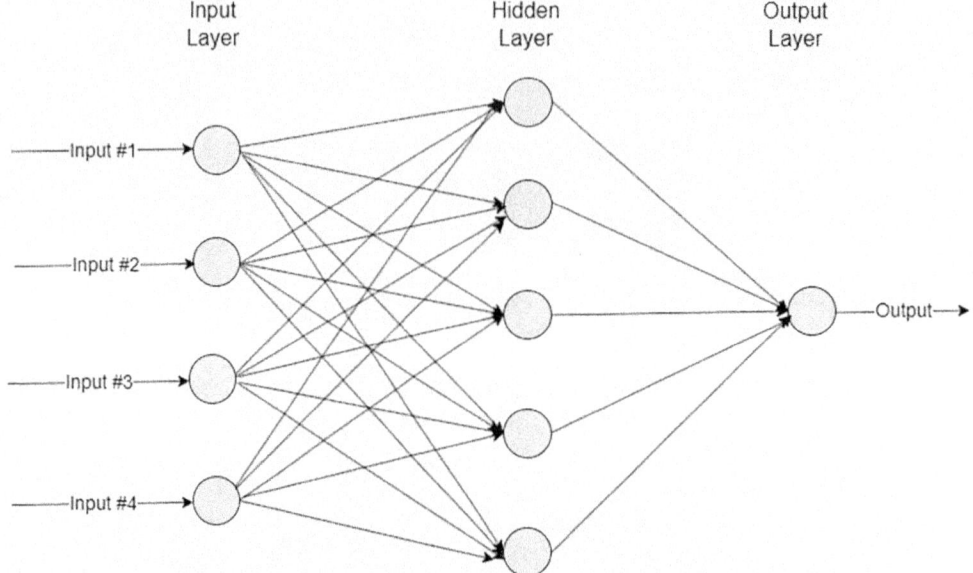

FIGURE 13.4 DL: Artificial Neural Networks with Many Layers.

Key points related to DL for better understanding are the following:

- *Inspired by the brain*: DL models are fundamentally artificial neural networks, and these models are constructed to resemble the structural and functional framework of the human brain.
- *Multiple layers*: The "deep" in DL refers to the use of many layers of interconnected nodes in the neural network. Each layer learns to recognize different features in the data.

- *Learns from data*: DL is the process of a model learning from extensive data, which may be visual, text, or voice. They can identify and differentiate between numerical or graphical patterns in the data that humans would not be able to remember or might miss.
- *Used for complex tasks*: DL is used for a variety of complex tasks, such as image recognition, speech recognition, NLP, and self-driving cars.

Computer Vision

This technology is used for images and videos and then provides information through object detection and image classification.

A computer vision symbolic picture can be seen in Figure 13.5.

FIGURE 13.5 Computer Vision Symbolic Picture (AI-generated image).

The majority of computer vision solutions relate to visual input coming from cameras, videos, or photographs, thus most computer vision technology is heavily based on this technology.

Common applications of computer vision include:

- Image classification
- Object detection
- Semantic segmentation
- Facial services

- Optical Character Recognition (OCR)

Natural Language Processing

An NLP symbolic picture can be seen in Figure 13.6.

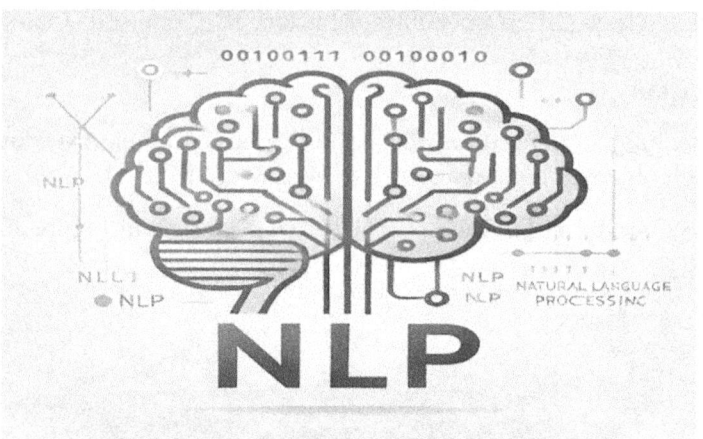

FIGURE 13.6 NLP Symbolic Picture (AI-generated image).

This is used to analyze text in documents or other text sources. It can interpret and generate speech. It also has the ability to translate spoken or written phrases between different languages.

NLP enables you to create software that can:

- Analyze text documents to extract key phrases and recognize entities (such as places, dates, or people).
- Perform *sentiment analysis* to determine how positive or negative the language used in a document is.
- Interpret spoken language and synthesize speech responses.
- Automatically translate spoken or written phrases between languages

Robotic Process Automation

Robotic Process Automation (RPA) is essentially using software robots to automate repetitive tasks on your computer. Imagine a tireless, digital assistant that can mimic what you do on various programs.

An RPA symbolic picture can be seen in Figure 13.7.

FIGURE 13.7 RPA Symbolic Picture.

Here's how RPA works:

- *Software robots*: RPA utilizes software programs called *bots* that can interact with digital systems and applications just like a human would.

- *Repetitive tasks*: These bots are designed to automate repetitive tasks that follow a defined set of rules. This can include things such as data entry, copying and pasting information between applications, generating reports, and moving files.

- *Increased efficiency*: By automating these tasks, RPA frees up employees to focus on more complex, strategic work. It can also improve accuracy and reduce errors since bots don't get tired or make mistakes.

Overall, RPA is a type of Business Process Automation (BPA), and it deals with automating well-defined procedures rather than using complex learning algorithms.

Generative AI

Generative AI is a powerful technology that enables machines to generate content, such as text, images, and videos, based on patterns learned from existing data. It has applications in various industries, including content creation, product design optimization, and operational efficiency.

Generative AI (or GenAI) is AI that is capable of generating text, images, or other media using generative models.

Generative AI models learn the patterns and structure of their input training data and then generate new data that has similar characteristics.

In simple terms, generative AI takes a bunch of data, uses it to gain hidden insights, and puts the data to work in various ways. It does this in a way that is very similar to how our brains work. It looks at all the data in all the different places, then says something based on what it saw.

These models can create new data points that have similar statistical properties to the training data they were exposed to. Generative AI models often use techniques such as neural networks, particularly Generative Adversarial Networks (GANs), Variational Autoencoders (VAEs), and autoregressive models. These models learn patterns and structures from a dataset and then generate new samples by either sampling from a learned probability distribution or by learning to produce outputs that are like the training data.

A generative AI symbolic picture can be seen in Figure 13.8.

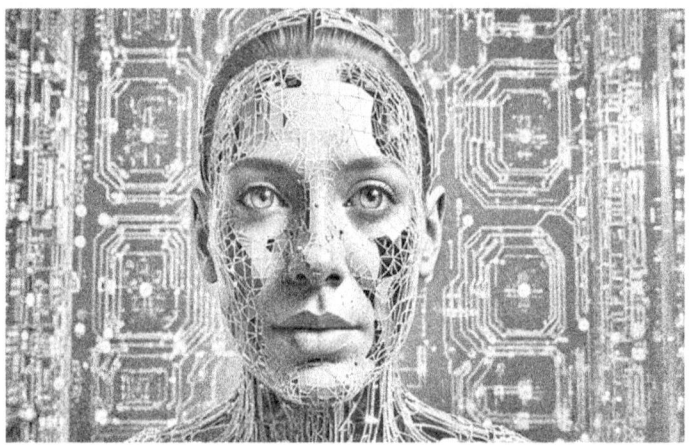

FIGURE 13.8 Generative AI Symbolic Picture.

Different Applications of Generative AI

Generative AI has numerous applications, as below:

- *Image generation*: Generating realistic images of people, animals, scenery, etc.

- *Text generation*: Producing human-like text, such as stories, poems, or even code snippets
- *Music generation*: Creating new music tracks or generating melodies
- *Video generation*: Generating video sequences, deepfakes, or synthetic training data for computer vision tasks
- *Data augmentation*: Generating synthetic data to augment existing datasets for training ML models

Relationship Between AI, ML, DL, and Generative AI

Generative AI falls primarily within the domain of ML and, more specifically, within DL. Generative AI techniques involve training models to generate new data samples that resemble a given training dataset. This can include generating images, text, audio, or even videos. Generative models, such as GANs, VAEs, and autoregressive models, are examples of DL techniques used in generative AI. Generative AI has applications in various domains, including image synthesis, text generation, music composition, and data augmentation.

ML is a core component of AI. Many foundational principles of AI are rooted in ML, making it essential to grasp basic ML concepts to understand AI effectively.

The relationship between AI, ML, DL, and generative AI can be seen in Figure 13.9.

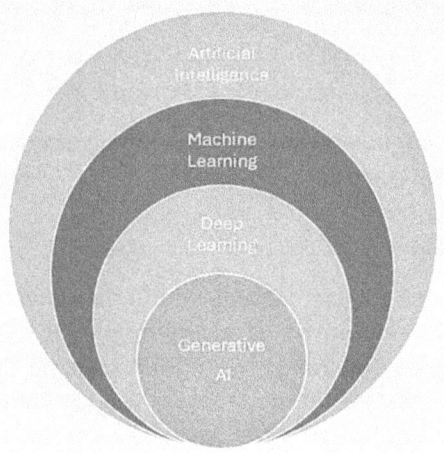

FIGURE 13.9 Relationship Between AI, ML, DL, and generative AI.

ML MODEL CREATION PROCESS

The process of establishing an ML model involves many steps, each of which is very important to the successful implementation of a system that can make predictions or decisions based on data. It is very important to know these steps for anyone interested in moving into the area of ML. This section will go through the main steps in this process: feature selection, feature engineering, model training, and model evaluation.

Feature Selection

Feature selection is a prerequisite to recognizing the most relevant variables (features) in your dataset that will be used as inputs for your model.

This step is critical because the quality and relevance of the selected features can significantly impact the model's accuracy and performance. Irrelevant or redundant features can introduce noise and reduce the efficiency of the model. Choosing a subset of relevant features will give the model the ability to transfer the learned knowledge more effectively to new data.

There are various techniques for feature selection, including statistical tests, the correlation matrix, and recursive feature elimination. For example, if you are building a model to predict house prices, important features might include the size of the house, the number of bedrooms, and the location, while less relevant features such as the color of the walls may be omitted.

The key objective of ML in feature selection is to create a good model based on the following steps:

- Provide inputs to the model.
- The model returns the prediction.

In this process, inputs are called *features*, and predictions are called *labels*. Refer to the feature selection example shown in Figure 13.10.

			FEATURES					LABELS
Pregnanci	Glucos	BloodPressu	SkinThickne	Insuli		BMI	Age	Diabetic
6	148	72	35	0	33.6	0.627	50	Yes
1	85	66	29	0	26.6	0.351	31	No
8	183	64	0	0	23.3	0.672	32	Yes
1	89	66	23	94	28.1	0.167	21	No
0	137	40	35	168	43.1	2.288	33	Yes
5	116	74	32	0	25.6	0.201	30	No
3	78	50	0	88	31	0.134	29	No
10	115	0	0	0	35.3	0.191	45	Yes
2	197	70	45	543	30.5	0.158	53	Yes
8	125	96	32	0	0	0.537	57	Yes
5	166	72	19	175	25.8	0.587	51	No
7	100	0	0	0	30	0.484	32	No

FIGURE 13.10 Feature Selection Example.

In the below example of a diabetes prediction model, the label and features are as follows:

- *Label*: Diabetic
- *Features*:
    - Pregnancies
    - Glucose
    - BloodPressure
    - SkinThickness

- Insulin
- BMI
- DiabetesPedigreeFunction
- Age

Feature Engineering

When the suitable significant features have been selected, then the next step is feature engineering. The art of adding new features that weren't there previously is known as feature engineering. This is the creation of new features from the already existing data to improve the model's performance. Feature engineering needs both the art of innovation and special knowledge of the domain because it manipulates the raw data in such a way that it becomes more relevant to the model.

Training data is necessary for ML algorithms. Developing the AI/ML models is a task for data scientists, and they must complete it first before the feature engineering stage. Engineered features are the features that record extra data that was not in the initial feature set. As a data scientist, you might need to do:

- Draw attention to crucial information in the data.
- Eliminate or isolate irrelevant information (e.g., outliers).
- Modify the data by adding your own subject-specific knowledge and experience.

Feature engineering takes up 80% of a data scientist's time. Training the model and optimizing the hyperparameters make up the easiest 20% of the remaining work. It is essential to undertake adequate feature engineering to enhance the performance of AI/ML models.

Data aggregation, calculating a moving average, and calculating the difference over time are a few examples of feature engineering. The following considerations must be addressed during the feature engineering process:

- The ML model's current capabilities
- Determination of the ideal features
- Whether domain knowledge can enable the use of fewer features
- Identification of new features based on existing data

Creating interaction terms, normalizing data, and generating polynomial features are common practices in feature engineering. For instance, if you are dealing with time-series data, you might create new features that represent the time of day, day of the week, or seasonality patterns. Additionally, complex features such as customer lifetime value or churn rate can be derived from simpler ones to add depth to the data used for modeling. An example of feature engineering can be seen in Figure 13.11.

Customer Id	Customer Name	Location	Age		Remarks
			Formatting Needed		
1	Ajit	India	Thirty Two		Duplicate Entry (Rows 2 & 4)
2	Steve	USA	25		
3	Abraham	France	40		
4	Steve	USA	25		
5	Francis	UK	(Missing)		Missing Information
6	Ankit	India	22		

FIGURE 13.11 Feature Engineering Example.

Model Training

Model training is when an ML algorithm acquires patterns from the data. This operation calls for the preprocessing and engineering of features, followed by their incorporation into the algorithm of your choice for training and subsequent adaptation of parameters. Various algorithms are useful for different types of problems. For instance, linear regression caused by environmental contingents is preferable for continuous target variables, but decision trees might be more fitting for classification tasks.

Over the training period, the algorithm modifies its internal parameters progressively to reduce the error between its predictions and the real target values. Optimization methods such as gradient descent are often utilized to modify these parameters close to perfect, always enhancing the model performance. The training data quality and the hyperparameters' selection are what define the training process.

Ensemble methods are another approach to model training that employs multiple models integrated to produce better results. Dissemination of methodologies such as boosting, bagging, and stacking creates a more robust and accurate prediction due to the synergy input by different models.

Model Evaluation

It is important to evaluate the performance of the model after training to see whether the model generalizes well to unseen data; this is called model performance evaluation. This procedure involves the usage of different indicators to ascertain the accuracy of the model, not in the training set but in the validation or test set, which has never been included in the training phase. This reveals whether the model has overfit the training data or whether it can generalize to new, unseen data after making accurate predictions. The kinds of errors in the evaluation process vary with the different tasks.

For instance, in the case of regression tasks, prediction accuracy is measured by Mean Absolute Error (MAE), Mean Squared Error (MSE), and Root Mean Squared Error (RMSE).

In classification tasks, *accuracy, precision, recall*, and *F1 score* are usually employed. Error types can be deduced from the confusion matrix. We can also use confusion matrices to comprehend the performance of classification models by assessing the types of errors the models are making.

Furthermore, cross-validation, which is the validation of the performance of a model independently of the data used in the training, can be also considered a more accurate technique for assessing the generalization of the trained model. In the case of k-fold cross-validation, for example, the training data is split into k subsets. Then, the model is trained k times, each time using a different subset as the validation set and the remaining data as the training set. This leads to an accurate picture of how the model performs and the data splitting issues that have been exposed are easily addressed the issues of data splitting.

Putting It All Together

The process of building an ML model from beginning to end takes different stages and modifies them back and forth. For example, you can identify some properties that will make it more adaptable, so you can design the process of selecting or creating features while changing settings. The use of non-optimal values for tuning the hyperparameters will lead to further iterations to explain the settings that yield inefficient combinations.

To summarize, the process involves:

1. *Feature selection*: Identifying the key variables that will significantly impact the model.

2. *Feature engineering*: Enhancing and creating new features from the existing data to improve model performance.
3. *Model training*: Using ML algorithms to learn patterns from the data.
4. *Model evaluation*: Assessing the model's accuracy and ability to generalize on unseen data.

TYPES OF ML

There are three types of ML: supervised learning, unsupervised learning, and reinforcement learning. To fully grasp ML, it's essential to distinguish between these approaches. Each method is unique in how it processes data and solves problems, making them suitable for different kinds of tasks:

- Supervised ML can apply what has been learned in the past to new data using labeled examples to predict the future.
- Unsupervised ML is used when the information used to train is neither classified nor labeled events.
- Reinforcement ML is a learning method that interacts with its environment by producing actions and discovering errors or rewards.

The different types of ML can be seen in Figure 13.12.

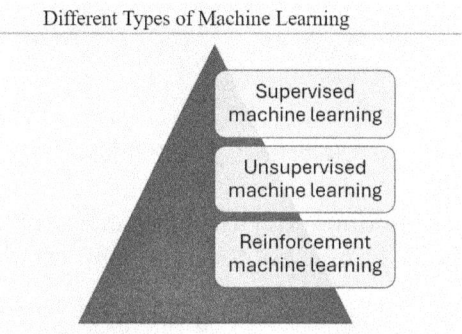

FIGURE 13.12 Different Types of ML.

Supervised Learning

Supervised learning in ML is an approach determined using labeled datasets. A label is an identifier of a piece of data. In this approach, models are trained using labeled data—that is, data that includes both input variables and their corresponding output labels. This setup allows the algorithm to be learned by example. For instance, if we want to predict real estate prices, we might provide the system with numerous examples of property features and their sale prices. The model then learns from these examples to predict future prices based on new input data.

In another example, fruit A has attributes or features of being green in color, round in shape, and the size of a soccer ball. Fruit B has attributes of being yellow in color, somewhat elongated in shape, and the size of a handspan. A fruit with attributes like those mentioned for fruit A is recognized as a watermelon, while a fruit with attributes like those mentioned for fruit B is identified as a banana. Therefore, the label for fruit A is watermelon and the label for fruit B is banana.

An example of features and labels can be seen in Figure 13.13.

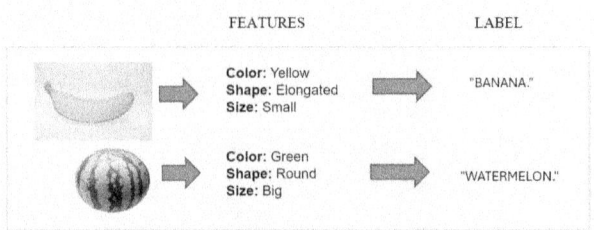

FIGURE 13.13 Example of Features and Labels.

Common algorithms used in supervised learning include neural networks, decision trees, linear regression, and support vector machines.

Supervised learning can be classified into two different categories:

- *Classification*: Classification involves categorizing data into predefined classes, such as determining whether emails are spam or not. In the case of classification, our labels are defined.

- *Regression*: Regression, on the other hand, deals with predicting continuous outcomes, such as estimating house prices based on features such as location, size, and age. In this case, labels are not defined.

Supervised learning finds applications in various fields. It can detect fraudulent bank transactions, forecast sales, identify disease risk factors, evaluate loan applicants, and even predict mechanical failures in industrial equipment. The key advantage here is the transparency and predictability provided by labeled data, which directs the model toward specific goals effectively.

Guidelines for supervised learning models include:

- *Labeled data collection*: Gather comprehensive datasets with clear labels.
- *Algorithm selection*: Choose an appropriate algorithm based on the problem type (classification or regression).
- *Model training*: Train the model using historical data while continually testing and tweaking for better accuracy.
- *Evaluation methods*: Use metrics such as accuracy, precision, recall, and F1 score for classification problems, and MSE for regression tasks.

Unsupervised Learning

In contrast, unsupervised learning deals with unlabeled data. The goal here is not to make predictions but to find hidden patterns and intrinsic structures within the data. Imagine sorting a box of mixed buttons into groups based on shape and color without any prior instructions. This is essentially what unsupervised learning does, leveraging algorithms to automatically discover patterns in data (Machine Learning 101: Supervised, Unsupervised, Reinforcement Learning Explained | Data Science Dojo, n.d.).

Algorithms that are popularized in unsupervised learning (k-means clustering, hierarchical clustering, Markov models (the so-called hidden models), and Gaussian mixture models) are introduced. Very often, when dealing with different problems such as clustering and association, the diversity of these algorithms is the most desirable quality.

Unsupervised learning can be used for purposes such as producing customer segments that are based on buying behavior, organizing inventory based on sales metrics, or revealing the relationship between data concerning customers. By doing this, organizations can produce more accurate and well-informed decisions regarding the customer's buying preferences, stock management issues, and data.

Guidelines for unsupervised learning models include:

1. *Data preprocessing*: Clean and prepare raw data for analysis.

2. *Algorithm selection*: Choose the right clustering or association algorithm based on the dataset's characteristics.

3. *Model training*: Apply algorithms to discover patterns and groupings in the data.

4. *Validation*: Use internal validation metrics such as the silhouette score or external criteria to assess the quality of the clusters.

Overall, we can represent different supervised and unsupervised techniques as shown in Figure 13.14.

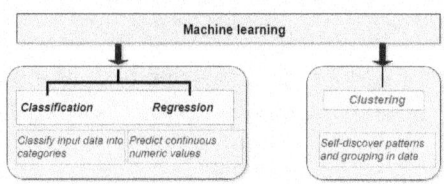

FIGURE 13.14 Different Supervised and Unsupervised Techniques.

Reinforcement Learning

Reinforcement learning is somewhat different from the previous two methods. It mimics the way humans learn by interacting with the environment and receiving feedback. Here, an agent learns to make decisions by performing actions and receiving rewards or penalties as feedback. Think of it like training a pet: good behavior is rewarded, while bad behavior is discouraged (Coursera, 2022).

Reinforcement learning is performed using some key algorithms, including temporal difference, deep adversarial networks, and Q-learning. These models can do the job based on the dataset with which they are trained without the aid of labeled data or supervised training sets. Instead, they teach themselves (in other words, each ML "agent" learns the optimal policy) which action is the best in a given situation via trial and error. Reinforcement learning is a method of training that is particularly effective in the context of environments that are highly dynamic or for continuous adaptation.

Reinforcement learning is typically used in many real-world applications such as autonomous vehicles, robotic control, and game playing. For example, self-driving cars use reinforcement learning to navigate roads efficiently by continuously learning from their surroundings and improving their driving strategies. The same effective approach can also be employed in gaming by AI agents through the application of reinforcement learning.

Guidelines for reinforcement learning include:

1. *Define environment and reward system*: Clearly outline the environment's parameters and establish a reward system.

2. *Algorithm selection*: Choose appropriate reinforcement learning algorithms based on the task's complexity and computational resources.

3. *Training*: Allow the agent to interact with the environment and learn from the feedback.

4. *Simulation and real-world testing*: Validate the agent's performance through simulations and eventually in real-world scenarios.

Comparative Characteristics and Applications

Each type of ML has unique characteristics and is suited for different types of data and problem-solving contexts. Supervised learning excels with structured, labeled data and clear prediction goals. Unsupervised learning shines when discovering hidden patterns in unlabeled datasets. Reinforcement learning thrives in dynamic environments requiring adaptive decision-making and continuous learning.

The ML overall picture can be seen in Figure 13.15.

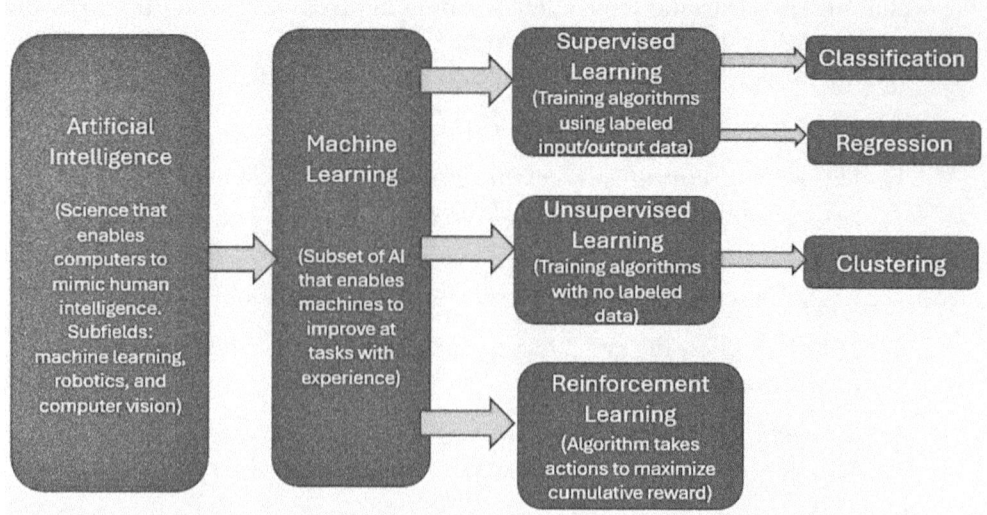

FIGURE 13.15 Machine Learning Overall Picture.

MACHINE LEARNING BUILDING BLOCKS

ML is the heart of existing AI technology. ML follows these steps:

1. Problem definition
2. Data gathering and preparation
3. Model selection or hypothesis generation
4. Training and evaluation
5. Hyperparameter tuning
6. Predictive modeling
7. Model deployment/implementation

DL has the same building blocks, as DL is a subset of ML.

ML building blocks can be seen in Figure 13.16.

Machine Learning Building block

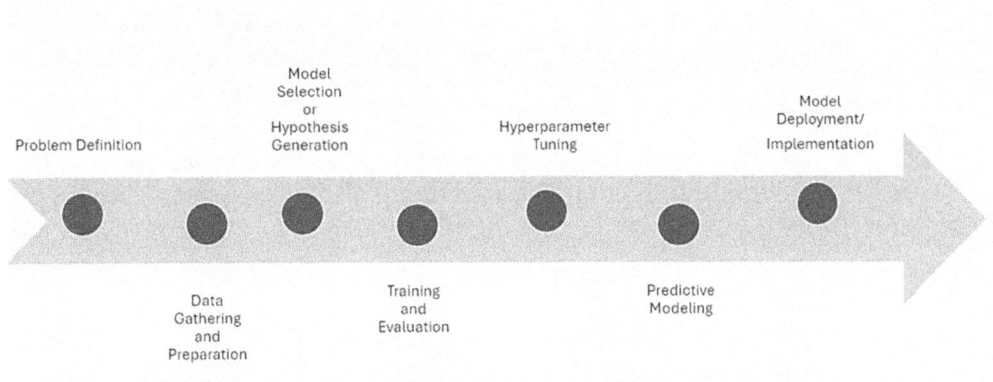

FIGURE 13.16 Machine Learning Building Blocks.

These are the seven important steps for building the ML model, so let's go over them one by one.

Problem Definition

The first step is to define the problem you want to solve and the success criteria. Some of the key questions that need to be answered in this stage are:

- What's the business objective that requires a cognitive solution?
- Which parts of the solution are cognitive, and which are not?
- Have all the necessary technical, business, and deployment issues been addressed?
- What are the defined "success" criteria for the project?
- How can the project be staged in iterative sprints?
- Are there any special requirements for transparency, explainability, or bias reduction?
- What are the ethical considerations?
- What are the acceptable parameters for accuracy, precision, and confusion matrix values?
- What are the expected inputs to the model and the expected outputs?

- What are the characteristics of the problem being solved? Is this a classification, regression, or clustering problem?
- What is the "heuristic" approach to solving the problem that doesn't require ML? How much better than that does the model need to be?
- How will the benefits of the model be measured?

Although there are a lot of questions to be answered during the first step, answering or even attempting to answer them will greatly increase the chances of overall project success.

Data Gathering and Preparation

Once the sponsor approves your ML project and the stakeholders are fully aware of the project and success criteria, then you can enter this step.

Data Collection

You must collect data from various sources in various formats, but you must ensure the data has the right format before it can be used in the ML project. Here are some key questions that must be considered:

- Where are the sources of the data that is needed for training the model?
- How much data is needed for the ML project?
- What is the current quantity and quality of training data?
- How are the test data and training data being split?
- For supervised learning tasks, is there a way to label that data?
- Can pre-trained models be used?
- Where is the operational and training data located?
- Are there special needs for accessing real-time data on edge devices or in more difficult-to-reach places?

Data Preparation

Once we can answer those questions, we need to prepare the data for future stages and do the activities as follows:

- Collect data from various sources.
- Standardize formats across different data sources.

- Replace incorrect data.
- Enhance and augment data.
- Add more dimensions with pre-calculated amounts and aggregate information as needed.
- Enhance data with third-party data.
- "Multiply" image-based datasets if they aren't sufficient for training.
- Remove extraneous information and deduplication.
- Remove irrelevant data from training to improve results.
- Reduce noise reduction and remove ambiguity.
- Consider anonymizing data.
- Normalize or standardize data to get it into formatted ranges.
- Sample data from large datasets.
- Select features that identify the most important dimensions and, if necessary, reduce dimensions using a variety of techniques.
- Split data into training, test, and validation sets.

Model Selection or Hypothesis Generation

Once you've defined the problem and extracted and prepared the data, you can list down all the possible hypotheses that might solve the problem. It's very important to make sure you fail on all possible hypotheses at this stage.

Remember, this is what you'll be working with to cast your idea netwide so include all ideas at the beginning.

This phase requires model technique, application, and appropriate algorithm selection. To accomplish all that, the following actions are required:

- Select the right algorithm based on the learning objective and data requirements.
- Identify the features that provide the best results.
- Determine whether model explainability or interpretability is required.
- Develop ensemble models for improved performance.

Algorithms for different types of ML can be seen in Figure 13.17.

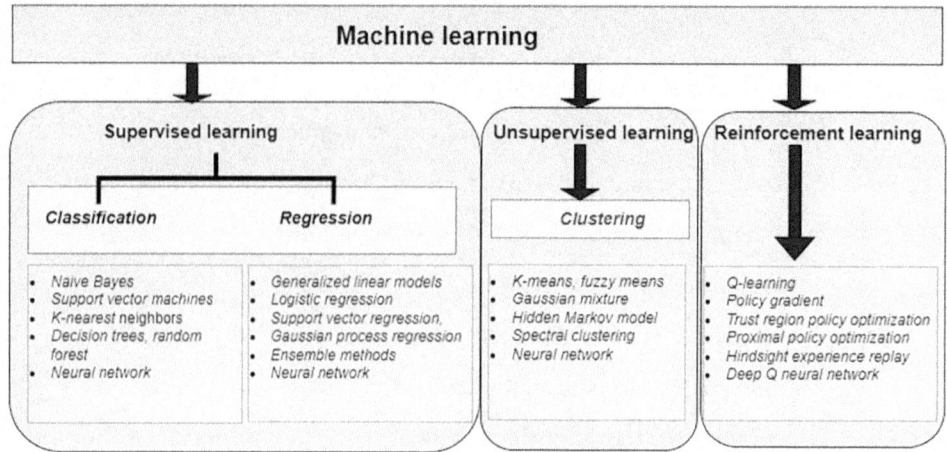

FIGURE 13.17 Algorithms for Different Types of ML.

Data Training and Evaluation

In this phase, we need to divide the available data into training and validation data. Training data is used for training the model, whereas validation data is used for evaluating the ML model. A word of caution is that data available in the training set should not be used for validation, as this can lead to overfitting and an overly optimistic assessment of the model's performance. Instead, the validation data should be a separate subset that accurately represents real-world scenarios, ensuring a fair evaluation of the model's ability to generalize to new data.

Training vs. validation data can be seen in Figure 13.18.

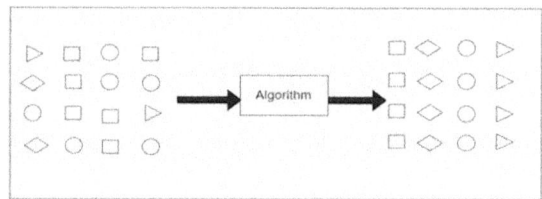

FIGURE 13.18 Training vs. Validation Data.

Training and validation data must be different to provide better results and accuracy in the final prediction. The training dataset is the largest sample of data used when creating an ML model. The validation dataset is a second sample of data used to provide an evaluation of the model to see whether the model can correctly predict, or classify, using data not seen before. The validation dataset is used to tune the model. It helps to get an unbiased evaluation of the model while tuning its hyperparameters.

A testing dataset is a set of data used to provide a final unbiased evaluation of the model. A test dataset is an independent sample of data and is used once a model has been completely trained with the training and validation datasets.

The dataset is generally divided into 70% for training and 30% for testing. Sometimes, we might include a validation dataset as well, and then we divide it into 70%, 20%, and 10% segments for training, validation, and testing, respectively (numbers may vary).

The division of a dataset into training, validation, and testing can be seen in Figure 13.19.

FIGURE 13.19 Division of a Dataset into Training, Validation, and Testing.

Hyperparameter Tuning

Once you've done the evaluation, you may want to see whether you can further improve your training in any way. You can do this by tuning your parameters. There were a few parameters we implicitly assumed when we did our training, and now is a good time to go back and test those assumptions and try other values. Differences can be seen depending on whether a model starts off training with values initialized to zero versus some distribution of values, which leads to the question of which distribution to use. As you can see, there are many considerations at this phase of training, and it's important that you define what makes a model "good enough;" otherwise, you might find yourself tweaking parameters for a very long time. These parameters are typically referred to as *hyperparameters* The adjustment, or tuning, of these hyperparameters remains a bit of an art, and is an experimental process that heavily depends on the specifics of your dataset, model, and training process. Once you're happy with your training and hyperparameters, guided by the evaluation step, it's time to finally use your model to do something useful!

Let us discuss some of the important hyperparameters.

Epochs Parameter

This parameter defines how many times we run through the training dataset during training. We can "show" the model our full dataset multiple times, rather than just once. This can sometimes lead to higher accuracies.

Learning Rate

Another parameter is the *learning rate*. This defines how far we shift the line during each step, based on the information from the previous training step. These values all play a role in how accurate our model can become, and how long the training takes. For more complex models, initial conditions can play a significant role in determining the outcome of training.

Accuracy and Loss

The loss value implies how poorly or well a model behaves after each iteration of optimization. An accuracy metric is used to measure the algorithm's performance in an interpretable way. The accuracy of a model is usually determined after the model parameters and is calculated in the form of a percentage.

Batches

A batch is a subset of the training dataset. It is used to train the model in smaller, more manageable chunks. This approach can:

- *Reduce memory usage*: Processing smaller batches requires less memory.
- *Improve computational efficiency*: Smaller batches can be processed faster.
- *Introduce stochasticity*: The randomness introduced by using different batches can help prevent the model from getting stuck in local optima.

Batch Size

The batch size is the number of data points in a batch. Choosing the right batch size is crucial for optimal training.

Large batch sizes:

- Can provide more stable gradients, leading to faster convergence.
- Require more memory and computational resources.

Smaller batch sizes:

- Can introduce more noise, which can help prevent overfitting.
- Are generally more computationally efficient.

For example, if you have a dataset of 1000 images, you could divide it into batches of 100 images each. This would result in 10 batches.

Iterations

An iteration is a single pass through the entire dataset, where each batch is processed once. For example, if you have 10 batches, one iteration would involve processing all 10 batches.

Epochs

An epoch is a complete pass through the entire dataset, considering all batches. If you have 10 batches and perform 3 iterations, that would be equivalent to 3 epochs.

In summary:

- *Batches*: Subsets of the dataset used for training.
- *Batch size*: The number of data points in a batch.
- *Iterations*: The number of times all batches are processed.
- *Epochs*: Complete passes through the entire dataset.

Choosing the right batch size and number of iterations is a hyperparameter tuning process that depends on factors such as dataset size, hardware, and the desired level of accuracy.

Predictive Modeling

ML uses data to answer questions. So, prediction, or inference, is the step where we get to answer some questions. This is the point of all this work, where the value of ML is realized. We can finally use our model to predict whether a given drink is wine or beer, given its color and alcohol percentage.

Model Deployment/Implementation

ML models' deployment refers to putting models in production, making your models available to various systems within the organization or the Web, thus allowing them to receive data and return predictions.

The deployment phase in the production environment should be the most cost- and performance-effective one.

An ML model vs. prediction example can be seen in Figure 13.20.

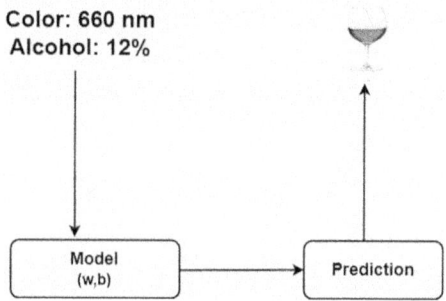

FIGURE 13.20 Machine Learning Model vs. Prediction Example 1.

The de facto standard for deploying ML models is as an on-demand prediction service. Batch prediction mode is considered. Also, some modern applications provide embedded models for edge and mobile devices. Therefore, we can classify the types of model deployment as follows:

- On-demand prediction mode
- Batch prediction mode
- Embedded model mode

A second ML model vs. prediction example can be seen in Figure 13.21.

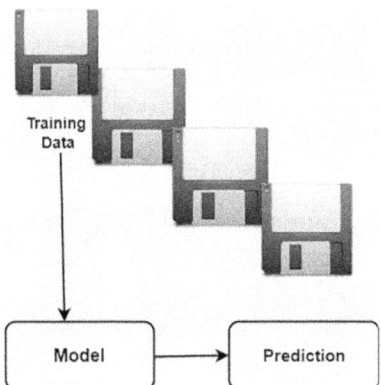

FIGURE 13.21 Machine Learning Model vs. Prediction Example 2.

Web services can provide cheaper and near real-time predictions. The maintenance of CPU power is not an issue when the program runs on the cluster or using an online service. API calls can easily make the model available to other applications. The best results of optimization in the batch processing scenario are sought in reducing the cost of model computing power. There is less need to rely on cloud services and external data sources. The computing of algorithmically complex models sometimes requires more power than is found in local processors. Embedded models are adaptable to our specifications and thus we can ensure the performance of a certain device by customizing it.

GENERATIVE AI DEFINITION AND COMPONENTS

Generative AI represents a transformative leap in AI by enabling machines to create content that is indistinguishable from that produced by humans. Unlike traditional AI models that primarily analyze data or perform specific tasks, generative AI can generate new and original outputs, such as text, images, music, and even entire videos.

At its core, generative AI refers to algorithms that can generate new content based on the data they have been trained on. This can include generating realistic images, natural language text, or even new musical compositions. By employing various underlying models, generative AI learns the underlying patterns and structures of data, allowing it to synthesize new, coherent content that mirrors human creativity.

How Does Generative AI Work?

Generative AI operates through advanced ML techniques that drive its functionality. The main steps in its methodology typically include the following.

Training

Training generative models is a complex and iterative process whereby the models are supplied with large datasets, and the input examples are studied to learn patterns and representations. This training process is critical for the models to be able to generate new, realistic data that is similar to the original dataset. Moreover, by constantly changing the parameters and structure of the model according to data, generative models can become better and quicker in the process of creating new content. In addition, the training of generative models often requires much computational power and time because of the high dimensionality and complexity of the model. Nevertheless, because of advancements in ML methods and techniques, researchers and programmers have been able to optimize the training procedures in order to boost the generative models' skills and their use in various fields including image generation, text synthesis, and even music composition.

Sampling

A model that has been trained on a dataset can learn the hidden patterns and structures of the data. The model can then generate new content from the patterns learned by the model. This step is called *sampling*, where the model can generate new content by randomly choosing sequences of data based on the patterns it has learned. The model produces not only the training data but also new and unique content, thus allowing it to use creativity and innovation. Sampling is the process of creating randomness and diversity in content generated by AI models, which makes them good tools for a wide range of applications.

Refinement

Generated content is often refined through feedback loops or additional model training to improve quality and coherence. Refinement of generated content is a crucial step in ensuring its quality and coherence. Through feedback loops and additional model training, any discrepancies or errors in the content can be identified and corrected. This iterative process allows for continuous improvement, as the feedback received from users or experts can be used to fine-tune the content and make it more accurate, engaging, and relevant. By refining the generated content, it becomes more valuable and trustworthy, ultimately leading to a more satisfying experience for the end users. Additionally, ongoing model training helps to keep the content up to date with changing trends and information, ensuring that it remains current and reliable. Overall, the refinement stage plays a significant role in enhancing the overall effectiveness and impact of the generated content.

By leveraging these methods, generative AI has unlocked new realms of creativity across multiple domains.

DIFFERENT APPLICATIONS OF GENERATIVE AI

Generative AI is making a significant impact in various fields. Let's look at some notable applications.

Different applications of generative AI can be seen in Figure 13.22.

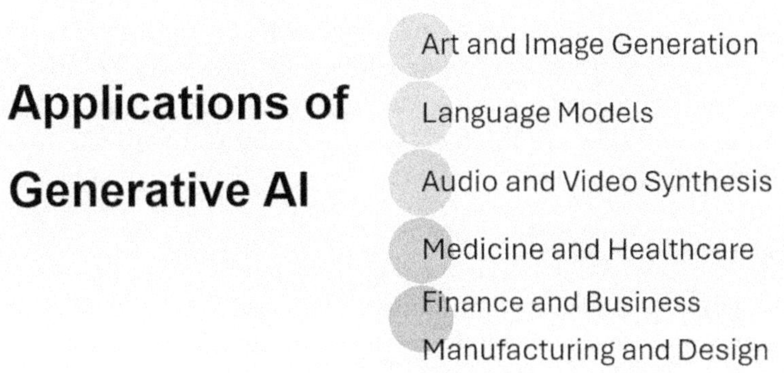

Applications of Generative AI
- Art and Image Generation
- Language Models
- Audio and Video Synthesis
- Medicine and Healthcare
- Finance and Business
- Manufacturing and Design

FIGURE 13.22 Different Applications of Generative AI.

Art and Image Generation

Artists use generative AI tools to create unique artworks, expanding the boundaries of traditional art forms. Artists are now showing great interest in manipulating generative AI tools that are beyond classical traditional art forms to come up with artworks that are really out of the ordinary. Through the power of AI, they can discover new styles and techniques that weren't even possible before. These AI tools enable artists to feel free to test different parameters such as color, shape, and texture to create unique images. Art and technology have become connected to such an extent that unique pieces of art are made that are not only seen but also challenge others to redefine the concept of art. With AI continuing to improve, the opportunities for artists who want to create exciting and brand-new works of art are practically unlimited. The incorporation of generative AI in art both offers novel outcomes in the artistic process and demonstrates the potential of the human-machine partnership in the creative stage.

Language Models

Language models have become the backbone of creating advanced applications that range from chatbots to content creation and communication to interaction across platforms. They are an important part of the process in the development of a wide range of applications that use NLP. These models, which can comprehend and produce human language, now form part of the technologies that include chatbots and content creation tools. Language models can allow developers to create dynamically intuitive conversational interfaces that will result in more effective and interactive experiences for users. These models are being developed and improved continuously so that more accurate and context-sensitive responses can be obtained in different scenarios. Language models have a huge impact on the development of technology, and they are the tools we use to interact with and use information on different platforms.

Audio and Video Synthesis

Generative AI can compose music and create realistic video content; thereby, a new entertainment media project can be achieved by bringing the concept of virtual reality into real life. Generative AI technology has transformed the process of audio content creation and consumption in the entertainment and media field to a great extent. An AI with ML algorithms can now create music and generate video content with precision and creativity; it is no longer just a dream. Not only are artists and creators assisted in producing high-quality, original work but new possibilities for interactive and immersive experiences for audiences are also introduced. With the use of computers, skills such as creating background scores for movies and designing virtual reality experiences can be developed; generative AI is innovating the entertainment industry.

The use of generative AI technologies has made movie production much easier and faster thanks to the fact that AI can adapt and improve over time. This changes the whole concept, blurring the lines between human and AI creativity that were previously fixed and clear.

Medicine and Healthcare

Generative models have become very important in the medical industry for early drug development, medical imaging, and accurately collecting and analyzing customer feedback, enabling customized treatment plans for individual clients. These models are key to a faster and more accurate drug discovery process by helping to predict and simulate the chemical structure and physiology of the possible new compounds and identify the most suitable candidates for further research. In the context of medical imaging, generative models make it possible to create high-quality images and enhance the visualization of internal structures, enabling doctors to increase the accuracy and efficiency of diagnostics.

Finance and Business

Generative AI is leading change in finance and business. In finance, it creates precise forecasts, simulates risks, and automates reports for data-based decisions. In business, it helps with marketing, gives executives real-time info, and automates tasks like data entry and inventory. It also improves customer service using chatbots, personalized advice, and sentiment analysis to tailor strategies. With Generative AI, companies can innovate, reduced costs, and work better in an increasingly data-driven world.

Manufacturing and Design

Generative design tools are employed by engineering and design professionals, enabling them to create optimized designs by means of parameter adjustments and simulations. Production and design have been significantly modified with the generative design tools.

With generative design, professionals can explore a wide range of design options and easily iterate through different possibilities to find the most effective solution. This has not only speeds up the design process but also leads to the creation of more innovative and efficient products. By harnessing the power of generative design, engineers and designers are able to push the boundaries of what is possible in manufacturing and design, leading to groundbreaking solutions that were previously unimaginable.

Defining Foundation Models, Prompts, and Prompt Engineering

Foundation Models (FMs) represent a groundbreaking advancement in AI, designed to handle a wide variety of input types and produce versatile outputs. These models are highly adaptable and can be specialized for specific modalities, such as text, video, audio, or images. Beyond these general capabilities, FMs can also be fine-tuned for specialized datasets, such as predicting DNA sequences or performing domain-specific tasks.

Large Language Models

Large Language Models (LLMs) are a subset of FMs uniquely optimized for language-related tasks. Trained on extensive text datasets, LLMs excel at generating coherent text, summarizing or extracting information, answering questions, and facilitating conversational exchanges. This proficiency makes them invaluable tools for diverse applications, ranging from automated content creation to interactive support systems.

Multimodal Capabilities

Some FMs extend their functionality to handle multiple types of input and output. For instance, a multimodal model might accept an image as input and produce a text description in response. This ability to bridge modalities expands the potential use cases of generative AI, enabling sophisticated interactions across diverse data types.

Understanding Prompts

Prompts serve as the mechanism for instructing an FM. By providing a prompt—a specific instruction or query—users can guide the model to generate relevant and tailored responses. For example, consider the prompt "Summarize this article in 300 words" accompanied by a link to an article on responsible AI. Submitting this prompt to an LLM might yield a concise summary of the content. Amazon Bedrock provides a convenient platform for experimenting with such prompts via its text playground feature. Users can select a model, input prompts, and observe the responses directly.

Building Generative AI Applications

Applications such as Amazon Bedrock benefit from generative AI techniques when developers send prompts through API calls to the service. The service receives the prompt and processes it through its model to deliver the results to the developers via the API. On the negative side, creating efficient prompts usually requires some sort of modification. Developers are forced to reasonably experiment and iterate on prompts to be sure that their produced outputs only correspond to the specific application. This creative, trial-and-error process is indispensable for tapping into the entire power of generative AI.

Prompt Engineering

Prompt engineering is the continued process of creating and perfecting prompts in order to make the best output. The context is very important in this amendment. One example is the way the initial prompt "a dog at a park" can be improved by introducing extra details: "a small curly-haired dog at a park with a fountain." At the same time, for text-based assignments, prompts can be customized to tone, style, or audience. For example, changing from "Summarize this article" to "You are an instructor teaching a course on Internet safety to sixth graders. Summarize this article for your students" provides the right traits to produce information with a purpose.

Prompt engineering often involves chaining prompts together for complex tasks. For example, after generating a summary of an article, the output could serve as the basis for a subsequent prompt: "Using this summary, create the text for five PowerPoint slides." This iterative approach enhances precision and enables the development of complex workflows.

Equipping developers with knowledge about FMs, prompts, and prompt engineering will lead to successful AI model training that will change the industry. With the help of these methods, people can direct models in AI by ensuring that the models are not only useful but also scalable and flexible for any required needs and objectives.

Defining Tokens, Embeddings, Vectors, and Transformers

The goal of LLMs is to predict what might come next by using the context of words in a sequence. So, for example, if you say, "The cat jumped onto the...," you might think that the next word could be "couch" or "table," based on contextual hints and previous knowledge of how cats behave. While the next word can be something unexpected like "kayak," this is far less likely. LLMs apply this same principle, using patterns and relationships they've learned from vast datasets to make predictions about the continuation of text. Four foundational concepts underpinning this process are tokens, embeddings, vectors, and transformers.

Tokens

    An LLM tokenizes text, which serves as a fundamental building block for processing. Every token could represent a word, part of a word, or even a single character. For instance, the sentence "10 cats jumped on to the table!" may be divided into eight tokens: one for every word and one for the exclamation mark. Tokens help the model to carve up text into manageable parts that can be further analyzed.

Embeddings

    Once segmented into tokens, embeddings are used to convert them to the numerical format. Embeddings store and express related information as high-dimensional vectors, enabling the model to capture semantic relationships. For example, for the tokens "cat" and "kitten" to be situated close to "cat" and "kitten" in the multidimensional space, they must be similar in meaning. At the same time, "cat" and "king" should be placed apart from each other.

Vectors

    A vector functions as a point of reference in a high-dimensional space, illustrating the semantic meaning of a token or sequence as a location. This capability enables the model to understand not only individual words but also complex relationships and patterns. The vectors enable the LLM to generalize, so it understands and draws inferences from text sequences, not just individual items.

Transformers

    Transformers refer to a type of neural network architecture that is designed to efficiently process vectors and work out the relationships among them. Unlike the previous neural networks, which process texts sequentially, transformers can analyze different parts of a sequence simultaneously, thus identifying the most critical components. As a result of this parallel processing capacity, transformers have become a core of modern LLMs, fostering their rapid development and broad usage.

Different Types of Generative AI

    Generative AI encompasses several types of models, each excelling in different areas of content creation. We'll look at the core types next.

Different types of generative AI can be seen in Figure 13.23.

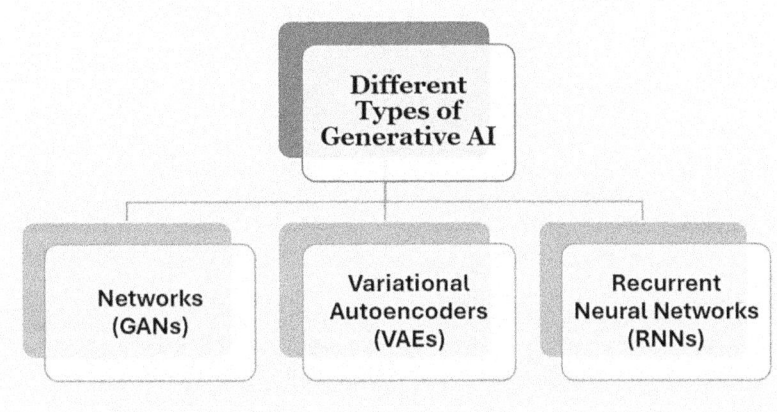

FIGURE 13.23 Different Types of Generative AI.

GANs

GANs have come into the spotlight in the worlds of AI and ML for their ability to generate high-quality images and videos. Generative Adversarial Networks (GANs) constitute a break through in AI by having two competing neural networks such as Generator and Discriminator. On one hand the Generator creates synthetic data through random input and on the other hand the Discriminator gets both real and generated data and judges them as real or fake. Both networks are getting trained in an adversarial way so the Generator gets better in producing fakes and the Discriminator acquires the skill to recognize them. This adversarial training gradually improves the quality of the generated data.

GANs can be seen in Figure 13.24., which clearly demonstrates this process. Fake and real examples are fed into the Discriminator, which guides the updates of both models. This competitive loop allows GANs to generate highly realistic outputs.

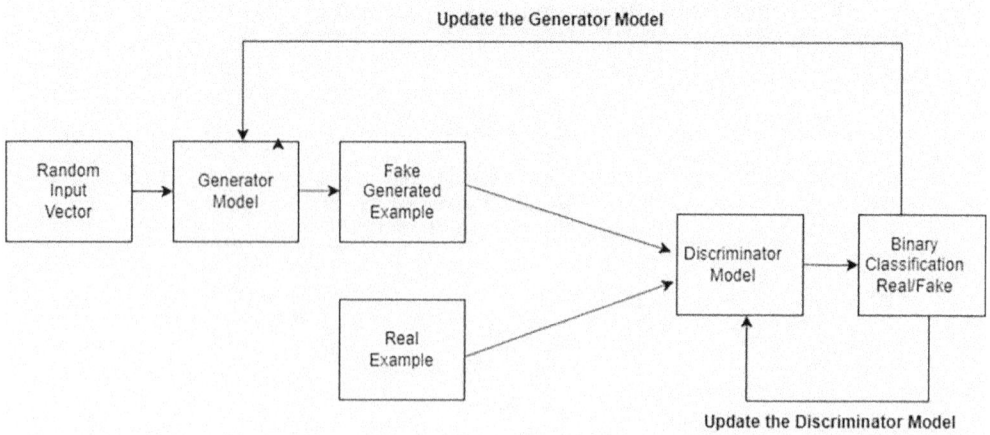

FIGURE 13.24 Generative Adversarial Networks (GANs).

GANs are used for many purposes; they are applied in voice synthesis, producing original music, or creating new pictures from text, to name a few examples. It is also possible to obtain realistic images of people or create fresh artistic styles by using them.

VAEs

A type of DL model, VAEs are a type of neural network that is developed with just one purpose, which is to find data patterns for creating new content. These automated data gathering and processing tools are well-established in image production and data compression. VAEs work by encoding input data into the latent space representing the features and relationships of the data. The information in the latent space is then decoded to yield new variations of the input data. VAEs have the potential to produce results that are very similar to the input data but also differ in the learning aspect by learning and capturing these patterns and relationships. This unique pattern in the data significantly highlights the VAEs' ability to develop new, realistic images from the original dataset in the process of image generation. Furthermore, VAEs are also beneficial for data compression as they can compress data in a very efficient manner without compromising the significant parts of the data while decoding it. In conclusion, VAEs are a dynamic and versatile tool for pattern recognition and data modification tasks.

VAEs are one of the most popular types of generative models that can generate new images that are closely related to the training data, by performing data compression and anomaly detection.

Recurrent Neural Networks

Recurrent Neural Networks (RNNs) are a specific kind of neural network that is used to process data in a certain order, which is perfect for generating and adapting language as well as creating musical notes that go along with it. With their unique structure, RNNs can store statistical patterns from past inputs and generate sequences that relate to the structure of the data they learned. This ability to capture dependencies regarding elements in a sequence makes RNNs a powerful tool for tasks that involve processing time series or generating new sequences after learning patterns from existing data. Whether it is writing music or completing the next word in a sentence, RNNs put their skill of ordering into practice, thus achieving extraordinary results across a wide range of applications.

Popular Tools and Web Sites for Exploring Generative AI

Several tools and platforms have emerged for users to experiment and create with. Some of the most popular are discussed next.

ChatGPT by OpenAI

ChatGPT by OpenAI is built around an excellent, highly effective conversational AI, which can write and engage with users in the form of text while also creating an environment to actively engage users in interactive dialogues. The most interesting feature of this state-of-the-art technology is that it can maintain a seamless conversation and reply to users as a human would. With ChatGPT, users can hold genuine and interesting conversations on various subjects, which makes it a useful tool for applications such as customer service, virtual assistants, and even entertainment, among others. ChatGPT utilizes the unparalleled power of AI to offer a service that is personalized and flexible, and consequently, users have a more complete and satisfactory experience. It is the first AI technology that is truly capable of understanding context, generating coherent responses, and adjusting to different conversational styles, and has drastically changed the way we relate to AI.

Visit *https://chat.openai.com* for more information.

DALL·E by OpenAI

DALL·E, created by OpenAI, is the most advanced image generation tool that shows the unlimited possibilities of AI. DALL·E redefines the potential of the combination of language and art through the processing of textual descriptions and the production of amazing visual creations. Such technological feats open up a whole new dimension of creativity, enabling deeper exploration in visual storytelling and artistic expression. The combination of language and visual art in DALL·E enables you to create genuinely mind-boggling images that were once only imagined. Its innovative approach could potentially change the world of visual imagery expression and the way we relate to images, leading to new forms of art and communication. DALL·E is an efficient tool to produce images and a testament to the ability of AI to transform the artistic process and inspire new ways of thinking.

Visit *https://openai.com/index/dall-e-3/* for more information.

RunwayML

RunwayML is an innovative platform that offers the creators of the art world a variety of generative tools that can be used to enhance their projects. With options such as image and video synthesis, RunwayML allows users to explore new ways of developing content that is visually stunning. From producing one-of-a-kind images to transforming video footage in innovative ways, this venue is a source of endless opportunities for artists, designers, and filmmakers. Through ML algorithms, RunwayML opens not only the road to creativity and personal development but also the opportunity to experiment with the most recent technology. Whether you are looking to add a futuristic touch to your designs or create mesmerizing visuals for your next project, RunwayML provides the tools and resources to bring your ideas to life in a whole new way.

Visit *https://runwayml.com* for more information.

Midjourney

Midjourney is a virtual platform that serves the purpose of getting users to think creatively by only concentrating on the artistic image generation process. It is a place for people to explore and play with different visual styles and express themselves in a visually dynamic manner. With a multitude of tools and features, you can efficiently modify images, attach effects, and beautify your art, subsequently creating magnificent projects that symbolize your personality. Regardless of whether you are an expert artist who is striving to boost your contribution to the worldwide artistic community or just beginning your first artistic adventure, Midjourney offers a supportive and inspiring environment for all levels of talent.

Visit *https://midjourney.com* for more information.

SOUNDRAW

SOUNDRAW is a wonderful tool that is transforming the world of music. With its advanced technology, musicians can now easily create entirely new and exclusive soundtracks. Gone are the days when you had to struggle for hours on end to come up with new and creative melodies and harmonies; SOUNDRAW will handle that for you. This tool has provided musicians with a wide range of new sound possibilities, allowing them to experiment with different sounds and genres. SOUNDRAW can be used by both professionals and beginners.

Visit *https://soundraw.io/* for more information.

GitHub Copilot

GitHub Copilot is a groundbreaking tool that is changing the way developers write code. By using the power of AI, Copilot shows code suggestions and reference code snippets, enabling faster and more efficient code. Developers no longer have to search for documentation or test everything at least once to find the best code solution. Using Copilot, developers can scroll through a whole set of ideas and get the right feedback at their fingertips, thus decreasing time and minimizing errors. This makes the whole coding process much easier. In addition, the code can be made available for other developers with the features of live sharing and recommendations. GitHub Copilot is a disruptor in the software sector, enabling developers to eliminate unnecessary code and write more precise and understandable code.

Visit *https://github.com/features/copilot* for more information.

Key Generative AI AWS Services

AWS provides a complete suite of fully managed services to support various methods of interaction with FMs, such as reusing, augmenting, customizing, or creating new models from scratch. The three AWS services that suit these methods are Amazon SageMaker, Amazon Bedrock, and Amazon Q.

Let's have a closer look at how these services support your needs.

Key generative AI AWS services can be seen in Figure 13.25.

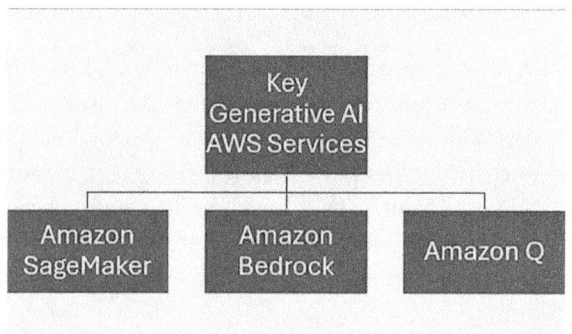

FIGURE 13.25 Key Generative AI AWS Services.

Amazon SageMaker

Amazon SageMaker is a comprehensive management service that is meant to help throughout the ML lifecycle. It assists data scientists and developers in building, training, and deploying models in a production-ready environment. SageMaker has an additional feature called Amazon SageMaker JumpStart, which is an ML center that has:

- FMs
- Built-in algorithms
- Prebuilt ML solutions deployable with just a few clicks

With SageMaker JumpStart, you can leverage innovative techniques such as Retrieval-Augmented Generation (RAG) and customize FMs to align with your specific requirements.

Amazon Bedrock

Amazon Bedrock ensures the accessibility of FMs by means of a unified API. It allows users to:

- Experiment with a variety of pretrained models to identify the best fit for their use case
- Enhance models using their own data sources for augmentation or customization

Bedrock has been designed with a focus on security, privacy, and responsible AI, ensuring that applications have strong safeguards. Moreover, its capabilities go beyond handling critical issues, such as compliance and ethical AI usage.

Amazon Q

Amazon Q is a set of customized tools that can help accelerate AI adoption:

- *Amazon Q Developer*: This simplifies development with features such as code generation and expert guidance for building solutions using AWS services.
- *Amazon Q Business*: This enables the creation of interactive chat applications that integrate LLM knowledge with enterprise-specific data.

These capabilities make Amazon Q a valuable asset for both technical and business-focused AI implementations.

Unified Security and Access Control

All these services come with integrated security measures and access controls managed through AWS's familiar tools. Key features include:

- Default encryption of data
- Granular encryption and access controls for enhanced data and model protection
- Assurance that customer data is not used to train Amazon or third-party models

By utilizing these AWS services, organizations can confidently manage the complexities of AI-powered cloud migration and prioritize both operational effectiveness and security best practices in the process.

Amazon SageMaker for Generative AI

Amazon SageMaker is a completely managed service designed for a wide range of ML applications, which include the development and deployment of generative AI models. It allows you to work in an integrated development environment that makes the process of building, training, and deploying ML models at scale (including FMs) simple. SageMaker provides powerful infrastructure and dedicated tools that give support to all the processes of the ML lifecycle, for example, training resources, MLOps as governance functions, and ML operations utilities. These tools are invaluable for ML engineers, data scientists, and developers.

Key Features for Generative AI

Two important features of Amazon SageMaker that are beneficial for AI generative are SageMaker Jumpstart and SageMaker Clarify:

- *Amazon SageMaker Jumpstart*:
    - A centralized hub offering easy access to publicly available FMs that can be deployed with minimal effort.
    - Facilitates advanced techniques such as prompt engineering, RAG, and model customization.
    - Accelerates the development process, enabling users to integrate generative AI capabilities seamlessly into their workflows.
- *Amazon SageMaker Clarify*:
    - Designed to support the evaluation of model quality and responsibility metrics, particularly for text-based FMs.
    - Provides insights into performance and fairness, ensuring that generative AI models meet both technical and ethical standards.

Flexible Pricing Model

SageMaker comes with a pay-as-you-go pricing model, where the cost is based on the consumption of resources such as computing power, storage, and other services for which you pay only when you use them. This methodology provides flexibility and reduces costs, although it also requires careful budget management, particularly for resource-intensive generative AI projects. Thorough planning and monitoring are essential to ensure the project stays within budget and meets its requirements.

Customization and Control

Amazon SageMaker's ability to provide granular control over model customization of the model, as well as the complete lifecycle of the training and deploying process, is one of its most outstanding advantages. This makes it an ideal choice for specialized cases. For example, a healthcare organization that develops predictive models for patient outcomes that are based on specific biomarkers can make use of SageMaker's features.

The decision to go with Amazon SageMaker means that you have a complete solution that you can use to design, personalize, and scale the most advanced DL AI models, while still maintaining control and flexibility. The main reason for that responsive environment is the precision of the tools and rich features that come with it, enabling users to introduce innovation in AWS cloud migration projects and other applications.

Amazon Bedrock for Generative AI

Amazon Bedrock, which is a managed service, enables the simplified creation of generative AI applications as it provides multiple FMs through a shared API. Such flexibility lets developers play with various models and thus integrate or improve them with small code modifications. Moreover, non-developers can engage in interactive playgrounds while using the console to investigate the models and practice prompting techniques, which makes Amazon Bedrock also convenient for those who are not adept at ML.

Key Features of Amazon Bedrock

Amazon Bedrock Knowledge Bases

This new addition facilitates the induction of the RAG system without the custom integration necessary for internal data sources. This will allow efficient access and retrieval of relevant information, which, in turn, will improve the user's understanding and experience.

Model Customization

Amazon Bedrock enables the private customization of FMs by using their own data. This method sets the right tone so that AI-powered applications are tailored to corporate requirements and thus deliver a more customized and useful solution.

Amazon Bedrock Guardrails

This feature commits to ethical AI practices by giving users the option to set up policies that will filter out undesirable or harmful content. Moreover, they can delete or mask private data such as sources of information or locations from which the news is received to avoid the possibility of the security of information being compromised.

Multiple guardrails could be set up for various use cases and used on all the FMs to maintain consistent safety and privacy controls that ensure the applications of creative AI across the board are secure.

Model Evaluation

To aid in selecting the most suitable FM, Amazon Bedrock supports model evaluation for text-based tasks. Automatic evaluation jobs or jobs involving human reviewers can be selected. This feature makes sure that the model that is picked fits the use case.

Pricing Model

Amazon Bedrock offers an on-demand pricing structure based on token usage—covering both input prompts and model responses. Image-based models use the number of images generated to calculate the price. Additionally, some FMs offer a provisioned throughput option, enabling users to be charged by an hourly rate calculated on the maximum number of tokens processed per minute. Separate pricing options exist in the case of customization or evaluation of the model to fit the users' needs and budget.

Benefits of Using Amazon Bedrock

Consider, for example, a customer support company that wants to improve its chat facility through AI-driven responses; it could use Amazon Bedrock to deploy advanced capabilities effectively and efficiently.

Through Amazon Bedrock, companies can easily accelerate the global usage of generative AI technologies, and maintain flexibility, privacy, and governed AI practices. This product is an example of how AWS can drive the innovation of AI-driven solutions and make sure that companies are still in the market as the world of technology changes.

Amazon Q for Generative AI

Amazon Q is a suite of generative AI apps that rely on Amazon Bedrock principles. They were created for a variety of purposes. Each application uses FMs constructed with predefined parameters according to specific tasks, ensuring optimal performance and results. The interconnectedness of Amazon Q to Amazon Bedrock means it inherits secure, reliable, and responsible AI mechanisms. This foundational infrastructure makes it possible for non-tech people to easily take advantage of advanced generative AI capabilities.

Core Applications of Amazon Q

The two primary applications of Amazon Q are Amazon Q Business and Amazon Q Developer. Additionally, it seamlessly integrates with certain AWS services such as Amazon QuickSight and Amazon Connect. Amazon Q has been further upgraded, enhancing the already high usability and flexibility of its different applications within operations.

Amazon Q Business

Amazon Q Business enables organizations to create an internal chat application environment that combines enterprise data with the knowledge of LLMs. Users benefit from immediate, permissions-aware responses that are cited, ensuring transparency and trust.

One prevalent use case for Amazon Q Business is powering departmental help desks, such as IT or HR support. By leveraging generative AI, these departments can streamline responses to common inquiries, enhancing efficiency.

Amazon Q Business operates on a subscription-based model. It offers two tiers: a Lite subscription and a Pro subscription with expanded features. The pricing structure also includes costs for the storage capacity required to house the application's document index.

For organizations with limited development resources or minimal generative AI experience, Amazon Q Business provides a low-effort entry point to harness AI-powered applications.

Amazon Q Developer

Amazon Q Developer is a generative AI-powered coding assistant available within popular Integrated Development Environments (IDEs) and the AWS Management Console. This tool supports developers by generating code, explaining program logic, identifying bugs, and creating functional tests. Additionally, it performs security scans and helps optimize AWS resources.

Amazon Q Developer also follows a subscription-based pricing model, offering a Free tier and a Pro tier. The Pro tier includes enhanced features and enterprise-grade controls. It is important to note that data in the Free tier may be used for service improvements, although users can opt out of this usage.

By accelerating development workflows, Amazon Q Developer empowers developers of all skill levels to streamline various stages of the software development lifecycle.

Benefits of Choosing Amazon Q

Amazon Q simplifies the adoption of generative AI technologies for diverse organizational needs. Whether through Amazon Q Business for non-technical roles or Amazon Q Developer for software engineers, this suite provides accessible and scalable solutions. Organizations can leverage these tools to boost productivity, reduce operational overhead, and unlock new possibilities with generative AI.

GENERATIVE AI IN AWS CLOUD MIGRATION

The rapid evolution of technology has made cloud migration an essential strategy for organizations seeking to optimize their operations and enhance business agility. One of the most transformative trends within this domain is the application of generative AI, particularly in the context of migrating to AWS. This section explores how generative AI can be leveraged in the key phases of AWS cloud migration—namely, the Assess, Mobilize, and Modernize phases—paving the way for efficient, innovative, and scalable cloud solutions.

How Generative AI Accelerates AWS Cloud Migration

Generative AI, a transformative technology, creates innovative outputs such as text, code, and data from defined inputs. By leveraging techniques such as LLMs, code generation models, and reinforcement learning algorithms, it drives automation and efficiency across various stages of cloud migration.

Automated Analysis of Existing Infrastructure

Generative AI simplifies the initial analysis of an organization's infrastructure. It can automatically scan and catalog servers, applications, and databases while mapping interdependencies. These capabilities also extend to generating detailed architecture diagrams and documentation, helping identify optimization opportunities such as re-architecting or consolidating systems for enhanced efficiency.

Streamlined Re-Architecting and Replatforming

Generative AI excels in transforming legacy systems to align with cloud-native architectures. It enables the redesign of applications for scalability and resilience, refactors legacy code bases to suit modern frameworks, and facilitates seamless data migration through automated ETL processes. Moreover,

AI-driven tools can generate test cases to validate functionality post-migration, ensuring that business continuity is maintained.

Simplified Redeployment and Validation

During the redeployment phase, generative AI automates the provisioning of cloud resources, optimizes application deployments, and generates data for functionality testing. It also conducts performance testing, ensuring the migrated system meets scalability and resilience requirements in the cloud environment.

By reducing manual effort and minimizing risks, generative AI not only accelerates the migration timeline but also enhances reliability, making it a game-changing asset in AWS cloud migration initiatives.

Evaluating Emerging AI-Assisted Migration Solutions

Several innovative startups are leveraging AI to streamline and accelerate cloud migration processes by automating complex tasks and enhancing efficiency.

StackPulse

This platform analyzes dependencies in legacy distributed systems, visualizes them, and recommends target cloud architectures and migration strategies. It also automates application redeployment and correctness verification using AI-generated tests.

Transposit

Utilizing abstract syntax tree analysis, Transposit documents legacy code and migrates it to cloud-native languages at scale. Additionally, it automates data transformations, enabling seamless integration of legacy formats into cloud platforms.

Astro

Astro scans legacy infrastructures to reverse-engineer architectures and identifies optimizations, such as decoupling monoliths into microservices. It also generates Terraform definitions to provision equivalent infrastructure on the cloud.

PolyAI

By ingesting enterprise documentation, PolyAI uses NLP to extract system topology, dependencies, and context. It answers queries in natural language, providing actionable insights for pre-migration planning.

Platform9

Platform9 ingests configurations and telemetry from legacy systems, automatically generates Terraform definitions for recreating environments in the cloud, and conducts validation testing to ensure post-migration correctness.

These AI-driven solutions significantly reduce manual effort and risk, enabling faster and more reliable cloud migration processes.

GENERATIVE AI IN DIFFERENT AWS CLOUD MIGRATION PHASES

AWS cloud migration is executed in three key phases: Assess, Mobilize, and Migrate and Modernize. In this section, we are going to look into how generative AI is used in the different phases. In addition, we are going to discuss the tools that are supported by AWS, and how they accomplish different tasks in each step of the migration process.

Generative AI in the Assess Phase of AWS Cloud Migration

This phase of AWS cloud migration is crucial as it helps you gain a comprehensive understanding of the current IT landscape. The main reason for AWS's smooth cloud migration is the detailed specification of the current IT environment. Organizations need to analyze their already existing applications to identify suitable infrastructure components and dependencies.

During the initial stage of the Assess phase, organizations must make sure that their current systems are examined and any potential hurdles or problems that may arise during the migration are considered. By conducting a thorough evaluation, businesses can make informed decisions about which applications are best suited for the cloud and what changes may need to be made before migration can occur. This stage is also a chance for the company to prioritize its most important applications and move them first. By taking the time to carefully analyze the existing IT landscape, companies can ensure a smoother transition to the cloud and avoid any unexpected complications. In summary, the first phase of the AWS cloud migration program lays the foundation for a successful and efficient migration.

Here are the main activities generative AI can help with in the AWS cloud migration Assess phase:

- Data analysis
- Cost estimation
- Risk assessment
- Documenting current architectures
- Optimizing target architectures

Generative AI in the Assess phase of migration can be seen in Figure 13.26.

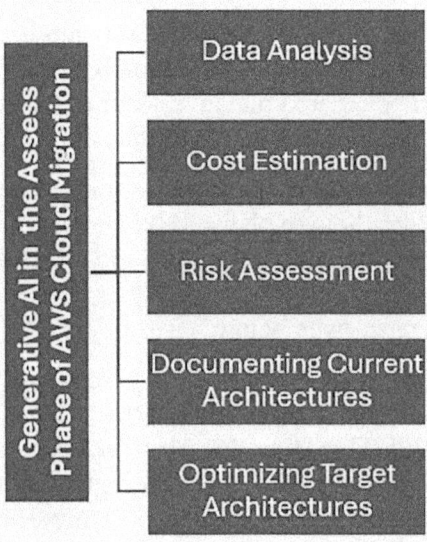

FIGURE 13.26 Generative AI in the Assess Phase of AWS Cloud Migration.

Data Analysis

Generative AI is capable of learning about usage patterns from past data and even finding potential bottlenecks in the currently used infrastructure. This insight enables organizations to decide which applications to migrate first.

The contribution of generative AI in data analysis lies in its ability to dive deep into historical data and extract valuable pieces of information, allowing organizations to make smart choices about the applications they should migrate. Resources are not only allocated effectively but the migration process also becomes more streamlined. Companies become more competitive by managing data effectively, aligning it with business objectives, and transforming it into comprehensive digital solutions. Together with data analysis, generative AI enables companies to be proactive, helping them become the best version of themselves by making intelligent adjustments in their operations for better performance and greater scalability.

Cost Estimation

Through the utilization of elaborate ML models, organizations can make forecasts associated with cloud migration. By using generative AI, more complex models can be created that give accurate information on additional costs determined by the fluctuating workload.

Cost estimation is a crucial factor for businesses looking to migrate to the cloud, as it enables them to plan and budget efficiently. Generative AI plays a critical role in providing more accurate and enhanced cost estimation models, thereby helping businesses make decisions about their cloud migration strategy. Key tools are as given below:

- AWS Migration Hub offers a wide range of services that recommend migration strategies and estimate the associated costs of moving workloads to AWS. The Migration Hub tool does a complete analysis of the application portfolio and provides high-level cost estimates of running standard workloads on AWS, which, in turn, helps in the process of planning and budgeting the migration of workloads effectively.

- AWS Pricing Calculator is a highly powerful tool for predicting the costs of AWS services based on custom configurations. The application allows users to model their architecture and estimate the costs of services, including EC2, RDS, and S3, with various offering options. By doing so, companies can strategically plan their cloud investments with precision.

- AWS Cost Explorer is a service that offers a clear visualization of potential AWS-related costs. It provides users with the capability to detect spending trends and simulate future costs based on utilization trends, resulting in better cost management.

- The AWS Total Cost of Ownership (TCO) calculator is a helpful tool that enables businesses to have a comparison between cloud costs and on-premises costs. The output of the calculator is a high-level comparison that includes factors such as hardware, software, labor, and energy expenses. Thus, companies have the opportunity to assess the financial benefits of migration to the cloud.

- AWS Trusted Advisor is a resource optimization tool that gives cost-saving recommendations for AWS workloads. It identifies underutilized or idle resources and offers suggestions for cost optimization, ensuring businesses get the maximum value from their migrated workload.

Risk Assessment

Generative AI can create various migration scenarios, identify potential risks, and propose the most appropriate ways to prevent those risks from happening. It can also be used to anticipate the possible effects of data breaches on network security, helping organizations strengthen their defenses before the migration process begins.

The potential of generative AI technologies to simulate various migration scenarios and assess the risks is crucial in revolutionizing the future of planning and the execution of data migration tasks. Companies can predict what information security breaches might occur in the migration process and prepare accordingly. These tools can analyze current security protocols and identify vulnerabilities, helping organizations to take efficiency-enhancing action to block those security gaps before migration work has started. This proactive approach not only contributes to cutting down the risks involved but also guarantees a secure and smooth migration. Organizations can make informed decisions and dynamically optimize their migration strategy to minimize disruption and ensure the safety of valuable data assets. Key tools include:

- AWS Application Discovery Service assists organizations in planning the migration of their on-premises applications to the cloud. It identifies the application dependencies and usage patterns and can identify potentially insecure aspects, including incompatible applications or interdependence, which could impact the migration process.

- By analyzing application complexity, AWS Migration Hub Strategy Recommendations gives you directions for migration and modernization strategies. It identifies potential threats that can arise and makes recommendations on possible modernization options to mitigate them as well as achieve a more efficient and secure migration.

- The AWS Well-Architected Tool is an advanced structure that assesses workloads in compliance with top AWS practices, focusing on operational excellence, security, reliability, performance, and cost optimization. This tool is an expert at identifying potential risks in these areas and it also offers the best remediation solution for improving the overall architecture of workloads.

- AWS Trusted Advisor provides a clear assessment and productive recommendations to enhance AWS environments. It identifies potential security threats, including issues such as open ports, weak IAM policies, and compliance gaps. At the same time, it brings attention to resources that are not used effectively and areas of possible expenses that are unnecessary. By providing these insights, organizations can be better shielded against security threats and reduce their costs.

- AWS IAM Access Analyzer analyzes the access control policies that are created to ensure secure resource management. The service can pinpoint the risks of over-granted access and guide organizations to the most effective ways of securing their data during and before migration, thus reducing potential vulnerabilities.

Documenting Current Architectures

During the Assess phase of AWS cloud migration, generative AI significantly contributes by automating the documentation of current architectures and performing comprehensive scans of existing environments. Generative AI tools are capable of scanning and analyzing complex IT landscapes, resulting in detailed topological maps that encompass servers, applications, and databases. These scans generate interactive visuals that help stakeholders easily understand the infrastructure, enabling better decision-making. Future documentation will provide a clear, dynamic view of the current architecture, making it easier to identify dependencies, assess risks, and plan migration strategies accordingly. Key tools include:

- The AWS Well-Architected Tool is utilized to evaluate workloads against AWS architectural best practices. It can recognize the strengths and weaknesses of the existing architecture by responding to structured questions and reporting. This enables organizations to generate complete and clear architecture documentation.

- AWS Application Discovery Service helps in the automatic detection of on-premises applications, infrastructure, and their dependencies. By gathering data related to servers, applications, and network dependencies, the tool illustrates the architecture of a system with its interdependencies, which, in turn, makes it simpler to document complex systems.

- The AWS Migration Hub dashboard centralizes migration tools and provides a consolidated view of applications and identified dependencies, while also monitoring progress. It also allows the documentation of workloads that are aimed for migration to be completed, so there is no interruption in the project management process during migration.

- AWS Config monitors and logs the configurations of AWS resources, including documenting their relationships to support hybrid architectures that include existing AWS resources. This full tracking is crucial for keeping the system documentation accurate and up to date.

Optimizing Target Architectures

Generative AI can be used to examine application dependencies to detect consolidation and modernization opportunities. It can also help with deciding which resources can be migrated to the cloud after an analysis of component interaction as well as identifying the parts of resources that are underutilized or even redundant. This is how optimization ensures that cloud resources are used efficiently, waste is reduced, and performance problems are avoided.

Additionally, generative AI can assist in the establishment of a migration strategy that also contains applicable AI-powered conversions and transformations to streamline the process. This targeted perspective helps in attaining a more cost-effective migration by addressing key factors that impact cloud efficiency and scalability. Key tools for this are as follows:

- The AWS Well-Architected Tool evaluates workloads against AWS architectural best practices and provides tailored recommendations to optimize security, performance, reliability, cost efficiency, and operational excellence. It not only focuses on the weakest spots of the objective architecture but also widens the opportunity for companies to effectively improve their cloud infrastructure.

- AWS Compute Optimizer examines the usage of resources to suggest the most appropriate computing resources for workloads. The algorithm suggests the instance type, size, and configuration, ensuring efficient resource allocation in the target architecture while balancing performance and cost.

- AWS Trusted Advisor provides valuable insights and recommendations to make the best use of AWS accounts. It identifies opportunities for improvement in cost, performance, and security in addition to highlighting areas where resources are underutilized. Potential risks that make the organization vulnerable are also identified, helping organizations maintain an efficient and secure cloud environment.

- AWS Cost Explorer helps in the analysis and forecast of the AWS services costs. It projects the future costs of the target architecture and gives details of the usage patterns, thus allowing organizations to allocate costs and manage their budgets.

- AWS Auto Scaling is a process by which computing resources for applications are automatically adjusted based on workload requirements, offering automation in the process of infrastructure optimization. It uses intelligent software to track resource efficiency, providing scalable "rightsizing" recommendations through accurate capacity planning aimed at improving performance and reducing costs in the target environment.

Generative AI in the Mobilize Phase of AWS Cloud Migration

Once the assessment is completed successfully, organizations are ready to enter the Mobilize phase, in which they start working on the migration plan. This phase is instrumental in transitioning applications to AWS seamlessly.

The Mobilize phase is a critical step of the migration process in which the migration plan is put into action. Organizations in this phase go through the smooth and efficient process of moving their applications to AWS. This involves migrating data, configuring settings, and ensuring that each component is properly configured in the AWS environment. The success of this phase allows organizations to take advantage of AWS features such as improved scalability, reliability, and cost-efficiency. This phase also minimizes the disruption of business operations during the migration process.

Generative AI in the Mobilize phase of migration can be seen in Figure 13.27.

Generative AI in the Mobilize Phase of AWS Cloud Migration

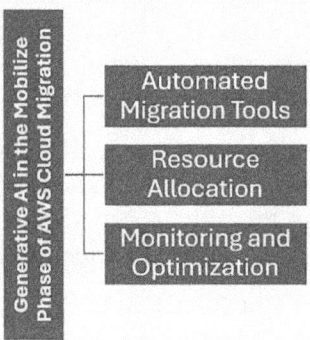

FIGURE 13.27 Generative AI in the Mobilize Phase of AWS Cloud Migration.

Here are the primary applications of generative AI in the AWS cloud migration Mobilize phase:

- Automated migration tools
- Resource allocation
- Monitoring and optimization

Automated Migration Tools

Generative AI can power automation tools that facilitate the migration of data and applications. Tools such as AWS Application Migration Service use AI algorithms to suggest optimal migration paths that minimize downtime.

A key application of generative AI is automated migration tools, which streamline the process of migrating data and applications. The use of AI during cloud migration ensures a smooth transition and saves time and resources, offering a hassle-free and reliable solution to organizations that want to modernize their systems. Key tools include the following:

- AWS Migration Hub is a centralized platform for tracking and managing migration progress. This platform closely works with all the other migration tools to provide a unified view that helps automate the process and tracks the progress of different workloads and services, ensuring streamlined project management.

- AWS Application Migration Service (MGN) is used to automate lift-and-shift migrations to AWS. It suggests the most efficient migration options by using AI algorithms. It provides real-time replication and cutover, which results in applications migrating without any interruption, making the migrations more efficient and reliable.

- AWS Database Migration Service (DMS) migrates databases to AWS by using automated schema conversion and data replication. It supports both homogeneous migrations (e.g., Oracle to Oracle) and heterogeneous migrations (e.g., Oracle to Aurora), leading to flexible database transitions.

- The AWS Schema Conversion Tool (SCT) aids in database migration by converting database schemas to AWS-compatible formats. This tool automates schema transformations and generates detailed assessment reports to ensure an efficient migration process.

Resource Allocation

AI plays an important role in resource allocation during the migration. It works by analyzing workloads to identify the best schedulers for the work and the appropriate instance types, optimizing costs.

Resource allocation is an essential factor affecting the successful migration of applications to the cloud. Organizations can use AI software to drive the allocation of resources based on the analysis of various workloads and recommending the most suitable instance types and configurations. AI tools can also provide insights into performance specifications and suggest solutions to reduce costs, enabling the organization to cut expenses. By using AI in resource allocation, companies can efficiently use their resources and effectively support their goals when migrating to the cloud to achieve a smooth and seamless transition. This not only results in potential cost savings but also ensures that the organization's applications are running at optimal performance levels. Key tools include the following:

- AWS Organizations provides centralized management of multiple AWS accounts. It streamlines resource allocation by managing permissions across accounts. This centralized account management manages permissions, which enables centralized billing and policy enforcement in all the AWS accounts in the company, ensuring efficient and consistent resource distribution.

- AWS Resource Access Manager (RAM) enables the secure sharing of AWS resources across accounts without duplication. Allowing shared access to resources such as VPCs and subnets ensures efficient resource utilization across an organization's accounts.

- AWS Identity and Access Management (IAM) is a centralized IAM service that provides a robust framework for managing access to AWS resources. It allocates permissions to the users, groups, and roles in a secure way that gives users controlled access while maintaining granular control over resource allocation.

- The AWS Service Catalog offers a pre-approved template for resource provisioning by standardized resource deployment. It ensures that all the regulations of an organization are fully met, and it also streamlines the resource delivery according to predefined policies.

- AWS Control Tower creates a secure and well-architected landing zone for multi-account environments. It allocates resources between accounts and enforces governance through guardrails, which helps to ensure compliance during resource provisioning.

Monitoring and Optimization

During the mobilization process, generative AI can continuously monitor performance metrics in real time, helping the team take action as soon as an issue arises. It can identify performance or security issues that require quick response, ensuring a smoother transition.

For example, AI can identify issues in performance metrics or security gaps that need immediate attention, ensuring that the mobilization process proceeds without interruptions. These ongoing monitoring and optimization processes ensure that systems are running at their best during the mobilization phase. With the assistance of generative AI, teams can anticipate any potential obstacles and make the necessary changes to the overall improvement of performance and security. Businesses can use AI technology in mobilization to optimize their process and enhance their operational capabilities.

During the Mobilize phase of AWS migration, the first activity is to monitor and optimize it. The main objective of this procedure is to ensure that resources, applications, and infrastructure are performing effectively and efficiently. AWS offers a comprehensive set of services designed to enhance the efficiency and visibility of monitoring and optimization, helping organizations manage the utilization of their resources:

- Amazon CloudWatch provides centralized monitoring for applications and infrastructure. It also gathers and visualizes metrics, logs, and events and provides alarms to detect anomalies as well as trigger optimizations. Customized dashboards enable zero-latency monitoring, enabling organizations to get the necessary information and actionable insights about their systems.

- AWS Trusted Advisor recommends ways to improve the performance of resources and reduce costs. It shows underutilized resources and suggests solutions to strengthen security, make the system fault-tolerant, and improve operational performance, enabling companies to optimize their cloud infrastructure.

- AWS Compute Optimizer provides tailored recommendations to optimize compute resources. By suggesting the most suitable EC2 instance types, auto-scaling groups, and EBS volumes, it improves performance while helping to reduce costs.

- AWS CloudTrail tracks API calls and activity across AWS accounts, offering a detailed record of access and changes to resources. It provides insights into usage patterns, enabling organizations to identify optimization opportunities and enhance resource management.

Generative AI in the Migrate and Modernize Phase of AWS Cloud Migration

This last phase prioritizes the actual migration work and optimizes the applications that were migrated to the cloud. This phase should be prioritized in order to get the most from the AWS cloud services.

Key applications of generative AI in this phase are:

- Architectural enhancement
- Continuous improvement
- Enhanced decision-making
- Predictive maintenance

Generative AI in the Migrate and Modernize phase of migration can be seen in Figure 13.28.

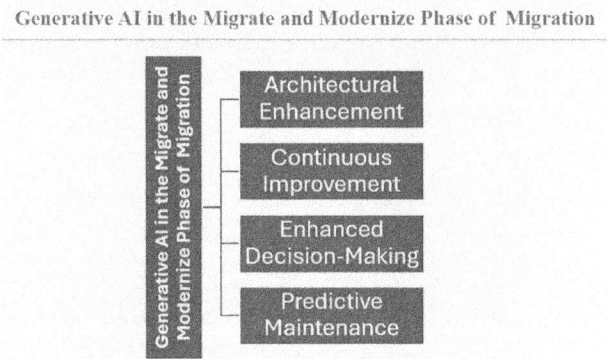

FIGURE 13.28 Generative AI in the Migrate and Modernize Phase of Migration.

Architectural Enhancement

Generative AI can recommend architectural improvements based on best practices and performance analytics. This recommendation includes serverless architectures or microservices to align with AWS's transformative capabilities.

The cutting-edge technology of generative AI is a game-changer for better architectural enhancement. It is smart enough to analyze how systems perform and suggest the best ways to improve them. For instance, it may recommend switching to serverless architecture or microservices, which are both compatible with AWS. Generative AI can handle complex designs and ensure that existing software can meet the demands of modern technology standards. Key tools are as follows:

- AWS Lambda runs code without the need for a server. It automatically scales code in response to events, eliminating server management tasks. This allows developers to focus on creating applications without worrying about infrastructure.

- Amazon RDS and Aurora are fully managed relational databases. They have features such as backups, read replicas, and automatic scaling, eliminating day-to-day database management tasks so no manual work is needed.

- Amazon DynamoDB is a serverless NoSQL database. It provides low latency and high scalability and is optimized for use cases such as real-time analytics and mobile applications, providing a fast and reliable database solution for dynamic workloads.

- Amazon ECS and EKS simplify the management of containerized applications. They support microservices deployment and management. They integrate with other AWS services to enable secure, scalable operations for modern applications.

- AWS Elastic Beanstalk fast-tracks application deployment by automatically handling the scaling process simultaneously. This means that teams can concentrate on writing code instead of managing resources, streamlining the work plan.

- AWS Step Functions help you manage complicated tasks without worrying about minor details, ensuring that everything runs smoothly. AWS Step Functions are more efficient than traditional methods, simplifying the management of complicated workflows, which is perfect for modern architecture.

Continuous Improvement

Continuous improvement is essential for organizations to stay competitive in today's fast-paced digital landscape. AI-driven feedback loops provide valuable insights into user interactions and performance data, enabling companies to make informed decisions about refining their applications. Generative AI goes a step further by suggesting necessary improvements and new features based on what users want. The process of looking at the data, making changes, and checking that they work helps businesses stay ahead and offers users great experiences.

Key tools for this are as follows:

- Amazon CloudWatch provides real-time metrics and logs. It identifies performance issues and helps create custom dashboards for tracking system performance over time, ensuring efficiency.

- AWS Trusted Advisor analyzes AWS workloads for best practices. It identifies potential issues and recommends improvements for cost savings, security, reliability, and performance, resulting in an optimized cloud environment for users.

- AWS Compute Optimizer evaluates the usage patterns of compute resources, giving suggestions on resizing and reconfiguring EC2, Auto Scaling, Lambda, and EBS based on performance needs as well as cost-effectiveness.

- AWS Cost Explorer tracks and analyzes cost trends over time. It helps users find ways to minimize their spending through budgeting and forecasting while improving financial management for their cloud services overall.

- AWS Systems Manager provides data centralized operational management, automating routine tasks such as patching and backups. It improves efficiency and minimizes the need for manual intervention.

- AWS Config tracks the compliance of resource configurations by monitoring changes. It ensures optimal configurations consistent with organization standards.

- AWS X-Ray helps debug distributed application performance by identifying bottlenecks and giving insights to enhance overall system performance.

Enhanced Decision-Making

AI technologies can analyze large amounts of data quickly and accurately, helping organizations make more informed decisions. Whether it's predicting market trends or identifying potential risks, AI can provide valuable insights to guide strategic planning.

Enhanced decision-making is one of the key benefits of AI technologies in organizations. With the ability to analyze vast amounts of data quickly and accurately, AI enables companies to make more informed decisions. Key AWS tools for this are as follows:

- Amazon CloudWatch

  A monitoring service that offers real-time insights into AWS resources, applications, and services. It is about the collection and visual representation of any metrics, logs, and events, which can assist the organization in detecting performance issues and optimizing resource utilization during cloud migration. The AI-based statistics are forward-looking; thus, they can fail or suggest solutions before human intervention is necessary.

- AWS Trusted Advisor

  AWS Trusted Advisor: An AWS tool that offers guidance on the basis of which clients can upgrade their AWS infrastructure according to the latest best practices, and at the same time, do it in no time. Through this platform, the companies can also learn about security, performance, fault-tolerance, and cost-efficiency best practices for their cloud migration.

- AWS Cost Explorer

    A cost management assistant that gives breakdown and forecast of AWS spending. Companies can see the trends of AWS usage, reuse resources, and find out cost hotspots by analyzing data obtained. Through AI-powered analytics, financial decision-making can be done timely and in a planned way to help achieve both migration and post-migration business objectives.

- AWS Migration Hub

    A centralized service for tracking and managing AWS cloud migration projects. The hub provides a unified dashboard which helps in understanding and facilitating the migration on AWS services. AI integrated it will be capable of forecasting, suggesting and even controlling the migration flow to end up with a successful transition to the cloud.

- AWS Application Insights automatically detects application issues during migration and modernization, supporting decision-making by monitoring applications and identifying performance anomalies. It offers actionable recommendations for resolving issues and ensures application reliability and optimal performance throughout the migration process.

- AWS Compute Optimizer

    An AWS tool that assesses AWS workloads and suggests ideas to improve the resource efficiency of the compute. It particularly employs AI to inform about instances that are rightly sized to the users of the cloud so as to reduce the cost of computing and increase the efficiency performance of most high-value cases. An important practice that is to be done while migrating is to seek assistance in getting the best configurations that balance both performance and cost-effective computation.

Predictive Maintenance

Predictive maintenance involves predicting issues before they occur. AI analyzes historical data trends and identifies patterns, alerting us when things might break down. This allows for planned maintenance, preventing interruptions.

By using AI predictions, businesses can improve their operational efficiency and reduce downtime costs. Key tools include the following:

- Amazon Lookout for Equipment analyzes equipment data with AI to predict whether it might break down. It shows you when to fix things before they stop working. This keeps machines operating smoothly and prevents unplanned downtime.

- AWS IoT SiteWise monitors machinery, showing both current and future conditions. It identifies patterns that suggest when something might go wrong. You can analyze the data together with other tools to assess overall system performance.

- Amazon SageMaker enables you to create AI models for the machine's operations. These models predict when things will break down or need fixing based on past and present data. They work smoothly with IoT systems.

- AWS Lambda automates the process of checking machine data. It identifies issues as they occur and sends out alerts or orders to fix them, enabling people to quickly solve problems when they arise.

- Amazon CloudWatch monitors systems and apps. It tracks their performance and monitors their health. It sends alerts when things go wrong and predicts issues using math models.

- Amazon QuickSight helps visualize data in clear, understandable ways. It creates charts and dashboards to show what is happening now and predict what might happen later, allowing teams to spot issues early and address them quickly.

- AWS IoT Core connects machines to the Internet. It collects data from sensors on machines for predictive maintenance. It sends alerts and takes actions automatically when issues arise, keeping machines running smoothly.

SUMMARY

Incorporating generative AI into the AWS cloud migration enhances the efficiency and effectiveness of the process. From detailed assessments that support risk management and cost estimation to automated migration tools that manage workloads smoothly, to modernizing applications through continuous improvement, generative AI is the main source of change in each phase of migration.

As organizations navigate the complexity of the digital world, embracing the latest technologies simplifies the migration process and positions them for survival in an increasingly competitive landscape. By taking advantage of the vast possibilities of generative AI within AWS, companies have the opportunity to achieve unprecedented levels of innovation and operational excellence, selecting the right path to the cloud and ensuring future success.

REFERENCES

[AWSGenAI23] Amazon Web Services, *"Transform your business with generative AI"*, AWS documentation. Available online at: *https://aws.amazon.com/generative-ai/*.

[AWSML22] Amazon Web Services, *"What is Amazon Machine Learning?"*, AWS documentation. Available online at: *https://docs.aws.amazon.com/machine-learning/latest/dg/*.

[AWSBedrock23] Amazon Web Services, *"Amazon Bedrock"*, AWS documentation. Available online at: *https://aws.amazon.com/bedrock/*.

[AWSLLM23] Amazon Web Services, *"AWS Machine Learning Blog"*, AWS blog. Available online at: *https://aws.amazon.com/blogs/machine-learning/*.

[AWSQ23] Amazon Web Services, *"Amazon Q – Generative AI Assistant"*, AWS documentation. Available online at: *https://aws.amazon.com/q/*.

[AWSMLWorkflow22] Amazon Web Services, *"Maximize business outcomes with machine learning on AWS"*, AWS documentation. Available online at: *https://aws.amazon.com/machine-learning/*.

[AWSMLOps22] Amazon Web Services, *"What is Amazon SageMaker AI?"*, AWS documentation. Available online at: *https://docs.aws.amazon.com/sagemaker/latest/dg/mLOps.html*.

[AWSCompute23] Amazon Web Services, *"Amazon EC2"*, AWS documentation. Available online at: *https://aws.amazon.com/ec2/*.

[AWSDataAI23] Amazon Web Services, *"Fuel innovation with data and AI"*, AWS documentation. Available online at: *https://aws.amazon.com/data/*.

KNOWLEDGE CHECK: MULTIPLE-CHOICE Q&A

Question 1

What is the primary purpose of generative AI in AWS cloud migration?

A. To generate creative content such as images and videos.

B. To automate infrastructure provisioning, application re-architecting, and data transformation.

C. To replace human decision-making in cloud migration.

D. To run virtual machines in the cloud.

Question 2

Which AWS service provides access to foundation models for building and scaling generative AI applications?

A. Amazon SageMaker.

B. Amazon Bedrock.

C. AWS Lambda.

D. AWS Glue.

Question 3

Which AI technique is commonly used in generative AI to generate realistic images and videos?

A. Reinforcement Learning (RL).

B. Variational Autoencoders (VAEs).

C. Generative Adversarial Networks (GANs).

D. Decision Trees.

Question 4

Which AWS service is primarily used for managing the machine learning lifecycle, including training and deploying generative AI models?

A. AWS Glue.

B. AWS Lambda.

C. Amazon SageMaker.

D. Amazon EC2.

Question 5

What role does generative AI play in the Assess phase of AWS cloud migration?

A. Predicts cost estimates and identifies potential migration risks.

B. Automatically provisions cloud infrastructure.

C. Deploys machine learning models without human intervention.

D. Creates new applications from scratch.

Question 6

Which of the following is a key feature of Amazon Q Business in generative AI applications?

A. Automates infrastructure deployment.

B. Provides AI-powered chat applications integrated with enterprise data.

C. Trains deep learning models from scratch.

D. Predicts customer behavior in cloud migrations.

Question 7

What is prompt engineering in generative AI?

A. A technique used to improve AI model responses by refining input prompts.

B. The process of designing cloud migration workflows.

C. A method for enhancing AI hardware performance.

D. A way to increase AWS cloud storage capacity.

Question 8

Which AWS service helps organizations estimate cloud migration costs and analyze workload dependencies?

A. AWS Cost Explorer.

B. AWS Migration Hub.

C. Amazon Bedrock.

D. Amazon Q.

Question 9

How does generative AI help in the Modernize phase of AWS cloud migration?

A. Automates data transformation and cloud-native application refactoring.

B. Replaces all cloud engineers with AI.

C. Reduces AWS service costs by 90%.

D. Creates cloud security policies automatically.

Question 10

Which AWS service enables businesses to use AI-powered development assistance for coding and software optimization?

A. AWS Glue.

B. Amazon Bedrock.

C. Amazon Q Developer.

D. AWS CloudFormation.

CHAPTER 14

ADDITIONAL AWS SERVICES FOR MIGRATION (AWS ORGANIZATIONS AND SERVICE CATALOG)

WHAT IS AWS ORGANIZATIONS?

AWS Organizations is a comprehensive account management platform that is designed to optimize the administration of multiple AWS accounts. It allows companies to improve budgetary control, enhance security, and comply with regulatory rules by consolidating accounts into the organization. By using AWS Organizations, businesses can set up various platforms within one consolidated bill.

As an administrator, you will also be able to create new accounts in the AWS Management Console, send invitations to new accounts, or even use AWS Control Tower to accomplish these tasks easily at your organization. With this solution, businesses can use resources effectively, group accounts, and enforce governance policies homogenously in the entire environment.

AWS Organizations allows the efficient use of AWS tools in a multi-account environment. By forming groups of accounts and presenting Service Control Policies (SCPs), clients can ensure compliance standards, streamline resource management, and govern access across accounts. This ensures that all accounts within the organization adhere to business policies, making multi-account environments easier to operate.

AWS Organizations is inherently cost-effective because no additional charge is made for the actual service. Customers pay only for the AWS resources used by their users and roles in the member accounts. For example, if users or roles within member accounts use Amazon EC2 instances, the respective costs will be reflected in the overall bill, but there is no overhead for using the AWS Organizations service.

What Problems Does AWS Organizations Solve?

AWS Organizations provides solutions for several challenges that businesses face while managing multiple AWS accounts, providing tools and different capabilities to streamline operations and enhance control in the AWS cloud environment.

Centralized Management

One of the key benefits of AWS Organizations is the provision of a centralized platform for managing multiple cloud environments, which enables you to continuously monitor any changes within accounts and keep them aligned with business processes. Using this approach, account administration can align seamlessly with business processes, offering flexibility while maintaining an organized structure.

Governance

Using AWS Organizations, businesses can establish control measures that are almost inviolable across their cloud environments. This is achieved by controlling privileges for accounts, AWS zones, and services during program operation, ensuring secure operations. Through the use of SCPs, AWS Organizations helps enforce access restrictions and maintain consistent governance.

Compliance

Security can be improved when organizations integrate tools that enforce compliance policies by monitoring account activities. With these technologies, organizations can ensure that all accounts abide by both regulatory and internal compliance requirements, promoting a secure and controlled working environment.

Resource Sharing

AWS Organizations enables rapid and secure resource sharing between groups of people. Developers have the necessary tools and services at their disposal without compromising the security system due to resource sharing. This leads to better compliance with central guidelines and faster project delivery.

AWS Organizations enables companies to manage their multi-account environments effectively, ensuring security, compliance, and operational efficiency.

What Are the Benefits of AWS Organizations?

AWS Organizations offers many benefits, which we'll look at in the following subsections.

Centralized Management Across Multiple Accounts

AWS Organizations simplifies the management of multiple accounts by consolidating them into a single organizational structure. It provides centralized control, enabling administrators to add, invite, or delete accounts easily. This structure also allows accounts to be grouped into Organizational Units (OUs), with unique access policies and permissions for each group. This flexibility supports seamless scalability and enhances the organization's ability to manage its cloud infrastructure efficiently.

Cost Optimization and Savings

One of the major benefits of AWS Organizations is its ability to optimize costs. Using consolidation billing across multiple accounts, businesses can take advantage of volume discounts on services that qualify. Financial teams gain visibility into the cost trends and usage patterns across accounts, enabling them to identify areas for potential cost savings. The ability to consolidate and track billing in this way ensures that organizations can maximize financial efficiency while maintaining transparency.

Customizable Environment Through Policies and Controls

AWS Organizations empowers administrators to tailor the cloud environment to their needs through the application of various policies and controls. Central administrators can use SCPs to manage service access, ensuring that only approved actions and permissions are granted. Additionally, administrators can implement tag policies for consistency across resources, set backup schedules to ensure regular data protection, and define other operational policies that ensure the environment runs in accordance with business needs.

Enhanced Security with IAM Integration and Support

AWS Organizations integrates seamlessly with AWS Identity and Access Management (IAM), adding an extra layer of granularity in setting permissions at the account level. This ensures that administrators can tightly control access to sensitive resources across accounts. Furthermore, AWS IAM Identity Center (formerly AWS Single Sign-On) simplifies user management by allowing centralized access to accounts, while AWS IAM Access Analyzer enhances auditing capabilities. Together, these features provide robust security controls that protect the organization's resources.

Global Operations with Unified Access Across Regions

AWS Organizations operates globally, making it easy for businesses to manage resources across all AWS Regions. It provides a unified endpoint, eliminating the need to select specific Regions for operations. This global access simplifies the management of resources spread across various Regions and ensures consistency in policies and configurations across the organization's entire cloud environment.

Secure and Comprehensive Auditing

With AWS Organizations, security and auditing are significantly enhanced. The service automatically activates AWS CloudTrail across all accounts, generating logs of every activity in the cloud environment. These logs cannot be turned off or modified by member accounts, ensuring that all actions are tracked and recorded for compliance and auditing purposes. This built-in auditing capability ensures that security policies are being enforced, and organizations can stay aligned with compliance requirements.

Efficient Resource Sharing Across Teams

AWS Organizations makes it easier to share resources across teams using AWS Resource Access Manager (AWS RAM), AWS Service Catalog, and other services. Resources, software applications, and directories can be shared across the organization or specific OUs, IAM users, and roles. This feature allows teams to collaborate more efficiently while maintaining security and control over who can access shared resources.

No Additional Cost for Using AWS Organizations

AWS Organizations is available at no extra charge. The service itself does not incur additional costs; instead, businesses only pay for the AWS services used by accounts within the organization. This cost-effective model allows businesses to take full advantage of the capabilities offered by AWS Organizations without worrying about hidden fees or overhead costs.

AWS ORGANIZATIONS: CENTRALIZED GOVERNANCE AND MANAGEMENT

AWS Organizations provides a centralized framework to govern and manage your cloud environment as your workloads scale. Whether you are a growing startup or a large enterprise, AWS Organizations simplifies account creation, resource allocation, and governance, ensuring efficient and secure operations.

With AWS Organizations, you can streamline your billing by consolidating all accounts under a single payment method. It allows you to log in to group accounts logically to align with workflows or business units and apply policies to these groups for governance. AWS Organizations also integrates seamlessly with other AWS services, enabling the definition of central configurations, security policies, and resource-sharing mechanisms across all accounts.

Key Components of AWS Organizations

The key components of AWS Organizations can be seen in Figure 14.1.

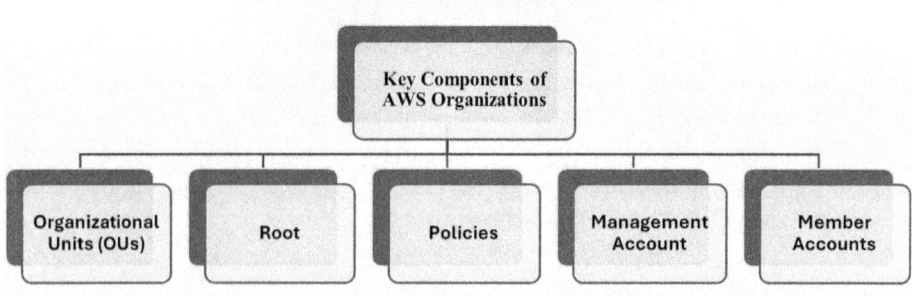

FIGURE 14.1 Key Components of AWS Organizations.

Organizational Units

OUs allow you to group AWS accounts under a common hierarchy, known as the root. An OU is a functional grouping that simplifies management by enabling the hierarchical application of policies. Accounts within an OU inherit the policies applied to their parent OU or root, ensuring consistent governance. OUs can be nested, with each OU having a single parent, and every account being a member of exactly one OU. This structure supports flexible and scalable management of accounts based on criteria such as departments, projects, or teams.

Root

The root is the top-level entity of an organization and acts as the central point of control. It serves as the anchor for all accounts and OUs within the organization. Any policies applied at the root level propagate downward to all associated resources, including OUs and member accounts, ensuring overarching governance.

Policies

Policies in AWS Organizations offer granular control over access to services, actions, and resources. These policies enhance security and operational consistency by enforcing governance across accounts. For example, SCPs can limit access to specific services for certain accounts, while tag policies help maintain consistent tagging practices for resources.

Management Account

The management account is the primary account responsible for overseeing the entire organization. It has elevated permissions that allow it to create and manage accounts, apply policies, and coordinate activities across the organization. This account ensures efficient control and governance throughout the multi-account environment.

Member Accounts

Member accounts are individual AWS accounts created or invited to join the organization. These accounts represent specific services, applications, or business units within the organization. Member accounts can either belong to OUs or be attached directly to the root, depending on organizational needs.

Hierarchical Structure and Policy Application

AWS Organizations supports a hierarchical structure where policies can be applied at different levels to manage access and resources effectively. For instance, a policy attached to a parent OU will cascade down to its child OUs and member accounts. This inheritance simplifies administration and ensures that governance policies are consistently enforced across the entire organization.

The diagram in Figure 14.2 illustrates a basic organizational setup:

- *Root*: The central point of control and the top-most level of the hierarchy.
- *OUs*: Functional groupings (e.g., based on teams or projects) nested under the root.
- *Member accounts*: Individual AWS accounts within OUs, inheriting governance policies from their parent hierarchy.

By leveraging these components, AWS Organizations enables centralized governance, efficient account management, and scalable security controls, providing businesses with the tools needed to manage their cloud environments effectively.

The hierarchical structure and policy application can be seen in Figure 14.2.

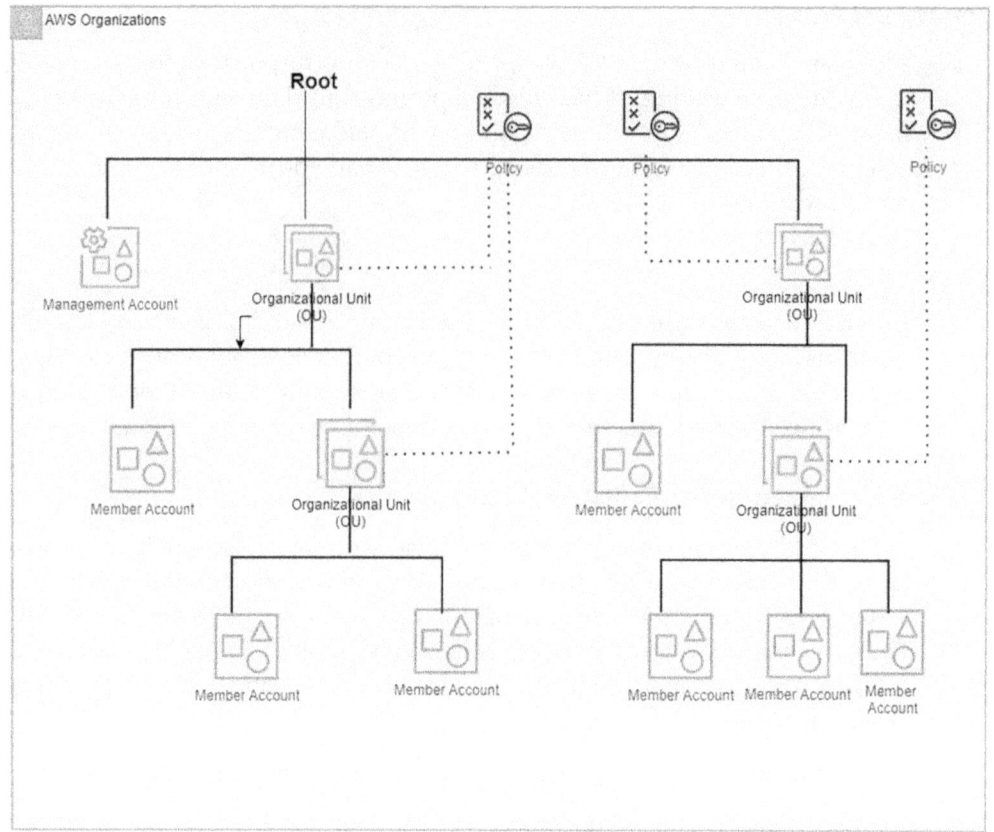

FIGURE 14.2 Hierarchical Structure and Policy Application.

OUs: Grouping for Governance and Security

OUs in AWS Organizations are not designed to mirror the reporting structure of your organization. Instead, they are intended to group accounts based on shared security policies and operational needs. The primary consideration when creating OUs should be the likelihood of accounts requiring a similar set of policies.

Below is an example of a common OU structure that enterprises might implement to meet operational and security requirements. Foundational OUs are critical to establishing a robust governance model, and additional OUs can be created as the organization evolves.

Foundational OUs

Foundational OUs form the backbone of an organization's governance model. They typically include:

- *Security*: This OU is dedicated to managing shared security services across multiple accounts and OUs. It ensures a centralized approach to implementing security measures.
- *Infrastructure*: This OU manages shared infrastructure resources used across multiple accounts and OUs, such as networking, identity services, and other foundational components.

Specialized OUs

These OUs typically include:

- *Sandbox*: This OU is reserved for developers and builders for experimentation and development. It provides an isolated environment where new ideas can be tested without impacting production resources.
- *Workloads*: Designed to manage production workloads, this OU ensures that critical applications and services operate in a controlled, compliant environment.
- *Policy staging*: This OU is used to test and refine policies before deploying them to production workloads. It provides a safe environment for validating governance models without disrupting operational systems.
- *Suspended*: Accounts that are temporarily inactive or non-compliant are placed in this OU. This includes accounts scheduled for deletion, legacy systems, or accounts flagged for review.
- *Individual business users*: This OU houses accounts for individual business users, such as those working on proofs of concept, running data queries, or managing limited-scope projects.
- *Exceptions*: Member accounts requiring exceptions or exemptions from common policies are grouped in this OU, ensuring that unique cases are handled without compromising the overall governance model.
- *Deployment*: This OU contains deployment pipelines and workloads, streamlining the process of launching applications and managing deployments across the organization.

- *Transitional*: Temporary member accounts created during organizational changes, such as mergers, acquisitions, or restructuring, are placed in this OU.

Different OUs can be seen in Figure 14.3.

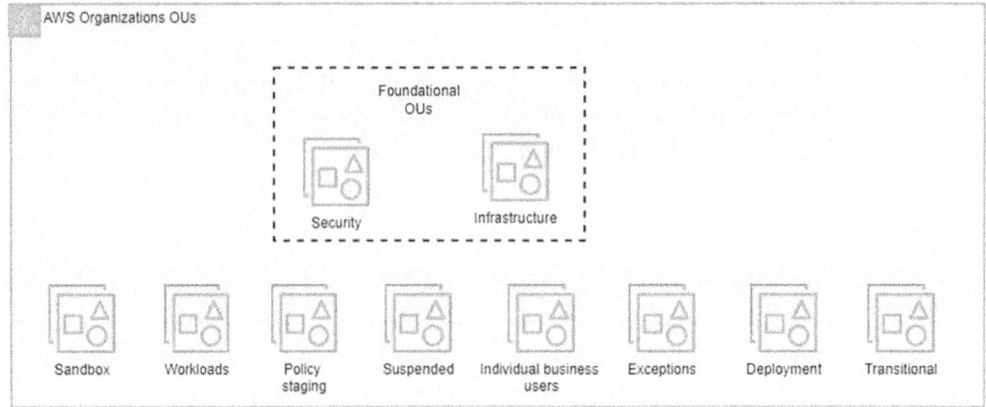

FIGURE 14.3 Different AWS Organizational Units (OUs).

While creating OUs, ensure that the structure aligns with governance and operational needs rather than organizational hierarchy. The flexibility of AWS Organizations allows you to adapt to the OU structure as your business requirements evolve. By grouping accounts with similar policy needs, you can implement streamlined governance and maintain security and compliance effectively.

Basic Technical Concepts of AWS Organizations

Understanding AWS Organizations requires familiarity with several key terms and concepts. Below is a detailed explanation of the fundamental elements to help you navigate this powerful account management service.

Organization

An organization is an overarching entity you create to consolidate and manage multiple AWS accounts as a single unit. Through the AWS Organizations console, you can centrally view, manage, and govern all the accounts within your organization, applying security policies and controls as needed.

Account

Accounts in AWS Organizations represent individual AWS accounts containing resources and user identities. These accounts fall into the following categories:

- *Management account*: The management account serves as the primary account responsible for creating and overseeing the organization. It manages resources such as OUs and policies and consolidates billing across all member accounts. Access to the management account must be tightly restricted to a small group of trusted individuals following the principle of least privilege. This account is not intended for hosting workloads or customer resources.

- *Member accounts*: Member accounts belong to the organization and operate under its governance. Billing for all member accounts is consolidated into the management account, simplifying financial management.

- *Delegated administrator accounts*: A delegated administrator account is a member account assigned specific administrative responsibilities for a particular AWS service or feature, as permitted by the management account. These accounts can manage services or features but cannot be deleted until they are deregistered. The workload typically resides in member accounts, with exceptions for centrally managed services located in either the management or delegated administrator accounts.

Invitation

An invitation allows an external AWS account to join an organization. Only the management account can issue an invitation, directed at the account ID or email address associated with the target account. The invited account must accept the invitation to become a member of the organization.

Handshake

A handshake is a multi-step process that facilitates secure information exchange between two accounts, most commonly used to implement invitations. Messages are exchanged between the initiator (management account) and the recipient to confirm the invitation.

FEATURES OF AWS ORGANIZATIONS

AWS Organizations offers two feature sets to suit different needs:

- All Features: This is the recommended configuration and includes advanced management capabilities, such as policy-based governance, integration with AWS services, and enhanced security features. By default, new organizations activate all features.

- Consolidated Billing Features: This basic feature set supports cost consolidation and billing management across accounts. It lacks the advanced management and security capabilities provided by the All Features set.

Service Control Policies

SCPs specify the maximum permissions that users and roles can utilize within an account, OU, or organization. SCPs act as guardrails rather than permission grants. They define the boundaries of what actions are possible but do not independently grant access. They ensure that administrators can only delegate permissions within the defined limits.

Management Policies

AWS Organizations supports various management policies to standardize and streamline operations across accounts:

- AI service opt-out policies: These policies allow you to enforce standardized opt-out settings for AWS AI services across all accounts in the organization.

- Backup policies: These policies define and automate backup strategies for resources in all member accounts, ensuring consistent data protection practices.

- Tag policies: These policies enforce tagging rules across resources, promoting consistent tagging practices throughout the organization. This standardization aids in better resource management and tracking.

By mastering these technical concepts, you can effectively use AWS Organizations to govern, secure, and optimize your multi-account AWS environment.

AWS ORGANIZATIONS USE CASES

AWS Organizations offers a range of use cases that help businesses efficiently manage their multi-account AWS environments. Below are some typical scenarios where AWS Organizations can be leveraged.

Organizing a Multi-Account Environment

For DevOps engineers, AWS Organizations simplifies the management of a growing cloud environment by allowing the creation of new accounts as you scale. These accounts can be grouped into OUs or logical groups representing a single application or service. Using tag policies, resources can be classified and tracked effectively, enabling attribute-based access control for users and applications. This structure ensures better organization, visibility, and access management within the cloud environment.

Centralized Security and Monitoring

Security engineers can use AWS Organizations to centralize tools and access for the entire security team, enabling them to manage security needs for the organization. SCPs can be applied to accounts or OUs to enforce granular control over access to AWS resources, services, and Regions. This central approach strengthens security governance and ensures compliance across all accounts in the organization.

Resource Sharing Across a Multi-Account Environment

System engineers benefit from AWS Organizations by enabling resource sharing within the organization using AWS Resource Access Manager (AWS RAM). For example, a single Amazon Virtual Private Cloud (Amazon VPC) can be created and its subnets shared across multiple accounts within the organization. This eliminates the need for duplication, reduces complexity, and improves operational efficiency.

Cost Management and Centralized Billing

For system managers, AWS Organizations offers centralized billing, providing a consolidated view of costs across all accounts. With tools such as AWS Cost Explorer, resource usage can be tracked and expenses can be analyzed to identify optimization opportunities. Additionally, AWS Compute Optimizer helps optimize compute resources, further enhancing cost efficiency across the organization.

By leveraging these use cases, AWS Organizations helps businesses simplify operations, enhance security, streamline resource sharing, and improve cost management in their cloud environments.

AWS ORGANIZATIONS ROLE IN AWS CLOUD MIGRATION

AWS Organizations plays a crucial role in facilitating and enhancing the migration process to AWS through its integration with various AWS services, particularly AWS Application Migration Service (AWS MGN).

The different roles of AWS Organizations in AWS cloud migration can be seen in Figure 14.4.

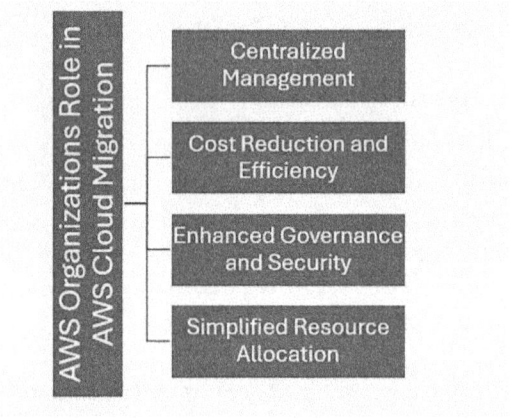

FIGURE 14.4 Different AWS Organizations Roles in AWS Cloud Migration.

Centralized Management: Streamlined Migration Across Multiple Accounts

AWS Organizations enables the centralized management of multiple AWS accounts, which is essential for large-scale migrations. By utilizing the global view feature of AWS MGN, organizations can oversee and manage migrations across different accounts efficiently. This centralized approach mitigates the complexities associated with handling migrations in disparate accounts, providing a unified interface for monitoring and controlling the migration process.

Cost Reduction and Efficiency: Reducing Migration Costs

The integration of AWS Organizations with AWS MGN not only simplifies the migration process but also reduces costs associated with migrating applications. Organizations can leverage consolidated billing, which allows them to manage expenses across all accounts under a single payment method. This financial management capability helps in optimizing costs during the migration phase.

Enhanced Governance and Security: Policy Enforcement and Compliance

With AWS Organizations, administrators can enforce policies across all accounts, ensuring compliance and governance during the migration process. This includes applying SCPs to manage permissions and access controls effectively. Such governance is crucial when migrating sensitive workloads to ensure that security protocols are adhered to throughout the migration.

Simplified Resource Allocation: Efficient Resource Management

AWS Organizations enables better resource management by allowing organizations to group accounts based on their workflows and operational needs. This grouping enables easier allocation of resources and management of dependencies during migrations. By organizing accounts strategically, companies can streamline their operations and enhance collaboration during the migration process.

AWS SERVICE CATALOG

Overview of AWS Catalog

AWS Service Catalog is a service that allows organizations to create and manage catalogs of IT services that are approved for use on AWS. It enables users to create a library of resources, including virtual machines, databases, and other applications, which can be easily deployed within their AWS environment. AWS Service Catalog streamlines the process for both IT administrators and end users, ensuring that only approved resources are accessed and reducing the likelihood of resource proliferation.

Why We Need AWS Service Catalog

The need for AWS Service Catalog arises from several key challenges faced by organizations, as given below:

- Governance: Maintaining control over cloud resources is essential. AWS Service Catalog helps enforce governance rules by allowing IT teams to define which services can be used and by whom. By centralizing service management, AWS Service Catalog enhances visibility, simplifies monitoring, and aids in enforcing governance rules, supporting secure and controlled cloud operations.

- Cost *m*anagement: By standardizing services and minimizing the usage of unapproved resources, AWS Service Catalog can significantly lower costs and prevent unexpected bills. With a centralized catalog of approved services and solutions, organizations can streamline their operations and ensure that all teams are utilizing the most cost-effective options available. This standardization also enables better tracking and management of resources, which helps in identifying potential cost-saving opportunities.

- Compliance and *s*ecurity: AWS Service Catalog plays a vital role in ensuring compliance and security by deploying only approved resources that adhere to industry standards and regulations. Acting as a central repository, it provides organizations with pre-approved, compliant AWS resources, such as Amazon S3 buckets and RDS instances, which have been rigorously assessed for compliance.

    With robust security controls such as encryption and IAM, AWS Service Catalog helps safeguard sensitive data and prevent unauthorized access or data breaches. Its centralized approach simplifies governance, enabling IT teams to monitor resource usage effectively and enforce policies across the organization.

    Furthermore, AWS Service Catalog stays updated with evolving compliance standards and security best practices, ensuring organizations can rely on its capabilities to maintain a secure, compliant infrastructure while focusing on their core operations.

- Resource *o*ptimization: AWS Service Catalog empowers businesses to optimize resources by ensuring efficient configurations tailored to their workloads. It provides detailed insights into performance and usage patterns, enabling organizations to scale resources up or down based on specific requirements. This proactive approach helps businesses avoid over-provisioning, reduce wastage, and achieve cost savings.

Additionally, AWS Service Catalog allows businesses to compare various configurations, evaluating their impact on both performance and costs. This enables organizations to fine-tune resource allocation and maintain an infrastructure that is both efficient and cost-effective. For instance, businesses can identify under-utilized instances or explore more suitable configurations to enhance workload performance.

By centralizing resource management, AWS Service Catalog streamlines operations, reduces complexity, and supports strategic decision-making. This not only minimizes costs and enhances efficiency but also ensures that organizations achieve optimal results, aligning resource usage with business goals.

Different AWS Service Catalog Features

AWS Service Catalog offers essential features that enhance resource management, streamline workflows, and maintain control, helping organizations optimize their cloud infrastructure.

AWS Service Catalog features can be seen in Figure 14.5.

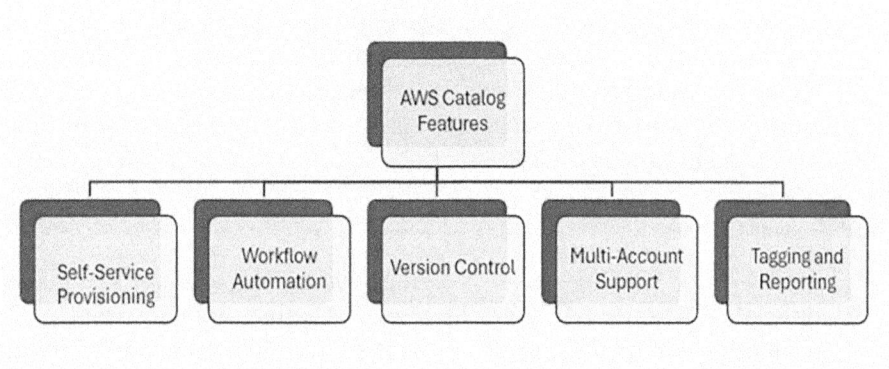

FIGURE 14.5 AWS Service Catalog Features.

Self-Service Provisioning

AWS Service Catalog enables users to quickly access and deploy resources without lengthy approvals. The self-service feature simplifies resource allocation for tasks such as creating test environments or adding storage, enabling faster application development. Predefined configurations ensure compliance and best practices, while customization options allow for tailored setups. This approach reduces administrative overhead, enhances productivity, and helps optimize costs by identifying underutilized resources.

Workflow Automation

With AWS Lambda integration, AWS Service Catalog automates product provisioning and other workflows. This eliminates manual steps, scales resources as needed, and minimizes errors. Businesses can integrate workflows with services such as S3 for storage or DynamoDB for database management, creating tailored, efficient processes that save time and improve reliability.

Version Control

AWS Service Catalog supports a version tracking tool that allows companies or organizations to manage multiple product versions, roll back changes, or upgrade seamlessly. By keeping a history of changes, it helps control the process, reduces disruptions, and enables smooth transitions between versions, enhancing product management and collaboration.

Tagging and Reporting

Standardized tagging in AWS Service Catalog allows users to track resources and usage more effectively. This mechanism provides detailed reports that highlight resource utilization, user behavior, and cost patterns. This information can be used for strategic planning, enhancing user experience, and resource allocation.

Multi-Account Support

AWS Service Catalog makes it easier for large organizations to manage multiple AWS accounts. It centralizes catalogs, ensuring consistent policies and promoting compliance. Multi-account support allows resources to be seen in a single view, providing better control to the IT department, reducing redundancies, and enabling efficient resource usage.

Benefits of AWS Service Catalog

AWS Service Catalog enables organizations to manage their cloud infrastructure effectively and securely, minimizing risk and optimizing resources.

The benefits of AWS Service Catalog can be seen in Figure 14.6.

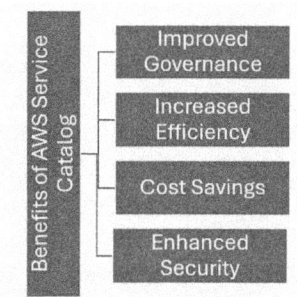

FIGURE 14.6 Benefits of AWS Service Catalog.

Improved Governance

AWS Service Catalog centralizes IT resources, enabling efficient management and ensuring they are utilized effectively. By setting up clear guidelines for the use of resources, it promotes compliance and ensures that tasks are completed within the scope. This enables businesses to manage their IT infrastructure more effectively, driving greater efficiency and increasing productivity.

Increased Efficiency

AWS Service Catalog allows users to provision resources directly, eliminating delays caused by manual administrative processes. This autonomy accelerates resource allocation while maintaining adherence to organizational policies, reducing the administrative burden and improving overall operational efficiency.

Cost Savings

AWS Service Catalog allows organizations to achieve cost savings by leveraging standardized provisioning of approved cloud resources and eliminates overspending on unauthorized or misconfigured services It regulates budget controls and cost policies. Furthermore, it also makes resource utilization more efficient by predefined configurations and hence, ensuring cost efficiency while maintaining compliance.

Enhanced Security

AWS Service Catalog enforces stringent security and compliance protocols, reducing risks associated with cloud services. Features such as access controls, data encryption, and real-time threat detection safeguard sensitive information. Compliance with industry standards such as GDPR and HIPAA further ensures data protection and builds trust with stakeholders.

AWS Service Catalog in AWS Cloud Migration

The AWS cloud migration process includes the important phases of careful planning, proper execution, and optimization. AWS Service Catalog is a critical tool that is used throughout the whole process, enabling enterprises to evaluate their current infrastructure. Launching with confidence, smoothly managing migrations, and optimizing cloud usage will lead to success, helping organizations keep up with the fast-changing business environment. The adoption of cloud technology plays a big part in digitizing and updating the system in real time, with AWS Service Catalog serving as a performance-boosting tool. These advancements will result in strategies that are centered on migration, with the goal of long-term operational resilience and innovation.

Assess Phase: Understanding Your Current Environment

Before any organization embarks on the journey to the cloud, a thorough analysis of the existing infrastructure, applications, and processes is essential. The Assess phase involves visualizing the scope of the operational activities and understanding how to move forward with the migration. Let's see how AWS Service Catalog contributes to this primary stage:

- *Inventory management*: AWS Service Catalog provides tools for creating an inventory of current applications and resources. This inventory helps organizations identify which applications are suitable for the cloud and which may require refactoring or redesigning.

- *Cost estimation*: AWS Service Catalog highlights potential cloud costs. By analyzing current usage patterns alongside AWS pricing structures, businesses will be able to predict their future expenditure and plan and budget accordingly.

- *Compliance and security*: AWS Service Catalog provides details about the compliance requirements for individual sectors through AWS services. It offers compliance framework templates that help organizations unfamiliar with regulatory requirements to understand them easily.

These capabilities not only provide organizations with the necessary information but also give them insights to help them make decisions that will lead to a successful migration.

Mobilize Phase: Preparing for Migration

Once organizations have assessed their environment, they reach the Mobilize phase, where they work out strategies for data transfer and prepare stakeholders for the transition. Here are the key areas that are essential for successfully migrating an on-premises IT solution to the AWS cloud:

- *Migration tools*: AWS provides a variety of migration solutions, such as AWS Application Migration Service and AWS Database Migration Service. These tools are cataloged for easy access and provide step-by-step guidance to facilitate the mobilization process.

- *Architectural guidance*: The AWS Well-Architected Framework, included in AWS Service Catalog, offers a set of best practices that can help organizations design their cloud environment efficiently. This guidance ensures that the migration strategy aligns with AWS's architectural best practices.

- *Training resources*: AWS Service Catalog includes a wealth of training materials and documentation. Businesses can make use of these resources to upskill teams in cloud technologies, ensuring they are ready to manage and optimize their new cloud infrastructure effectively.

Several solutions can be helpful when using AWS Service Catalog during the Mobilize phase, enabling us to lay the foundation for an organized and successful migration.

Migrate Phase: Executing the Transition

The Migrate phase is where the actual migration of resources takes place. This phase can seem daunting, but AWS Service Catalog simplifies the process:

- *Automated migration solutions*: AWS provides a collection of automated tools that are designed to be very easy to use. These tools assist in the transition process and application deployment with minimal downtime, reducing the risks associated with manual migrations.

- *Data management*: AWS Service Catalog includes tools such as AWS DataSync and AWS Storage Gateway, making them available for organizations to migrate large volumes of data reliably and securely, ensuring data integrity throughout the process.

- *Monitoring during migration*: AWS cloud monitoring tools allow businesses to keep track of application performance and health during migration, ensuring that any issues are detected and mitigated promptly.

AWS Service Catalog provides a comprehensive toolbox for companies, facilitating a smoother migration process.

Optimize/Modernize Phase: Enhancing Your Cloud Environment

Once the migration is complete, the Optimize or Modernize phase focuses on enhancing resource management efficiency and performance in the new environment. This is how AWS Service Catalog helps in this final stage:

- *Performance management*: Tools such as AWS CloudTrail and AWS Config allow you to see resource usage and application performance metrics, which helps companies configure more accurately and optimize resources.
- *Cost management*: The AWS Cost Explorer service that is included in AWS Service Catalog enables organizations to analyze their spending to find cost savings opportunities through resource optimization and usage patterns.
- *Innovation opportunities*: Organizations can leverage AWS Service Catalog to extend their AI-driven machine learning and big data analytics capabilities, enabling them to migrate traditional applications to a cloud environment.

In the Optimize/Modernize phase, AWS Service Catalog continuously enhances and maintains the cloud environments of organizations.

SUMMARY

This chapter focused on AWS Organizations and AWS Service Catalog, two of the key services that facilitate cloud migration through centralized governance, security, and resource management. AWS Organizations enables companies to handle multiple AWS accounts more effectively by implementing security policies, unifying billing, and ensuring compliance with the help of SCPs. It promotes cost optimization, resource sharing, and unified operations across Regions, making large-scale migrations easier. AWS Service Catalog enables organizations to produce and manage authorized IT service catalogs, which guarantees compliance by allowing only standardized deployments while maintaining security and cost control. It also facilitates self-service provisioning, workflow automation, and version control, enhancing operational efficiency. These AWS services are essential for successful cloud migrations, resource optimization, and the safety and compliance of the whole process.

REFERENCES

[AWSOrg24] Amazon Web Services, *"What is AWS Organizations?"*, AWS documentation, 2024. Available online at: *https://docs.aws.amazon.com/organizations/latest/userguide/*.

[AWSGov24] Amazon Web Services, *"Organizing Your AWS Environment Using Multiple Accounts"*, AWS whitepaper, 2024. Available online at: *https://docs.aws.amazon.com/whitepapers/latest/organizing-your-aws-environment/organizing-your-aws-environment.html*.

[AWSBilling24] Amazon Web Services, *"What is AWS Billing and Cost Management?"*, AWS documentation, 2024. Available online at: *https://docs.aws.amazon.com/awsaccountbilling/latest/aboutv2/*.

[SCPCtrl24] Amazon Web Services, *"Service control policies (SCPs)"*, AWS documentation, 2024. Available online at: *https://docs.aws.amazon.com/organizations/latest/userguide/orgs_manage_policies_scps.html*.

[WAF24] Amazon Web Services, *"AWS Well-Architected Framework"*, AWS whitepaper, 2024. Available online at: *https://docs.aws.amazon.com/wellarchitected/latest/framework/*.

[AWSRAM24] Amazon Web Services, *"What is AWS Resource Access Manager?"*, AWS documentation, 2024. Available online at: *https://docs.aws.amazon.com/ram/latest/userguide/*.

[CloudTrail24] Amazon Web Services, *"What Is AWS CloudTrail User Guide,"* AWS Documentation, 2024. Available online at: *https://docs.aws.amazon.com/awscloudtrail/latest/userguide/*.

[AWSMigrate24] Amazon Web Services, *"Strategy and best practices for AWS large migrations"*, AWS whitepaper, 2024. Available online at: *https://docs.aws.amazon.com/prescriptive-guidance/latest/strategy-large-scale-migrations/welcome.html*.

[AWSServiceCatalog24] Amazon Web Services, *"What Is Service Catalog?"*, AWS documentation, 2024. Available online at: *https://docs.aws.amazon.com/servicecatalog/latest/adminguide/introduction.html*.

KNOWLEDGE CHECK: MULTIPLE-CHOICE Q&A

Question 1

Which of the following is a key benefit of AWS Organizations?

A. Decentralized account management.

B. Centralized management and governance of multiple AWS accounts.

C. Increased operational complexity.

D. Reduced security policies across AWS accounts.

Question 2

What is the primary function of Service Control Policies (SCPs) in AWS Organizations?

A. To grant permissions to IAM users.

B. To enforce compliance and restrict access to AWS services across accounts.

C. To store backup policies for AWS resources.

D. To monitor EC2 instances.

Question 3

Which AWS service allows organizations to create and manage catalogs of IT services approved for deployment?

A. AWS Service Catalog.

B. AWS Lambda.

C. AWS Organizations.

D. AWS CloudFormation.

Question 4

In AWS Organizations, what is the purpose of the management account?

A. It hosts application workloads.

B. It is responsible for overseeing the entire organization, creating accounts, and applying policies.

C. It is used to run only billing-related activities.

D. It is restricted from making changes to policies.

Question 5

Which of the following AWS services automatically integrates with AWS Organizations to provide consolidated billing?

A. AWS Cost Explorer.

B. Amazon CloudWatch.

C. AWS Billing and Cost Management.

D. AWS Config.

Question 6

Which feature in AWS Organizations allows companies to logically group accounts for policy enforcement?

A. AWS Identity and Access Management (IAM).

B. Organizational Units (OUs).

C. Amazon Virtual Private Cloud (VPC).

D. AWS Resource Access Manager (RAM).

Question 7

What is the role of AWS CloudTrail in AWS Organizations?

A. It provides automatic auditing and logging of API activity across all member accounts.

B. It restricts unauthorized access to AWS resources.

C. It helps in provisioning EC2 instances across multiple accounts.

D. It is used only for monitoring cost and billing.

ANSWER SHEET: KNOWLEDGE CHECK

CHAPTER 1

Question 1

The term "hybrid cloud" refers to?

Answer: C. Combination of Public and Private Cloud.

Question 2

Which of the following is a cloud platform by Amazon?

Answer: C. AWS.

Question 3

In which cloud service model does the provider manage the infrastructure, operating system, and applications?

Answer: C. SaaS (Software as a Service).

Question 4

Answer: B. Private cloud.

Question 5

Answer: C. Bare metal servers and networking resources.

CHAPTER 2

Question 1

Which of the following are the advantages of AWS?

Answer: E. All of the above.

Question 2

Which AWS service category encompasses tools for building and deploying applications?

Answer: A. Compute.

Question 3

What makes an AWS Region different from an Availability Zone?

Answer: A. Regions are geographical locations, while Availability Zones are isolated locations within a region.

Question 4

Which of the following is NOT a frequent approach to access or connect to AWS?

Answer: D. On-premises Data Center connection.

Question 5

What of those given are AWS (Amazon Web Services) infrastructure components?

Answer: E. All of the above.

Question 6

What is the definition of a region in AWS?

Answer: A. A region is a geographical area or collection of data centers.

Question 7

What is the Availability Zone in AWS?

Answer: B. An Availability Zone is an isolated logical data center in a region.

CHAPTER 3

Question 1

What are the benefits of AWS IAM?

Answer: D. All of the above.

Question 2

What feature in AWS IAM allows you to group users with similar permissions?

Answer: C. Groups.

Question 3

Which AWS service is not based on AWS Compute Services?

Answer: A. Amazon S3.

Question 4

What is the most important benefit of IAM Roles in AWS?

Answer: B. Providing temporary permissions to entities.

Question 5

Which feature of IAM is chosen to add an extra layer of authentication to users' accounts?

Answer: B. Multi-Factor Authentication (MFA).

Question 6

What will be the cheapest pricing model for workloads that have steady and predictable usage in Amazon EC2?

Answer: C. Reserved Instances.

Question 7

What are the three main categories of Amazon Machine Images (AMIs)?

Answer: B. Community, AWS Marketplace, and My AMIs.

Question 8

Which of the following is an advantage of AWS Lambda?

Answer: A. Pay-per-use pricing.

Question 9

What is the role of a Security Group in Amazon EC2?

Answer: B. Acting as a virtual firewall to control traffic.

CHAPTER 4

Question 1

Which of the following does AWS NOT offer as one of its storage types?

Answer: D. SQL storage.

Question 2

Which AWS storage service is the best for accessing data, websites, and mobile applications?

Answer: B. Amazon S3.

Question 3

Which Amazon S3 feature is capable of changing storage classes and transferring data aligned with defined lifecycle policies on its own?

Answer: B. S3 Lifecycle Policy.

Question 4

Which functional element is dedicated to the management of traffic flow as well as routing in a VPC?

Answer: C. Route Table.

Question 5

What is Amazon Glacier mostly used for in the storage?

Answer: B. Long-term archival storage.

Question 6

Which AWS service do enterprises primarily use for hybrid cloud storage and connecting on-premises environments to AWS?

Answer: B. Amazon Storage Gateway.

Question 7

What is the maximum number of S3 buckets an AWS account can have by default?

Answer: C. 100.

Question 8

Which of the following VPC components is responsible for filtering traffic at the subnet level?

Answer: C. Network Access Control List (NACL).

Question 9

What does S3 Intelligent-Tiering optimize?

Answer: C. Storage costs based on access patterns.

Question 10

Which of the following is NOT a feature of Amazon S3?

Answer: C. SQL query processing.

CHAPTER 5

Question 1

Which kind of databases does Amazon Web Services support?

Answer: E. All of the above.

Question 2

What is the main feature of Amazon ElastiCache?

Answer: A. In-memory data storage for ultra-fast access.

Question 3

Which AWS service is ideally suited for analyzing large-scale datasets?

Answer: C. Amazon Redshift.

Question 4

Which of the following database engines are also present in the case of Amazon Aurora?

Answer: D. Both A and B (MySQL and PostgreSQL).

Question 5

Which one of the following databases is most suitable for databases with a lot of connections between them?

Answer: A. Amazon Neptune.

Question 6

What are the reasons for having databases that are managed by AWS over the ones that are hosted by EC2?

Answer: D. All of the above.

Question 7

Which database system uses JSON or XML to store data as records?

Answer: B. Document stores.

Question 8

What does Multi-AZ deployment in Amazon RDS provide?

Answer: A. High availability and durability.

Question 9

Which AWS service provides a tamper-proof and auditable record of transactions?

Answer: B. Amazon Quantum Ledger Database (QLDB).

CHAPTER 6

Question 1

Amazon CloudFront helps reduce latency by:

Answer: B. Caching content at edge locations closer to users.

Question 2

Which of the following is NOT a feature of Amazon CloudWatch?

Answer: B. Automatically caching content at edge locations.

Question 3

AWS CloudTrail primarily helps with:

Answer: C. Auditing and tracking API activity.

Question 4

What is the primary purpose of AWS Systems Manager?

Answer: C. To manage AWS resources and automate operational tasks.

Question 5

Which AWS service provides a unified dashboard for operational data across multiple accounts and regions?

Answer: B. AWS Systems Manager Explorer.

Question 6

What is a key feature of Amazon CloudWatch Alarms?

Answer: B. Automatically triggering actions based on metric thresholds.

Question 7

AWS Systems Manager Agent (SSM Agent) is required for:

Answer: A. Managing and automating operational tasks on managed nodes.

CHAPTER 7

Question 1

What is the first step in a cloud migration process?

Answer: B. Assessing workloads and configurations.

Question 2

Which of the following is a core component of cloud migration?

Answer: D. All of the above.

Question 3

The "Rehost" migration strategy is also referred to as:

Answer: A. Lift and shift.

Question 4

What is the main advantage of re-platforming during cloud migration?

Answer: B. Improved performance and scalability.

Question 5

Which cloud migration strategy involves moving applications to a SaaS-based solution?

Answer: B. Repurchase.

Question 6

What is the purpose of creating Total Cost of Ownership (TCO) reports during cloud migration?

Answer: B. To calculate long-term operational costs and savings.

Question 7

Which phase in the migration process involves testing and validating applications in the target environment?

Answer: B. Validation.

Question 8

The "7R's" of cloud migration strategies do NOT include:

Answer: C. Reassess.

Question 9

What is a disadvantage of the "Retain" strategy in cloud migration?

Answer: B. Resource expenditure on managing on-premises systems.

Question 10

Which tool is used in the discovery phase of AWS cloud migration?

Answer: B. AWS Discovery Service.

CHAPTER 8

Question 1

The primary purpose of Cloud Adoption Framework (CAF) is:

Answer: B. Provide a structured approach to cloud adoption.

Question 2

Which of the following is NOT a key component of the Cloud Adoption Framework?

Answer: C. Application Deployment.

Question 3

The first step in the Assess phase of AWS migration is:

Answer: B. Developing a business case.

Question 4

Which tool is used to automate the migration of on-premises databases to AWS?

Answer: A. AWS Database Migration Service (DMS).

Question 5

In the Mobilize phase, setting up a secure AWS landing zone involves:

Answer: B. Establishing governance and security frameworks.

Question 6

The six perspectives of the AWS Cloud Adoption Framework include:

Answer: B. Business, Governance, Operations, Security, People, and Platform.

Question 7

What is the main objective of the Optimize and Innovate phase in cloud migration?

Answer: C. Continuous improvement and innovation.

Question 8

Which AWS service is best suited for transferring large amounts of on-premises data to AWS?

Answer: C. AWS Snowball.

Question 9

The Well-Architected Framework by AWS is based on how many pillars?

Answer: C. Six.

Question 10

What is the primary goal of refactoring applications during the modernization phase?

Answer: B. To align applications with cloud-native capabilities.

CHAPTER 9

Question 1

Which of the following is a key component of the Assess Phase in AWS Cloud Migration?

Answer: B. Determining what to migrate and performing TCO analysis.

Question 2

What does the AWS Cloud Adoption Framework (CAF) help organizations assess?

Answer: B. Readiness for cloud adoption across multiple perspectives.

Question 3

Which tool provides an initial assessment of an organization's cloud adoption readiness?

Answer: B. Cloud Adoption Readiness Tool (CART).

Question 4

Which of the following statements about AWS Migration Evaluator is true?

Answer: C. It evaluates on-premises workloads and provides migration cost analysis.

Question 5

What is the primary difference between Cloud Readiness Assessment Tool (CART) and Migration Readiness Assessment (MRA)?

Answer: A. CART is used for self-service readiness assessment, while MRA is a deeper evaluation conducted by AWS professionals.

Question 6

Which AWS tool helps analyze an organization's IT landscape for cloud migration and includes business case development?

Answer: C. Migration Portfolio Assessment (MPA).

Question 7

What is the key benefit of the AWS Migration Evaluator tool?

Answer: B. It provides insights into cost optimization and right-sizing workloads for AWS.

CHAPTER 10

Question 1

What does the primary goal of the AWS Migration Mobilize phase?

Answer: B. To develop a detailed business case and prepare resources for migration.

Question 2

Which of the following activities is NOT part of the Mobilize phase?

Answer: C. Migrating all workloads to AWS.

Question 3

What is the purpose of the AWS Control Tower in the Mobilize phase?

Answer: A. To set up a Landing Zone for a secure AWS environment.

Question 4

Which AWS service helps collect data from on-premises environments for migration planning?

Answer: C. AWS Application Discovery Service.

Question 5

What is a key component of AWS Control Tower that helps enforce compliance?

Answer: B. AWS Guardrails.

Question 6

Which method of application discovery is best suited for VMware environments?

Answer: B. Agentless discovery.

Question 7

What does the Landing Zone in AWS refer to?

Answer: A. A secure and scalable AWS environment for migrated workloads.

Question 8

Which AWS service provides a centralized dashboard to track migration progress?

Answer: B. AWS Migration Hub.

Question 9

What is the role of the Operations Runbook in the Mobilize phase?

Answer: B. To provide detailed instructions for managing AWS applications post-migration.

Question 10

Which of the following is a major focus of security in the Mobilize phase?

Answer: B. Checking security and compliance of the AWS Landing Zon.

CHAPTER 11

Question 1

What does the term "hybrid cloud" refers to?

Answer: C. Combination of Public and Private Cloud.

Question 2

Which of the following is a key advantage of cloud migration?

Answer: C. Cost optimization.

Question 3

In cloud migration, which phase involves assessing the existing IT landscape?

Answer: C. Assess.

Question 4

Which of the following is NOT a cloud migration strategy?

Answer: D. Redistribute.

Question 5

Which AWS service is primarily used for migrating databases to the cloud?

Answer: C. AWS Database Migration Service (DMS).

Question 6

What is the primary advantage of using microservices in cloud-native design?

Answer: B. Easier scalability and maintainability.

Question 7

Which cloud service model provides infrastructure components such as virtual machines and networking?

Answer: C. IaaS.

Question 8

Which AWS service provides automatic scaling for applications?

Answer: B. AWS Auto Scaling.

Question 9

What is the purpose of Google's BigQuery in cloud computing?

Answer: B. Serverless data warehouse.

Question 10

What is the key characteristic of a serverless computing model?

Answer: B. Auto-scales based on demand.

Question 11

Which component is essential for Change Data Capture (CDC) in database migration?

Answer: B. Transaction logs.

Question 12

Which tool is commonly used in the assessment phase of cloud migration?

Answer: B. Azure Migrate.

Question 13

Which cloud security feature ensures access control and identity management?

Answer: A. AWS IAM.

CHAPTER 12

Question 1

What is the main goal of the Modernization Phase in AWS migration?

Answer: B. To transform the current environment into one that is more adaptable, elastic, and reliable.

Question 2

Which of the following is NOT a key objective of the modernization phase?

Answer: D. Retaining all legacy systems.

Question 3

What does refactoring for cloud-native design primarily involve?

Answer: B. Decomposing monolithic applications into microservices.

Question 4

Which AWS service is used for monitoring applications and resources?

Answer: B. AWS CloudWatch.

Question 5

What is the purpose of using AWS Database Migration Service (DMS) in the modernization phase?

Answer: C. To ensure secure and efficient database migration with minimal downtime.

Question 6

Which of the following is an AWS managed service used to enhance application performance by reducing database load?

Answer: C. Amazon ElastiCache.

Question 7

What is a key feature of AWS Elastic Load Balancing (ELB)?

Answer: B. Distributing incoming traffic across multiple EC2 instances.

CHAPTER 13

Question 1

What is the primary purpose of Generative AI in AWS Cloud Migration?

Answer: B. To automate infrastructure provisioning, application re-architecting, and data transformation.

Question 2

Which AWS service provides access to foundation models for building and scaling Generative AI applications?

Answer: B. Amazon Bedrock.

Question 3

Which AI technique is commonly used in Generative AI for generating realistic images and videos?

Answer: C. Generative Adversarial Networks (GANs).

Question 4

Which AWS service is primarily used for managing the machine learning lifecycle, including training and deploying Generative AI models?

Answer: C. Amazon SageMaker.

Question 5

What role does Generative AI play in the Assess Phase of AWS Cloud Migration?

Answer: A. Predicts cost estimates and identifies potential migration risks.

Question 6

Which of the following is a key feature of Amazon Q Business in Generative AI applications?

Answer: B. Provides AI-powered chat applications integrated with enterprise data.

Question 7

What is prompt engineering in Generative AI?

Answer: A. A technique used to improve AI model responses by refining input prompts.

Question 8

Which AWS service helps organizations estimate cloud migration costs and analyze workload dependencies?

Answer: B. AWS Migration Hub.

Question 9

How does Generative AI help in the Modernize Phase of AWS Cloud Migration?

Answer: A. Automates data transformation and cloud-native application refactoring.

Question 10

Which AWS service enables businesses to use AI-powered development assistance for coding and software optimization?

Answer: C. Amazon Q Developer.

CHAPTER 14

Question 1

Which of the following is a key benefit of AWS Organizations?

Answer: B. Centralized management and governance of multiple AWS accounts.

Question 2

What is the primary function of Service Control Policies (SCPs) in AWS Organizations?

Answer: B. To enforce compliance and restrict access to AWS services across accounts.

Question 3

Which AWS service allows organizations to create and manage catalogs of IT services approved for deployment?

Answer: A. AWS Service Catalog.

Question 4

In AWS Organizations, what is the purpose of the Management Account?

Answer: B. It is responsible for overseeing the entire AWS Organization, creating accounts, and applying policies.

Question 5

Which of the following AWS services automatically integrate with AWS Organizations to provide consolidated billing?

Answer: C. AWS Billing and Cost Management.

Question 6

Which feature in AWS Organizations allows companies to logically group accounts for policy enforcement?

Answer: B. Organizational Units (OUs).

Question 7

What is the role of AWS CloudTrail in AWS Organizations?

Answer: A. It provides automatic auditing and logging of API activity across all member accounts.

INDEX

A

accelerated problem detection, AWS Systems Manager, 161
Access Control Lists (ACLs), 91–92
accuracy and loss, 446
additional EBS volumes, 67
agent-based application discovery process, 272
agent-based data collection, 273–274
agent-based *vs.* agentless collection, 277–278
agentless application discovery process, 272
Agentless Collector, 275
agentless data collection, 273, 275
agility
    cloud computing, 4
    resilience and, 405
Amazon Aurora, 130, 407
Amazon Bedrock, 462–463, 465–466
Amazon CloudFront, 30, 34, 147–149
Amazon CloudWatch, 404, 410, 415, 482–483
    alarms, 152–153
    Amazon CloudWatch Logs, 153–154
    EC2 instance, 154–155
    metrics, 151–152, 404
    monitors systems and apps, 485
Amazon Database Migration (DMS), 335–336
Amazon DocumentDB, 124, 127, 130
Amazon DynamoDB, 124, 130, 481
Amazon EBS, 378
    snapshots, 312
Amazon EC2, 408–409
Amazon ECR, 86–87
Amazon ECS and EKS, 482
Amazon EFS, 378
Amazon ElastiCache, 130
Amazon Elastic Compute Cloud (EC2), 41, 53–61
    instances, 56–58
    preparation for use of, 65
    pricing models for, 58–59
Amazon Elastic Container Service (ECS), 54
Amazon Elastic Kubernetes Service (EKS), 41, 54
Amazon Elasticsearch service, 411
Amazon FSx, 370, 378
Amazon Glacier, 86
Amazon GuardDuty, 415
Amazon instance user data, 60–61
Amazon Kinesis, 335
Amazon Lookout for Equipment, 485
Amazon Machine Images (AMIs), 55, 59–60, 65
Amazon Managed Streaming for Apache Kafka, 335
Amazon MemoryDB for Redis, 130
Amazon Neptune, 124, 130
Amazon Q, 463, 466–468

Amazon Quantum Ledger Database (QLDB), 130
Amazon QuickSight, 276, 485
Amazon RDS, 407
    Aurora and, 481
Amazon Redshift, 123, 130
Amazon Relational Database Service (RDS), 130, 133–136
Amazon Route 53, 30
Amazon S3, 370, 378, 380
Amazon SageMaker, 462–465, 485
    for generative AI, 463–465
Amazon S3 File Gateway, 383–384
    architecture, 384
    benefits, 385
    scenarios to use, 385–386
Amazon S3 Glacier, 371
Amazon Simple Storage Service (S3), 83, 87–91, 101–105, 335
    Transfer Acceleration, 105–107
    versioning, 94–95
Amazon SNS, 408
Amazon SQS, 408
Amazon virtual private cloud (VPC), 107–117
    with all components, 113–114
    AWS Site-to-Site VPN, 116–117
    AWS Transit Gateway, 114–115
    components, 108–112
        Elastic IP (EIP) addresses, 111
        endpoints, 111–112
        Internet gateways, 110–111
        NAT instances and NAT gateways, 112
        Network ACLs (NACLs), 110
        peering connections, 112
        route tables, 109–110
        security group, 110
        subnet, 109
        Virtual Private Gateways (VPGs), 112
Amazon Web Services (AWS), 7, 23
    cloud history, 25–26
    creating AWS account, 36–37
    Gartner Magic Quadrant, 23–25
    global infrastructure, 29–34
    methods to access or connect to AWS, 35–36
    method to choose the right AWS region, 34
    products and services, 27
    services and key characteristics, 26–29
application, 177
    configuration and dependency mapping, 239
    dependencies, 277–278
    management, AWS Systems Manager, 159
    mappings, 179
    migration, 264
    modernization, 224–225, 402–404
    sizing, 179–180
Application Discovery Service (ADS), 226, 265, 270–280
Application Discovery Service Agentless Collector, 272, 284
Application Migration Service API, 311
architecture(al)
    of EC2 Instance, 67
    enhancement, generative AI, 481–482
    patterns, AWS Prescriptive Guidance, 296
art and image generation, generative AI, 451–452
Artificial Intelligence (AI)
    computer vision, 425–426
    deep learning (DL), 424–425, 429
    definition, 421–422
    Generative AI, 427–430
    machine learning (ML), 423, 429
        model creation process
            feature engineering, 432–433
            feature selection, 430–432
            model evaluation, 434
            model training, 433

natural language processing, 426
robotic process automation (RPA), 426–427
assess phase of cloud migration
assessment, 239–240
database migration, 337–338
generative AI, 470–476
migration evaluator and MPA, 257
Migration Portfolio Assessment (MPA), 254–256
migration readiness assessment, 245–254
readiness, 239
reasons for migrating, 237–238
tools used in, 240–245
what we want to migrate, 238–239
Astro scans, 469
Athena, 276
audio and video synthesis, generative AI, 452–453
auditing, IAM, 42
augmented reality, 398
Aurora MySQL target endpoint, 360–361
authentication, IAM, 42
authorization, IAM, 42
automated backups, 134
automated discovery, 271
automated maintenance, 407
automation capabilities, 287
automation for repetitive tasks, AWS Systems Manager, 168
auto scaling, 150, 152, 408–409
Availability Zones (AZs), 30, 55
AWS Application Discovery Service (ADS), 270–280, 288, 473, 475
agent-based *vs.* agentless collection, 277–278
architecture, 272–276
benefits, 278–279
features of, 271
integration with migration tools, 277
key features and considerations, 276–277
planning data center migrations, 271–272
tutorial, 279–283
AWS Application Insights, 484
AWS Application Migration Service (AWS MGN), 227, 297–298, 305–319, 478, 504
with added replication servers, 312–313
with added replication servers and data encryption, 313–314
application migration service lifecycle, 308–309
AWS MGN architecture, 311–319
benefits of, 306–307
with conversion server, 315–316
fundamental attributes of, 306
implementation, 309–310
with migrated resources, 316–317
network connectivity architecture, 318–319
Server Migration Service (SMS) and its comparison, 310
source and target environments, 311
tutorial, 321–334
application migration service console, access, 323
applications and waves, 331–332
cleaning up after final cutover, 334
cutover instance launching, 330–331
IAM user, 323
launch settings, 327–329
launch template configuring, 324–325
post-migration modernization, 332–334
replication template/tags, 323–324
test instance launching, 329–330
WordPress Content and AWS replication agent, 326–327
types, 305
AWS Audit Manager, 157
AWS Cloud Adoption Framework (AWS CAF), 239–240
business stakeholders, 208
Environmental, Social, and Governance (ESG) performance, 208
perspectives, 208–209

AWS CloudFormation, 403
AWS cloud migration
  automation for repetitive tasks, 168
  compliance monitoring, 169
  generative AI in, 468–470
  integration with other AWS migration tools, 169
  pre-migration assessment, 168
  resource management, 169
AWS Cloud Readiness Assessment Summary Report, 244
AWS CloudTrail, 155–157, 494
AWS CodeBuild, 225
AWS CodeCommit, 403
AWS CodeDeploy, 225
AWS CodePipeline, 225, 403
AWS Command Line Interface (CLI), 35, 371
AWS Compute Optimizer, 476, 482, 484
AWS Config, 157, 483
AWS Config monitors and logs, 475
AWS Control Tower, 226, 265, 479
AWS Cost Explorer, 473, 476, 483
AWS Database Migration Service (DMS), 227, 297–298, 300, 414, 478
AWS Database Migration Service Fleet Advisor, 277
AWS database services
  Amazon Aurora, 136
  Amazon RDS, 133–136
  AWS-managed databases, 132–133
  data warehouse databases, 125
  EC2-hosted databases, 131–132
  key database services, 130–131
  memory-based databases, 125
  non-relational databases, 124
    column-family stores, 128–129
    document stores, 127–128
    graph databases, 129–130
    key-value stores, 127
  relational databases, 124–126
  Relational Database Service (RDS) database
    delete, 140–141
    instance, 138–139
    modification, 141–142
    solution architectures, 136–138
  types, 124
AWS data storage mapping
  AWS data migration services, 378–383
  AWS migration services (migration tools), 377
  AWS Snow Family, 386–390
  AWS Storage Gateway, 383–386
  AWS storage services (target storage systems), 378
  file systems (source storage systems), 377
  with traditional storage systems, 375–376
AWS DataSync, 298, 300, 379–383
  Amazon S3, 380
  architecture, 379–380
  archiving cold data, 382
  benefits, 381–382
  data protection, 382
  online data migration, 382
  timely data movement for in-cloud processing, 382–383
  Transport Layer Security (TLS) version 1.2, 380
AWS DMS, 339
AWS DMS Fleet Advisor, 364–366
  architecture, 364–366
AWS DMS Serverless, 362–363
AWS Elastic Beanstalk, 482
AWS Fargate, 54
AWS GovCloud, 32
AWS IAM Access Analyzer, 474
AWS IAM (Identity and Access Management), 411, 479
AWS IAM Identity Center, 269
AWS Identity and Access Management (IAM), 494
AWS Inspector, 415
AWS IoT Core connects machines, 485
AWS IoT SiteWise monitors machinery, 485
AWS Lambda, 41, 54, 405, 481, 485

AWS-managed database services, 407
AWS Managed Services, 227, 404
  in cloud modernization, 408–409
  scalability and elasticity, 408–409
AWS Management Console, 35, 287–288
  integration, 306
AWS Marketplace AMIs, 60
AWS MGN, 299
AWS migration evaluator, 240
AWS Migration Hub, 226, 265, 277, 284–287, 472, 475, 484
  console, 283
  tutorial, 287–288
AWS migration phase tools, 297–298
AWS migration services (migration tools), 377
AWS Organizations, 491–492
  AWS Service Catalog, 505–512
  benefits, 493–495
  centralized governance and management, 495–501
  components
    management account, 497
    member accounts, 497
    organizational units, 496
    policies, 496
    root, 496
  features of, 502
  grouping for governance and security, 498–500
  hierarchical structure and policy application, 497–498
  organizations role in AWS cloud migration, 504–505
  solutions for challenges, 492–493
  technical concepts of, 500–501
  use cases, 503–504
AWS prescriptive guidance in migrate phase, 294–297
  components, 295
  industry-specific scenarios, 297
  large-scale migrations, 296
  risk reduction, 297
  tool-specific guidance, 297
AWS Pricing Calculator, 472
AWS Replication Agent, 311
AWS Resource Access Manager (AWS RAM), 495
`AWS-RunShellScript`, 164
AWS SAML provider, 36
AWS Schema Conversion Tool (SCT), 478
AWS SCT, 339
AWS Security Hub, 415
AWS Security Services, 411–412
AWS Service Catalog, 479, 505–512
  in AWS cloud migration, 510–512
  benefits, 508–510
  features, 507–508
AWS Services
  Amazon Bedrock, 462–463, 465–466
  Amazon Q, 463, 466–468
  Amazon SageMaker, 462–465
  for data migration, 227, 297–298
AWS Single Sign-On (SSO) experience, 36
AWS Snowball Edge, 387
  benefits, 388–389
  scenarios, 389–390
  workflow, 387–388
AWS Snow Family, 86, 298, 300, 379, 386–390
AWS Software Development Kits (SDKs), 35
AWS Step Functions, 482
AWS Storage Gateway, 298, 379, 383–386
  Amazon S3 File Gateway, 383–384
AWS storage services
  and migration phases, 369–375
  target storage systems, 378
AWS Systems Manager, 157–160, 483
  benefits, 160–169
    accelerated problem detection, 161
    enhanced visibility and control, 162
    robust security and compliance, 163
    seamless hybrid environment management, 162–163
    streamlined automation, 162

capabilities, 160
cases
    configuration management, 167
    operations management, 167
    patch management, 166
    session management, 166–167
core technical concepts of
    managed nodes, 163
    resource groups, 164
    Systems Manager Agent (SSM Agent), 163–164
documents
    compliance and configuration management, 165
    parameters and parameter store, 164
    patch manager and baselines, 165
facilitates AWS cloud migration
    automation for repetitive tasks, 168
    compliance monitoring, 169
    integration with other AWS migration tools, 169
    pre-migration assessment, 168
    resource management, 169
AWS Total Cost of Ownership (TCO) calculator, 473
AWS training & certification, 254
AWS Transfer Family, 299–300, 379
AWS Transit Gateway, 114–115
AWS Trusted Advisor, 473–474, 476, 482–483
AWS Well-Architected Framework, 211, 295
    AWS migration phases with, 216–225
        assess phase, 217–220
        migrate and modernize phase, 217, 222–225
        mobilize phase, 217, 220–222
    continuous improvement, 212
    cost optimization, 215
    for migration, 212–213
    operational excellence, 213
    performance efficiency, 214
    reliability, 214
    security, 214
    strong cloud foundations guidance, 212
    sustainability, 215
AWS Well-Architected Tool, 474–475
AWS X-Ray, 483
Azure, 369
Azure Cosmos DB, 127
Azure Well-Architected Framework, 212

B

batch, 446
batch size, 447
blockchain, 398
block storage, 85
Bring Your Own License (BYOL), 252
broad network access, 17
building applications, 454–455
business case
    development, 256
    for migrating to AWS, 264
    migration, 219
business requirements, assess phase of cloud migration, 237
business value, 253

C

caching, modernization phase, 407
capabilities, AWS Systems Manager, 160
centralized configuration, AWS Systems Manager, 160
centralized logging and reporting, 269
Change Data Capture (CDC), 341–342
change management, 229–230
    AWS Systems Manager, 159
    strategy, 206
ChatGPT by OpenAI, 459
classic port in Windows and Linux, 62–64
Classless Inter-Domain Routing (CIDR), 107
cloud adoption framework (CAF)

adoption and migration, 206
AWS CAF, 208–211
AWS migration phases with AWS well-architected framework, 216–225
cloud migration success mantra
  people, 229–231
  process, 231
  technology, 231–232
governance, 204–205
migration phases and associated tools, 225–227
optimization and innovation, 207
people and processes, 205–206
phases of AWS cloud migration, 215–216
strategy and planning, 204
technological dimension of, 205
Well-Architected Framework, 227–228
Cloud Adoption Readiness Tool (CART), 240, 242, 270
cloud assessment tools, 231
cloud computing
  applications, 2
  benefits of, 4–5
  characteristics, 16–18
  cloud deployment model characteristics, 14–16
  definition, 1–2
  deployment models of, 9–14
  ecosystem, 1
  on-premises infrastructure *vs.*, 2
  on-premises/traditional IT infrastructure, 2–3
  3-4-5 principles of, 5
  service models, 5–9
Cloud Endure, 298
CloudFront (Amazon's CDN), 33
Cloud Infrastructure and Platform Services (CIPS) graph, 24
Cloud migration workloads
  application migration, 174
  change management, 175–176
  compliance, 176
  configuration management, 175

cost management, 176
database migration, 175
data migration, 174
infrastructure migration, 175
migration strategy, 182–185
migration strategy identification, 196–198
refactor (re-architect), 189–190
rehost (lift and shift), 185–186
relocate, 186–187
replatform (lift and reshape), 187–189
repurchase (drop and shop), 191–192
retain (revisit), 193–196
retire, 192–193
testing, 175
traditional approach to
  data collection and analysis, 176–178
  execution and migration, 181–182
  mappings and dependencies, 178–179
  planning and assessment, 179–181
cloud-native design, 227
Cloud Readiness Assessment (CRA), 226
Cloud Readiness Heatmap report, 244–245
CloudTrail, 155–157
CloudWatch, 403; *see also* Amazon CloudWatch
  alarms, 153
CloudWatch Logs, 153–154
CloudWatch Logs Insights, 410
cold migration, 304
column-family stores, 128–129
communication and change management, migration process, 296
community AMIs, 60
community cloud, 13–14
comparison of different S3 storage types, 91
complexity, 3
compliance and configuration management, AWS Systems Manager, 165
compliance and governance, 375
compliance monitoring, AWS Systems Manager, 160, 169
computer vision, AI, 425–426

configuration items/workloads, 173–174
configuration management, AWS Systems Manager, 167
Configuration Management Database (CMDB), 173–174, 239
containerization, 406
Content Delivery Network (CDN), 30, 147
continuous data replication, 338
continuous improvement, generative AI, 482–483
cost-effectiveness, modernization strategy, 406
cost-efficiency, 270
cost estimation, 472–473
cost optimization, modernization, 409–412
cost reduction potential, 306
cross-cluster migrations, 305
customer gateway device, 116
customer ID, 125
customizable data collection, 271
customizable thresholds and sampling, 153
cutover phase, 183

D

DALL·E by OpenAI, 459–460
data
    center divestment, 254
    collection, 255
    collection, ML, 442
    gathering and preparation, ML, 442
    handling, AWS Systems Manager, 160
    integrity, 308
    inventory, 255
    migration, 224
    preparation, ML, 442–443
    protection, AWS Managed Services, 411
    security, 277
    security and validation, 373
    sovereignty, 34
    storage, 2
    training and evaluation, ML, 444–445
    volume tiers, 370
    warehouse services, 335
database migration
    Amazon Database Migration (DMS), 335–336
    AWS Database Migration Service (DMS), 300
    AWS DataSync, 300
    AWS DMS homogeneous architecture, 345–346
    AWS Snow Family, 300
    lift-and-shift database migrations, 344
    replatforming, 345
    replication instance, 346
    replication tasks and CDC, 346–347
    source and target endpoints, 346
    three-phase approach to
        assess phase, 337–338
        migrate and modernize phase, 338–339
        mobilize phase, 338
        native database migration tools, 339
    tool or approach for, 336–351
    types
        heterogeneous migrations, 339, 341
        homogeneous migration, 339–340
Database Migration Service (DMS), 288
decoupling
    components, 408
    monoliths, 405
Dedicated Hosts, 58–59
deep discovery, 220
deep learning (DL), 424–425, 429
deployment models of cloud computing, 9–14
    community cloud, 13–16
    hybrid cloud, 12–13, 15
    private cloud, 11–12, 15
    public cloud, 9–11, 15
deployment summary, 253
digital transformation and cloud adoption, 176
discovery, 174

Discovery Agent process, 282
Distributed Denial of Service (DDoS), 415
DMS fleet advisor, 339
document stores, 127–128
DynamoDB, 123

E

EBS volume, 68
EC2-hosted databases, 131–132
EC2 launch templates, 306
edge location, 149
edge locations, AWS, 30, 33
Elastic Block Store (EBS)
    for block storage, 83
    volumes, 65, 136
Elastic Compute Cloud (EC2), 25
Elastic File System (EFS) for file storage, 83
Elastic IP (EIP) addresses, 111
Elastic Load Balancing (ELB), 409
embeddings, generative AI, 456
endpoints, VPC, 111–112
enhanced decision-making, generative AI, 83–484
enhanced visibility and control, AWS Systems Manager, 162
Enhanced vMotion Compatibility (EVC), 305
epochs, 446
    parameter, 446
error management and recovery, 373
event-driven model, modernization strategy, 405–406
execute high-performance computing (HPC) workloads, 2

F

file storage, 85
file systems (source storage systems), 377
finance and business, generative AI, 453
flexibility, cloud computing, 5
flexible retention, 154

Foundation Models (FMs), 454
frameworks and methodologies, AWS Prescriptive Guidance, 295
full load migration, 338

G

Generative Adversarial Networks (GANs), 457–458
generative AI, 427–430
    Amazon SageMaker for Generative AI, 463–465
    applications of
        art and image generation, 451–452
        audio and video synthesis, 452–453
        finance and business, 453
        language models, 452
        manufacturing and design, 453
        medicine and healthcare, 453
    in assess phase of AWS cloud migration, 470–476
    in AWS cloud migration, 468–470
    AWS Services
        Amazon Bedrock, 462–463, 465–466
        Amazon Q, 463, 466–468
        Amazon SageMaker, 462–465
    building applications, 454–455
    embeddings, 456
    Foundation Models (FMs), 454
    Generative Adversarial Networks (GANs), 457–458
    Large Language Models (LLMs), 454
    in migrate and modernize phase of AWS cloud migration, 480–485
    in mobilize phase of AWS cloud migration, 476–480
    multimodal capabilities, 454
    popular tools and web sites for exploring
        ChatGPT by OpenAI, 459
        DALL·E by OpenAI, 459–460
        GitHub Copilot, 461
        Midjourney, 460
        RunwayML, 460

SOUNDRAW, 461
prompt engineering, 455
Recurrent Neural Networks (RNNs), 459
refinement, 450–451
sampling, 450
tokens, 456
training, 450
transformers, 456
understanding prompts, 454
unified security and access control, 463
Variational Autoencoders (VAEs), 458
vector, 456
GitHub Copilot, 461
Google Cloud, 369
Google Cloud Adoption Framework, 295
Google Cloud Platform (GCP), 7, 42
Google Cloud Well-Architected Framework, 211–212
GovCloud, 32
graph databases, 129–130

H

Hadoop file system, 369
heatmap, 243
heterogeneous AWS database migration service, 351–362
    AWS Schema Conversion Tool, 354
    database schema, 354
    homogeneous database migration, 298, 352–353
heterogeneous database migration, 298
heterogeneous migrations, 339, 341
High initial Capital Expenditure (CapEx), 3
High-Performance Computing (HPC) experiments, 56
homogeneous database migration, 298, 352–353
homogeneous migration, 339–340
horizontal scaling, 4
hybrid cloud, 12–13
hyperparameter tuning, ML, 445–447

I

Identity and Access Management (IAM) service, 78, 163, 210
    access key, 52–53
    adding user to an available group, 47
    AWS compute services, 53–78
    AWS IAM group creation, 46–47
    AWS IAM user creation, 44–45
    benefits, 43
    groups in AWS work, 45–46
    identity and access management, 42–53
    MFA in, 51–52
    policy, 50–51
    role, 47–49
    user, 44
    users, groups and roles, 43
immersion days, 254
Infrastructure as a Service (IaaS), 6–7
Instance Metadata Service (IMDS), 60–61
integration
    with COEs, 307
    with migration tools, 271
    with other AWS migration tools, AWS Systems Manager, 169
Internet gateways, 110–111
Internet of Things (IoT) services, 28, 398
inventory data import, 273
inventory process, 218
iteration, 446
IT modernization, 402
IT snapshot, assess phase of cloud migration, 237

K

Key Management Service (KMS), 164, 411
key pair, 66
Key Performance Indicators (KPIs), 151
key-value stores, 127
KPIS for successful implementation, 319–321
    cutover, 321
    implementation, 320

initial replication, 320
ready for testing, 320
testing, 320

L

Lambda functions, 151
landing zone, 221–222, 264, 266–267
    with AWS Control Tower
        accounts and deploying resources, 269
        benefits, 270
        consolidated management and governance, 269
        establishing, 268
        optional components, 269–270
    greenfield *vs.* brownfield deployments, 267
language models, generative AI, 452
Large Language Models (LLMs), 454
large-scale data migration, 371–372
latency end users, 34
leadership, 230
learning rate, 446
lift-and-shift focus, 306
live migration, 305
local zones, AWS, 31
logical data migration, 337

M

machine learning (ML), 423, 429
    building blocks
        data collection, 442
        data gathering and preparation, 442
        data preparation, 442–443
        data training and evaluation, 444–445
        hyperparameter tuning, 445–447
        model deployment/implementation, 448–449
        model selection or hypothesis generation, 443–444
        predictive modeling, 448
        problem definition, 441–442
    comparative characteristics and applications, 439
    model creation process
        feature engineering, 432–433
        feature selection, 430–432
        model evaluation, 434
        model training, 433
    reinforcement learning, 438–439
    supervised learning, 436–437
    unsupervised learning, 437–438
maintainability, 405
managed nodes, AWS Systems Manager, 163
manual import, 272
manufacturing and design, generative AI, 453
measured service, cloud computing, 17–18
medicine and healthcare, generative AI, 453
metadata management, AWS Systems Manager, 160
microservices architecture, 405
Microsoft Azure, 7
Microsoft Azure Cloud Adoption Framework, 295
Microsoft Remote Desktop, 73
Midjourney, 460
migrate and modernize phase, database migration, 338–339
migration
    evaluator, 226, 247–249, 270
        executive summary, 251–252
        obtaining access, 248
        reports, 250–254
        workflow of, 249–250
    execution, 181–182
    governance, 264
    path decision, 183
    patterns, 296
    plan and scripts, 373
    planning, 256
    project plans, 180–181

strategy, 231
    development, AWS Prescriptive Guidance, 295
  task
    creation, 361–362
    monitoring, 362
  tools, 232
migration phase
  associated tools and, 225–227
  AWS Application Migration Service (MGN), 305–319
    tutorial, 321–334
  AWS DMS Fleet Advisor, 364–366
  AWS DMS serverless, 362–363
  AWS prescriptive guidance in, 294–297
  cold migration, 304
  database migration
    Amazon Database Migration (DMS), 335–336
    tool or approach for, 336–351
  data migration, 294, 299–300
    to AWS, 366–369
    framework and AWS data storage mapping, 375–390
  different AWS migration phase tools, 297–298
  generative AI, 480–485
  heterogeneous AWS database migration service, 351–362
  KPIS for successful implementation, 319–321
  live migration, 305
  optimization and modernization, 294
  targeting AWS storage services, 369–375
  VMware to AWS cloud migration, 301–303
  warm migration, 304–305
  workload migration, 293, 298–299
Migration Portfolio Assessment (MPA), 226, 240, 254–256
Migration Readiness Assessment (MRA), 226, 240, 245–254

minimal downtime, MGN, 306
ML, *see* machine learning (ML)
mobilization phase
  agent-based application discovery tutorial, 280–283
  application discovery service (ADS), 270–280
    agentless collector, 284
  AWS Control Tower, 265–270
  AWS Migration Hub, 284–287
    tutorial, 287–288
  benefits, 278–279
  database migration, 338
  objectives, 263–264
  tools, 265
model deployment/implementation, ML, 448–449
model selection or hypothesis generation, ML, 443–444
modernization
  challenges and solutions in, 412–416
    compliance, 415
    data migration, 414
    security, 414–415
    technical debt, 413–414
  choice for application, 400–401
  DMS, 339
  generative AI, 480–485
  objectives, 398–400
    agility, 399
    collaboration, 400
    cost saving, 399
    innovation, 399–400
    scalability, 399
  rehosting, 412
  replacement of legacy applications, 412
  stages, 401–404
    application modernization, 402–404
    IT modernization, 402
  strategies, 404–412
    AWS managed services in cloud modernization, 408–409

cost optimization, 409–412
   refactoring for cloud-native design, 405–406
   replatforming on managed services, 406–408
MongoDB, 127
monitor migration progress, 288
multi-AZ deployments, 134
multi-AZ RDS deployment, 137
multimodal capabilities, generative AI, 454
multi-protocol communication platform, 408
multi-tenancy and resource pooling, 17
My AMIs, 60

N

NAT instances and NAT gateways, 112
native database migration tools, database migration, 339
native migration tools, 340
natural language processing, 426
network access control, 306
Network ACLs (NACLs), 110
network dependencies, 178
Network File System (NFS), 369
Network Load Balancers, 409
network stability and bandwidth, 374
node management, AWS Systems Manager, 159
non-disruptive testing, 307
non-relational databases, 124
   column-family stores, 128–129
   document stores, 127–128
   graph databases, 129–130
   key-value stores, 127
NoSQL database services, 335

O

object storage, 84
offline data migration, 337, 368–369
On-Demand, 55
on-demand self-service, 16–17
One-Time Password (OTP), 51
online data migration, 337, 367–368
on-premises environment, 252
operate phase, 184
operational expenditure (OpEx), 3
operational model for cloud services, 206
operations management, AWS Systems Manager, 159, 167
operations runbook, 264
optimization
   and innovation, CAF, 207
   and modernization, 294
   patterns, 296
Oracle source database endpoint, 359–360
organizational units (OUs), 268
outposts, AWS services, 31

P

parameters and parameter store, AWS Systems Manager, 164
partner migration tools, 288
patch management, AWS Systems Manager, 166
patch manager and baselines, AWS Systems Manager, 165
pay-as-you-go model, 3, 399, 401
peering connections, VPC, 112
people and processes, CAF, 205–206
performance
   information, assess phase of cloud migration, 238
   insights, RDS, 134
   optimization, 374
phased approach, 231
phased migration, 344
physical data migration, 337
Platform9, 470
Platform as a Service (PaaS), 7–8
point-in-time recovery, 134–135
Points of Presence (PoPs), 33–34
PolyAI, 470

portfolio
   analysis, 255–256
   discovery, 264
practical implementation guides, AWS Prescriptive Guidance, 295
predictive maintenance, generative AI, 484–485
predictive modeling, ML, 448
pre-existing inventory data, 275–276
   data analysis and visual, 276
   data storage and processing, 275–276
pre-migration assessment, AWS Systems Manager, 168
pre-packaged software, 55
private cloud, 11–12
problem definition, ML, 441–442
prompt engineering, generative AI, 455
proof of concept (POC), 254
public cloud, 9–11
PuTTY application configuration, 73–78

Q

QuickSight, 276

R

radar chart, 243
rapid elasticity and scalability, cloud computing, 17
RDBMS, 335
read replicas, 134
real-time monitoring, 154
recognition, 231
Recurrent Neural Networks (RNNs), 459
Redshift, 125
Refactor cloud migration strategy, 189–190
refactoring for cloud-native design, 405–406
refinement, generative AI, 450–451
regional edge caches, 30, 33–34, 149
region selection, 277
regions in AWS, 31–32
Rehost cloud migration strategy, 185–186
rehosting, modernization, 412

Relational Database Service (RDS) database
   delete, 140–141
   deployment with read replicas, 138
   instance, 138–139
   modification, 141–142
   solution architectures, 136–138
reliability, cloud computing, 5
Relocate cloud migration strategy, 186–187
replacement of legacy applications, modernization, 412
Replatform cloud migration strategy, 187–189
replatforming on managed services, 406–408
replication servers, 312
Repurchase cloud migration strategy, 191–192
Reserved Instances, 55, 58–59
resource grouping, AWS Systems Manager, 160, 164
resource management, AWS Systems Manager, 169
resource utilization, 277–278
Retain cloud migration strategy, 193–196
Retire cloud migration strategy, 192–193
Retrieval-Augmented Generation (RAG), 462
robotic process automation (RPA), 426–427
robust security and compliance, AWS Systems Manager, 163
root volume, 67
route tables, VPC, 109–110
RunwayML, 460

S

sampling, generative AI, 450
S3 bucket policies, 92–93
scalability, 3–4, 270
   elasticity and, 401
scaling capability, 136
Schema Conversion Tool (SCT), 338
score chart, 243

seamless hybrid environment management, AWS Systems Manager, 162–163
security
   cloud computing, 4
   in cloud environment, 232
      and compliance, AWS Control Tower, 270
      groups, 66
         VPC, 110
   risk and compliance, 264
   risks, traditional IT infrastructure, 3
serverless functions, modernization strategy, 405–406
serverless messaging deployment, 407–408
Server Message Block (SMB) servers, 369
Server Migration Service (SMS), 288
servers, 177
      readiness, 288
Service Control Policies (SCPs), 492–493
service integration, MGN, 306
service integration management, AWS Systems Manager, 160
Service-Level Agreements (SLAs), 239
session management, AWS Systems Manager, 166–167
7 Rs of Cloud Migration Strategies, 184
Simple Storage Service (S3), 25
single-AZ RDS deployment, 136–137
Site-to-Site VPN connection, 114–115, 117
skill-building programs, 205–206
skills and expertise, 230
S3 Lifecycle policy, 95–101
small-scale data migrations, 371
software, 178
Software as a Service (SaaS) solution, 8–9, 412
Software-Defined Data Center (SDDC), 301
software development and testing, 2
software inventory, 277–278
SOUNDRAW, 461
speed and simplicity, AWS Control Tower, 270

Spot Instances, 58–59
StackPulse, 469
staging volumes, 312
stateless design, 405
Storage Area Networks (SANs), 369
storage assessment model, 253
Storage Gateway, 85
storage system in AWS, 83–101
   Access Control Lists (ACLs), 91–92
   Amazon ECR, 86–87
   Amazon Glacier, 86
   Amazon S3, 87–91
   Amazon S3 versioning, 94–95
   AWS Snow Family, 86
   block storage, 85
   comparison of different S3 storage types, 91
   file storage, 85
   object storage, 84
   S3 bucket policies, 92–93
   S3 Lifecycle policy, 95–101
   Storage Gateway, 85
streamlined automation, AWS Systems Manager, 162
subnet, VPC, 109
supplementary AWS services, 254
supportive culture and continuous learning, 230
Systems Manager Agent (SSM Agent), 163–164
System V init tools, 282

T

task automation, AWS Systems Manager, 160
testing dataset, 445
third-party providers, Transit Gateway to, 115
third-party replication tools, 304
three-phase approach to database migration
   assess phase, 337–338
      migrate and modernize phase, 338–339

mobilize phase, 338
native database migration tools, 339
time estimation and planning, 374
time-series system performance, 272
tokens, generative AI, 456
tool or approach for, 336–351
Total Cost of Ownership (TCO), 271
    analysis, 237
    reports, 180
traffic distribution, 409
training, generative AI, 450
transaction logs, 342
transformers, generative AI, 456
transit gateway, 116
Transmission Control Protocol (TCP)
    network connections, 282
Transport Layer Security (TLS) version 1.2, 380
Transposit, 469
TSO Logic, 248

U

understanding prompts, generative AI, 454
unified inventory view, AWS Systems Manager, 160
unified security and access control, generative AI, 463
Unix commands, 283
user data, 60–61

V

validation, 183
Variational Autoencoders (VAEs), 458
vector, generative AI, 456
vertical scaling, 4
Virtual Private Clouds (VPCs), 107–117, 266
    with all components, 113–114
    AWS Site-to-Site VPN, 116–117
    AWS Transit Gateway, 114–115
    components, 108–112
        Elastic IP (EIP) addresses, 111
        endpoints, 111–112
        Internet gateways, 110–111
        NAT instances and NAT gateways, 112
        Network ACLs (NACLs), 110
        peering connections, 112
        route tables, 109–110
        security group, 110
        subnet, 109
        Virtual Private Gateways (VPGs), 112
Virtual Private Gateways (VPGs), 112
Virtual Private Network (VPN), 373
    connection, 116
    tunnels, 116
Virtual Tape Library (VTL), 369
vMotion, 305
VMware Cloud on AWS, 298–299, 303
VMware environments, 278, 288
VMware HCX, 304
VMware SDDC, 302–303
VMware to AWS cloud migration, 301–303
    relocate strategy, 301–302
    VMware Cloud on AWS, 303
    VMware SDDC, 302–303
VMware vSphere Replication, 304
VPGs, *see* Virtual Private Gateways (VPGs)

W

WAN (Wide Area Network) connections, 367
warm migration, 304–305
wavelength zone, AWS, 31
wave plans, 180
web and application hosting, 2
Web Application Firewall (WAF), 30
Web service, *see* Amazon Elastic Compute Cloud (EC2)
Well-Architected Framework, 240
Windows and Linux servers, 277–278
workload
    management, 232
    migration, 222–223, 293, 298–299